INJUSTICE

AND THE
CARE OF
SOULS

INJUSTICE

AND THE
CARE OF
SOULS

Taking Oppression
Seriously
in Pastoral Care

Sheryl A. Kujawa-Holbrook and
Karen B. Montagno, Editors

Fortress Press
Minneapolis

INJUSTICE AND THE CARE OF SOULS
Taking Oppression Seriously in Pastoral Care

Reprinted by permission of the author from Monnett, Mikel Ryuho. "Developing a Buddhist Approach to Pastoral Care: A Peacemaker's View." *Journal of Pastoral Care*, 59, no. 1: 57-62. (Spring, 2005).

Cover photo © Steve Schapiro/Corbis
Cover design: Danielle Carnito
Book design: Jessica A. Puckett

Library of Congress Cataloging-in-Publication Data
Injustice and the care of souls : taking oppression seriously in pastoral care / Sheryl A. Kujawa-Holbrook and Karen B. Montagno, editors.
    p. cm.
  Includes bibliographical references and index.
  ISBN 978-0-8006-6235-6 (alk. paper)
  1. Church and social problems. I. Kujawa-Holbrook, Sheryl A. II. Montagno, Karen Brown, 1955-
  HN31.I55 2009
  206'.1--dc22
                            2009000227

The paper used in this publication meets the minimum requirements of American National Standard for Information Sciences—Permanence of Paper for Printed Library Materials, ANSI Z329.48-1984.

Manufactured in the U.S.A.

CONTENTS

Part Two: Oppression-Sensitive Pastoral Practice

PART ONE

CONTEXT, COMMUNITY, AND PASTORAL CARE

INTRODUCTION

How does oppression manifest itself in the structures of society? What are the implications for pastoral care? This book developed out of a course taught at the Episcopal Divinity School in Cambridge, Massachusetts, called "Pastoral Care As If Oppression Matters." Each time we teach this course, we search for pastoral care books and articles that speak to the largest section of our society, marginalized people. Although we find many general resources on pastoral care, it is difficult to find one text that speaks to the diversity of concerns of marginalized persons. The desire to give an alternative and prophetic voice to these concerns was the birth of this project.

Injustice and the Care of Souls seeks to broaden and inform the paradigm for pastoral care in a variety of contexts and communities, including the poor, the homeless, the abused, the aged, and racial/ethnic communities. The appropriate construction and use of ritual in pastoral care included here is often overlooked. Though it is impossible to include chapters on all marginalized groups, we made an effort to include the work of diverse authors writing on pastoral care in a wide variety of contexts, communities, faith traditions, and pastoral situations.

An underlying assumption of this book is that pastoral care is inextricably linked to justice and compassion. In the face of interlocking social oppressions, those engaged in prophetic pastoral ministries cannot approach pastoral care solely from the perspective of white, Western, middle-class models disconnected from the realities of people of color and marginalized people. Overall, the purpose of this book is *constructive*—that is, to provide readers with an opportunity to inform and broaden their knowledge and skills in pastoral care, to respond more effectively to the needs of oppressed persons, and to reflect on ways that the pastor's social location has an impact on pastoral ministry. The focus is *not* on individual pastoral counseling per se, but on pastoral care within the context of marginalized communities and faith communities. How are the realities of racism, sexism, classism, heterosexism, ageism, ableism, and the like prevalent within our faith communities? How can we develop more oppression-sensitive forms of pastoral care?

Theologically, this book assumes that the bias of most faith traditions is with the marginalized: God sees, hears, knows, and lives in the midst of the poor and the oppressed. The primary work of faith communities, then, is human *freedom*—to provide an opportunity for wholeness for all people. While it is true that all human beings struggle and experience pain, the realities of oppression mean that within the system of human structures some persons have more advantages than others. Skilled pastors will have the ability both to recognize and analyze the impact of oppression on individuals and faith communities and to know how to utilize their prophetic role to bring healing, voice, and wholeness to the marginalized.

This volume is a collection of essays that focus on a variety of aspects of pastoral care and oppression. Two introductory essays by the volume editors begin the first section, which sets a broad overview of topics related to the relationship between injustice and pastoral care. While not exhaustive, the second section exposes the reader to a number of communities and discusses pastoral care in relationship to marginalization. Although it would not be possible in a single volume to address pastoral care in the context of every form of injustice, it is our hope that the topics here will provide an introduction to the need for oppression-sensitive pastoral care, and will spark interest in further work in these areas.

We would like to thank the authors of the articles here for their generosity of time and talent. David Lott believed in this project and helped us organize it and get it published. John Ratti's editorial skills helped us refine the articles and preserve the voice of the authors. Many thanks also to our families, friends, and the Episcopal Divinity School community who offered their support throughout this project.

Sheryl Kujawa-Holbrook
Karen Brown Montagno

Midwives and Holy Subversives: Resisting Oppression in Attending the Birth of Wholeness

Karen B. Montagno

But the midwives feared God; they did not do as the king of Egypt commanded them. . . .—Exod. 1:17

My mother believed babies were more likely to arrive when the sky was filled with rain clouds than when it was clear. . . .—Chris Bohjalian (1998)

Consonant with the understandings of their African forebears, African Americans have always known that persons cannot flourish apart from a community of belonging.—Peter J. Paris (1995)

Context and community have shaped my ministry and approach to pastoral care. From the time I was a youth, my experiences and the values of my community were shaping forces. In his foreword to Edward Wimberly's *Relational Refugees*, Gilbert H. Caldwell writes about the innate nature of context: "Whenever we put pen to paper or fingertips to key board, we do so in a particular historical and cultural context" (Wimberly 2000, 11).

"Why you talk so proper? You need to get back to your roots, gal, and I ain't meaning your hair!" These are phrases I remember from childhood—my southern cousins questioning my "proper" northern way of speaking. Getting back to your roots, to where you came from (in my case, the South), was as important as taking proper care of new growth in hair. Knowing your roots, your community of people, and where you come from was critical to being whole, knowing who you were and where you were going.

My story is one of overlapping contexts. I am an African American woman, a descendent of African people enslaved in North Carolina. Currently, I am an instructor and practitioner of pastoral care, an Episcopal priest in a local parish, a seminary dean, and a parent. My communities are multiple, significant, and formative.

Although my current context is diverse, my African American heritage forms my worldview. My school days in the North were spent during the turbulent struggles for civil rights and the Vietnam era, the 1960s and '70s. My father, a research scientist, and my mother, a nurse, faced many of the barriers, frustrations, and humiliations of African American professionals who tried to move forward and make a contribution during that time. Like many other African American professionals, they raised funds, marched, and were involved in organizing for the struggle for civil rights.

Our neighborhood was in flux. It was a changing mix of African Americans, white Americans, and Italian and Puerto Rican Americans. It was a time of throwing off old racial norms and labels and claiming a self-defined identity. It was a time of struggle, reclamation, protest, and resistance. In the midst of turmoil, our little neighborhood Episcopal church (an African American congregation) was a place of quiet beauty, nurture, and graciousness.

Equally formative were the seasons of my childhood spent where I was born and bred, in the rural Baptist South. Peter J. Paris lifts up the practical wisdom of elders as an important source of training for African American children: "Whenever their children were separated from their grandparents by geography (as when African Americans had emigrated to the cities), many generations of parents sent their children to live with their parents during school holidays. . . . spending the summer in the care of one's grandparents enabled the child to learn about their values and experience the practical import of these values" (1995, 144).

Worship, prayer meeting, Bible study, choir practice, and visiting formed the fabric of the week. Neighbors checked from house to house and lent their collective expertise to the issues that emerged. The blazing heat of the sun gave way to the mysteries of the black, black night. Into the night their voices echoed, carrying stories about great-grandparents, grandparents, aunts, uncles, and cousins.

In the midst of growing pains, adolescent angst, these stories of life, death, crisis, recovery, despair, and joy gave me a perspective and sense of wholeness that continues today. It is these overlapping contexts that help shape my approach to pastoral care.

Context and the community of the caregiver as well as the care seeker set the stage for the pastoral care encounter. For example, here are some of the perspectives I bring:

- The challenges and strengths borne in the historic and continuing oppression of African peoples and other oppressed communities in this country, especially the plight of African American men and boys
- The baby boomer era as a matrix where the tension between conformity and human rights and political action took place
- Geographical diversity—North/South, city/rural, cyclical poverty/upward mobility
- Concerns of African American women and families
- Episcopal ministry and seminary communities

No, only does my context and community inform what I bring to pastoral care, it also gives clues about challenges (both blind spots and sore spots) I may face as a pastoral caregiver. Caregivers from oppressed populations often bring their own struggle with oppression to the pastoral care encounter. Self-care and mindfulness regarding the impact of oppression are critical. While shared oppression can provide valuable insight and solidarity, it also presents challenges. Verna Dozier speaks from her own experience: "One of the great tragedies of being an oppressed people is that you take on, almost without intending to do it, the evaluation of the controlling community . . ." (Dozier 2006, 21).

Valerie Batts (1998) and Suzanne Lipsky (1991) each write about "internalized oppression." Lipsky tells us that the evaluations and patterned behaviors are created by oppression and racism: "Internalized oppression is this turning upon ourselves, upon our families, and upon our own people the distress patterns that result from the racism and oppression of the majority society" (1991, 3–67). Taking on the negative evaluation of others shatters the self-esteem, authority, and confidence of the caregiver.

Batts describes five expressions of internalized oppression:

- System beating—attempting to get over or around the system through manipulation.

- Blaming the system—deflecting responsibility for one's action; putting all the blame on the other.
- Anti-white avoidance of contact—avoiding contact with whites; distrusting all whites.
- Denial of cultural heritage—distrusting one's own group, accepting that one's own group is inferior.
- Minimization of the political significance of racial oppression—feeling powerless (learned helplessness); misdirecting anger to persons with less power (Batts 1998, 9–11).

Operating from internalized oppression can limit growth and new learning if used habitually or unconsciously. Ultimately, internalized oppression does not address the root cause of the strategy that is oppression itself. Batts relates internalized oppression to what she calls modern racism (1998, 12). Modern racism is old-fashioned racism expressed covertly at personal, interpersonal, institutional, and cultural levels. The two forms of racism play off and trigger each other. The task, then, is to become aware of dysfunctional old patterns of racism and internalized oppression and strategize new options for interrupting all oppression.

The overlapping and interrelatedness of context and community suggests an approach that is holistic, addressing the physical, spiritual, and psychological equally. By holistic, I mean the equally interrelated spirit, body, and mind. These spirits, bodies, and minds cannot remain whole if not integrated and related to community.

Emmanuel Lartey writes about holism, saying that it involves working with other caregivers for the "total well-being of all persons" (2003, 108). This totality includes social networks and the relevant psychosocial, theological, and ethical disciplines.

As a Christian African American, this holism comes together, takes shape, and derives meaning through my faith life. Pastoral care is one way I live out my call to faith. Community and Scripture are reference points. Wimberly points out that the African American encounter with liberative themes in Scripture has fostered a legacy of protest against oppression (2000, 38).

In Scripture, there are many images that have been used as models for the work of pastoral care. For many Christians, Jesus is the chief model of pastoral care as savior/liberator, teacher, healer, and prophet. Further, throughout Scripture there are a variety of models of pastoral caregiving—the divine transformation in lives of people and communities. Creator, shepherd, the gardener, potter, and wounded healer are common images of pastoral care.

The model that speaks most clearly to me is that of the Hebrew midwives found in Exodus. This story is positioned at the beginning of the iconic story of God's work of liberation from oppression, forging of community, and ongoing presence among the Hebrew people. This story of freedom and conquest may raise political and justice issues for contemporary readers if approached uncritically. All Scripture must be read critically as well with the eyes of faith. Further, there is debate about whether the midwives were Egyptians or Hebrew themselves. For my purpose here they are Hebrew.

The exodus story has been formative and a source of strength for many African peoples in the diaspora as we continue the struggle of freedom in our own contexts:

> Therefore they set taskmasters over them to oppress them with forced labor. . . . But the more they were oppressed, the more they multiplied and spread, so that the Egyptians came to dread the Israelites. The Egyptians became ruthless in imposing tasks on the Israelites, and made their lives bitter with hard service in mortar and brick and every kind of field labor. They were ruthless in all the tasks that they imposed on them.

> The king of Egypt said to the Hebrew midwives, one of whom was named Shiphrah and the other Puah, "When you act as midwives to the Hebrew women, and see them on the birthstool, if it is a boy, kill him; but if it is a girl, she shall live." But the midwives feared God; they did not do as the king of Egypt commanded them . . . (Exod. 1:11a, 12-17b).

This story is rich with themes that inform my approach to pastoral care. In this reading, women working as a team are models of pastoral care. The agency of women, teamwork, and collective resources are important themes. The women "act" against the powers of the world (the king) because of their fear (or taking seriously the call) of God. There are other themes: oppression, solidarity, resistance, transformation, liberation, and blessing. The context is one of urgency, peril, challenge, and promise.

The function of the midwife is seemingly simple and practical, to attend to birth. In reality, it is quite challenging and complex. Trained in practical knowledge, collective wisdom, and experience, the midwife is a mentor who offers strategy to empower and bring about the birth. The midwife seeks to preserve health and ensure safety—attending, listening, witnessing to the process and what is emerging. The midwife honors what is being birthed by encouraging and urging the one giving birth to use collective resources necessary for birth. There is attention to forces not seen, but at work. This is much the role of pastoral caregivers.

Any birth is transformative and the work of the pastoral caregiver is to attend that transformation. One aspect of this story that makes it particularly relevant to my context and community is that the midwives take "subversive," risky, and strategic steps to interrupt and dismantle oppression and to ensure the wholeness and future of their community. They preserve the lives of the male children.

In real time, for my community, there is a sense of urgency, peril, challenge. The liberative acts of African Americans struggling against oppression have been part of the unfolding story of this country. Has the ongoing legacy of oppression and internalized oppression subverted our confidence and power to take risky and strategic steps? Have we turned against ourselves? Has oppression kept us from observing and witnessing to the promise we hold? Has the spell of mobility seduced us from the power of solidarity in community?

Despite many gains, we continue to stagger under the weight of systemic economic and social disparities. African American males have become an endangered species disproportionately predisposed to poverty, prison, violence, and stress-related disease. Salim Muwakkil (2006) describes it as a social emergency.

The theme of resistance suggests a challenge for the field of pastoral care. Moreover, Carroll A. Watkins points to an overlooked role for the field of pastoral care, that of advocacy and agency in dismantling oppressive systems (1999). Taken a step further, the strategies used to attend to oppressed populations are useful in attending, liberating, and transforming all populations. Speaking specifically about the African American situation she says,

> . . . the pastoral care of African Americans is not just a situation that African American pastoral theologians and pastoral caregivers need to address. The existential problems that confront African Americans today are as much an American problem as the institution of slavery was an American problem. Hence the crisis in Black America presents a ministry situation that the field of pastoral theology and care needs to come to terms with, collectively. (1999, 136)

Pastoral caregivers must be agents of the scriptural vision spoken about in the book of Isaiah. Here lamb and lion exist in safety together. Another vision is a sumptuous banquet table with enough for all and to which all are invited. The vision compels us to midwife the birth of a place for all. This is the challenge for pastoral care. These visions suggest this promise is available in combined contexts and community.

As a pastoral caregiver, I have been surrounded by a community of pastoral care colleagues. Their collective voice has been urgent, formative, wise, and supportive. Collectively, they represent my context and community. They have been a source of authority and accountability, as well as challenge. In the final words of this essay they will speak.[1]

They are people of color who are caregivers to oppressed as well as dominant populations. They represent a variety of contexts. They are African, Asian, Native, and Caribbean American. They are lay and ordained. They provide pastoral care in a variety of settings: prison communities, faith communities, seminaries, community organizations, immigrant populations, and mental health communities. They are male and female and span a wide age range. As caregivers they demonstrate commitment to care of community, witness, compassion, and justice in God's name.

For me, they are the community that Verna Dozier calls a Scripture community: "As I reflected on the images of community in scripture, it seemed to me that there were five characteristics that marked them: a scripture community is a community with a memory, with a ritual life that keeps the memories fresh, with a passion for justice, with a commitment to love, and with a mission" (2006, 94).

I asked these colleagues five questions. Their answers represent many of the issues raised in this essay. The major points of their collective wisdom are paraphrased under each question below. The answers are not listed in order of priority.

1. What comes to mind when you hear the phrase "pastoral care as if injustice or oppression really mattered?"
   - An understanding of oppression, power, and privilege is key.
   - In an ideal world pastoral care in the face of injustice might mean a redundancy of care. However, there is a profound and deep recognition that, sadly, many do not experience a redundancy of care.
   - Pastoral care is a sacred practice that considers how the Spirit is working in various levels: mind, spirit, body, and community. Pastoral

care has the goal of transformation, salvation, liberation, redemption, healing, and restoration.

- Care takes place within a particular social, cultural, historical context. It asks the questions, What are the norms, strengths, or challenges of the situation, individual, or group? What does health look like in this context?
- Being present and available to listen, comfort, mentor, encourage, witness, and advocate is important.
- Being a practical resource assessing concerns of safety, food, health, shelter, clothing, and livelihood.
- Pastoral care at its best comes naturally from the community.

2. What skills have been important to you as a pastoral caregiver of color?
   - Recognizing that the person or group brings gifts and solutions to the situation as well as challenges.
   - Respect, mutuality, and compassion.
   - Presence, listening, and witnessing. Patience to let the story unfold in its own time.
   - Networking, resource development, and team and coalition building.
   - Credibility is important, which means knowing the person or community and being known.
   - Spiritual practice, prayer, faith, and reliance on God.
   - Counseling and other skills that can be transferred to a variety of contexts.
   - Knowledge or a willingness to explore other contexts, history, cultures, and norms, as well as a willingness to explore assumptions and learn, relearn, or unlearn information.
   - Ability to work as part of a team, share leadership, and empower all ministries. Pastoral care is not the private domain of ordained ministers.

3. What have been particular challenges for you as a pastoral caregiver of color?
   - Making sense of the variety of definitions and images of pastoral care.
   - Maintaining and sustaining credibility and dealing with what seems to be rejection. Facilitating care when there is rejection.
   - Resources that can't be accessed because of delivery constraints or inflexible systems.

- Exhaustion, which means knowing personal limits and maintaining a balanced life. Demands are greater because the needs are greater.
- There has been a paradigm shift; many of the old models of care and ministry are no longer effective.
- Internalized oppression may be unavoidable, but at least be conscious of when it is happening. Practice other options.

4. What are critical issues that you address as a pastoral caregiver?
   - The survival of at-risk populations—urban youth, black men, gay, lesbian, and transgendered people.
   - Domestic and other forms of violence.
   - Addiction.
   - Spiritual formation.
   - Mutual ministry, team ministry, pooling wisdom and talent.
   - Extended aging and end-of-life issues.
   - Nurturing marriage and other relationship concerns.
   - Race and fear of the other, xenophobia, and the current fear of brown-skinned people.
   - Accessing funding resources.

5. What recommendations do you have for students of pastoral care?
   - Get experience by encountering a variety of people and situations. Keep learning and growing.
   - Develop and guard a healthy mind, body, and spiritual life.
   - Get to know your community and be known by the community.
   - Gather a toolbox of resources and a network with whom you partner. Ministry in community means teamwork.
   - Develop a regular pattern of contact with a community of support.
   - Develop communication skills. Listen attentively and develop the tactfulness to say the hard things that people need to hear. Honesty and straightforwardness with compassion are important.
   - Develop integrity and confidentiality without secrecy. Develop the ability to hold information and know when situations call for reporting and how to relay the necessity of reporting.
   - Develop some grief counseling skills. Know the dynamics of loss and letting go.
   - Be able to make assessments and develop a plan of action.

Pastoral care for oppressed populations requires taking the impact of oppression seriously. It is a call to solidarity and the work of justice. Context and community are interrelated and inform the perspectives of both caregiver and receiver. Serious consideration of these reveals challenges as well as wisdom and insight. Further, the interrelated nature of context and community suggest that pastoral care is a holistic practice that attends to whole persons—mind, spirit, and body—in community.

The Hebrew midwives are a powerful model of pastoral caregiving; their story offers a way of viewing pastoral careg in community and in the context of oppression.

TWO

Love and Power:
Antiracist Pastoral Care

Sheryl A. Kujawa-Holbrook

. . . power without love is reckless and abusive, and love without power is sentimental and anemic. Power at its best is love implementing the demands of justice, and justice at its best is power correcting everything that stands against love.—Martin Luther King Jr. (1967, 247)

All love and power are central to God, so, too, they must be central to all who walk in God's way and are concerned about pastoral care. When Dr. King spoke of love and power, he was talking about the "connective tissue" that holds together all of the human community. As the stories from the articles featured in this book suggest, pastoral care that recognizes the realities of oppression is also an exercise in love and power. That is, authentic healing and reconciliation in a world of vast inequities not only requires sharing in God's great love, it also necessitates the power to accomplish genuine human community, hopefully and intentionally.

Love and power together transform pastoral care and make an impact on the larger human community. One of the reasons why so many attempts at pastoral care fail to bring authentic healing and reconciliation is that the overall dominant culture within American society often does not recognize or strive to correct the deep power imbalances experienced by all marginalized people. Antiracist pastoral care emanates from the collective concern that we are all, despite the divisions we perpetuate, part of one human community; if life is improved for one person, all benefit. Justice does not admit of partitioning. In the Jewish tradition, this practice is known as *tikkum olam*, or the healing and repair of the world. Within the Christian tradition it is the belief that we are all called to live in communion with each other, to be transformed for the sake of one another and the world.

Despite the official repudiation of racism throughout most faith communities, including the Christian church, Dr. King observed that eleven o'clock on Sunday mornings is the most segregated hour in America. He believed that churches play a fundamental role in shaping the values and changing the oppressive forces of our societies. Yet overall, our faith communities, as well as the models of pastoral care they support, have historically mirrored rather than transformed the biases of our society. Generally speaking, the experience of Dr. King's "beloved community" is a vision that remains elusive within most faith communities. Racism and other forms of oppression have prevailed as an organizing principle of religious life throughout American history. The problem is not that racism can be confined to fringe religious groups and only embraced by persons who subscribe to a faith based on hate. Such groups are flagrant in their racism and bigotry and therefore fairly easy to disavow. Rather, the racism at the very core of our faith communities is the ongoing challenge to pastoral care.

If we examine the *actual* level of diversity that exists in the United States today, the critical nature of antiracist pastoral care is obvious, as well as an essential ingredient to our survival and participation in our own communities and the world:[1]

- At the beginning of the twenty-first century, five billion of the earth's six billion people are people of color.
- There are over five thousand living languages in the world; there are more bilingual than monolingual people; and, more people speak English as a second language than as a first language.
- In the United States, 40 percent of bias crimes are against blacks and 13 percent are antiwhite crimes. The highest growth in hate crimes in recent years is against Asians and homosexuals. Every hour someone commits a hate crime. Every day eight blacks; three whites; three gay, lesbian, or transgendered people; three Jews; and one Latino become hate crime victims. Every week a cross is burned.
- Thirty percent of African Americans and Hispanics live in poverty, compared to 12 percent of European Americans. For African

Americans, unemployment is twice as high, and their paychecks are half as much as those of their white counterparts. Infant mortality among African American babies is more than double that of European Americans.

- Presently, there are over a million students in the New York City school system representing the following groups: 38 percent black, 35 percent Hispanic, 19 percent white, and 7.9 percent Asian. In some California school systems, twenty languages are represented. In the rural community of Hall County, Nebraska, with a population under fifty thousand people, thirty different languages are spoken in homes.
- If recent trends continue, between the years of 2025 and 2050 whites will no longer be the voting majority in several states. By 2050, Asians, Hispanics, non-Hispanic blacks, and American Indians together will account for almost half the total U.S. population.

At a time when hatred is growing between religious groups worldwide, how can religious leaders enact healing and reconciliation? How can pastors and pastoral caregivers become agents of transformation? How can those of us who live lives of privilege develop an ethic of pastoral care that offers both love *and* power? How can we effectively care for those different from ourselves, particularly the poor, the marginalized, the oppressed, those who live outside our homogeneous communities? How can pastors and pastoral care be the catalysts for religious and social change?

Developing a Beyond-Racism Tradition

Although it can be argued that many pastors seek justice as a personal vocation, and while it is true that individuals can and do make a difference, their impact is short-lived and temporary if not connected to faith communities empowered by God's healing presence. To be sure, antiracist pastoral care is ultimately a corporate reality. More than secular political movements, economic theory, or social analysis (although all three are essential), faith communities can become sources of healing and reconciliation on the personal, interpersonal, institutional, and cultural levels of human society.

The development of a beyond-racism tradition depends upon a multiple-strategy approach to change in the way we envision pastoral care. The challenge is to further personal and structural change at the level of pastors, individual believers, faith communities, religious organizations, as well as in daily expressions of spiritual life. To be achieved, the spirit of antiracist pastoral care needs to embrace the whole of religious life—worship, hospitality, evangelism, formation for all ages, and social action. We need to push beyond seeing pastoral care exclusively as an individual-to-individual, pastor-and-client relationship, to seeing it as integral to the vocation and mission of the whole people of God. This vision of pastoral care must encompass moral values as well as public policy making through which individual pastors and faith communities relate to other religious traditions and to the broader society.

Finally, pastors and religious faith communities must develop a theological perspective on pastoral care that offers people a sign of hope in an enduring culture of oppression. As the U.S. population grows increasingly diverse, the need for a greater awareness of difference within a dynamic of privilege and oppression is a challenge facing all people of faith who will live, work, and pray within this changing context.

Understanding Antiracist Pastoral Care

Antiracist pastoral care is based in hope. To be sure, models of pastoral care that take seriously both love *and* power are risky; however, then the question becomes whether or not we believe that our faith communities are resilient enough to confront the evils of our world. As Catherine Nerney and Hal Taussig write, "The building of community in America is our primary work and calling; through it we share the very life and work of God" (2002, 238). I believe that religious communities are in fact among the few places in the world where people of diverse backgrounds can join together constructively for the good of all humankind. This conviction comes from the knowledge that people from different traditions are now confronting oppression in the midst of dangerous circumstances, struggling through it, and ultimately moving closer to the reality of Dr. King's "beloved community." To do so requires intentionally choosing to live in hope, despite the pain, the loss, and the risks. Transformation always means that we must face the reality of death. The confrontation itself is hope embodied. William Stringfellow once wrote that "hope is known only in the midst of coping with death. Any so-called hope is delusory and false without or apart from the confrontation with the power of death. . . . Resistance to death *is* the only way to live humanly in the midst of the Fall" (1973, 138).

While antiracist pastoral care will not look the same in every context, the values that support it are based in the liberation tradition, and thus are consonant with other models of liberatory pastoral care. Some of the indicators of antiracist pastoral care include:

- focus on helping all people achieve their full potential and the tools for using it; supporting their autonomy and connecting them into broader community;
- balance between the need for individual freedom and mutual responsibility for others;
- recognition that freedom requires people to make their own choices;
- emphasis on pastoral care that values *shared power*, rather than *power over* people;
- skill development in the arts of listening, compromise, and mediation;
- emphasis on integrity and accountability in relationships through alignment of individual and communal values, such as generosity, accountability, forgiveness, and so forth;
- treating everyone as a person of dignity and value, not someone to be used or controlled;
- belief that racial differences, as well as other forms of difference, enhance life and community;
- recognition that all people have a right to food, clothing, shelter, education, health care, and a just income (adapted from Pharr, 2000, 450–51).

Antiracist pastoral care takes into account white privilege, and examines the impact of racism in pastoral care situations and what faith communities can do to address it. One scholar argues that "race is perhaps the most visible of all cultural differences [in America] . . . and has been and continues to be the ultimate measure of social exclusion and inclusion, because it is a visible factor that historically and currently determines the rules and bounds of social and cultural interaction" (Carter 1998, 3). This focus on race and racism is not in any way intended to minimize the other forms of oppression discussed throughout this book. Certainly, sexism, classism, heterosexism, ageism, ableism, and other "isms" also have a profound impact on pastoral care. Indeed, all forms of structural oppression share certain characteristics, namely, exploitation, marginalization, powerlessness, cultural imperialism, and violence (Young 2000).

Because of the "interlocking" nature of oppression, it is not possible to address fully one form of oppression and not another. None of us is free until all God's people are free. In other words, in order to fully examine our racism, we must also examine our sexism, classism, heterosexism, and so forth. For European Americans this challenge is in understanding the power dynamics inherent in "whiteness" and how the resultant social power has an impact on our role as a pastor caregiver, as well as an impact on persons of other races and cultures with whom we relate. For people of color this challenge includes understanding the impact of internalized oppression on the role of the pastoral caregiver, as well as on individuals and communities within a society where the dominant culture remains white. Overall, antiracist pastoral care demands that both white people and people of color grow more culturally competent and aware of how the history of racism in the United States has influenced our models of pastoral care.

For pastors committed to antiracist pastoral care it is crucial to recognize the persistence of racism in predominantly white religious institutions. It is quite possible to find white pastoral caregivers who self-describe as "progressive," or even as "justice centered," but who have done little or nothing to address their own racism, particularly on a structural level. In fact, in many cases such pastors are often pastorally concerned with one or several groups of marginalized persons. In no way do I discount these efforts. Nor am I suggesting that racism has anything to do with the labels of "conservative" or "progressive" extant in many faith communities. Racism is embedded in U.S. faith communities from the colonial era, and the process of maintaining it remains in place to the present day. Although the U.S. demographic reality has changed, the historical legacy of racism remains constant.[2]

An important goal here, then, is to focus on how pastoral caregivers can deal with the impact of racism on their lives, how this learning leads to greater understanding of other marginalized people, and how racism undermines all pastoral care. This essay is predicated on the belief that racism is a profoundly *spiritual* concern and a central issue for all pastoral care. For those of us who are Christians, racism robs us of our wholeness as the body of Christ. Although many faith communities support the need for racial reconciliation, such a vision can only be built on a foundation that recognizes the impact of centuries of racism and discrimination on people of color, and the relative and unequal effect of this legacy on white people. Inherent in this view is the assertion that faith communities are intended to be instruments of human freedom, rather than instruments of oppression.

Antiracist pastoral care demands nothing less than reenvisioning our faith communities through the eyes of God. Some of the questions that need to be considered by pastoral caregivers include: What impact do my attitudes and behaviors regarding racism have on my call as a pastor? How do the models of pastoral care within my faith community or religious organization perpetuate racism? Who are the marginalized in my midst and how am I called to care for them? How do I begin to turn aside my ingrained racist vision of pastoral care and begin to live into a vision where one group is not dominant over other groups? What will pastoral care rooted in love and power look like in my faith community?

Telling Stories

Integral to antiracist pastoral care is the telling of stories. The telling of stories not only unmasks the various levels of personal history within a pastoral situation, it shows how the experiences of entire communities differ when told from the perspective of varying social locations. Personal narratives are at the root of how we experience difference, as well as how we experience God. "Telling my story is not itself theology but a basis for theology," writes Jung Young Lee, "indeed the primary context for doing my theology. This is why one cannot do theology for another. If theology is contextual, it must certainly be at root autobiographical" (1995, 7).

My own family of origin is Polish American, which includes a distinctive racial, ethnic, cultural, and social class heritage. I was raised in a large midwestern city during the 1960s and 1970s, where my family worked in a variety of agricultural, factory, and service occupations. The reality of ethnic discrimination against Polish people—even in areas where we comprised a large portion of the white population—combined with discrimination based on economic class, served to reinforce within my family and ethnic community a fierce determination to survive and to keep the culture alive. My grandparents spoke little English and throughout their lives held on to the hope that their grandchildren would have access to higher education, professional advancement, and leisure pursuits. A by-product of the discrimination my family and neighbors experienced was the growth of our own prejudices against other ethnic groups, as well as a deeply ingrained racism against people of color.

It was not until I attended graduate school at an elite, predominately white, eastern college, without another person with a similar ethnic or class background in sight, that I realized it was possible to be raised as a white person in the United States without a distinctive sense of ethnicity or a specific cultural identification. Although my academic and professional successes are partially due to my abilities,

I am also aware that they have everything to do with my whiteness. My ability to "pass" as someone from middle-class, English-speaking, white, "American" culture assured my acceptance in classrooms, in professions, and in a Christian denomination defined by the dominant culture, while my Polish American, working-class, inner voice always felt like a fraud. While I felt isolation due to my family's economic marginalization, I also had personal support and access to resources that were not shared by the students of color in similar situations.

Reflection on my own personal story teaches me lessons about the privilege of whiteness, and at the same time gives me a "window" into what it might be like for those who experience racial oppression. Although I have experienced oppression and marginalization, as a woman and as someone from a working-class background, as a white person I will never experience, firsthand, true racism. My whiteness means that I do not have to face the unremitting racial oppression that people of color face every day of their lives.

As an ordained minister and faculty member at a denominational seminary, I continue to ask myself about the impact of white privilege on my ministry and how I can better use my institutional power to enhance the lives of all people. In particular, as a white professor I see it as part of my responsibility to challenge white students to identify their unearned racial privilege and then offer examples of how they can use that privilege for the good of all people through pastoral ministry. After more than twenty years of antiracism training among many predominately white Christian groups, I have seen the fear, the anxiety, and the hostility expressed when the need to address our racism is raised. White people in the United States with little multicultural education or vocabulary may feel inadequate to discuss the "stories" of their own racial and cultural heritage. Discussions of racism often evoke feelings of shame and guilt in white people. Others fear intercultural communication, and feel like they are "walking on eggshells." Yet the fact remains that neither white people nor people of color are *personally* responsible for racism. Racism is an oppressive system that predates our personal histories. However, we *are* personally accountable for how we perpetuate racism and internalized oppression—how we are complicit—and for our failure to take action against them.

Challenging the Melting-Pot Theory

The twenty-first century is a global society with a high degree of mobility. Until fairly recently much of the written American history either minimized or denied racial differences. The "melting pot" theory envisioned that racial, ethnic, class, regional, religious, and other cultural differences could be subsumed under the inclusive identity "American." However, the efficacy of this vision as applied to pastoral care has been challenged by pastoral theologians such as Donald Chinula, who writes, "That no social order is unicultural is axiomatic" (1997, 77). The melting-pot view of the social order is discarded, not only because it is a fictitious construct, because assimilation is a symptom of sociocultural intolerance and imperialism. It annihilates desirable diversity in the human and physical ecology and promotes and maintains maladjustment among the poor and oppressed.

Although the "melting-pot" theory has proved untenable, its assumptions continue to exercise influence over the way racial differences are approached. Many white Americans are still raised to believe in the well-intentioned but misinformed "melting-pot" vision of American society—that is, the consideration of racial differences is negative and the ideal American society should not consist of discreet racial groups. Works in multicultural studies also point to the limitations of this perspective, including its racist bias. As Edward W. Rodman notes:

> All this adds up to a situation in which the so-called majority in this country is really to be understood as a coalition of European ethnic groups who have dropped their ethnic identity, and have chosen to become that homogenized "American" that we call white. This in turn is then portrayed as the norm for the society, and is identified as the melting pot. The only problem is that those who are not European cannot melt, and that the numerically average person in the world is an eighteen-year-old Asian woman. (1995, 155)

Mary Elizabeth Hobgood, in *Dismantling Privilege,* illustrates the negative effects of racism on white people:

> The race system is a complex web of social institutions that devastates people of color economically, politically, and culturally. The race system, which gives whites dominance over other racialized groups, also restricts whites emotionally and damages us morally. White dominance, or white supremacy, harms people socially constructed as white in ways most whites neither see nor understand. That said, the truth is that whites gain at the expense of communities of color, which is the primary reason for the construction of whiteness and the racial system. (2000, 36)

The automatic privilege received by white Americans within the United States is the topic of Peggy McIntosh's influential study, "White Privilege: Unpacking the Invisible Knapsack." McIntosh says that she was taught about racism as a phenomenon that puts others at a disadvantage, but not taught how it gave her, as a white person, personal and societal advantages. These advantages are what McIntosh calls "white privilege." McIntosh uses the metaphor of white privilege as an invisible, weightless knapsack of special provisions, maps, codebooks, visas, tools, and blank checks. White privilege is given to us because we are born white; we do not choose it. Similarly, white privilege is experienced as oppressive to people of color, whether we beneficiaries choose to be oppressive to them or not. White people are socialized, according to McIntosh, "to think of themselves as mentally neutral, normative, and average, and also ideal, so that when we work to benefit others, this is seen as work that will allow 'them' to be more like 'us'" (1990, 4).

Most of the privileges McIntosh lists are those things that a white person living in the United States can and does take for granted. For instance, we can, if we wish, arrange to be in the company of our own race for most of the time. We are educated knowing that the accomplishments of our own race will be included in the canon. We can extrapolate the privileges received by individual white people, and extend them to religious life. For instance, those of us who are white can enter our religious community and expect to hear the hymns that we like to sing, eat the food we like to eat, listen to sermons relevant to the way we operate in the world, and experience pastoral care resonant with our own experience from someone of our own racial background.

It is possible for white seminarians to have many role models of their racial background outside their immediate family. Theological education holds up many aspects of white culture, whereas it is not yet a given that persons of color will learn anything about their own culture within the same setting. The impact of white privilege on people of color is so pervasive that it is experienced even in contexts where no white people are present. As bell hooks illustrates:

Nowadays, it has become fashionable for white and black folks alike to act like they do not have the slightest clue as to why black folks might like to separate, to be together in some corner, or neighborhood, or even at some dining table in a world where we are surrounded by whiteness. It is not a mystery. Those of us who remember living in the midst of racial apartheid know that the separate spaces, the times apart from whiteness, were for sanctuary, for re-imagining and re-membering ourselves. In the past separate space meant down time, time for recovery and renewal. (1995, 5–6)

Letting go of white privilege in pastoral care means acknowledging that our well-intended ministrations are not necessarily as welcoming or effective as we would like to believe; and perhaps, too, that our models of pastoral care need to be reshaped if antiracist pastoral care is to be a reality. Increasing mobility and access through international travel and electronic communication have opened the way to increased cultural diversity throughout the United States. While there are individuals and groups within European American culture who have undeniably suffered from negative prejudice and discrimination, whiteness carries with it unearned entitlements that make the domination of institutions, like churches and other faith communities, possible. Rather than holding onto the vision of a melting pot, we are called into a new vision of a "mosaic," or "salad bowl," or "symphony." In these visions difference is considered valuable and enriching for relationships in community. While white pastors are born into racial privilege without a choice, what we decide to do with these advantages *is* a matter of choice.

Developing Cultural Competence

Cultural competence—the ability to recognize and respond to varying aspects of racial and cultural differences, and to remain thus engaged long term—is an integral step toward antiracist pastoral care. People of color who are pastoral caregivers are also challenged to become more culturally competent as the demographic diversity of the overall population increases. It is also an important skill for communities of color in responding to the effects of racism on them. Cultural competence in pastoral ministry is a *learned skill*, not an automatic part of theological education. Although often left unincorporated into practice, research has shown that sound mental health is correlated to strong ethnic identification, and by extrapolation, the same holds true for pastoral care (for example, Pinderhughes 1990).

One of the most rewarding aspects of antiracist pastoral care is to learn about other racial and cultural groups. Such work provides opportunities for lasting relationships between individuals of diverse racial and ethnic backgrounds and confronts the isolation of those outside the dominant culture. Marginalized groups have a history of courage in the midst of racism that can strengthen communities of faith when recognized. An inadequate understanding of how race and ethnicity work within a religious context hampers multiracial coalition building in the larger community. African Americans, Asian Americans, Hispanic Americans, American Indians, or European Americans all bring distinctive cultures and positive contributions to pastoral care situations.

Promoting antiracist pastoral care requires a commitment on all levels of institutional life. Cultural competence is the outcome of a multilevel process of multicultural and antiracism awareness, which enables pastoral caregivers and religious communities to:[3]

1. *Know the difference between race, ethnicity, and culture—that culture is more than race and ethnicity—and gain expertise in applying this knowledge within pastoral care contexts.* While the focus of this essay is on racism, which to a large degree remains the most divisive issue in U.S. society, other dimensions of culture include ethnicity, gender, geography, age, ability, social class, sexual identity, religion, nationality, immigration status, and so on. We need to acknowledge that these differences are real. As Larry Kent Graham suggests, "God is big enough to let each entity be itself, rather than something else. So must we be, if we reflect God's love" (1997, 176). On a personal level, this means that white pastoral caregivers understand how culture shapes their white identity, how whiteness dominates our culture and religious institutions, and how the reshaping of our identities is a lifelong process. We also need to recognize the multitude of cultural differences between people of color. Here pastoral caregivers need to get in touch with their individual cultural backgrounds, share and reflect on their own personal stories, and listen and reflect on the stories of others with the goal of building shared pride in commonness and differences.

2. *Get in touch with issues of prejudice and stereotypes.* Cultural competence requires each pastoral caregiver to examine his or her own biases, and to develop an understanding about what impact these characteristics have on pastoral relationships with persons of different cultures. When dealing with issues of race and culture, feelings of anxiety, awkwardness, fear, and discomfort are natural. Often there is a prevailing sense that acknowledging difference is wholly negative, or that a lack of a multicultural vocabulary is uncomfortable. Internal biases about different racial and cultural groups are often based on

a feeling level, rather than on a cognitive level. Here pastors may benefit from reflection on their families of origin and what was taught them about racial and cultural differences.

3. *Challenge the myth of "color blindness," and be aware of the reality of "color consciousness" as it pertains to race and pastoral care.* People of color have suffered many injustices at the hands of white people, and continue to do so within religious institutions. The reality of oppression is present whether the dominant culture chooses to recognize it or not. Thus, pastoral caregivers concerned with gaining cultural competency need to be aware of how racial identity informs power relationships. Further, it is important for white pastors to learn when and how it is appropriate to advocate on behalf of marginalized persons and those from different racial groups.

4. *Understand that race, ethnicity, gender, economic class, sexual identity, age, ability, religion, nationality, immigration status, and so forth are organizing principles for good or ill in everything we do.* It is important for those working for systemic change within pastoral care to have a grasp of the "interlocking" nature of oppressions. That is, oppression, the use of power by one group against another, is expressed in many different interrelated ways. Racism, sexism, classism, heterosexism, ableism, and ageism are terms used to describe various forms of oppression. All too frequently, people concerned with social inequities focus on only one or two of these "isms," often at the price of disregarding the others. *Everyone* has experienced some form of oppression, and all forms of oppression damage, not only those in marginalized groups (people of color, women, disabled people, etc.), but those in the dominant culture as well. Cultural competence suggests knowledge of the complex nature of interlocking oppressions, rather than focusing on all forms of oppression through the lens of a single issue.

5. *Recognize there are multiple centers of truth, whose legitimacy is often determined by the amount of power any given perspective may have in a particular context.* The human tendency to universalize our own experience notwithstanding, it is important to understand that what we value as "objective truth" may not be perceived the same way by persons of different racial groups who have their own experiences of truth. As Elaine Graham argues, "Those who reduce 'truth' to their own image actually distort that inherent complexity and

heterogeneity of human experience. This, embracing the Other and celebrating, not repressing, diversity, is the avenue to genuine, non-coercive identity and truth" (1996, 200). For those of us who are white Americans, this means that we can never *really* know what it means to be anyone other than a white person, and that part of the skills needed are those that help us identify how to become an effective ally with people of color given our own experience, attributes, and limitations. Although people of color generally know a great deal about white culture because it is critical to survival, they, too, need to develop strategies on how to recognize and cultivate helpful white allies. As Emmanuel Lartey states, "Every human person is in some respects (a) like all others (b) like some others (c) like no other" (2003, 171).

6. *Develop a rich symbolic life.* "Spiritual liberation is necessary for, and the base of, the imagination for material liberation. In these spaces, the technologies of the sacred, art, music, oral and written literature all express the needs and struggles of the community seeking the transformation of oppressive conditions" (Smith 1993, 160). Part of the challenge of antiracist pastoral care is adapting the symbolic life of our congregations in terms of worship, music, education, art, and architecture to reflect different races and cultures. In your faith community, does pastoral care reflect racially and culturally diverse language and content? Are prayers, music, and symbols from a variety of cultural and religious traditions welcomed? Are the religious holidays celebrated and the heroes of the faith reflective racially, and culturally diverse? Does the "sacred space" reflect a multicultural, rather than a homogeneous, reality? The symbolic life is a powerful ingredient in antiracist pastoral care, but not all symbols are experienced as positive and healing in all contexts.

7. *Cultivate spiritual stamina.* God calls humankind to a life of rich diversity. Our spirituality reflects the relationships we have with God, other people, and the world, and are consistent with our racial, ethnic, and cultural heritages. The process of living out antiracist pastoral care transforms our hearts, and minds, and lives, and brings about new attitudes and behaviors about God, oneself, and our larger society. It requires a great deal of spiritual stamina. A disciplined life of prayer and reflection rooted in a faith community is perhaps the greatest source of support for the challenges ahead.

In his book *The Color of Faith: Building Community in Multiracial Society,* Fumitaka Matsuoka offers advice to people of faith compelled to build pastoral relationships across difference: "The starting point is not to find ways of uniting people divided by fear and violence, but to recognize, celebrate, and learn from God's gift of one creation embodied in varied cultures, languages, religions and races. It is to restore moral integrity in the midst of the culture of decay by restoring freedom and dignity to the captives we held" (1998, 104).

People of faith today are called to respond to a world that is groaning under the weight of injustice and broken relationships. Our differences and our interdependence are intended to be a source of strength and a gift from God. As people of faith, we know that the reign of God will not ultimately be built on separatism or political arguments, but on the transformation of hearts—*new* life, not just reordered life. As the people of God who believe in justice, forgiveness, and reconciliation, we can resist the temptation to stop at the political, social, or even emotional level of racial awareness. Rather, through antiracist pastoral care we can work to bring about the healing and wholeness that the world craves.

THREE

Engaging Diversity and Difference: From Practice of Exclusion to Practices of Practical Solidarity

Brita L. Gill-Austern

One of the most stunning facts of being human is that each individual shares 99.9 percent of the same DNA with all other humans. Yet it is that less than one-tenth of 1 percent of difference that creates a good deal of the havoc, conflict, war, and oppression in our world. The differences between us lead to many acts of dehumanization and practices of exclusion toward the one or ones we consider "other." The human race is still struggling with learning how to deal with its differences in ways that can contribute to the beauty, richness, and meaning of life, rather than be the source of such unrelenting oppression and suffering.

In this essay, I argue that the vitality of life and creation rests upon the interplay of difference and unity. Drawing upon the work of Miroslav Volf, I will show how human beings unable to maintain the creative tension between difference and unity consistently turn to various practices of exclusion to deal with difference. These practices of exclusion further the disconnections between us that dehumanize us all and contribute to oppression and the suffering that follows in its wake. I will argue that one form of exclusion, poverty, is maintained through the practice of abandonment and indifference. Finally, I will develop a definition of practices of practical solidarity and show how in the face of oppression they can move us away from practices of exclusion to practices of practical solidarity.[1]

Diversity, Difference, and Unity are the Dance of Creation

The Mexican writer Octavio Paz wrote: "What sets the worlds in motion is the interplay of differences, their attractions and repulsions. Life is plurality, death is uniformity" (1985, 17). This truth is also built into our common creation story. As theologian Sallie McFague reminds us:

> The common creation story radicalizes both oneness and difference. From one infinitely hot, infinitely condensed bit of matter (a millionth of a gram) some fifteen billion years ago, have evolved one hundred billion galaxies, each its billions of stars and planets. . . . Biologists have found in a single square foot of topsoil an inch deep an average of 1,356 living creatures, including 865 mites, 265 springtails, 22 millipedes, 19 adult beetles and various numbers of other forms. From one millionth of a gram of matter, unimaginable unity, has evolved unimaginable diversity. (1993, 38)

If anything can be said about the creative source of the world, it is that the Source of All loves diversity and unity. The common creation story tells us that the basic dynamic of the universe is a constant dance between distinctiveness and communion, with every distinctive part of the universe being attracted to another part. The basic dynamic of the universe is also at the heart of genuine care and justice making. Care, pastoral theologian Peggy Way reminds us, "seeks embrace, the embrace of difference and hence the embrace of the possibility of community" (2005, 59).

The problem of difference, of seeing "the other" as object rather than subject, permeates our individual and communal lives. As a species we still need to work on the dance that makes distinctiveness and difference belong to the experience of communion rather than disconnection. All too often we interrupt the dance of creation that binds difference and communion, diversity and unity together, by treating difference as a threat to both identity and community. Too often we deal with differences by and through practices of exclusion, which also foster systemic oppression. To bring creative change, we must address directly the practices of exclusion that oppress others based on perceived and real differences and find ways to model and incarnate for others practices of practical solidarity.

Practices of Exclusion

Carl Sandburg called "exclusion the ugliest word in the English language,"[2] no doubt because of all that ugliness it spawns in human life. Exclusion results from a failure to hold in creative tension what we know of reality from the beginning of creation: we are both distinct and differentiated from everything else and also a part of and drawn into an inescapable web of interdependence, reciprocity, and mutuality that yearns for communion.

We deal with difference, according to Volf in his book *Exclusion and Embrace,* through the violence of exclusion. To heal the disconnections that divide us we must look at what Volf calls "the powerful, contagious and destructive evil of exclusion" (1996, 30). Practices of exclusion are rooted in our interpersonal and familial histories. They thrive, as do weeds in a garden, when identity is seen exclusively through the lens of our own tribe or culture, when we are blinded by our captivity to that culture, and when the narcissism of self-absorption prevents us from recognizing the historical realities of others.[3]

Volf identifies four forms of the violence of exclusion in the ways in which we deal with difference, each of which can make life hell on earth.

First, he names the *violence of expulsion,* when we intentionally and often violently exile others from community or proclaim that "they" do not belong. In such objectification of the other, we create a rationale for violence. Some of the most horrific practices of expulsion depend upon hatred and evoking it in others (1996, 74). Expulsion takes its most extreme form through the elimination of "the other" in such historical events as the ethnic cleansing in the Balkans, the Holocaust, the genocide of Rwanda. The exclusion of expulsion says fundamentally: You do not belong to the family of humanity; you are "other," you are vermin, rats, scum, and therefore I have a right to kill you. The exclusion of expulsion can also be found in discrimination, in the workplace, in ghettos and white suburbs, in schools of privilege, and in prisons filled with those made poor by structures that perpetuate economic inequality.

Second, we deal with difference, according to Volf, by the *violence of assimilation.* This is a milder form of eliminating the identity of the other, which occurs when we incorporate the other into our reality by obliterating his or her reality. The other only exists through the lens that the assimilator creates in order to make him or her become like oneself. Distinctiveness is swallowed up, repressed, or denied. Volf, drawing on Claude Lévi-Strauss, says that exclusion by assimilation rests on a deal: "we will refrain from vomiting you out, if you let us swallow you up" (ibid.). We see this in the United States when acceptance of immigrants is based on their becoming just like "us," giving up their language, customs, and culture.

Another common pattern for dealing with difference is through *subjugating the other*. We designate others as inferior in some way, then use them or exploit them to increase our wealth, or inflate our egos (1996, 75). When we do this we are often operating out of an ideology of scarcity, whereby we exclude others from scarce goods be they economic, social, or psychological. This is exclusion made concrete in practices of domination, revealing our desire to be alone at the center. We see these patterns of exclusion in the history of colonization, in much of our global market economy, and in gender relations in many parts of the world.

Finally, Volf says, we practice *exclusion by the indifference of abandonment*. Here we deal with difference by pretending we just do not see. We see, but pass over to the other side. We see, but we keep our distance so that the other has no claim on us. We see, but we divert our attention to other things. We see, but we feel powerless, so we push this seeing from consciousness. The exclusion of indifference, when the "other" becomes anonymous or invisible to us, grows like mold in a basement. Volf reminds us that when the other lives at a distance, indifference can be more destructive than hate (ibid., 77).

Underlying most forms of oppression and practices of exclusion are persistent and pervasive patterns of disconnection. These patterns of disconnection not only lay a foundation for oppression, fundamentally they also create an attitude that we are not responsible. Patterns of disconnection are at the root of some of our most intractable social problems: violence, war, racism, ecological devastation, homophobia, and the increasing economic inequality in our world. These problems and others are maintained and exacerbated by patterns of exclusion that reify such feelings of disconnection.

The Exclusion of the Practice of Abandonment of Those Made Poor

An attitude of indifference lies beneath the practice of abandonment and we see its expression most vividly in the abandonment of those who have been made poor. I focus on the practice of indifference and abandonment and the patterns of disconnection that give rise to it for three reasons: first, I believe it is the practice of exclusion to which the majority of U.S. citizens are most susceptible; second, in our historical moment it has the most power to spawn suffering and evil; and finally, I believe this is the practice of exclusion where faith communities and our practices of care can make the greatest impact. The Gospels are permeated with Jesus' concern for exclusion. The good news of Christ's welcoming embrace comes again and again to those who are abandoned to live on the margins of exclusion.

The problem of abandonment stems from a lack of connection. We exclude and abandon others when we feel no connection with them or we fail to recognize our connection. When there is no sense of connection, the expected common reaction is indifference, which leads to abandonment. Without relationship, we lose a sense of responsibility to the other.

Where is the place in our world where the exclusion of indifference and abandonment is most evident? Many would argue that it is in the growing gap of economic inequality that allows an increasing abandonment of the poor. Only indifference and abandonment of the poor would allow the richest 10 percent of the world's population to receive 49.6 percent of the world's total income, while the bottom 60 percent receives 13.9 percent.[4] Economic inequality eventually leads to more social breakdown and disconnection (Collins and Yeskel 2005, 30).

Salvadoran theologian Jon Sobrino points to the fact that, quantitatively, poverty constitutes the most painful suffering on this planet. He calls its day-to-day, death-dealing reality "the world's most serious wound" (1992, 22). The greatest weapon of mass destruction in our world today is poverty; nothing else comes close. All the casualties of all the wars in the world do not equal those who die because of causes related to poverty. The oppression of those whom minister Delle McComick, executive director of the experiential educational organization Borderlinks, calls "the made poor," the largest percentage of whom are persons of color, by the vast economic inequalities of our nation and our world, is one of the most urgent moral issues of our time and the greatest challenge to the witness of faith communities.

Way reminds us in her book *Created by God: Pastoral Care for All God's People* (2005) that pastoral care is faithful living by finite creatures in their particular historical context. Our particular historical context demands that we give increased attention to the exclusion practiced through abandonment by the "haves" of the "have-nots" of our world. How can one billion people, almost one fifth of the world's population, live on less than a dollar a day unless much of the world simply accepts their fate with indifference and abandons them to their plight?

Behind the statistics of poverty from all corners of the world are millions of stories of individual women, children, and men whose exclusion from power and the world's resources has resulted in lives of unbelievable hardship and premature death. In the United States it is becoming harder to deny the death-dealing power of the exclusion of indifference and abandonment. In this country we have seen that the poorest were most at risk by Hurricane Katrina. One out of six persons in New Orleans did not own an automobile, and therefore were dependent upon public or government-provided transportation to evacuate. They lived in the lowest, most flood-prone parts of New Orleans. Some think Katrina has begun to shake us out of our slumber. But if you look at the slow rebuilding of New Orleans and what has happened to many of its former residents, we need to wonder. We give generously immediately following a crisis, we write checks, we gather food for food banks and open our doors for soup kitchens, but the underlying structures that continue to fuel inequality, and are the most resistant to change, remain in place.

The indifference of abandonment, and the form of politics it generates, comes at least in part because we have lost a sense of connection to those who suffer from the impact of poverty. The great divide between the "haves" and "have-nots" in our world can only be crossed by building connective bridges that foster relationship and a sense of community with those outside our immediate circle. Because we are knit together in an inescapable web of mutuality and interdependence, we need each other to be fully human. Without recognition of this interdependence, the self and other are dehumanized. A "re-humanization" of the self and other can happen through connection with those outside of our immediate circles or "lifestyle enclaves."[5] This movement can be facilitated by practices of practical solidarity in congregations that deepen our sense of connection to those who live on the margins.

Practices of Practical Solidarity

How do we weave the ties that bind us to others beyond our own cultural boundaries and economic class? How do we awaken from our patterns of exclusion of "the made poor" by expulsion, subjugation, assimilation, and the indifference of abandonment? How do we create practices of practical solidarity in order to heal the disconnections that divide us, and that contribute to genuine justice making? How do we do this within the context of faith communities that can nurture, foster, sustain, and call forth such practices?

These questions do not assume that the brokenness of this world can be fully overcome, or that redemption lies at the end of history, or in some utopia, but they do assume that we can incarnate love, mercy, and justice in the moments that are given us to share with others on this earth and that such moments may be engendered by practices of practical solidarity.

While there is no one answer to the questions I pose, at least part of our task consists in shaping and forming persons and communities: first, who have the emotional and intellectual maturity and skills to live constructively with difference and who are enriched rather than threatened by otherness; second, who are able to open the doors of their hearts and minds to those who have been excluded; and third, who can understand that justice, as Martin Luther King Jr. once said, "is love enfleshed in history," and who make a commitment to justice-making in a concrete and particular arena, while at the same time seeing its connections to other arenas.

So what does this shaping require? One way we can begin to shape such persons and communities is through "practices of practical solidarity." Practical solidarity means we do not simply feel compassion and empathy for others, but commit ourselves to be in the struggle for justice with them. We do not simply suffer with people; we also struggle alongside of them. One Nicaraguan summed up for me what is at the heart of practical solidarity, "to make mine the problem of the other and together to find a solution, while giving myself to the other."

Practices of practical solidarity require developing a capacity to recognize our common humanity and our common need of one another for individual wholeness and for the healing of our world. The prophet Isaiah reminds us that when we feed the hungry, clothe the naked, bring the homeless poor into our own houses, and do not hide ourselves from our own kin, then our light will shine and our wounds will speedily heal (Isa. 58:6-9). Only with the recognition "that interdependency sustains the life of the planet" (Bellah 1985, 130) will we be able to build genuine solidarity with those made poor.

Practices of practical solidarity also require what Sobrino describes as the "principle of mercy":

The ideal human being, the complete human being, is the one who interiorizes, absorbs in her innards, the suffering of another—as in the case of the parable (The Good Samaritan)—unjustly afflicted suffering in such a way that this internalized suffering becomes a part of her, is transformed into an internal principle, the first and the last, of her activity. Mercy, as re-action, becomes the fundamental action of the human being." (1994, 17)

For Sobrino, mercy is what defines the human being. We cannot therefore become human without recognizing our connection to the other, a connection that happens when the suffering of another moves us enough in our viscera that we must act. Mercy is a precondition for real justice, for it never loses the face of the other's suffering. Mercy, for Sobrino, is the particular Christian "praxic love that swells within a person at the sight of another person's unjustly inflicted suffering, driving its subject to eradicate that suffering for no other reason than that it exists, and precluding any excuse for not doing so" (1994, 18). To eradicate suffering, for Sobrino, begins with being so moved by the suffering of another that one cannot help but act. But he makes very clear that we cannot confuse the principle of mercy with the works of mercy:

> When mercy is taken seriously as the first and the last, it becomes conflictive. No one is thrown in prison or persecuted simply for having practiced the works of mercy. Not even Jesus would have been persecuted and put to death, had his mercy been mere mercy—without being mercy as the first and the last. But when mercy becomes the first and the last, then it subverts society's ultimate values, and society reacts." (1994, 24)

We cannot truly care for those who are oppressed without being moved by their suffering. But mercy as a principle also requires closer proximity to those who suffer. We must struggle alongside of the suffering in the pursuit of justice-making, knowing that by being in closer proximity relationally and physically more may be asked of us than we had anticipated.

The practice of practical solidarity is not simply the practice of an individual. At its best it calls forth the commitment of faith communities who recognize that the "place of the church is with 'the other,' and with the most radical otherness of that other—his suffering—especially when that suffering is massive, cruel and unjust" (Sobrino 1994, 21).

Three Movements and Three Practices of Practical Solidarity

Three movements and three practices of practical solidarity can begin our conversion to the principle of mercy and help move us beyond the practices of exclusion and abandonment.

First Move: Know Home

We cannot work with those who suffer from oppression of any sort without being willing to become "ruthlessly self-aware" and to confront the baggage that each of us brings to this work (Meyers 1999, 158). This means, first, as poet Adrienne Rich once said, to "understand the assumptions in which we are drenched" (1979, 35). This means our assumptions about the poor, about poverty, and about why poverty exists. It also includes understanding our assumptions about privilege. We cannot undo the yokes of oppression and exclusion without clearly recognizing how systems of privilege and power in which we participate support structures of oppression. We cannot reach out to the other without a radical openness to examining our own complicity in structures of oppression.

To connect with those outside our own immediate circle, we need to know and own our familial home, cultural home, economic home, and our faith home. We need to know the landscape of where we have been dwelling all these years and bring it to full consciousness. As bell hooks says, "To work for change we need to know where we stand" (2000, 9). And where many of us stand is in the landscape of privilege; without being able to name this reality and identify its consequences we cannot know home.

To know our familial home means to see the patterns and habits of being and doing that have been passed down from one generation to the next, and how and where we have been shaped and misshaped by our parents' and family's culture, attitudes, and actions. We need to know and own the cultural milieu in which we have been formed and rooted. We need to see the network of commitments that bind us to a place and a people and the social arrangements in which we are inextricably linked that disconnect us from the lived realities of others. Knowing our economic home means grasping how our economic well-being or lack thereof, our class, has shaped the way we see the world. How does it influence our values and priorities? How does it open or close us to cultural worlds outside our own? To know our faith home is to wrestle with what is absolutely foundational and to ask what the implications of that faith are. In each of these arenas we need to ask the question: How has this home (familial, cultural, economic, faith) influenced our own practices of exclusion and how and in what ways can our home help promote practices of practical solidarity?

First Practice: Self-Examination, Confession, and Repentance

The first movement, knowing home, leads to the first practice of practical solidarity: self-examination, confession, and repentance. Before we can scale the walls that divide us, we have to see what bricks we are living behind.

One of the bricks we need to confront is what Walter Wink calls the "delusional system" that makes us believe lies about ourselves and others: "The rulers of the earth do not know that they too are held in thrall by the delusional system. They do not know whom they serve" (1992, 97). Only when the delusions of both the poor and the nonpoor are addressed and the web of lies is exposed and confronted by God's truth can the structures that support poverty be dismantled (B. Meyers 1999, 79). Only through honest self-examination can we move to confess where and how we have practiced exclusion in our own lives. Only then can we begin to withdraw projections, confess to our moral self-righteousness, and take the first step to seeing others in their distinctiveness and not simply as our projection. The bottom line is the need to stop seeing evil as "out there," but rather as Volf writes about it, "exclusion as barbarity within civilization, evil among the good, crime against the other right within the walls of the self" (1996, 60). This practice leads us to see that nothing that is human can be totally alien, for we see the stranger and "other" lives within us. In them, I see me; in me, I see them. In self-examination, we see the connection within and between.

Repentance and confession include the need to confess our own spiritual poverty. David Meyers writes, "More than ever, we have big houses and broken homes, high incomes and low morale, secured rights and diminished civility. We excel at making a living, but often fail at making a life. We celebrate our prosperity, but yearn for a purpose. We cherish our freedoms, but long for connection, in an age of plenty, we feel spiritual hunger" (quoted in De Graaf et al. 2005, 114). We cannot move toward the marriage of justice with mercy, without confronting the emptiness of our own lives and asking ourselves the cost of the disconnections in our own lives. One such cost is the growing rate of addiction, a rate that is growing faster among the affluent than among those living lives of economic marginalization. Yet addiction in all its forms—drugs, alcoholism, compulsive conspicuous consumption, gambling, "workaholism"— seeks to address a gnawing emptiness, a lack of meaning and purpose, and in the process destroys relationships and contributes to patterns of disconnection.

For those of us who stand among the privileged in our society and in our world, we need to begin the inoculation against the virus and addiction of *affluenza*. Conspicuous over-consumption is a disease and an addiction that is a "painful, contagious and socially transmitted condition of overload, debt, anxiety, and waste resulting from the dogged pursuit of more" (De Graaf et al. 2005, 2). We need to confront and expose the idolatry of gluttonous consumption that teaches us to choose things over people. As we buy more, we seem to become increasingly spiritually empty. The average American parent spends six hours a week shopping and forty minutes playing with his or her kids (De Graaf et al.

2005, 7). *Affluenza* is a seductive and infectious virus because it makes us believe that we are what we possess, equating worth with possessions. Simultaneously, it mars the true identity of those who have little and of those who have much. "Without a fundamental core belief that we are always more than our material possessions, we doom the poor to a life of meaningless struggle. This is a form of psychic genocide. To honor the lives of the poor, we need to resist such thinking. We need to challenge psychic assault on the poor with the same zeal deployed to resist material exploitation" (hooks 2000, 130).

Affluenza is rooted in what hooks has called "predatory capitalism," which is rooted in greed (2000, 67). *Affluenza* punishes the poor twice. The rich get richer and the poor get poorer. While we are all conditioned to want the good life, a large segment of our society and the world is given very little possibility of getting that good life. The result is that "ostentatious materiality, the flaunting of excess, erodes community no matter whether it is done by the greedy rich or the suffering poor" (Bellah et al. 1985, 62). Only in confronting the culture of greed and standing up to it in the personal moral choices of our lives will we restore a sense of identity that is not based on overidentification with material objects.

Repentance, confession, and self-examination have to include the examination of our sense of entitlement in relationship to the world's needs. We need to confront our practices of giving, which are often from our overabundance, from what is left over, rather than asking just how much am I permitted to have when so many live with so little. One needs to ask oneself: How can I begin to move my life into more conscious practices of practical solidarity with others in the world? There are many such practices: choosing to buy consciously and frugally, committing to buy fair trade whenever possible, recycling faithfully, and using consciously the world's resources by reflecting on "just what is my fair share?" Such reflection also leads to pledging a more significant distribution of one's own economic resources to help create a more equitable society. Self-examination also has a communal dimension, for instance, challenging our own nation to examine its practices of giving in the form of international aid. Although the United States is the wealthiest nation in the world, we are twentieth among industrial nations in the percentage of the GNP that we give to developmental assistance (Collins and Yeskel 2005, 54). Communal self-examination includes a concern for how our economic policies (like a minimum wage that keeps full-time working people below the poverty line), our health-care policies, our tax laws, and the barriers to forming unions contribute to practices of exclusion and abandonment.

Second Move: To Make Pilgrimage

We never fully know home until we have left it, until we have made a pilgrimage to somewhere else. In many ways, the second movement deepens the first. Just as God said to Abraham, "Go from this land, to a land that I will show you," we, too, are to make pilgrimage and leave home, because God calls us to a new future that is always more than our past. Pilgrimage, then, becomes a way to deconstruct the home that has built borders to keep others out, as well as to see clearly where it has created space to receive others. If we are not careful we can slip into the exclusion of assimilation, coming to see the "other" only through our own lens, instead of getting ourselves a new set of glasses.

Pilgrimage was an ancient spiritual practice that was not simply a metaphor, but a literal spiritual practice in the Christian tradition by which people achieved dehabituation from their accustomed environment. Margaret Miles talks about spiritual practice as "a way to deconstruct the socialization and conditioning inscribed on the body, mind and heart by the world and to produce a new organizing center of the self" (1990, 51). Pilgrimage, as a spiritual practice, requires some kind of displacement that dislodges us from the known and familiar and allows us to see what has been inscribed on our own body, mind, and heart by our own socialization and conditioning. Pilgrimage, as a spiritual practice, becomes transformative when it displaces the self from the center of reality and creates a new organizing center of the self.

To overcome the practices of exclusion that undergird oppression we need to find ways to weave ties of connection and relationship with those outside of whatever we call home. This requires that we adapt the practice of pilgrimage for our own time, in what I am calling the second practice of practical solidarity, the practice of constructive engagement with otherness.

Second Practice: Constructive Engagement with Otherness

In the book *Common Fire: Leading Lives of Commitment in a Complex Age*, the authors set out to discover what shaped and formed people who had sustained a commitment to work on behalf of the common good (Daloz et al. 1997). They interviewed over a hundred people who had sustained a long-term commitment to the common good, most for more than twenty years. The criteria for interviewing people included: a commitment to the common good; perseverance and resilience; ethical congruence between life and work; and engagement with diversity and complexity. The common thread they identified in the life experience of each person they studied was a "constructive engagement with otherness." Each person told some story about a constructive engagement in which they experienced a "sympathetic identification" where they felt that the "other" experienced some fundamental aspect of life in the same way they did (1997, 67). Through this, they gained an ability to recognize both difference and commonality. Such experiences came in many forms, such as an artist working with the elderly poor to realize their artistic talents, a man deeply engaging with a person with a disability, or a woman crossing through the gates of a prison from her privileged upbringing to be involved in an "Alternatives to Violence" program. Each of these experiences involved encounters where people had the opportunity to get to know others deeply and develop an empathic connection.

The practice of constructive engagement with otherness can take many forms, but if the church is serious about shaping and forming people who can move toward practices of justice and mercy instead of practices of exclusion, it must develop multiple opportunities for people to experience constructive engagement with otherness.

Over the last five years, I have led seminary students on immersion trips to Nicaragua, El Salvador, and Mexico, and I have seen the kind of shifts that can take place through constructive engagement with those who were not previously in their circle of awareness or concern. Such formation by immersion experiences or service learning trips can deepen and promote the experiences of solidarity, commitment, and community, provided that the students approach the experience as learners and know they have as much to receive as to share. As an aboriginal woman once said, "If you came here to help me, please go home, but if you came because you know that somehow your destiny is tied up with mine, please stay and we can work together." People who have had the chance to cross borders in their lives and experience the impact of poverty and oppression on others through a relationship of working side-by-side often find themselves profoundly changed (Swedish and Dennis 2004). For immersion experiences to provide constructive engagement with otherness, however, they need to create space for critical reflection and opportunities to make connections to one's home.

Travel outside the United States is not required for such an encounter or experience of constructive engagement with otherness. It can be around the corner. As Harold Recinos (1992) reminds us, global encounters can be on our doorsteps. Jonathan Kozol named the encounter that we avoid that is right around the corner from where we live: "The ultimate terror for white people is to leave the highway by mistake and find themselves in East St. Louis as nightmare. The nightmare to me is that they never leave that highway so that they never know what life is like for all the children here. They ought to get off that highway. The nightmare isn't in their heads. It's a real place. There are children living there" (1991, 18). We cannot engender real concern for the other or move toward practices of mercy and justice if we do not even have social contact with others that allows some constructive engagement to happen.

To have a constructive engagement with otherness requires that we step out of the familiar into an unknown place where we have to struggle alongside others and learn to see the world from their perspective, and in so doing simultaneously find ourselves developing empathic identification. Our entry places may be different, but the commitment is to grow the circle of our concern. Such engagements seem to lead to successive experiences of people rediscovering shared common bonds (Daloz et al. 1997, 68). The practice of constructive engagement with otherness can take many forms, pilgrimage being one. If congregations are serious about shaping and forming people who can engage in practices of practical solidarity that increase mercy and justice, then they need to offer opportunities for constructive engagement with otherness through some form of modern-day pilgrimage that helps people cross borders of class, nationality, ethnicity, and worldviews where they develop empathic identification with the other. But pilgrimage also requires returning home.

Third Move: Returning Home

Every pilgrimage, every constructive engagement, ends with a return home. Here, too, there is work to be done. Returning home requires that we find ways to weave new connections with those we have left; that we bear witness to what we have seen and what we have learned. Whether it is an adult who has been working with autistic children, or teaching on a Native American reservation, or returning from an immersion trip overseas, we create more porous borders to community in the doing and in the sharing. We must go through the discomfort and upheaval that comes, as the return also means we may have to shift the arrangements of our allegiances. Such shifting of the arrangement of our allegiances may mean that we inhabit new spaces and places in our lives that help us keep company with those who suffer from the unjust structures of oppression and poverty. Transformative pilgrimage will mean we can't return home as the same people who left. Inevitably it will lead to the necessity of breaking the silence around the slow, wordless death that comes in the wake of extreme poverty and to confront in very personal and practical ways our complicity in structures of privilege and oppression. To return is to have to face our complicity in the status quo and to name it, but also to risk the tension and conflict that comes from making new commitments given what we have experienced and witnessed. "To ignore evil," Martin Luther King Jr. once said, "is to become an accomplice to it" (1967, 246). Returning home requires empowering those we have met on the margins to have a public voice.

Third Practice: Partnering with Others

Many Americans tend to be strong individualists with tendencies toward being "Lone Rangers." Peggy Way reminds us that "the first duty of the Christian is to confess not to be God" (2005, 20). Partnering with others reminds us again and again that the world's healing does not depend on us alone and that we cannot change the world alone. Humility requires our recognition of the need of the other. The more deeply we move into the work of mercy and justice, the more we come to realize that we cannot do this work alone. Most of us will discover that many people were involved in the struggle before we ever showed up.

Oppression happens when individuals and groups are powerless. Partnership is an essential practice of practical solidarity because practices of practical solidarity require an intention to help further the empowerment of those who have been disempowered. Partnering begins with the humility to know that we do not know what is best for the other.

Only by seeking genuine partnership can we protect others and ourselves from unnecessary harm. Bryant Meyers speaks of the importance of participation in transformational development and names three critical questions about participation (1999, 148). I paraphrase these to address the issue of partnership: (1) Who are the partners? Who is being included, excluded? (2) What kind of partnering are we talking about? What are the agreements underlying the partnering? How are decisions being made? Are there limits placed on the partnership? (3) How is the partnership being enacted? What evidence will we see that this is a real partnership of equity? Is the partnering integral and central and not simply erratic and formal? Is the result of the partnership empowerment for those who have been disempowered? Partnering requires ownership of the process by all being involved from beginning to end, which includes research and analysis, planning, implementing, and evaluating (ibid.). Partnership requires intentionality that incorporates inclusion in all processes, and that builds the means by which empowerment happens. Partnership develops community when there is equal participation, clear communication, and respect for what all participants bring to the process.

Repeatedly, I have seen those living in poverty "keep on keeping on," in large part because they stay close to one another. They persevere in the suffering and find the courage to resist and persist, because they stay in connection with one another, because they lean on one another. They know how to reach out and partner with others to do whatever it is that needs to be done. It is learning the power of "one plus one."

Recently in listening to a group traveling here from Nicaragua I heard a man say, "We just can't believe the millions of cars everywhere, and there is only one in each one."[6] In Nicaragua you can't travel down a rural country road without stopping and picking someone up until there is simply no more room. We have lost an essential truth to becoming human: our mutual survival and well-being depends on interdependency, not going it alone.

To learn how to partner with others in the building of communities that embody lives of mercy and justice, we need to learn how to lean on each other. Jesus did not do his work alone. He found disciples, formed a community around him, and sent people out two by two. We can only keep practices of practical solidarity when we join with and alongside others in the struggle. Poet Maya Angelou (1975, 25) reminds us again and again of what we forget:

> *Nobody, but nobody*
> *Can make it out here alone*

Maya Angelou etches in our hearts the truth we know, that we only live through and by the grace of God and others. We are inextricably woven in a web of mutuality that requires us to acknowledge our mutual interdependence. Ultimately, the future of our country and our world depends upon our capacity to see that practical solidarity with those made poor is the only means by which we can help lead our country and world back to a "vision of community that can effectively challenge and eliminate violence and exploitation" (hooks 2000, 49).

As we confront our practices of exclusion and forge practices of practical solidarity, we discover that good news is proclaimed in bad-news places, that transformation of life often happens on the margins of life, that the joy and goodness of God breaks out in hospitality to the stranger in communities where practices of exclusion have been replaced with practices of practical solidarity. When this happens we are all born anew, the doors to our hearts are unlatched, and instead of disconnection we experience love, mercy, and justice flowing into our lives and into the world.

FOUR

Pastoral Care with African American Women: Womanist Perspectives and Strategies

Marsha I. Wiggins and Carmen Braun Williams

Pastoral care in the twenty-first century is shaped not only by values and commitments of individual pastors and caregivers, but by the complex levels of pluralism, multiculturalism, and oppression that characterize U.S. communities. Historically, pastoral care has been defined as the provision of religious leadership in a faith-based group (Everly 2000, 69–71). The tasks generally associated with pastoral care include personal support, religious education, community organization, worship, ethical decision-making, and spiritual guidance (ibid.). In general, clergy and others who provide pastoral care have focused largely on *individual need* rather than on *social realities*, on personal pain rather than corporate suffering. Moreover, pastoral care developed primarily within white, Western Christian denominations, and thus much of its theology and worldview reflects these roots. The purpose of this essay is to suggest that offering pastoral care to African American women requires that caregivers acknowledge their possible positions of power and privilege in relation to those to whom they provide care. They must also take seriously the challenge of providing pastoral care for both individual African American women and acting prophetically as regards oppressive systems. Here, we propose a *womanist* approach to pastoral care that validates African American women's experience as the crucible for pastoral care of both individuals and systems struggling under the burdens of oppression.

The Womanist Perspective as a Key to Pastoral Care

"Womanism," a term coined by Alice Walker in her book *In Search of Our Mother's Gardens,* when applied to theology holds a key to pastoral care with African American women. Walker describes what she means by "womanist" in this excerpt:

> Womanist, from womanish (Opposite of 'girlish,' i.e. frivolous, irresponsible, not serious). A Black feminist or feminist of color. From the Black folk expression of mothers to female children, 'You acting womanish,' i.e., like a woman. Usually referring to outrageous, audacious, courageous, or willful behavior. Wanting to know more and in greater depth than is considered 'good' for one. Interest in grown-up doings. Acting grown-up. Being grown-up. Interchangeable with another black folk expression: 'You trying to be grown.' Responsible. In charge. Serious. (1987, xi)

Further, Walker says that a "womanist" loves women's culture, but is not a separatist. She claims that womanists oppose homophobia and colorism (value judgments made on the basis of how light or dark one's skin is). They also eschew class hierarchy because they are committed to the survival of the whole people. Womanism is all about black female emotional flexibility and strength (D. S. Williams 1993). Womanist theology is a way of thinking about God and ministry from the African American female perspective. It is a response to the reality that "Black women at best are invisible in Black theology and at worst exploited by African American men" (Hopkins 2005, 20). Womanist theology is rooted in and grows out of black theology, feminist theology, black women's experience, and the biblical witness (Crawford 2004). Ultimately, the goal of womanist theology is to address the multidimensional oppression in African American women's lives related to racism, classism, sexism, and heterosexism. As such it "challenges the structures, symbols, and socio-political realities that foster oppression/domination of Black women in particular, as well as Black men, humanity in general and nature" (ibid., 214).

African American Women's Experience

African American women share in a legacy of kinship, but their place in this cultural legacy is distinctive due to their experience of dual oppression by virtue of being caught in the double bind of racism and sexism. Typically, when mental health and social systems address the concerns of marginalized groups, these groups are compartmentalized into categories such as race, gender, class, and sexual orientation. As a result, people who carry multiple stigmatized identities are thrust into fragmented cultural groupings that do not reflect their multidimensional real-life experiences (Constantine 2002; Croteau et al. 2002; Moradi and Subich 2003). African American women are faced with all of the challenges of being female in a male-dominated society as well as the tremendous stresses of being persons of color in a world characterized by white privilege.

This dual stigma results in personal and psychological distress for many African American women. Emotional isolation is one such difficulty (Greene 1994). African American women are taught early on to be self-reliant within the context of social support and kinship networks (Turner 1997). Yet, as greater numbers of African American women enter professional work settings, they report feeling alienated from sources of support (Greene 1994). Many also feel guilty for moving into the middle class; abandoning their families, friends, and communities; and for becoming successful (ibid.; Mays 1985). Others, despite their professional success, "feel diminished, devalued, unappreciated, and mainly 'unknown' in a full sense by those around them" (Turner 1997, 84). This tension between competing cultural values is salient for many middle-class African American women.

Another major issue for African American women is internalized oppression. Internalized oppression is "the internalization of conscious or unconscious attitudes regarding inferiority or differentness by the victims of systematic oppression" (Batts and Landrum-Brown 2003, 5). This internalized oppression means that people of color and other target groups come to accept the negative attributions made about them by the dominant culture. Pervasive and unrelenting racism is complex and multidimensional and has an ongoing negative impact that must be countered deliberately and repeatedly. African American women constantly must struggle with self-doubt because they have absorbed the denigrating racial messages of white society and culture.

Racial identity is another theme closely related to internalized oppression. For African American women to establish a healthy sense of self in a white-dominated context is extremely challenging (Jordan 1997). In the process of moving from racial self-devaluation to positive self-esteem, African Americans must pass through an established developmental process (Helms 1990). This process is more complicated for African American women, who are also confronted with gender images and standards of beauty that are not affirming of them. "African American women have suffered the blotches of bleaching creams and the harshness of hair straighteners, all in futile efforts to be accepted as attractive, as women" (Jordan 1991, 53). Because many women connect self-worth with physical attractiveness, African American women's concerns about body size, hair texture, facial features, and skin color are ever-present realities of their experience (Frame, Williams, and Green 1999).

Low self-esteem is another emotional issue for black women regardless of their economic circumstances (Greene 1994; Jordan 1991). This situation may be partially a result of the ways in which African American women feel torn between meeting their own needs and the needs of others, especially those of African American men. Greene indicated that this conflict between self and others is more strident where mistreatment by African American men is tolerated or excused out of empathy for black men's victimized status in the culture and society of the United States (Greene 1994).

Despite these difficulties, African American women's experience also includes the theme of empowerment arising from women-centered networks of communal care, spiritual bonding, and social activism. Katie Cannon, in addressing black women's moral agency, states, "Black women have created and cultivated a set of ethical values that allow them to prevail against the odds, with moral integrity" (1998, 75).

Communal care and support is a means of survival for African American women. They rely on networks of female and male family members and friends who assist them with activities of daily life, and give them the emotional support to confront life's problems. Nurturing, too, is central among African American women. They have nurtured self, children, community, and their whole racial group (Greene 1994). The concept of "motherhood" in this tradition transcends biology and nuclear family, extending kinship ties and connection in the struggle for freedom from both internal and external oppressive forces (Frame, Williams, and Green 1999). Alice Walker captures this notion powerfully in her essay "One Child of One's Own":

> It is not my child who tells me: I have no femaleness white women must affirm. Not my child who says: I have no rights black men must respect. It is not my child who has purged my face from history and herstory, and left mystory just that, a mystery; my child loves my face and would have it on every page, if she could, as I have loved my own parents' faces above all others. . . . We are together, my child and I. Mother and child, yes, but *sisters* really, against whatever denies us all that we are. (1979, 75)

African American Cultural and Spiritual Traditions

A profound sense of spirituality and transcendence characterizes African American women's experience. These women acknowledge and celebrate the mysterious connections between self, others, identity, and power. These cultural and spiritual traditions have always held a central place in African American communalism, and emerged from a history of forced migration and enslavement, followed by systemic discrimination and victimization (Mbiti 1990; Boyd-Franklin 1989; P. H. Collins 2000; Kwok 2001). Two major themes characterize African American spirituality: the pursuit of liberation from injustice, and the belief that the spiritual is present in every aspect of life (Hopkins 1993; Mbiti 1990; Mitchell and Mitchell 1989). The "operative force of this worldview is to find God in all of God's creation" (Mitchell and Mitchell 1989, 103). Rather than compartmentalizing religion and spirituality, among African Americans in general and African American women in particular, it is seen as intimately related to all of life's experiences (Boyd-Franklin 1989).

The black church, born during slavery, is, as a unique cultural institution, the central focal point and container for African American spirituality. As a result, the black church embodies for many African Americans a feeling of hope, an experience of community, and a locus for social justice. The black church also functions as an educational center, a resource of economic support, and a command post for political organizing (Quarles 1964). In addition, in it black children find role models and opportunities for leadership and responsibility that improve self-esteem (Boyd-Franklin 1989; Richardson 1991). The black church, therefore, has been called "the most organized, visible, and nurturing institution in many African Americans' lives" (Hopkins 1993, 1).

African American women have a history and tradition of social activism. In their culture, speaking and doing justice are powerful balms against oppression and depression. African American female leaders such as Sojourner Truth, Harriet Tubman, Ida B. Wells, and Mary McLeod Bethune are held up as role models and examples of hope (Giddings 1994; Williams, Frame, and Green 1999). It is this corporate commitment to social justice in the face of marginalization, discrimination, and oppression that offers a wellspring of possibilities for pastoral care in this community.

The Interplay of Privilege and Oppression

Providing pastoral care first requires caregivers who are typically white to become aware of and acknowledge their location in the web of power and privilege (social, political, economic, racial, gendered, heterosexual) and the ways in which location in the power sphere shapes one's worldview and consequent actions. To begin the process of developing an inclusive, justice-based stance toward pastoral care demands a look at the structures of society that focus on difference among particular groups and how those structures use difference as a means of systematically rewarding or punishing the groups' members.

Understanding the concept of "privilege" is critical if compassionate, committed pastoral caregivers are to be successful in expanding the notions of their work beyond responses to *individual* need to the larger, global issue of oppression. "Privilege" refers to the situation in which "one group has something of value that is denied to others simply because of the groups they belong to rather than because of anything they have done or failed to do" (Johnson 1997, 23). Privilege means males, whites, financially solvent persons, able-bodied people, and heterosexuals are afforded the "luxury of obliviousness" because these groups wield social power in society (ibid., 24). For example, when seeking jobs, shopping, socializing, or applying for promotions people from privileged groups have an unspoken advantage over women, people of color, the poor, gays, lesbians, and transgender persons. Such privilege is as if those from privileged groups are permitted to walk through life as if they were entering through the automatic doors of a grocery store: the doors open for them and they never give those doors a second thought. People from marginalized groups, including African American women, are all too aware of doors that are slammed shut in their faces. Peggy McIntosh, in what is now a classic essay, gives concrete examples of how white privilege is experienced in everyday life:

- I can if I wish arrange to be in the company of people of my race most of the time.
- I can turn on the television or open to the front page of the paper and see people of my race widely represented.
- When I am told about our national heritage or about "civilizations," I am shown that people of my color made it what it is.
- I can do well in a challenging situation without being called a credit to my race.
- I am never asked to speak for all the people of my racial group.

- I can easily buy posters, postcards, picture books, greeting cards, dolls, toys, and children's magazines featuring people of my race. (McIntosh 1998)

What is important here, as Allan Johnson notes, is that privilege doesn't have to do with characteristics of individual persons; it is more about the fact that they belong to groups who are powerful and more esteemed than other groups (Johnson 1997). That is, individual white males may not feel privileged on a personal level, particularly if they are poor. Nevertheless, they benefit socially from being white skinned in ways people of color simply do not.

In essence, according to Johnson:

Privilege generally allows people to assume a certain level of acceptance, inclusion and respect in the world, to operate within a relatively wide comfort zone. Privilege increases the odds of having things your own way, of being able to set the agenda in a social situation and determine the rules and standards and how they're applied. Privilege grants the cultural authority to make judgments about others and to have those judgments stick. It allows people to define reality and to have prevailing definitions of reality fit their experience. Privilege means being able to decide who gets taken seriously, who receives attention, who is accountable to whom and for what. And it grants a presumption of superiority and social permission to act on that presumption without having to worry about being challenged. (Ibid., 33–34)

Oppression is intimately related to privilege. In the presence of privilege, there is oppression. They are two sides of the same coin. According to Johnson, oppression "points to social forces that tend to 'press' upon people and hold them down, to hem them in and block their pursuit of the good life" (ibid., 39–40). Like privilege, oppression is an equally important reality for pastoral caregivers to comprehend. Oppression happens when a privileged group has power over another group. Again, oppression is a reality that occurs between groups of people in a society, rather than simply individuals who happen to belong to privileged groups (ibid.). African American women, as a group, experience oppression when privileged groups (males and whites, for example) behave in ways, often subtle, that limit their access to education, jobs, relationships, or resources and/or act in socially prescribed ways to devalue their race, culture, or ways of being in the world.

To wear the mantle of privilege is to march through life assuming that one's values, beliefs, assumptions, and experiences are normative for everyone. It is to be able to ignore and devalue the cultural traditions, values, literature, spirituality, and social and sexual mores of groups who are different from those in privileged groups. For pastoral caregivers to attempt to be about their work without acknowledging the ways that they are privileged is to participate in the very oppression they seek to eradicate.

Womanist Themes

There are several prevailing themes that emerge from womanist theology that have direct application to the work of pastoral care among African American women. Some of these themes include African American women's experience as the center of analysis, liberation, and survival; Jesus as the incarnation of suffering; support for justice in the global community; and sexuality (P. H. Collins 2000; Lewis 2004). In addition, the use of narrative, especially the biblical narrative, and contemporary African American women's literature also shape womanist thought (Baker-Fletcher 1993; D. S. Williams 1993).

African American Women's Experience as Epistemologically Sound

African American women's experience is a legitimate starting point for constructing meaning and we extrapolate this notion to the work of theology and pastoral care (P. H. Collins 2000; Howell-Baker 2005). For Patricia Hill Collins, the day-to-day survival of African American women determines their epistemology (ways of knowing) and validates the wisdom of their insights. According to Collins: "For most African American women, those individuals who have lived through the experience about which they claim to be experts are more believable and credible than those who have merely read or thought about such experiences" (2000, 209).

African American women's daily lives are circumscribed by the need for survival and the desire for increased quality of life. In their workplaces, homes, communities, churches, and in their relationships, African American women may feel "pressed" and "oppressed" by societal structures and racial/gender attitudes that get in the way of their vision of how life could and should be. Black women's unique experience is captured in oral traditions, autobiographies, novels, and scholarly writings (Lewis 2004). Listening to and learning about the challenges and celebrations these women face is one of the ways pastoral caregivers can begin to take seriously African American women's reality.

Liberation and Survival

African American women resonate with these themes that reflect their life experience. Marjorie Lewis noted that the focus on liberation and survival characterizes much of the writing and community work labeled "womanist" (ibid.). Delores Williams spoke of biblical characters to underscore the ways the scriptural story intersects with black women's stories. Biblical women such as Hagar symbolize the oppression African American women face. Moses' mother is viewed as a sign of liberation for the Hebrews from their bondage in Egypt (D. S. Williams 1993).

In addition, African American women who made significant historical contributions to recent history in terms of liberation for African American people are noted and revered: Harriet Tubman, Milla Granson, Sojourner Truth, Frances W. Harper, and Mary Church Terrell (ibid.). These foremothers used courageous and sometimes subtle strategies to liberate themselves and their communities from racial oppression. Tapping into their legacy has ongoing power for African American women. Learning and applying these ancestral witnesses' stories to modern dilemmas is one way pastoral caregivers can guide and give value to continuing the struggle for liberation and survival.

Jesus as the Incarnation of Suffering

In Christian circles, Jesus is a central figure related to liberation from suffering. Jesus' plight is often compared to that of African American women: he experienced "unjust and undeserved humiliation and suffering" but also became for many Christian black women a symbol of empowerment against all forms of oppression (Lewis 2004, 91). The metaphorical language of the Bible describes Jesus as a rock, the bread of life, the door to the abundant life, the shepherd, the friend, the shelter, the great physician, the mother to the orphan, the way to wholeness. Though black (male) theology has pointed to Jesus' ultimate liberation in the crucifixion/resurrection event, womanist thinkers such as Delores Williams suggest that the liberating power in the person of Jesus comes from his vision of social justice in his earthly ministry rather than at the cross (Hopkins 2005; D. S. Williams 1993). Lewis referred to Jesus as a "co-sufferer" with African American women (2004, 91). It was Jesus' notion of a sociopolitical reality in which the last should be first and his concern for the whole person that make him a viable participant in African American women's journey toward freedom and improved quality of life.

Pastoral caregivers working with African American women should note that it is not simply the meek and mild Jesus who gains attention and becomes a role model for black women in the Christian tradition. Rather, African American women find solidarity with the Jesus who took on political and religious authorities and bureaucratic structures and who was willing to suffer with the poor and the marginalized of his time because he believed in a God whose justice, love, and mercy were offered to all.

Support for Justice in the Global Community

African American women know their plight is not confined to the historical and contemporary realities of racism and sexism in the United States. Although the times and places are diverse, womanists stand in solidarity with the wider global community (Lewis 2004). As a result of their double bind by race and gender, womanists acknowledge they must stand with other women (including white feminists and women from developing nations) against men and others who perpetuate sexism, and they must stand with black men (and other people of color and white allies) against white racism (CRC 1983). On individual and group levels, pastoral services may involve peer counseling and spirituality groups that address issues of internalized oppression, racial identity, and self-esteem (Lewis 1994; Frame, Williams, and Green 1999). In the corporate dimension, pastoral care from a womanist perspective involves the intersecting nature of the "isms" that keep various segments of the global population marginalized and oppressed. This global orientation pushes pastoral caregivers to recognize and confront the deeply entrenched structures of economics, politics, colonization, and religion in which they participate and from which they benefit. To stand in solidarity with the global community means that nationalism in all its forms must take a back seat to the justice needs of all humanity.

Sexuality

Lewis noted that a womanist posture must take seriously disenfranchised African American women who also happen to be lesbian or bisexual (Lewis 1994). Such a posture has created difficulty in some segments of Christian communities, and among self-identified womanists who view homosexuality as incompatible with Christianity. This issue frequently divides the African American community, and yet it is related to the notion of supporting justice initiatives in the larger, global context and understanding that all forms of oppression are interrelated. Pastoral caregivers must come to terms with their own understanding of homosexuality and struggle with the cries for justice and inclusion that come from the gay, lesbian, and bisexual community. Creating safe spaces for gay, lesbian, and bisexual African American women to gather, gain support, and advocate for civil rights would be considered an act of pastoral care from a womanist perspective.

Making Use of Narrative

Narrative—including songs, poems, Scripture, autobiography, drama, novels, oral tradition, and female slave narratives—forms a centerpiece for African American women's self-knowledge, validation, and liberation. This literature is the core of African American culture and, as such, it is more connected with nature, more egalitarian, more respectful of female knowledge than bourgeois views that characterize much of white, Western culture (D. S. Williams 1993). Because of its centrality in the African American culture and community, this indigenous literature may be used as a source for personal comfort and strength as well as for building communities of care and justice.

In her article "Tar Baby and Womanist Theology," Karen Baker-Fletcher gives a concrete example of the ways in which novelist Toni Morrison uses African American women's experiences to forge a positive valuation of their reality. Baker-Fletcher argues that the image of the Tar Baby is grounded in an ancient African myth with a similar name, the "tar lady." This mythical figure was a symbol of black womanhood. Indeed, the tar lady was the black woman who holds things together. She is the container for black female spiritual power and moral wisdom (Baker-Fletcher 1993). What is required, then, is recovering the myths of the ancestors and claiming their power for the present day. Indeed, it is the communal strength and sisterhood of African American women that holds together their churches and other spiritual communities (Hoover 1979). Pastoral caregivers can immerse themselves in the rich literature of this community and can share the emergent themes and metaphors so that African American women may claim them as powerful tools for personal and societal transformation.

Strategies for Women-Based Pastoral Care

The womanist themes described above give clues to ways pastoral caregivers might intervene with African American women who are struggling with individual and corporate oppression.

First, to respond faithfully and ethically to the call to provide pastoral services for this population, caregivers must take seriously their social location. They must assess and come to terms with the dimensions and degrees of privilege they are afforded in U.S. society by virtue, for instance, of being male, white, heterosexual, financially secure, able-bodied, young, or Christian. Second, they must acknowledge the ways in which they embody racism, sexism, classism, heterosexism, and the other "isms" that divide the world's people into the haves and have-nots. And further, they must take steps to confront those "isms" in themselves, their colleagues, family members, and friends. Third, in order to offer effective pastoral care from a womanist perspective, caregivers must take responsibility for learning about African American female culture, traditions, spirituality, sexuality, community, politics, and relationships. They must avoid the tendency to take the easy and privileged path of asking African American women to teach them these concepts. Fourth, pastoral care from a womanist perspective requires that caregivers expand their worldviews, and be open to a lifelong process of self-awareness and growth regarding issues of racism and sexism and the intersection of these oppressions.

Finally, pastoral care from a womanist perspective demands a heightened and deepened sense of empathy that results in a commitment to personal and social change for all those involved in the endeavor. Only when these initial steps have been taken can specific individual or social strategies be employed with any effectiveness.

Individual Strategies

We have discussed elsewhere specific, womanist strategies for effecting personal and psychological change (Frame and Williams 1996; Frame, Williams, and Green 1999). Some of these interventions include using the musical and literary traditions of African and African American communities to extract themes of power, hope, and survival. In addition, we suggest emphasizing the communal nature of African American experience through the development of spiritual support groups for African American women. Other interventions include using the biblical narrative as a witness to the strength and resiliency of African American women, as well as gaining support of the black church's ministries to women within and beyond its walls. We believe these strategies and others like them can be useful tools for pastoral care among individual African American women. However, we are also convinced that the individual approach to pastoral care, even from a womanist perspective, is not sufficient to address the structural and societal realities that promulgate and perpetuate racism and sexism. Therefore, we turn to corporate strategies that must be used in tandem with the individual approaches if the totality of the womanist view is to be adequately applied in pastoral care.

Corporate Strategies

The most challenging and significant dimensions of pastoral care from a womanist perspective have to do with confronting the corporate reality of the unrelenting "isms" (in this case, the interplay between racism and sexism). This is not a journey for those who seek an easy answer or a quick fix. It is also not an endeavor that can be engaged in alone or from an ivory tower or a church steeple. To address the reality of oppression from a womanist worldview means to assemble like-minded colleagues who are willing to put themselves on the line in pursuit of social justice. It also involves immersion in African American communities and getting skilled consultation and supervision from persons with expertise in community building and organizing.

One strategy in addressing the corporate aspects of womanist pastoral care is to follow the lead of Allan Johnson who advised readers to "get on the hook" by becoming committed, obliged, and involved (1997, 135). He urged privileged "helpers" to give up the myths that things will never change and that whatever they attempt in the name of justice will have little effect. As simplistic as it may sound, Johnson called for people to "do something" rather than nothing, and to confront the social systems that support privilege to the detriment of those on the margins (ibid.). This approach means developing a prophetic voice and calling institutions, organizations, businesses, government, and other systems into accountability with regard to race and gender and the double bind they often create for African American women. For example, Johnson advocated offering support for workplace equality, equal pay and promotion, access to child care and health care, and the development and enforcement of antiharassment policies and other economic and political initiatives that address the everyday oppression African American women experience.

In a similar vein, David A. Thomas and Robin J. Ely call for a new paradigm for managing diversity in business and other corporate settings. They noted that sheer numbers of women and persons of color in the workplace do not guarantee equal treatment or equal opportunity for advancement. Increasing the presence of African American women without diversifying the work is not ultimately effective. Moreover, this approach propagates the "color-blind, gender-blind" ideal where important cultural differences do not count. Another existing attempt at increasing diversity involves celebrating differences, but not allowing those differences to have any real impact on how business gets done. Approaches are needed that incorporate difference (in this case gender and race) such that the experience of African American women is welcomed and considered meaningful and valuable to the organization (Thomas and Ely 1996). Pastoral caregivers as consultants to businesses, churches, and other organizations may have the opportunity to employ womanist perspectives in pursuit of corporate justice.

Summary

We have argued that pastoral care in the twenty-first century requires more than an individual approach to human suffering. A womanist perspective on pastoral care involves naming the double bind in which African American women are caught by the forces of racism and sexism. It means understanding African American women's experience from the inside out, including their personal pain and triumph and their corporate suffering and survival. Pastoral care from a womanist perspective means owning one's place in the systems of power and privilege and acknowledging the ways in which caregivers themselves participate in the very racist, sexist, and classist structures they desire to dismantle. Pastoral care from a womanist perspective involves discovering and celebrating African American female "herstory," traditions, institutions, religion, rituals, practices, music, and literature and employing these powerful modalities in the service of healing and personal and societal transformation. Pastoral care from a womanist perspective means joining with others to advocate on behalf of all marginalized groups—not only in the United States, but in the global community as well. Pastoral care from a womanist perspective invites caregivers to become advocates in their work settings and among their colleagues, families, and friends in order to confront the systems that perpetuate the "isms" that oppress so many people.

Pastoral care from a womanist perspective means echoing in word and deed the prophetic words of Amos: "Let justice roll down like waters, and righteousness like an ever-flowing stream" (Amos 5:24).

FIVE

Pastoral Care From
the Latina/o Margins

Miguel A. de la Torre

When the Pope made a papal visit to Miami, Florida, in 1987, delighting that city's large Hispanic Roman Catholic community, a local enterprising European American shirtmaker decided to capitalize on this important event. He made thousands of shirts bearing Spanish words that were suppose to read, "I saw the Pope." Unfortunately, he didn't bother to check his quote with those who knew the language, and as a result something was lost in the translation. Rather than using the masculine definitive article *el*, the shirtmaker used the feminine definitive article *la*. Hence, the shirts instead read, "I saw the Potato."

The Miami shirtmaker's costly mishap is often repeated in a number of ways by churches within the dominant European American culture. Although European Americans attempt to reach out to the Hispanics in their communities, a lot can get lost in the translation. In an age of political correctness, many predominately Anglo churches are scrambling to erase centuries of exclusion by now appearing to be multicultural, making "diversity" the church buzzword of our time. Three-hundred-year-old German hymns are quickly translated into Spanish and flashed on overhead screens; sermons are preached to instruct the European American congregations why it is their Christian duty to reach out to their less fortunate Latino/a neighbors with the gospel message of salvation; and attempts are made to appear culturally sensitive by offering Taco Bell dinners at the congregational fellowship meal.

Although I do not question the sincerity of those European American churches that wish to see their congregations better reflect the diversity of humanity, many still attempt to include Latinos/as without necessarily changing the congregation's cultural milieu. All too often, when the predominately white, middle-class congregation wrestles with issues of inclusiveness, they unwittingly revert to a multicultural facade for the sake of political correctness. All are welcomed, as long as the church power structures that privilege the predominantly Euro-American congregation remain intact. The underlining meaning of politically correct congregations is that Hispanics can join, as long as they first convert to European Americanism and respond appreciatively to whatever way their culture gets "translated."

The Ideal Church Structure

John, an apostle of Jesus the Christ, was led by an angel to gaze upon God's revelation to humanity. Before the heavenly throne stood a multitude of people, too great to count. They represented every tribe, being black, yellow, red, white, and brown. They spoke many languages—Serbian, Swahili, Spanish, Sioux, and so many others that they outnumber the stars in the sky. They were from a multitude of peoples, some of which were Asians, Aborigines, Aryan, African, Arab, and every possible combination of blend and mixture. And they came from every nation—Iraq, Israel, India, Indonesia, Ireland, Italy, and Iceland, just to name a few. And this uncountable multitude gathered as one body, united to praise the Lamb that sits upon the throne. Clothed in white robes with palms in their hands, they cried out in one voice saying, "Salvation to our God sitting on the throne, and to the Lamb!"[1]

Multicultural Church

The beloved apostle John records this apocalyptic vision of the kingdom of heaven in all its glory in the seventh chapter of the book of Revelation. He witnesses the mission of Christ coming to fruition in the form of a multicultural church—a church ransomed from "every tribe, language, people, and nation." John is not solely testifying about some future hereafter; he is providing a model, a pattern for the church of Christ to be imitated in the here and now. What begins at Pentecost finds its completion in heaven.

According to Acts 2:4-11, Peter, filled with the Holy Spirit, preaches his first sermon to a crowd gathered "from every tribe, language, people, and nation." Although those among the crowd represented Parthians, Medeans, Elamites, Mesopotamians, Judeans, Cappadocians, Pontusians, Asians, Phrygians, Pamphylians, Egyptians, Libyans, Cyrenes, Romans, Cretans, and Arabs, each heard the message of salvation in his or her own language. If we recognize that language is a cultural symbol rooted within the social context of a particular people, then the miracle of Pentecost is not that the crowd representing various nations understood the language spoken by Peter, but, rather, that they heard the message in their own tongue. In this way, the curse of the Tower of Babel (Gen. 11:1-9) is reversed. What was used to separate people—language—now ushers in the unification of God's people. As a result, three thousand were converted, all of whom represented the first Christian church, a very multicultural church indeed. Hence, from Acts to Revelation, from the alpha to the omega, the first church as well as the last, as the body of Christ, is multicultural (De La Torre 2003, 57).

When we compare the typical church of today with the ideal illustrated in Revelation, we are struck with how far we are from the mark. The homogeneity prevalent in most congregations bears testimony to our refusal to accept Christ's mission of establishing his church on earth. If our congregations fail to reflect a body of believers who come from "every tribe, language, people, and nation," then the church has failed to emulate what it is called to be. We simply cannot live in a culturally diverse city or town and have everyone in church look, believe, and worship in the same way. To do so only confirms Martin Luther King Jr.'s observation that the church hour remains the most segregated hour of the week in America.

The task facing the church is not how to convert the world, making believers out of nonbelievers. Rather, the task has to do with how much must the church be converted to become relevant in a hurting world. This is the lesson learned by that first Christian community, which was forced to convert away from its prejudices in order to reach the world for Christ. The book of Acts depicts how that first church had to change (i.e., accept Gentiles as fellow believers, renounce circumcision, appoint women to lead churches) in order to keep abreast of the movement of God's Spirit. As this early church began to encounter the wider world around it, Christians were forced to change, becoming multicultural so that others could come into a salvific relationship with the God, not the sociopolitical culture, of that first church. The Acts of the Apostles becomes the story of how God's Spirit acted in subverting any self-imposed religious superiority of the church.

Circumcision

One of the first challenges faced by the early church dealt with the inclusion of non-Jews in the body of believers. Must these Gentiles convert to Judaism to become Christians? More specifically, do the men first need to be circumcised before becoming a follower of Jesus Christ? Acts 15 records the controversy, which took place at Antioch. "Unless you are circumcised in the tradition of Moses, you cannot be saved," cried out those who came from Judea to disrupt the mission of Paul and Barnabas.

Even the most faithful to God can reveal the prejudices lurking in their hearts. When Peter, the rock upon whom the church was built, was visiting Antioch, he, too, refused to eat with the Gentiles. This is the same Peter who faced criticism for visiting the home of the Gentile Cornelius, a Roman centurion. That visit led to the first baptism of Gentiles (Acts 10–11). Still, some time later while in Antioch, when certain men of Jerusalem arrived to insist that Gentiles must first be circumcised before being saved, Peter withheld breaking bread with brothers and sisters in Christ because the males among them were uncircumcised Gentiles. Even Barnabas, Paul's co-laborer, joined Peter in this pretense (Gal. 2:11-14). Paul's rather earthy rebuttal is worth noting. He tells those Gentile men who are being hounded to be circumcised that they need not to be concerned. Specifically, he states, "I wish that the ones causing you to doubt would castrate themselves" (Gal. 5:12).

Modern Circumcision

The controversy was eventually settled in Jerusalem in favor of the Gentiles. They could become Christians without first having to become Jews. Nevertheless, the circumcision controversy, in another form, still exists today. The debate no longer centers on cutting off one's foreskin. Instead, what Hispanics are often called upon to do is cut off their identity, their culture, the symbols by which they perceive the Divine. In many cases, Latinas/os (as well as all other people of color) must first become European American before becoming Christians. They must adopt European American theology, hermeneutics, philosophy, liturgy, and, most importantly, ecclesiastics (church structures). They must prove their Christianity by describing their faith and salvation in the cultural symbols taught to them by the dominant culture. To insist in believing through one's own Latino/a symbols only proves (like the uncircumcised Gentiles of old) that they are not *really* believers, and even if they are, it is a more primitive and backward form of faith than that of their European American superiors.

Unfortunately, pastoral care made accessible to these "uncircumcised" Hispanics has been offered within European American cultural structures in the belief that it is for their own good. That is, pastoral care has assumed the superiority of European American paradigms and methodologies, even when they directly contradict Hispanic culture and identity. However, any pastoral care based on the individualistic characteristic of European Americans will be destined to fail among a people who place greater emphasis on the communal. Our question is, What would pastoral care look and sound like if it were rooted in the cultural symbols of the Hispanic community? In other words, how does one do pastoral care in "Spanglish"?

One Body

The apostle Paul saw the importance of diversity among the fellowship of believers. He surmised that such diversity provided healing to the overall church body. In his first epistle to the Corinthians, Paul wrote, "There are a variety of gifts yet the same Spirit, there are a variety of ministries yet the same Lord, there is a variety of working in all sorts of different people yet the same God who is working in all of them" (12:4-6). For Paul, because we represent different communities of people, we all offer different gifts, different ministries, and different forms of pastoral care. One size does not fit all. Our unity as one body does not come from "circumcising" different races and ethnicities so that they can become Euro-American in thought and action; rather, unity comes in one Spirit, one God, one Christ. It is our diversity that makes unity possible. Paul reminds us that just as the human body is made up of different parts yet remains a single unit, so it is as well with Christ's church. Therefore, it would be ridiculous for the foot to insist that the eye also be a foot. Likewise, it is ridiculous for the European American to insist that the Latino/a must also sing three-hundred-year-old German hymns, recite a similar conversion experience, or worship with a European American liturgy in order to be more spiritual or closer to God. God put all these separate parts into the church body on purpose. If all parts conform to the will of one of its parts, how then could it be a body? The parts may be many, but the body remains one. In fact, Paul insists that the parts of the body that seem to be the weakest are the ones that are indispensable. The least honorable parts of the body receive the most attention, as they are clothed with great care because they show that they do not need God. Meanwhile, God arranges the body so that more dignity is given to the parts that are lacking (12:12-26). While those parts that have always assumed their importance to the overall body continue to insist that their lesser parts conform, God has arranged the body so that pastoral care can flow from the least of the body parts to those that have placed themselves in the self-imposed center. It is the least among the body parts that have much to offer those who insist on their cultural and racial superiority.

Structures Preventing Pastoral Care

Before examining what the dominant European American culture can learn from the Latino/a margins concerning pastoral care, it is important first to explore how the church's power structures inhibit and prevent proper pastoral care from taking place. I recall that while doing my pastoral work in rural Kentucky, I was invited by a church within my denomination to come and preach. They invited the migrant workers (who were stripping tobacco on the farms owned by church members) to worship with them. After the service, the migrants treated the white congregation to a lunch. This was to be their way of saying thank you for the invitation to worship with their *patrons*. I confess excitement at the opportunity of preaching to a congregation composed of the European American parishioners and the visiting migrants (mostly Mexican), anticipating good home cooking afterwards as Hispanics shared bread with their Anglo hosts. Unfortunately, when I arrived at the church I was ushered to the fellowship hall located in the basement. While the white church members worshiped upstairs in the ornate sanctuary, we Latinas/os were crowded in the church basement. In a separate part of the church, sitting on folding chairs, we worshiped the same God that those who were sitting above us were worshiping. After my sermon, the Hispanics laid out a feast. Sadly, of the one hundred-plus individuals worshiping upstairs, only a handful thought it was worth their time to join the Latinos/as in the fellowship hall.

White Supremacy

In Revelation the angel tells John, "You must again prophesy about many tribes, languages, peoples, and nations" (10:11). In the past, it was understood that the "white man's burden" was to bring civilization to the margins, a civilization that includes the gospel message. The message went from the center to the margins, from the parts that deemed themselves superior, to the parts that were viewed as inferior. This message was presented via missionaries and evangelists. Yet here the angel is telling John to go to the center, his Jewish community, and tell them *about* the margins. The center incorrectly assumes that its task is to bring the gospel to the margins (Gonzalez 1999, 86–91). How do we reach *them*? What must we do to bring *them* into the fold? What programs must we initiate so as to bring *them* under our tutelage? In reality, the gospel is thriving on the margins of society. The real question facing the center, accustomed to confusing its interpretations with the biblical text itself, is whether those at the center will also participate in the body of Christ, which already exists at the margins of society.

The question should never be, "How do we attract more of their kind?"—where "their kind" is here understood to be Latinos/as. The real question that must be asked is, "How must we change so that all can become the body of Christ—where if one part of the body hurts, all hurt, and if another part rejoices, all rejoice." The challenge facing the church truly wishing to encompass "every tribe, language, people, and nation" is how to create *community* in a European American culture that is so individualistic. If those who consider themselves superior would humble themselves to learn from those they perceive as their inferior, they may discover that the Hispanic church community has much pastoral care to offer European American Christianity, specifically in the area of *comunidad*, a central aspect of how Latinos/as demonstrate their Christian faith.

Individualism

But what if the church today rejects the model presented by the books of Acts and of Revelation? Then it risks being impotent in ministering to a hurting world torn apart by the sins of racism, classism, and sexism. The danger of a hyper-individualistic society is that Christianity is simplified to a set of rules insuring personal piety, ceasing to be the universal force that binds strangers and enemies together as family. A Christianity solely focused upon the individual tends to reduce pastoral care to self-help, ignoring the suffering of the community as a whole. Ministering to those on the margins of society, prevented from experiencing the abundant life promised by Christ (John 10:10), is defined as "social services," and thus discarded as outside the mission of the church. This disturbing trend was witnessed in the mid-1990s at Southern Baptist Theological Seminary in Louisville, Kentucky (my alma mater), and can serve us as an illustration.

Newly elected President Albert Mohler and the seminary's board of trustees launched a study to determine whether the seminary's social work school was congruous with the Christian faith. After much "(de)liberation" the trustees and Mohler concluded that the tenets of the social work profession were incompatible with the seminary's core beliefs. Ironically, as the social work school was being closed, the Billy Graham School of Evangelism was opened, with the mission of training future evangelists to convert those (among others) in predominantly Roman Catholic Latin American countries who believe in God differently. The emphasis of converting Latin American Catholics to a European American understanding of Christianity (assuming that Roman Catholics are not Christian in the first place) testifies how far the foot is willing to go to make the eye into a foot! Circumcising the other to European Americanism was deemed more Christian than training Christian social workers, who were called to the ministry of clinical praxis. The "doing" of pastoral care, binding the wounds caused by the oppressive social structures that perpetuate injustices, is dismissed for apparently appearing to engage in politics. Notwithstanding, that for the church to consider seriously its role of pastoral care, it has no choice but to walk in accompaniment with the disenfranchised—those on the underside of power and privilege.

Power and Privilege

Actions taken by the churches of the dominant culture demonstrate how the political power they hold in society is at times responsible for creating religious doctrines, thus reinforcing oppressive structures while justifying the privilege held by European American Christians. Talad Asad reminds us that doctrinal "truth" is born at the intersection of church power and ideology (1983). The position within society held by the religious leaders and institutions of the dominant culture ensures that their doctrinal beliefs will prevail, beliefs that are more a product of their social location than any biblical "truth" gleaned from the scriptures. In this fashion, the biblical text is reduced to a form of prooftexting that provides the necessary justification for maintaining the present social structures.

In spite of the good intentions and religious fervor of well-meaning Euro-American Christians, it is difficult to escape the prevailing racism, classism, and sexism prevalent in the overall culture into which they are born. Not only are they shaped by their culture, but most live out their lives, either consciously or unconsciously, preserving the fundamental assumptions upon which the dominant culture is based. Through their self-imposed view of themselves as God's representatives on earth, they are able to exert the necessary disciplinary procedures within the power context of the church hierarchy to dictate what is "truth." The "authorized truth" dictated from the European American pulpits realized through the coercive conditions that exist within the overall dominant culture are preserved through authorized chastisement, that is, spiritual ostracization. Succinctly stated, the religious doctrines of the dominant culture, which so often are detrimental to those who are not white heterosexual males, become a reality when the power existing within the churches of the dominant culture intersects with the knowledge created by the early church theologians, who are themselves highly influenced by their own racist, sexist, and classist social locations.

This ideology motivates the populace in general to act in certain ways that validate the supremacy of structures created by the dominant European American church for survival reasons (their own and their children's). Even some of the marginalized learn to see and perceive reality through the eyes of the dominant European American culture. Historically, the church has needed to foster doctrines that safeguard their preeminence. If all humanity is in need of the saving grace as defined by European American churches (because the consequences of not obtaining this grace through the church is eternal damnation), then the church, which controls how redemption is to be defined (i.e., "circumcision" to European Americanism), has temporal, if not eternal, significance. In this fashion, the liberation from oppression found in Christ is exchanged for conforming to how European American churches choose to define Christianity.

Such an exchange leads to oppression, not just for those who are marginalized by the social structures, but for those who benefit from them as well. Although they do not necessarily suffer from physical or material depravation, and their "whiteness" provides opportunities within society denied to most people of color, still, those of the dominant culture (including Christian churchgoers) lack "dis(cover)ing" their full humanity in Christ Jesus. The overall structures of oppression also dehumanize the oppressors, subjugating them to the same structures they and their progenitors created to ensure their privilege within society. The existing socially oppressive structures also prevent the dominant culture from obtaining an abundant life (specifically in the spiritual sense). They are just as much in need of the gospel message of salvation and liberation. Their liberation can be made possible by the pastoral care that can be offered to them from their margins. To do pastoral care in "Spanglish" is not only crucial for the well-being of the Hispanic community, but it can also restore the humanity of the privileged who have falsely constructed their identity through the negation of their other.

Pastoral Care in Spanglish

God can use whomever God chooses to proclaim God's message of liberation to those God wishes to reach. If the congregation is indeed a body of "priest and priestesses," then the responsibility to provide pastoral care can never be limited to a trained professional—it becomes the responsibility of the entire church community. To pick one person (usually a man) to serve as the official pastoral caregiver undermines the responsibility and obligation of those who join together to form the body of Christ. Pastoral care in Spanglish rejects the salient individualism found in the dominant culture in favor of a more communal form of ministering to the needs of the congregation, needs caused by the prevalent racism, sexism, and classism found within the dominant culture. But how does communal pastoral care develop within both a highly individualistic society and church structure? What can such a culture learn from how Latinos/as do pastoral care?

Pastoral en Conjunto

The concept of *pastoral de conjunto* emerged from pastoral experiments in Latin America in the 1960s and 1970s. The Latin American Roman Catholic bishops adopted it as the preferred pastoral strategy to meet the exigencies of evangelization on that continent. This strategy calls for full participation by every level of the faith community. The goal, according to the bishops, was for the church to learn "how to analyze reality, how to reflect on this reality from the standpoint of the Gospel, how to choose the most suitable objectives and means, and how to use them in the most sensible way for the work of evangelization" (CELAM 1968, 1307). This Roman Catholic notion implies a quasi-Christendom, as it calls for numerous pastoral agents to work together under a bishop. Because no full analogy of *pastoral de conjunto* exists in North America, there is no adequate translation of the term. At best, the term connotes a form of group pastoring.

The U.S. Latino/a version of this Latin American concept (referred to as *teología en conjunto*—doing theology as a group) reaches deep into the Hispanic existential location to forge an evangelistic methodology that assumes direct involvement by Hispanics in analyzing their reality, a reality tied to a theological perspective that demands a sociopolitical response to oppression, both internal and external. They take care to avoid the representation of a Latino/a theology as a spontaneous single eruption from Hispanics. Rather, *teología en conjunto* shows the relationship that has developed between oppressed Hispanics and intellectuals who are aware of the structural crises Hispanics face in the United States. *Teología en conjunto* connects the pastoral care done by ministers (both Roman Catholic and Protestant) with those domesticated by the normative structures of oppression existing within the dominant culture. These ministers attempt to learn from the disenfranchised how to do pastoral care while serving them as "organic intellectuals," in the style of the twentieth-century Italian political thinker and philosopher Antonio Gramsci, and acting in the consciousness-raising process of the faith community.

Teología en conjunto moves away from professional clergy focusing the movement of God's Spirit among those who are on the margins of church power structures—those who are usually ignored, yet mightily used by the Spirit of God as pastoral caregivers. The experience of most faith communities is that the greatest wisdom appears to emanate from the underside of the church, rather than from seminary-educated pastors, deacons, or other ministers, who are at times chosen due to their personal piety and standing within the community. All too often, those chosen to lead are men who approach pastoral care from that particular social context—a context that, for example, usually reinforces sexism within the church.

We have all heard of male pastoral caregivers who have advised women who are physically abused by their husbands to stay within the marriage because this is the cross they are called to carry. Others are told they have no choice but to submit to their abusive husbands because God hates divorce. Still others are interrogated as to what they did to cause their husbands' outbursts of anger. Nevertheless, Latina theologian Elizabeth Conde-Frazier illustrates how from the margins of church power, God chooses modern prophets to declare God's word to those who are abused. She speaks of a woman of faith in her seventies by the name of Doña Inez. One day a woman, who bore the evidence of physical abuse, came to a Bible study in which Doña Inez was participating. Doña Inez caressed the abused woman, attempting to soothe her body and spirit. Finally, in a public whisper, she said,

> Because the Bible says that what we loose on earth will be loosed in heaven and what we bind on earth will be bound in Heaven, in the name of Jesus I loose you from your bonds to this man who has done this to you. You are not guilty of anything he has done. Go now to your cousin's house and start a new life. Don't look back or go back like Lot's wife. In God's name, we will provide for you all your needs. (Conde-Frazier 1997, 139–40)

Her words not only set this oppressed woman free, but also bound the rest of the faith community to support and provide for her. Pastoral care becomes not what one trained professional does for the hurting, but what the community of faith does for each other.

Creating *Familia*

Church can never be reduced to a building, for in reality it is a *familia* (a family). Even within the diversity of the Hispanic Christian community existing along lines of national origins, race, language, denominations, and class, still the experience of community remains a unifying factor and a resource for pastoral ministries. Go to any Hispanic church and, if you pay attention, you'll hear the congregation greet each other with the terms *hermano* or *hermana* (brother or sister). The congregation becomes, in effect, a family in order to provide support, stability, and hope in the lives of those who must confront the trials and tribulations of a society hostile to the Hispanic presence. When Latinas/os gather for church, it becomes a source of strength rooted in the *familia* model. The church becomes a family where no one need feel pressure to leave. Everyone must greet everyone in *la familia* and visit before leaving, even though they were probably already greeted prior to the service. In fact, an unhealthy church can always be recognized by how fast it takes for the church parking lot to empty after the service. Only within dysfunctional families are members in a hurry to get away.

Compadrazgo

Familia moves beyond the blood bonds. The concept of *familia* encompasses a broadly extended network of relatives and fictive kinship. Even when there may not be literal blood relations, there often is a recreation of family through the *compadrazgo* system. Baptism is more than simply an initiation sacrament for the one entering the faith; it becomes a bonding ritual among Latinos/as, an intentional bonding of God's people with the baptized person and with each other. Among Latina/o Roman Catholics and some Hispanic Protestants that practice infant baptism, the sponsoring godparents (*padrino, madrina*) become "co-parents" (*compadres, comadres*) and enter into lifelong relationships, not only with the child, but also with the family. Separate families become one *familia*, committed to providing each other pastoral care in difficult times. In this fashion, the *compadres* and *comadres* (literally co-fathers and co-mothers) become part of an extended family committed in nurturing the child, being reliable companions to the parents, ministering to each other's needs, and assuming parental responsibility should the parents die (De La Torre and Aponte 2001, 66).

The Eucharist

Like baptism, community creates the means by which strangers in church can become *familia*—a body of believers charged with ministering to each other's pastoral needs. Among Hispanics, communion becomes more than simply a ritual of remembrance. Partaking in the elements signifies the creation of community. To have "bread with"—the Spanish is *con pan*—is the derivation of the Spanish word *compañero*: "companion." Bread is the substance you eat for the nourishment of your body, and it is the same substance I use to nourish my body; we both, you and I, are sustained (fed) by the same bread. For this reason, one "has bread with" one's companions. We do not break bread with our enemies.

Roberto Goizueta introduces us to a theology of accompaniment, a theology in which *caminemos con Jesús* ("we walk with Jesus"). For Goizueta, to walk with Jesus on his way to Calvary is to accompany him physically, in all his humanity, during his greatest need of pastoral care. Tortured and broken by the oppressive structures of his time, we walk beside him in accompaniment. Goizueta says it best:

> It is this accompaniment that constitutes us as individual persons and as a community. More precisely, it is in our common accompaniment of Jesus on the cross that *he* constitutes *us* as individuals and a community. Again, this community is not an abstraction, nor a merely "spiritual" reality; it is mediated by a mutual, bodily presence. Such a community of accompaniment is not possible in a disembodied way any more than it is possible for me to break "bread *with* another" (the literal meaning of *ad-cum-panis*) if I am not actually sitting at the same table with him or her. The *act* of accompaniment is what defines this community. (1995, 68)

Like Jesus, who was accompanied during his time of trial and tribulation, the one in need today is never truly alone, for the body of believers with whom they break bread are there to accompany them, that is, provide substance and pastoral care in their hour of need. Not only do we accompany Jesus; Jesus accompanies us as community, for it is in our *comunidad* that Jesus becomes "in-fleshed" (incarnate). We do not find Jesus in the academic halls of prestigious seminaries, nor in theological books written by renowned religious scholars. We find Jesus within a hurting community accompanying each other in their struggles against oppressive structures, ministering to each other's pastoral needs.

Testimonios

For Hispanics, worship can never be considered complete until the *testimonios* (testimonies) are shared.[2] *Testimonios* are very emotional and private experiences shared within the safety and security of the church's *familia*. They become a crucial means by which Latinos/as participate in pastoral care. This is the time during the worship experience when both the joy experienced from answered prayers and the trials and tribulations to be faced are shared in the form of prayers with the congregation. These *testimonios*, when shared by the disenfranchised, provide insight into the daily struggles they experience. *Testimonios* show how God, who is in their midst accompanying them, can still answer their concerns. Sharing these *testimonios* creates the opportunity for the people of the congregation, the *familia*, to either share in the joy of their fellow congregants' good news or offer assistance in carrying their burdens. The *testimonio* of answered prayers, on the one hand, reinforces the good news of a living God in the lives of believers. It creates a time for rejoicing and celebrating. A *testimonio* of hardship, on the other hand, mobilizes the church to assist the *hermanos/as* in their difficulties—in visitations, food delivered, connections made to those who can help. The congregation is provided with the opportunity to move beyond pious prayers and instead learn how to accompany the sufferer, offering encouragement, assistance, companionship, and pastoral care.

Although *testimonios* testify to a God who assists the downtrodden during their time of need, it would be an error to think that *testimonios* only attest to miraculous deliverance. Regardless of the prayers offered and the willingness of the church's *familia* to share in the struggle, good and faithful people still die, lose jobs, go bankrupt, go through divorces, and endure tragedies, more so if they are dispossessed. The *testimonio* is just as powerful when it attests to the strength and courage displayed by the afflicted even in the midst of their trials and tribulations. To demonstrate peace and trust in God in spite of the wretched circumstances facing the believer becomes itself a most powerful testimony.

Romanticization

There is a danger in romanticizing the Latina/o experience. Instead, we must recognize that how the Hispanic believers minister to each other's pastoral concerns is still but one part of the overall body of Christ. While not claiming exclusivity in having the one and only way of providing pastoral care, we do claim that some of our approaches and methodologies are a needed gift to a dominant culture obsessed with Eurocentric "circumcision" and individualism. What Latinos/as (as well as other races and ethnicities) offer can contribute to a more holistic church body. Listening to the margins moves all of us away from a strictly Eurocentric methodology of providing pastoral care that often fails to connect with the vast majority of the world's people, subsisting on the underside of power and privilege. Instead, a communal paradigm is offered, and an opportunity is created to do pastoral care in such a way that we can minister to "every tribe, language, people, and nation."

SIX

Pastoral Care in the Context of North American Asian Communities

Greer Anne Wenh-In Ng

While acknowledging the historical functions of pastoral care as "healing, sustaining, guiding, and reconciling" (Clebsch and Jackie 1964, quoted in Clinebell 1984, 20), and that "pastoral care and counseling seek to empower growth toward wholeness in all of the six interdependent aspects of a person's life,"[1] this essay also takes seriously the critique that genuine pastoral care needs to move beyond helping individuals to cope with their crisis situations to getting involved in effecting social change to ameliorate and/or eradicate those unjust conditions that give rise to the problems in the first place (Pattison 1988).[2] The need to integrate a prophetic dimension of ministry into pastoral care is especially applicable in the case of racial-cultural minorities such as Asians in North America, since their opportunities for wholeness and growth—both as individuals and as communities—are often circumscribed by the often unjust treatment they receive in what is a predominantly white, Eurocentric, and still fairly patriarchal society.

External Factors

Asian Communities in North America and the *Han* of Systemic Racism

In discussing Asian communities here, I make no attempt to cover all of the people who have settled in North America from the whole range of countries across the continent of Asia from Afghanistan and Iran in the Middle East to the far eastern shores of Japan and Korea. Instead, I have dealt more modestly with those Asians now living in the United States and Canada who originally came from three significant regions: Far East Asia (China, Korea, and Japan); Southeast Asia (the Philippines, Vietnam-Cambodia-Laos, and Malaysia-Singapore); and to a lesser extent South Asia (India, Pakistan, Sri Lanka, and Bangladesh). As much as possible, I will use the term "Asian North American," a designation that gained prominence during the 1960s and 1970s as a term of resistance inspired by the U.S. civil rights movement, to refer to communities and individuals whose ancestors came from those regions, but who themselves were born in North America ("subsequent generations").

Historically, Chinese and Japanese laborers came as early as the mid-nineteenth century to California and British Columbia, first to try their luck in gold prospecting and then remaining to work in the lumber, fishery/canning, and other coastal industries. The earliest Koreans (1903), Filipinos, and East Indians came to work in the sugar cane plantations in Hawaii and to do other harsh and low-paying jobs. Historically, these were the groups who were discriminated against—not only by the exploitation of unfair labor practices, but also by discriminatory, oppressive legislation against them. Most notoriously, the latter included relocating Pacific Coast residents of Japanese ancestry (including citizens born in the United States or Canada) to internment camps during World War II, and passing a series of exclusion acts severely limiting and prohibiting would-be immigrants from entering the United States from Asia between 1882 and 1943. In Canada, one special ethnic group, the Chinese, was targeted with both an exclusion act and a "head tax."[3] One can only imagine the accumulated suffering, mostly unarticulated and unrelieved, that shadowed the hard lives of these early Asian "sojourners."

The Korean concept of *han* aptly describes such suffering as "a critical wound," explains Korean American theologian Andrew Sung Park, "generated by unjust psychosomatic, social, political, economic, and cultural repression and oppression" (Park 2003, 42). Such *han* persisted even after many generations had struggled and succeeded in moving out of the urban ethnic ghettos of their ancestors, and even when the liberalization of immigration laws in both the United States and Canada after 1965 saw better educated and socioeconomically better-off Asian immigrants arriving in increasing numbers. At present, they are often regarded by the non-Asian U.S. population as the "model minority," a group who send their sons and daughters to Ivy League colleges and are believed to be steadily climbing up the social and corporate ladder by dint of innate intelligence, disciplined hard work, and an enterprising spirit. Yet, as the criminal FBI investigation and solitary confinement (with no trial and no proof of guilt of being a spy) of Taiwan-born American citizen scientist Wen Ho Lee demonstrates, both naturalized and American-born Asian citizens continue to be perceived and treated by the majority population as outsiders and foreigners, even to the fourth and fifth generation.[4] Such continuing discrimination and exclusion lie at the heart of much of the *han* endured by Asian communities and individuals. As Park points out, "In this so-called melting-pot society, Asian Americans have been unwelcome and 'unmeltable.' This enduring rejection by society is *han* for Asian Americans" (Park 2003, 42).

As a survival technique, North American Asians have had to come together in mutual help groups such as business associations and clan societies in traditional Japantowns and Chinatowns in San Francisco, New York, Vancouver, Toronto, Chicago, and Boston. Those who converted to Christianity in the early days, and who came as Christians after 1965, formed faith communities in which they could worship in their own language and pass on their cultural traditions to their children. In this way, "ethnic" churches extend pastoral care to one another. In a recent account, Su Yon Pak and others describe how Korean Americans come together in "ricing" communities to seek protection from the alienation and estrangement their members often experience. These Christian groups meet from house to house, sharing not only hospitality and food ("rice") but also exchanging news about family, friends, business, and church, as well as engaging in Bible study. In this way they provide mutual nurture physically, socially, and spiritually in a holistic care of the soul (Pak et al. 2005, 88–90).

To help strengthen the cultural identity of their younger members, Asian ethno-specific faith communities hold ancestral language classes so that younger generations do not totally lose their linguistic and cultural heritages. At the same time, these faith communities also provide care to newcomers such as refugees and recent immigrants by connecting them with social and government resettlement agencies to ease their integration into the host society. The most recent groups to follow this path are Southeast Asian refugees from Vietnam, Laos, and Cambodia. A case study of the establishment of new religious organizations of each of these national groups in California and New Orleans confirms the central motivation of "providing a sense of cultural identity and continuity to people who are struggling to make sense of new lives in a new world" (Zhou et al. 2002, 66; see also Warner and Wittner 1998; Yoo 1999; Ebaugh and Chafetz 2000; Iwamura and Spickard 2003).

Regarding the provision of pastoral care more specifically,

> First generation Cambodians who suffer from post-traumatic stress and long-term depression as the result of war and resettlement can . . . turn to the monks for help. . . . Through offering mental and spiritual help, the temple contributes to the rebuilding of the Cambodian community. . . . By rebuilding the Khmer cultural heritage, the Cambodians are able to renew trust, rebuild their self-esteem and dignity, and achieve gradual reunification with each other. . . . (Zhou et al. 2002, 62)

Yet, owing to continued unequal acceptance by the majority society, many Asian North American Christians continue to meet in ethno-specific churches, even if they no longer need to communicate primarily in their ancestral languages. Such is the case with the movement among subsequent generations to form pan-Asian or multiethnic congregations where they can share their experiences, and where they can affirm their cultural roots and styles in safe sacred spaces (D. Ng 1996b).[5] Supporting and strengthening such faith communities, therefore, is one way to provide pastoral care for these communities, something Protestant denominations also try to do by establishing Asian caucuses or ethnic specific ministries.[6]

Pastoral Response to the *Han* of Racism

To address effectively the *han* of racism for Asians and Asian North Americans, therefore, involves both individual action and structural change. In cases where members of a minority community suffer overt or covert racial harassment or discrimination, active advocacy and support in the form of backing up a victim's filing of a complaint and accompanying them through the process offers the more immediate kind of care that matters. Standing in solidarity with Asian Americans where there is a climate of "Asian bashing" is another expression of such care. To provide more "radical" care, however, the root causes of such discrimination must be addressed. Depending on the location of the potential caregiver, action can range from putting in place antiracism training to auditing existing employment practices to ensure employment equity for minorities in places where such legislation exists. It can take the form of working for legislation that facilitates the credentialing of immigrant professionals (how many times, in our respective states or provinces, have we talked to immigrant taxicab drivers from South Asia who turned out to be physicians or lawyers or holders of other advanced academic degrees?).

These long-term efforts involve whole institutions, whether they be business, academic, nonprofit organizations, or churches. In fact, moving a church body such as one's own denomination from the initial stage of being an "exclusive" church and a church of the status quo through the intermittent stages of being a self-declared "open" and "awakening" church, to actually redefining itself and finally becoming a "transformed church" where diversity is seen as an asset incorporating the interests and gifts of diverse racial-cultural constituents in its mission and ministry, policy and practices, may elude most of the institutions we know today.[7]

Healing the Internalized Racism of Asians and Asian North Americans

A further response in attempting to release and resolve the *han* of racial discrimination for Asians/Asian North Americans (as indeed for other racial-ethnic minority persons), is to bring about their souls' healing at a more fundamental level by uncovering the insidious harm caused by internalized racism. This kind of injustice oppresses by making its victims doubt their own worth and the worth of their racial-ethnic peers: it is like a "poison that seeps into the psyche of people of color and aboriginals," leading them to accept Euro-centric values as superior and indeed as universal "norm" (G. Ng 2004b, 81). It can be seen as the opposite of the equally damaging "invisible knapsack" of white privilege lodged unconsciously in the psyche and socialized into the behavior of white folk (McIntosh 1990/1998).

The Rev. Wesley Mubasa, a Methodist minister from South Africa, told the story of how once, upon boarding a flight to Kenya, he found himself growing nervous upon discovering that the pilot was African rather that white/European. Mubasa confessed that he had been shocked by the realization that he had internalized within his psyche the superiority accorded white people (hence pilots) the world over, and how spiritually damaging such internalization could be. His story, told in a small group at an antiracism workshop, had the effect of freeing a participant to share her own story of how she was once reluctant to be seen reading a newspaper in Chinese on the subway ride home, even though she had wanted to read the Chinese version of a news story that had originated from China the day before.[8]

Internalized racism often takes the form of a "hierarchy of color," whereby the lighter skinned (and therefore closer to appearing "white") get better treatment than the darker skinned, even within the same racial-cultural group. Among Asians, for example, fairer-skinned Chinese, Korean, or Japanese, Middle Easterners, and Southeast Asians like the Vietnamese or Hmong, are seen as higher on the color hierarchy than darker-skinned Filipinos/as and South Asians. White or fair-skinned Latinos/as would occupy a higher position than African Americans and black Canadians (whether they be descendents of United Empire Loyalist ancestors moving to eastern Canada in the 1700s or immigrants from the Caribbean), ending with darker, more recent refugees from the continent of Africa on the lowest end. How to recognize one's complicity in benefiting from such a hierarchy and working actively to expose its injustice becomes both an educational and pastoral imperative for people of color (G. Ng 1996a, 229–37; 2004b, 40–50; D. W. Sue 2003, 254–76; 2004, 49–50). The post–Rodney King strife in south central Los Angeles involving African Americans, Hispanics, and Korean shopkeepers showed not only how injustices of class and race intersect, but also how cross-racial hostility perpetuates the *han* of one minority group against another.

One specific area of minority relating requiring both repentance and education on the part of Asians in North America involves learning how to relate in a just manner to Native Americans/Canadians (the current acceptable term in Canada is "Aboriginal") in light of the shameful history of colonization, land appropriation, plus linguistic/cultural genocide and physical and sexual abuse in boarding/residential schools of native peoples in both Canada and the United States. In this case, the attempt to establish "right relationships" can result in healing, not only for the victimized and abused, but also for Asians in North America who share the guilt by benefiting from the legacy of white settlement in these lands (United Church of Canada 2000; G. Ng 2007).

Tensions and Injustices within Asian North American Communities

Oppression from external forces is not the only kind faced by persons of Asian heritage: within their own families, churches, and communities members with less social power—namely, those who are younger in age (whether male or female), those who happen to be girls or women, and those of lower economic status—usually find themselves having to submit to the wishes of more senior members, male members, or members of a higher economic class. This is especially true of those ethnic groups originating in East Asia among whom Confucian values are still viably strong, namely, Chinese—including Vietnamese who are ethnically Chinese—Japanese, and Koreans. The Confucian ideal is to achieve "harmony" in family and social relationships by following strictly a set of values tending toward the "high context" end of the values continuum; prizing collective belonging (family, community) and interdependence over individual independence; hierarchical ways of relating and respect for seniority and authority over egalitarian relating; and domination of males over females with clearly defined gender roles for each, to mention just the major values.[9] This is, however, not meant to imply that similar values do not apply to South Asian (Indian, Pakistani, Bangladeshi, Sri Lankan) communities.

Tensions between the Generations

When we place these high context values over against "low context" values on the other end of the continuum prevalent in modern Western society—values that more acculturated second and subsequent generations are apt to espouse—inevitable tensions arise between younger generations and more "traditional" first-generation immigrant parents, grandparents, and elders in the community, who benefit from the Confucian concept of "filial piety" that continues to be practiced in the Asian diaspora. For young persons up to college years, family pressure to excel in school (a combination of Confucian valuing of education and "workaholism" and the myth of Asian Americans as the "model minority") becomes a source of intrafamily oppression, bringing an extra dimension to the usual teen angst of testing limits and attempts at asserting autonomy—what Korean American pastoral theologian Young Lee Hertig calls a "cultural tug of war."[10]

For young adults, issues involving career choice ("Doctor or Lawyer?" as one of the authors of *Following Jesus without Dishonoring Your Parents* puts it [Yep et al. 1998]) and mate selection and marriage (with overt and covert pressure to marry within one's ethnic group) easily become occasions where personal preferences and choice come up against parental preferences and decisions.[11]

One peculiar oppression in immigrant Korean families described by Young Lee Hertig pertains to faith practice or family devotions, where parents trying to impose rigid programs of "faithing" at home by insisting on practices they themselves regard as the only valid ones, such as family prayer time and family Bible reading in Korean, and proscribing any "work," including studying, on Sundays, without negotiating with their children or taking the latter's needs and wishes into account (Lee Hertig 2001, 90–97).

This kind of tension extends beyond the family to the church, where "1.5" and second-generation English-speaking worshiping youth and young adults experience similar power dynamics between themselves and the first-generation heritage-language-speaking portion of the same congregation. Where matters of faith are concerned, first-generation leaders (pastors, elders) often expect younger people to "assimilate to the first generation's cultural expression of faith and [to] regard that faith as sacred" (ibid. 107). At the same time, decisions about church government and congregational practice, programming and use of space, may be made without adequate consultation with younger members: even when there is representation on the church board or parish council, younger members may not be able to participate fully if meetings are always conducted in the ancestral language. English service pastors and workers are often marginalized. When conflict arises, tensions are exacerbated by divergent styles of managing conflict. More traditional older members prefer a nonconfrontational, more indirect style while keeping any conflict within the church family to "save face." Younger, more acculturated members would normally not hesitate to be direct or confrontational with their peers, and might accept the mediation of an outside consultant, but might feel constrained to fall in with their elders' ways so as not to appear disobedient or disrespectful, thus adding to their inner frustration (G. Ng 1997b, 206).

Pastoral Response for Generational Tensions

What kind of pastoral care response is called for in a generational tension/conflict situation? Asian American psychologists Derald Wing Sue and David Sue point out the importance of involving the family, not just the individual, in cases of family conflict, and of opting for a more actively engaged role (including that of educator or advocate in contrast to the usual, more objective, "neutral" role) for social service providers. Such advice can be useful for pastoral caregivers as well (Sue and Sue 2003a). In the case of parental pressure for academic success, for instance, it may be necessary to help parents, and indeed the wider ethnic community, to realize that they can be proud of their children's nonacademic achievements as well. In the related matter of parental pressure to conform to a narrow range of professions and careers (medicine, law, the hard sciences) versus individual children's personal gifts and desires (the arts, the humanities, or some kind of helping profession), Derald Wing Sue and David Sue suggest framing this kind of conflict as a culture conflict issue and trying to present the child's case to the parents (ibid., 328–42).

Ironically, disapproval seems to be particularly severe when children of Christian parents show signs of desiring to opt for some kind of Christian ministry. By pointing out that, from a faith perspective, such pressures and attempts to control the next generation's lives could be interpreted as usurping

God's place in their children's lives and thus seen as being idolatrous, pastors have an opportunity to tend to the spiritual health of the older generation as well as the real-life, professional/career and emotional/psychological needs of the younger. Such attention to the "soul health" of both generations requires of caregivers a "bicultural" (awareness of the cultures of both generations) sensitivity.

Addressing the *Han* of Asian/Asian North American Women in Family and Church

Valuing the male over the female (*zong nan quing nu* in Chinese, or *nam jo nu bi* in Korean) is the major thrust of gender relations in a society governed by Confucian values.[12] One traditional manifestation is that of "the three obediences" ("Obey your father [when not yet married], obey your husband [when married], obey your son [when widowed]"). Even though the more extreme forms of these injustices may no longer be legal or practicable when transported to North America (for instance, the obliteration of women's names once they are married, the custom of *sati* or widow burning in India, or the abandonment of girl babies in contemporary China), an overarching patriarchal ethos still obtains among the Asian communities of present-day United States and Canada. In serious cases, such continued subordination of women could result in domestic violence, especially in homes of recent immigrants in which husbands feel they are "losing face" by seeing their wives find employment and advancement while they themselves remain unemployed or underemployed, as documented in the case of Korean women in urban areas (Sung-Kim 1992).

In most Asian churches in North America, such an overall ethos is coupled with a conservative theological stance and a tendency toward literal interpretations of Bible passages such as Ephesians 5:22-24 ("Wives, be subject to your husbands . . .") to justify patriarchal attitudes and behaviors. Abetted by an atonement theology that sanctions endurance and suffering modeled on Christ's sacrifice on the cross, women's *han* is reinforced by pastors who counsel uncomplaining endurance, or forgiveness when sought by an apparently repentant spouse over and over again, rather than seeking a way out of the abusive situation.[13]

One way *nan jo nu bi* is expressed in Asian churches lies in the way women's leadership in the church is often confined to traditionally acceptable roles of service, whether at table, in fundraising activities such as running the annual bazaar/ rummage sale, and in teaching church school. In many Korean North American churches, women may still not be ordained as elders, the most powerful spiritual office to which a layperson can aspire in a Presbyterian congregation. And, in spite of the increasing number of women of Asian heritage graduating from theological schools in this new century, they are only rarely ordained to serve professionally in Asian churches; instead they end up working in their denominational structures, or serving "majority" Anglo-American/Canadian congregations.[14]

Feminists contend that pastoral care for women and girls is "care in the context of justice," the premise on which this volume is based. Such soul care "listens to voices that are easily thrust aside" and, as in cases of sexually abused women or women suffering from domestic violence, not only takes care of the immediate and material needs ("dressing the wounds") but actually becomes an ally of the victim (Bons-Storm 1996, 202). In cases of Asian women's thwarted leadership potential, responses could include helping women to "choose their battles," inviting them to develop a holistic spirituality and to act as role models and mentors (G. Ng 2002). A further, and more radical (in the sense of getting at the root of things) pastoral response is to open up possibilities of interpreting Scripture in ways that are life-giving for women. It could be a simple lifting up the roles of women leaders in the early church such as Prisca, Phoebe, and Junia (Acts 18:1-4 and 24-26; 1 Cor. 16:19; Rom. 16:1-2), or more complex attempts at analyzing how ethnically nondominant women (Rahab, the Syrophoenician woman) have been traditionally represented and what alternative interpretations might be.[15]

One area that Asian Christians, both women and men, have tended to ignore is the matter of gender-inclusive language. One reason for this is that many Asian languages have gender-inclusive terms for humanity (for example, *ren* in Chinese) and no gender distinctions for the third person singular (he/she). What they do not realize is that father/lord language and images continue to reinforce hierarchical, repressive relationships between the divine and the human, which then get transferred to human males in the community. Raising consciousness around this current "null curriculum" in Asian communities then becomes a radical act of soul care.[16]

Resources for Pastoral/Soul Care in Asian North American Communities

Asian North American churches extend pastoral care not only to their own members, but often also to persons from their ethno-cultural and immigrant communities. How Christian resources shape the approach of such care, whether consciously or unconsciously, has consequences in that care's effectiveness.

Reading and Interpreting Scripture from the Experience of Victims/the Colonized

Pastoral care workers in a Christian setting often rely on the Bible to comfort and heal those people who are in pain. Yet the Bible as a resource can be an ambiguous one. Depending on how it is interpreted, the Bible could be liberating or oppressive not only for girls and women, but also for "racialized" minorities, including Asian men and seniors, as pointed out by postcolonial biblical scholars R. S. Sugirtharajah, Musa Dube, and others (Sugirtharajah 1998, 2001, 2003; Dube 2000).[17] Traditional interpretations that follow the Bible's usual recounting of a narrative from the point of view of the victors (for instance, that of the Israelites over against that of the Canaanites in the story of the entry into Canaan, the "promised land" for the former only) ignore, or at least neglect, the experience of those who are victims or conquered. For those suffering personal or systemic injustices, therefore, a different way of reading the Bible—learning to uncover its problematic, contradictory nature and learning to read it from the margins over against from the center—is crucial.[18]

For Asian North American Christians, most of whom have inherited their Christianity from the Western missionary involvement in their home countries, indigenous spiritual traditions and practices have also been devalued or prohibited outright. Learning to reread and reinterpret traditional "mission texts" (for instance, "the great commission" in Matt. 28:28-30) to uncover their imperialistic orientation and harmful effects on the "missioned to" can help to restore the dignity of these colonized Christians and make whole their multilayered spiritual legacies (Dube 1998, 2002).

Doing Theology from the Side of the Sinned Against

"For the past two thousand years," declare Korean American theologian Andrew Sung Park and Susan L. Nelson, "we have inadequately treated the victims of by neglecting to formulate doctrines for them . . ." (Park and Nelson 2001a, 2). A more adequate formulation will focus on the need of the sinned against to resolve their *han* rather than on the need of the sinner or perpetrator of injustice to absolve their guilt. Park invites us to notice that in teaching his disciples to pray, Jesus was doing so from the perspective of those who had been offended, since only these could be asked to forgive others: ". . . the forgiving of the injustice of the oppression precedes the forgiveness of God for the oppressed. Had Jesus been concerned about the oppressors, he would have said that . . . you must

ask the forgiveness of others (your victims) prior to asking God's forgiveness."
(Park 2001, 55). To do theology from this perspective can and should result
in concrete ecclesial practices, including ethical decisions, faith formation, and
church education, pastoral counseling, and liturgy. In Park and Nelson's volume
The Other Side of Sin, theologian Marie Fortune is quoted as lifting up the call
of a theological conviction that "asks us to side with the victim who beckons
bystanders to action, engagement, and remembering," while Ruth Duck is
quoted as calling for "hospitality for victims" in worship with the double-sided
potential of the Eucharist/Holy Communion "as an act of confession for sinners,
of forgiveness for violators, but as a medium of welcoming into the community
of faith or celebrating joy, life, abundance, community, and grace for healing the
wounded" (Park and Nelson 2001a, 18–20).

Integrating Asian Religio-Cultural Practices with Christian Practices

One powerful resource in the spiritual care of Christians of Asian ancestry is
to recognize and affirm important rituals they still practice in their lives by
"institutionalizing" these rituals in the life of their faith community. Russell
Jeung describes how a memorial ritual (still practiced by most families on the
anniversary of the deaths of family members) has become part of the monthly
communion service at Park Avenue United Methodist Church in New York
City. At such a service, the pastor reads out the names of those who have died in
the same month either that year or in years past, telling a little of their lives, and
having a child place a flower in a bowl for each person remembered. This ritual
accomplishes several things. First, it makes concrete for children the connection
with elders and ancestors of their community; second, locating such a central
Asian spiritual practice in a Christian liturgical setting, such as the Eucharist or
Holy Communion, legitimizes what may be seen as a "pagan" cultural practice
by linking it to the Christian concept of the Communion of Saints; and, third
but not least, it helps with the grieving process (Jeung 2005, 132–33).

Cultural festivals, which are filled with religious meaning, are also resources
when they both honor the identity of those who practice them and interlace
them with Christian meaning, as when the annual Chinese spring festival of
Qing-ming ("Clear and Bright"), commemorating ancestors by cleaning up their
graves and its autumn counterpart *Qong-yang* ("Double Nine"), is linked to the
ideas of "rising again" (Easter) and the Communion of Saints around All Saints
Day (G. Ng 1989, 1996c, 2006).

Connections between the living and their dead are themselves a resource for spiritual care in the lives of Asian American Canadians. Sociologist of religion Jung Ha Kim has made an interesting study of the relationship of "ghosts" to the protagonists of Asian American fiction and their effect on the latter's spiritual life. Kim points out that ghosts are "at once marginal and central to the protagonists. The ghosts guide, critique, sustain, and heal the protagonists. . . . By selectively remembering the painful past at times and by learning to tell their own 'talk-stories' at other times, the protagonists demonstrate the spirituality of resistance and resilience in Asian America" (J. H. Kim 2006, 246; Brock et al. 2007). At the same time, Kim's use of fiction "for better understanding a racialized people's construction of reality"(J. H. Kim 2006, 247 n.1) is a powerful reminder of the resource literature depicting the experience of Asian Americans/Canadians and how significant an influence this literature can be for these people in their search for meaning in their lives as well as for the healing of painful memories. Where feasible, encouraging people who have suffered injustice to write their own life narratives can be a viable and empowering pastoral and spiritual strategy (G. Ng 2003).

Racial-Cultural Identity and Social Location of the Pastoral Caregiver

Pastoral care to individuals within an Asian ethnic or faith community in North America is likely to be given by persons of a similar ethno-cultural group. In areas where persons of Asian origin do not congregate in significant numbers, however, non-Asian pastors, pastoral visitors, or counselors will be called upon to extend care. Because relations between persons may vary according not only to cultural styles and values but also to a differential in social power, it is important to be aware of the dynamics that occur between pastoral caregivers and recipients so that such relationships do not themselves become oppressive.

When these identities are similar, it is generally assumed that caregiving will likely be culturally appropriate and therefore effective. Someone who understands the communal orientation of most Asians, for instance, is less likely to ignore the family in any encounter with an individual. Such an assumption may not always be correct. Owing to the pervasive Western-oriented clinical pastoral education and training given to everyone, pastors/pastoral caregivers of Asian heritage may find that the approach they have learned will be inappropriate in spite of the identification the person receiving the care may feel. Canadian Lutheran pastor Alan Lai discovered this to his dismay when he applied what he had learned in his CPE course to his visit to a hospitalized female Chinese immigrant woman. The emphasis on getting the patient to articulate how she was feeling just did not work because of the accepted Chinese behavioral norm of not sharing emotions and feelings verbally—and certainly not with strangers (Lai 2003).

Another challenge is the power differential between pastoral caregiver and recipient/s even of the same ethno-cultural group. Thus, a senior male pastor (and most pastors in Asian and Asian American churches are still male), unless he is very careful, may bring his own "high context" orientation to any guidance he might give. In a situation involving career choice, he might unconsciously privilege parental authority over the children's struggle for autonomy. A dilemma arises when the pastor/pastoral caregiver is a younger male ministering to older males, or when a woman pastor/pastoral caregiver (even if older) ministers to males. The most challenging case would be when the pastor is both younger and female.

Both cultural identity and power differential also apply to the care extended on a North American college/university campus, in a hospital, or the only Presbyterian church in town, by a chaplain or pastor (or pastoral care team) of non-Asian ethno-cultural heritage as they engage in pastoral care with students, patients, and church members, some of whom may be Asian or Asian North American. Society in both the United States and Canada today continues to accord more social power ("involuntary" power ascribed to individuals without their earning or even wanting it) to persons of Anglo-European origin (and thus "white"), whether born in North America or not, whose native or at least working tongue is English, than to persons of non-Anglo-Euro descent, or who are recent immigrants for whom English is their second or third language. Indeed, so significant is the "race" factor that such power discrepancy would persist even if the latter were born in North America and had functioned in English all their lives, or even if their educational background and socioeconomic standing were equivalent.[19]

When such power differential exists between a white pastoral caregiver and a nonwhite recipient, there is danger of racial and cultural oppression/injustice even if perpetuated unintentionally. Conversely, when the pastor or pastoral caregiver is a racial minority, the dynamics would be reversed: there might be discomfort or resistance in students, patients, and church members who are of Anglo-Euro ancestry to accepting pastoral care from someone whom they have been socialized to regard as less authoritative.

Power differential exists, therefore, not only to position and authority, but also to white privilege. Whites have been socialized from earliest childhood to regard the way things operate in the world in their style and favor as "the norm." When the knapsack of white privilege remains invisible, white pastoral caregivers may inadvertently engage in cultural oppression when dealing with Asian North American and other nonwhite persons. It is therefore imperative that antiracism training be mandatory for all service providers, including pastoral caregivers. Central to such training would be an understanding of white racial identity development so that individuals could locate themselves on the continuum and ultimately develop a nonracist or racially just identity.[20]

Such a nonracist identity would be indispensable in developing cultural and multicultural/intercultural competence, a viable vehicle in moving toward achieving greater justice in intercultural soul care. Derald Wing Sue lists four components of cultural competence for social workers, which would be just as applicable to pastoral caregivers and educators. These are: (1) becoming aware of one's own assumptions, values, and biases about human behavior (awareness of one's own Euro ethnocentric monoculturalism); (2) understanding the worldview of culturally diverse clients (knowledge); (3) developing appropriate intervention strategies and techniques (skills); and (4) understanding organizational and institutional forces that enhance or negate cultural competence (sociopolitical know-how). Culturally aware service providers (or pastoral caregivers) will not impose their values or standards, which unaware ones would see as superior, on culturally diverse groups, nor would they regard differences as being deviant. Instead, they will respect cultural differences, including accepting indigenous approaches to healing (D. W. Sue 2006, 23–40).

Persons from the dominant culture whose consciousness has been raised and who are on the journey toward developing an antiracist identity can be strong pastoral care providers to "racialized" Asians and Asian North Americans on an individual level, and eventually come to be real advocates and allies as they work for structural change in the institutions whose policies and practices discriminate against minorities. Such alliances are particularly crucial in attempting any structural change. The power in most, if not all, institutions in our present context is concentrated in the hands of European American/Canadians. White allies working within institutions will attempt to move these institutions from being monocultural and exclusive to being truly inclusive or multicultural, with intermediate stages of being merely passive or nondiscriminatory.[21]

Looking Beyond the Present

As North American society in the twenty-first century becomes more pluralistic in both racial-ethnic and multifaith makeup because of globalization and increased immigration from the South, Christian communities can learn to redefine and reframe traditional faith stances and practices, including their practices in pastoral/ spiritual/soul care, toward repentance for past injustices and working toward greater justice. Asian communities in the United States and Canada exemplify only one aspect of this new changing context. It is also important to point out that in such a contemporary context, there is no longer any homogeneity even within the same ethno-cultural groups, no "cultural essentialism," since cultural change is accelerated by global migration. As cultural critic Lisa Lowe reminds us, "interpreting Asian American culture exclusively in terms of the master narratives of generational conflict and filial relation essentializes Asian American culture, obscuring the particularities and incommensurabilities of class, gender, and national diversities among Asians" (Lowe 2003, 135).

SEVEN

Pastoral Care
from a Jewish Perspective

Howard Cohen

All good pastoral care involves compassionate, nonjudgmental listening, careful questioning, and patience. Regardless of religious orientation, all pastoral caregivers strive to comfort the afflicted, offer hope, and preserve the dignity of those to whom they are ministering. What makes an ordinary pastoral caregiver an exceptional one is the ability to access religious systems beyond his or her own, whether for the benefit of a coreligionist or people of a different faith. In this essay I will present an approach to essential pastoral skills and values from a Jewish perspective. Since the techniques and methods of good pastoral care are universal, the purpose of this discussion is not to offer new skills, but, rather, to provide an introduction to Jewish language, imagery, and textual references that will enable the non-Jewish chaplain to be more effective when called to serve someone who is Jewish.

Chaplaincy Lessons from the Bible

The starting point for understanding a Jewish approach to chaplaincy is found in Genesis 1:27: "And God created man in His image, in the image of god He created him. . . ."[1] Judaism understands this in a nonliteral sense. We do not actually look like God, but rather possess an intangible essence that inexplicably makes us godlike. Judaism further assumes that this is a prescriptive, not descriptive, statement. In other words, it does not tell us what God looks like (to say God looks like everyone is essentially meaningless); rather, it suggests how we might act God-like. What then does it mean to act God-like? To approach an understanding of this directive let us look closely at how God is depicted intervening in the lives of some biblical personalities.

Let us begin with what I consider to be the first recorded pastoral intervention in history, God's response to Adam and Eve after their having tasted the fruit of the tree of knowledge of good and bad. They violated God's very specific instruction, but there is no immediate response in the Bible. Though this lack of immediate response may lead us to believe that the violation was no big deal, in fact, a crisis of biblical proportion (pardon the pun) has begun to unfold. This delay or hesitant response provides the first lesson in how to approach a pastoral situation in a God-like way. In a word: cautiously. A crisis is by definition a situation where we have no choice but to learn or accept that change is inevitable. A crisis does not necessarily require an immediate or urgent response. If we assume that God is omnipresent and omniscient, then of course God knows what has happened and what will happen as a result of Adam and Eve's action. Note, however, that God's response is slow and cautious. Our first lesson in acting God-like, then, is that not only is it appropriate to respond to a crisis cautiously and slowly, but quite likely that is the best way. The critical event has occurred. Now our job as caregiver begins as we figure out how best to guide the person in crisis.

Once again, God models for us an appropriate response to an unfolding crisis. Let's look at how God is described as responding to Adam and Eve's transgression. It is easy to enter into relationship with a person in crisis with all the answers. After all, they are looking for answers and we have them, right? Wrong—at least from a Jewish perspective it is rarely about the answers; rather, it is all about the questions we ask. How did God respond to Adam and Eve? First, God responded slowly and cautiously, "moving about in the gardens at the breezy time of day," according to Genesis 3:8. One gets the impression that God was meditating, so to speak, deciding how to respond to this crisis at hand. Finally, God calls out, "Where are you?" as if an omniscient, omnipresent God did not know. This then is our second lesson: enter into pastoral relationships with questions, not answers. Good questions, such as the one God asked, are open-ended and are subject to interpretation by the hearer. For example, does God's question mean "Where are you physically at the moment?" or does it mean "Where are you in relationship to the crisis you are facing?" It is easy to assume that we know how a person must be feeling in response to a crisis. After all, it is a crisis and so it must be terrible. Actually, this is not always the case.

In an earlier stage of my life I was very involved with mountain rescue. Our training included plenty of technical and mechanical knowledge, ranging from how to set a bone to initiating a complicated lowering system. It also involved extensive training in asking questions, both of the victim and of ourselves. Paralleling God's slow response to Adam and Eve, we were also taught that upon arriving at the scene of an accident, instead of rushing to respond we should sit down, take a drink of water, and carefully and cautiously assess the situation before acting. Sometimes what we first encountered was not always the real crisis. For example, there might be one person holding his leg and moaning loudly while just ahead and out of sight another person might be unconscious and bleeding profusely. In addition, we had to learn how to assess personal risk as we approached the accident scene to avoid making a bad situation worse. Although the circumstances are different, both a chaplain's and rescuer's response reflect the lesson God is depicted role-modeling for us: respond to a crisis cautiously and with questions, not answers.

Here is an example of how an assumption was misguided. When I was a young prison chaplain, I met an inmate about my same age who was serving a life sentence with no chance for parole. During one of our pastoral conversations I voiced my assumption that my client must surely find incarceration depressing and that he must undoubtedly struggle with having wasted his life. Whatever he had on his mind at the time it was not this, because he looked at me and said emphatically, "God, no. I am wickedly sorry for the crime I committed, but if I had not been caught and convicted I know I would be dead by now. Look what I've managed to accomplish." He then proceeded to tick off a long list of accomplishments, all achieved only after incarceration. He came to me for pastoral counseling and I made the mistake of assuming I knew what must be on his mind, rather than asking him.

There are at least two more lessons that we can glean from God's response to the crisis of Adam and Eve: compassion and subjectivity. Adam and Eve made a huge mistake with profound ramifications. God did not back away from the promised consequences and so they were banished from the garden of Eden and as a result came to know death. However, God also did not withhold compassion for them. Remember, "the two of them were naked" (Gen. 2:25). Instead of sending them out into the world naked and alone, "God made garments of skins for Adam and his wife, and clothed them" (Gen. 3:21). It was not enough that God made them clothing, but from the words "and clothed them" one has the sense that God lovingly dressed them in preparation for their journey. In this example, God role-models compassion, an important quality for good chaplaincy work.

As a prison chaplain I often found myself providing guidance and comfort to men who, frankly, had committed terrible crimes. It was helpful for me to remind myself that the courts had determined the inmate's punishment. My duties had nothing to do with this punishment. My job as a chaplain was to treat each inmate as a person created in God's image. One need not be a prison chaplain, however, to find oneself providing pastoral care to someone who needs support, not judgment. For example, a hospital chaplain might be called to meet with someone who caused a terrible accident while under the influence of alcohol. As chaplains our task is to act God-like and be compassionate, not judgmental.

The next lesson from the Adam and Eve story that I want to highlight is *subjectivity*. To Judaism the banishment of Adam and Eve from the garden of Eden was a blessing that made possible all of the other blessings and miracles that have since filled each and every day. On the other hand, Christianity looks upon their banishment as the "original sin" for which humankind must always seek forgiveness. This is not the place in which to discuss these two points of view. I mention it only to reiterate a point I made earlier about making assumptions. People respond to crisis differently, just as Christianity and Judaism view the impact of Adam and Eve differently. Therefore, it is important to remember that individuals respond to crisis in their lives differently than we as chaplains might expect.

The Bible is replete with many more prescriptive or instructive examples for chaplains to glean. Here are three more. The first has to do with conditions of ritual cleanliness (*tahor*) and impurity (*tamai*), two of the more perplexing themes found in the Bible. In truth, we do not know what these words actually mean; however, we do know that they are not inherently negative. In fact, in the biblical context they describe conditions that everyone experiences (see Leviticus). These conditions are natural and accepted parts of life, and include such examples as the priest after a day's duties in the temple; a woman after giving birth; and a person who cares for a dead body. The Bible goes on to describe how a *tamai* person must be separated from the rest of the community until the condition passes. This might be only the short time it takes to change clothing—or weeks, depending on the presumed cause. In any case, properly understood, this is not a punishment but a necessary period of healing or transition. In some cases this is a "medical" healing and in other instances it is more spiritual. From this we learn the importance of creating sufficient space and time for the "healing" that is needed.

With the help of Rashi (Rabbi Shlomo Yitzhak), the classic eleventh-century Jewish scholar from Troyes, France, we find two more examples of God demonstrating for us what it means to be God-like. In the opening sentence of Genesis 18, "G-d appeared to Abraham in Elonei Mamrei, as he was sitting at the entrance to his tent in the heat of the day." Why does God suddenly appear? The text offers no explanation—or does it? Remember that this encounter follows immediately after Abraham's self-performed circumcision, a painful experience at any age but certainly all the more so at the advanced age of ninety! Rashi gives us two answers. The first is straightforward: visiting the weak, infirm, and ill is holy work. This, of course, is obvious to anyone pursuing the work of chaplaincy. However, too often we avoid this important responsibility because we do not know what to say when meeting someone who is in pain or ill. Herein lies God's second role-modeling lesson, according to Rashi. God appears without words and fanfare: "G-d appeared to Abraham in Elonei Mamrei. . . ." God's mere appearance is healing enough. This teaches us that sometimes as chaplains just being present, even in silence, is healing.

This reminds me of another very powerful experience I had while working in the prison. I arrived on a restricted housing block and announced my presence. An inmate I did not know called me over to his cell. On this block the men were not allowed out of their cells so we had to speak through the small openings in his door. Since he did not want his cell-mate to overhear us he spoke in a hushed tone. If hearing him was not hard enough, to complicate matters he had a very strong Spanish accent. I stood outside his door with my head cocked toward his voice for a good fifteen minutes, but I confess that between his heavy accent and hushed tone of voice and all the background noise, I could not understand a word he said to me. Finally, he lifted his head, with tear-filled eyes looked at me, smiled, and said, "Thank you, *gracias*, thank you." He turned and went to his bunk. My silent presence was all he needed to find the strength within himself to go on.

My experience reminds me of a story one of my teachers once told. When he was a young man and going through a difficult period he felt an urgent need to speak with his pastor, so he called him in the evening at his home. His pastor reluctantly agreed to meet in his office. My teacher arrived and settled into a comfortable chair. With head in his hands he immediately began a long soliloquy. This pastor liked to sit in a big, oversized leather swivel chair. When it was turned so the back of the chair faced into the room it was almost impossible to see him. Well, after a long time of emptying his heart my teacher looked up and noticed that the chair was turned away from him. He stopped speaking and peeked around the edge of the chair. His pastor was sound asleep. Quietly my teacher turned and slipped away. When asked if his pastor falling asleep like that insulted him, he answered, "Not at all. I only needed his presence, nothing more, to find my own inner strength."

The last biblical lesson I want to explore is one that gives caregivers a real challenge. This is the teaching of boundaries. To keep Adam and Eve from returning to the garden of Eden God stationed "east of the Garden of Eden the cherubim and the fiery ever-burning sword, to guard the way to the tree of life" (Gen. 3:24). In preparation for experiencing the great theophany at Mt. Sinai, Moses relays these instructions from God: "You shall set bounds for the people round about, saying, "Beware of going up the mountain or touching the border of it" (Exod. 19:12). Creating and respecting boundaries are critical skills to master. They are essential to the health and well-being of both client and chaplain. The Bible puts it in the strongest terms of life and death. Yet, as important as it is to respect boundaries, at times our task involves asking our clients to explore their own boundaries and even inviting them to consider redefining where they are drawn. How does one do this? In a word: cautiously. The other aspect of respecting boundaries deals with those that we as caregivers create to protect ourselves. Too often we tend not to establish clear boundaries between the people we serve and ourselves, leading to a myriad of problems, not the least of which is ineffectiveness. It is good to remember God's role-modeling for us and to create healthy boundaries for ourselves as well as respect those of the people we serve.

Chaplains must also be careful to respect the boundaries between different religions. A person ordained to perform rites and rituals in one religious system does not have any right or obligation to assume these duties while providing chaplaincy service to a client. Nevertheless, this does not mean that one cannot participate or even preside over the fulfillment of a ritual or rite for someone of a different religion. A chaplain based in one faith should assume such a responsibility for someone of another religion only with their consent and clear parameters so as to maintain the integrity of both religious systems. Let me be clear that I am not referring to an interfaith service or ritual. For example, as the chaplain of our local fire department I am occasionally called upon to officiate at funerals for firefighters or their family members if they have no specific religious affiliation. When this happens I lead a standard Protestant service, choosing readings from the book of Psalms and other passages in the Old Testament. For specifically Christian prayers, I call upon either a past chief or another senior officer. This kind of interfaith work is very rewarding but requires careful attention to working so closely to the boundaries that separate one religion from another.

Chaplaincy Lessons from the *Siddur*

I would like to now shift to the Jewish prayer book, known as the *Siddur*, for more examples of a Jewish approach to chaplaincy.[2] Over the centuries men and women have shaped the prayer book in response to the myriad of moments when one seeks guidance, counsel, and wisdom. As a result, the *Siddur* provides a wealth of insight for a Jewish approach to chaplaincy. A well-rounded chaplain expected to provide succor to someone who is Jewish will need at least an introduction to the *Siddur*.

Let me begin with the language of the prayers contained within the *Siddur* because it is instructive. The prayers are unevenly divided between first person singular and first person plural. In fact, the vast majority of the prayers are in the first person plural. Only the opening, preliminary section of the daily morning service is composed in the first person singular. This is also the most corporally orientated part of the entire Jewish worship service. For example, it includes references to "removing slumber from my eyes" or "who made me in your image." It also describes a prayer known as the "bathroom" prayer, which I consider in more depth below. This initial physical orientation serves to remind both the chaplain and client that there is a uniquely inner strength within each individual (the "I" language) that must be tapped. However, the imbalance in the language of the prayer book in favor of the first person plural emphasizes that a Jew need never be alone when facing crisis. He or she is inextricably part of a larger community from which additional support may always be drawn. This not only makes sense intuitively, it also mirrors one of the initial tasks of a chaplain when entering into relationship with a client, namely to convey the message that the person does not have to face his or her challenge alone. Anyone who has experienced personal travail—whether illness, incarceration, problems in a relationship, or trauma—knows that it is often accompanied by an overwhelming sense of aloneness. At the same time we also need to help our client seek the inner strength that she must access for meeting the challenge she faces. Literally, as a caregiver one of the first "lifelines" we are likely to throw out is that of a caring connection that pierces the loneliness of coping with crisis. A fundamental task of a chaplain is to dispel loneliness and begin the process of drawing the client back into community. The language of Jewish prayer does this.

Beyond language, the *Siddur* also contains innumerable passages and blessings that are very useful to the chaplain. One of my personal favorites is found in the opening section of the morning service. It is occasionally referred to as the bathroom prayer because it is traditionally recited after a visit to the bathroom.

> Blessed are you, Adonai, our God, the sovereign of all worlds, who
> shaped the human being with wisdom, making for us all of the openings

and vessels of the body. It is revealed and known before your Throne of Glory that if one of these passage-ways be open when it should be closed, or blocked up when it should be free, one could not stay alive or stand before you. Blessed are you, Adonai, the wondrous healer of all flesh. (*Kol Hanishama*, 21)

The literal meaning of the prayer is an expression of gratitude for our ability to open up our bodies and discharge waste. On a deeper level, however, it speaks to the wondrousness of our bodies. Without any conscious effort on our part we are host to an infinite number of miracles taking place within our bodies; our cells open and close as needed, as do the valves in our heart and other organs. Rabbi Arthur Green sums up the importance of this passage by pointing out that "We do not need to stand before any greater wonder of nature than our own bodies in order to appreciate the intricacy and beauty with which our world is endowed. A sense of awe at our own creation is a starting point . . ." (*Kol Hanishama*, 20). For me this blessing brings to light how we are infused with the divine presence, a gift of pure grace.

I was once meeting with an inmate who suffered tragically because of a drug addiction. He had recently violated his condition of release because of his addiction problem and was back in prison. He was utterly crushed. He felt devastated because he believed he let down all those who had worked so hard to help him gain his release. Back in the prison he was feeling his life was worthless. Instead of trying to argue with him that this was not the case I invited him to say this blessing with me. I explained to him that even though he was having so much trouble controlling certain aspects of his life, other parts were safely in God's hands. By taking time to meditate on this passage he was slowly able to see that even though he thought God had abandoned him, indeed this was not the case. I cannot say that this revelation cured him of addiction problems. But I can say that it helped him to regain the strength to start therapy again.

Prayer language is metaphorical. Conscious use of metaphors can be extremely helpful in many cases. However, one must be careful to use the right metaphor at the right time. For example, the "bathroom" prayer might not be the best metaphor to use with a patient suffering heart or kidney failure. In such cases it is advisable to use alternative metaphorical prayer language. There is another passage in the opening section of the morning service that conveys a similar message but does not focus specifically on bodily functions. This passage states: "My God, the soul that you gave to me is pure. You have created it, you shaped it, and you breathed it into me and you preserve it deep inside of me. . . ."

For a person suffering from physical ailments, self-loathing, excessive guilt, or shame, repeating these words can be transformative. No matter how impure or unholy or dirty a person may feel, this passage is a reminder that deep within us is a pure, God-given soul. In Hebrew the word for soul also means "breath." Thus, on another level this simple sentence can also be understood as saying with each breath one takes one inhales a godly gift of the pure breath of life and hope. Both this sentence and the "bathroom" prayer are profound yet simple passages from the daily Jewish prayer service that have tremendous healing potential. Their universal themes make them valuable tools in the hands of a chaplain, regardless of religious orientation or training.

Another quintessential Jewish blessing is called the *shechiyanu*: "Blessed are you, Eternal One our God, the sovereign of all worlds, who gave us life, and kept us strong, and brought us to this time." It celebrates and affirms the uniqueness and holiness of each new day. It is traditionally said whenever we experience something for the first time. The blessing means that we are grateful for having been sustained with life so that we might make it to this moment in time. It also is a celebration of encountering something for the first time. However, if we loosen its traditional application it becomes an alternative mantra to the familiar "live one day at a time." Instead of living one day at time, by reciting the *shechiyanu* we bless and express gratitude for each day, hour, or minute with a new frame of mind or attitude. Like the first passages from the *Siddur* already explicated, the *shechiyanu* can be a simple but powerful tool to build self-esteem and courage to face crisis.

Jewish Perspectives on Certain Chaplaincy Issues

I want to briefly touch on Jewish perspectives on a variety of topics a chaplain may encounter. Keep in mind that in Judaism, like life in general, there is rarely one right response to a situation. For deeper and more nuanced examinations of issues please consult a rabbi. However, please note that even among rabbis responses will vary. Your client or his/her family will be the final judge in determining which rabbinic point of view to follow.[3]

Abortion. Judaism is not categorically opposed to abortion. Judaism does not presume that life begins with conception. Since almost all Jewish precepts and ordinances can be violated in order to save a life, an abortion is permissible if carrying the fetus to term can in some way threaten the life of the mother. How to define what is life threatening, and when life begins, may be ambiguous. As a chaplain you may be called in for guidance to help determine this.

Alcohol. Judaism recognizes that the consumption of alcohol can lead to harmful addictive behavior. Despite the potential harm it can cause, drinking is not prohibited within Judaism. In fact, in Jewish tradition wine is closely associated with the act of consecrating time or activities. For example, special blessings are recited over wine in order to sanctify the Sabbath. Some people maintain that the popular Alcoholics Anonymous Twelve-Step program is "not Jewish." This is not true. There is nothing in the AA Twelve-Step program that contradicts Jewish values or teachings. Alcohol consumption becomes problematic when its use leads to such things as violation of the value of *shalom b'bayit* (peace in the home), self-destructive behavior, and/or inability to meet personal responsibilities.

Autopsy. Traditionally, autopsy is strongly discouraged. However, when state or local law mandates, it is permissible. The principle or underlying value is that the body should be kept as intact as possible and treated with the highest regard. When an autopsy might contribute to saving the life of another person it is also considered permissible. Defining the parameters of what it means to save the life of another person is subject to discussion. Does this include general research or education (for doctors in training, for example), or must it be more specific?

Contraception. There are no specific restrictions regarding the use of contraception. However, among observant Jews there are concerns about "wasting seed" (Gen. 38:9) and a desire to fulfill the blessing to "be fertile and increase, fill the earth . . ." (Gen. 1:28). On the other hand, the Bible also instructs us to be responsible stewards of the land: "The Lord God took the man and placed him in the Garden of Eden, to till it and tend it" (Gen. 2:15). With overpopulation a very serious environmental problem it is evident that there is potential conflict between these two commandments. Similarly, the use of contraception also affects another Jewish value, *pikuah nefesh*, saving a life. The use of contraception not only reduces the chance of pregnancy but also the spread of life-threatening diseases such as HIV/AIDS.

Cremation. Traditionally, Judaism has opposed cremation. There are two main reasons for this. One is that the idea of "dust to dust" reminds us that Adam (humankind) was created from earth and to earth we are destined to return upon death. (Note that in Hebrew the word for earth, *adamah*, is linguistically closely related to the word for humankind, *adam*). Second, since the Holocaust when millions of Jews were murdered in Nazi crematoria, cremation has taken on a new level of meaning. For many liberal Jews, however, environmental and economic factors have given the option of cremation a new value and relevance.

Domestic violence. Judaism has a core religious value called *shalom b'bayit* or peace in the home. Domestic violence comes in many forms—verbal, emotional, psychological, and of course physical—all of which destroy peace in the home. Also, domestic abuse violates the value of *b'tzelem Elohim*, that we are all created in the image of God. In principle, Judaism is intolerant of domestic violence. Unfortunately, identifying it is often difficult. Across the religious spectrum it is laden with much social stigma. Victims often feel somehow responsible for their victimization, while perpetrators contradictorily feel embarrassed by their actions, yet perversely justified. Consequently, people are often reluctant to admit abuse is going on. Also, without obvious physical injuries, identifying abuse can be highly subjective. This can be additionally challenging for someone not familiar with observant Judaism's often clear and distinct gender roles.

Ending life support. Judaism maintains that time and cause of death are in God's hands alone. However, compassion and concern for prolonged suffering, quality of life, and definitions of life and death mitigate against a formulaic response to whether or not it is acceptable according to Jewish tradition to end life support. The importance of a living will and medical directive cannot be understated with respect to issues surrounding whether or not to end life support. In general, the law of the land supercedes religious law.

Euthanasia. In general the Jewish view on euthanasia is relatively straightforward. Time and cause of death are in God's hands alone. Compassion and concern for prolonged suffering complicate this relatively cut-and-dried answer and invite questions about the extent of medical intervention necessary to comport with tradition. However, in no situation does Judaism permit the taking of one's own life to avoid future pain and suffering.

Gambling. Judaism recognizes that gambling, like alcohol, can lead to harmful addictive behavior. Despite the potential harm it can cause, gambling is not prohibited. In fact, Jewish tradition includes games of chance, the most well known being *dreidle*, a game closely associated with the holiday of Hanukkah. As with alcohol consumption, gambling becomes problematic when it leads to such things as violation of the value of *shalom b'bayit*, self-destructive behavior, and/or inability to meet personal responsibilities.

Homosexuality. The Jewish people are divided on the issue of homosexuality. Some people base their opposition to homosexuality on one interpretation of Leviticus 18:22 that states, "Do not lie with a male as one lies with a woman; it is an abhorrence." Others argue that there are different ways to read this passage, some more literal than others, that do not support opposition to homosexuality. Still others maintain that the biblical passage ought to be secondary to the foundational value that we are all created *b'tzelem Elohim*, in the image of God. While traditional doctrine opposes accepting homosexual behavior, it does not permit the mistreatment or abuse of any kind toward gays or lesbians. Regardless of theology, hostile homophobic behavior is not acceptable.

Interfaith worship. Interfaith worship presents particular problems for chaplains. For many Christians, worship that does not include the opportunity to witness their belief in Jesus is at best insipid and at worse sacrilegious. For many Jews, evoking the name of Jesus or closing a prayer in Jesus' name creates an uncomfortable situation, and an untenable one for others. Interfaith worship is certainly possible. Sometimes it helps to call the gathering something other than "worship." However, careful thought as to what to include can easily mitigate most problems. Christian prayer is often more spontaneous than Jewish prayer, which tends to follow a set structure. This in itself is typically not a problem if the closing of such a prayer is not sealed in the name of Jesus. Awareness of this is important.

Life after death. Judaism's views on life after death are complex and often contradictory. Insofar as Judaism does not maintain a concept of an eternal hell, it does not make much of a link between how one lives his life and what happens in death. At a minimum, Judaism promotes the notion that each person's soul will be reunited with God upon death, while the body will return to the earth. The idea of "divine punishment" is left as a mystery. Judaism does not address the issue of life after death for a non-Jew.

Organ donations. There is no restriction on organ donations when the organs will be used imminently to save a life. There are reservations over donating organs that will be stored until needed. It is noteworthy that traditionally organ donation was discouraged. This is not the case anymore.

Sin/Forgiveness. Making a mistake is considered a necessary part of life. Within Judaism, therefore, sinning—while not desirable—is never the end of the world, so to speak. Judaism distinguishes between two broad categories of sins: sins between people and sins between a person and God. For sins between people, God does not intervene with forgiveness. Only a person against whom a transgression was executed can forgive the transgressor. For sins between God and humankind, however, Judaism teaches we may expect forgiveness from God if we seek it.

The soul. Judaism's views on the nature of the soul are so complex that it teaches that we actually each have five souls! The most operationally important points for a chaplain to understand about the Jewish view of the soul are that it is pure; it is a gift of grace from God; and, finally, "someday God will take it back."

Conclusion

Judaism is a complex system of historical and religious traditions rich with a wide variety of, and often conflicting, values. It is rarely easy to know when one value takes precedence over another in determining the best response to a situation. Indeed, sometimes the right response for one person may be exactly the wrong one for someone else. Both perspectives may well be perfectly legitimate and appropriate Jewish responses. A well-trained, multifaith chaplain will understand that his or her Jewish clients are often wrestling with these many different Jewish points of view. Judaism, it should again be mentioned, favors questions over answers.

When in doubt, ask your client what he or she thinks about a situation or wants or expects from it. Also, do not hesitate to contact any rabbi for insight, clarification, or information. It is not advisable to ask a Jewish friend because there is much folklore that circulates among well-intended people as "tradition." A chaplain will never go wrong if he or she goes back to the basic Jewish core values that we are all created in the image of God and one good question is worth much more than a dozen bad answers.

EIGHT

Light at the End of the Tunnel: Pastoral Care for Muslims

Ahmed Nezar M. Kobeisy

The United States is a microcosm of humanity. No other country has a greater diversity of races, nationalities, ethnic, cultural, and religious groups. Although the United States offers a great asylum for diverse people, cultures are always encouraged to assimilate and even disappear into what is called the "melting pot." According to A. Mazrui in *The Report of The New York State Social Studies* (1991), many cultures have been, at best, marginalized. There is no doubt, however, that both pluralism as well as the awareness of pluralism and diversity are on the rise. The task for all of us, especially the service providers among us, is to learn how to understand people of other communities as we understand ourselves, and how to be inclusive of those who are different from us through skillful and sensitive service.

The marginalization of Muslims in various aspects of American society is evident, particularly in pastoral care. Since most Muslims are unaware of pastoral care to begin with—its services and benefits—they are often deprived of the benefits and services it could offer them. This chapter, therefore, will be of use to health-care professionals, pastoral care providers, and the Muslim communities they may serve.

It is the consensus of Muslim scholars as well as scholars of other faiths and societies, that the Muslim community is little understood, and is underserved in the United States (Kobeisy 2004). Unfair treatment of Muslims in the United States has damaged and continues to threaten the mental health of American Muslims.

This chapter seeks to help pastoral and health care professionals understand the most significant features of Islam, and of Muslim culture, and to equip them with the tools they need to help their Muslim clients in their particular settings. Furthermore, it describes what pastoral caregivers and other helping professionals need to do in order to enhance their skills and sensitivity in dealing with people of different cultures in general. For Muslim individuals and communities, I will try to explain the basic elements and goals of pastoral care so that they may come to benefit from its services.[1]

The Case for Including Muslims

Islam is one of the fastest growing religions in the world and in the United States; by the year 2010, Muslims will be the second largest religious group after Christians (Haddad & Lummis 1987; Bagby 1994; Melton 1993; Waugh, Abu Laban, and Qureishi, 1991). The rapid growth of the Muslim community is attributed mainly to immigration, a high fertility rate, and conversion. Despite this tremendous growth, the group continues to be understudied (Ghayur 1981; Rashid 1985). Research and recent polls indicate that Muslim Americans face what is known as "Multiple Oppression Syndrome" more severely and more frequently than other communities. Muslims suffer the various forms of discrimination prevalent in American society at large on the basis of religion, color, national origin, gender, age, and sex among other factors, but in exacerbated ways. Several years after 9/11, Muslims continue to be treated with suspicion and continue to hear negative characterizations of Islam and Islamic tradition from high-ranking public officials and influential persons in the media. Travel, particularly by air, has been documented and reported to single out Muslims, Arabs, and those who look like them with harassment, intimidation, and sometimes prevention from travel altogether. For instance, according to *USA Today* reporter Marilyn Elias:

> Motaz Elshafi, 28, a software engineer, casually opened an internal e-mail at work last month. The message began, "Dear Terrorist." The note from a co-worker was sent to Muslims working at Cisco Systems in Research Triangle Park, N.C., a few days after train bombings in India that killed 207. The e-mail warned that such violent acts wouldn't intimidate people, but only make them stronger. "I was furious," says Elshafi, who is New Jersey-born and bred. "What did I have to do with this violence?" (Elias 2006)

The same report states,

A *USA Today*/Gallup Poll of 1,007 Americans shows strong anti-Muslim feeling, and the hard feelings are damaging the mental health of U.S. Muslims. . . . Thirty-nine percent of respondents to the *USA Today*/ Gallup Poll said they felt at least some prejudice against Muslims. The same percentage favored requiring Muslims, including U.S. citizens, to carry a special ID as a means of preventing terrorist attacks in the United States. About one-third said U.S. Muslims were sympathetic to al-Qaeda, and 22% said they wouldn't want Muslims as neighbors. (Ibid.)

Yale University researcher and psychologist Mona Amer concludes in the same report that because many Muslims have different names, or dress differently, they end up being ostracized all the more. Furthermore, harassment and discrimination against Muslims is leading to poorer mental health among Muslims (ibid.). In Amer's new study of 611 adults, thought to be the largest study ever done on Arab-Americans, she concludes that they had much worse mental health than Americans overall. About half had symptoms of clinical depression, compared with 20 percent in an average group of Americans.

Obstacles to Pastoral Care Among Muslims

The two most important obstacles to be discussed here are (1) the lack of information on pastoral care among Muslims, and (2) the lack of sensitivity among pastoral care providers to Muslim concerns and problems.

Muslims are often unaware of pastoral care and its services. When they are made aware of it, they are, at best, suspicious of its origin, motivation, and practices. Of the most frequently mentioned concerns by Muslims about pastoral care are (a) its Christian origin, (b) suspicion of proselytizing intent among caregivers, (c) fear of religiously based bias, and (d) lack of sensitivity due to misunderstanding the principles, values, and practices of Islam and Muslims by many pastoral care providers.

In order to address Muslims' fear and suspicion of pastoral care, more information about the service must be provided to Muslim communities and individuals in an organized and systematic way. Although pastoral care does indeed have a Christian origin, it is no longer a Christian-only profession. Pastoral care refers nowadays to the overall care for the social and personal well-being of individuals through ministry, counseling, and other support provided by clergy or trained laypeople of any religion, and caregivers may include pastors, chaplains, rabbis, and imams. Such services can be offered in places of worship (the mosque for Muslims), home, hospitals, and so forth. Clergy who are not legally required to be licensed before providing counseling should, however, acknowledge limitations in their training. There is always the risk, when dealing with troubled individuals and families, of missing important psychological indicators pointing to deeper clinical problems. It is very important for pastoral care providers and counselors to acknowledge limitations when they reach a psychological "roadblock," and refer persons under care (with their consent) to the appropriate professional or agency that can address their problem at greater depth.

The elements of pastoral care include: therapy, ministry, social action, empowerment, and personal interaction as its most important elements (Lartey 2003). Any skillful clergy and pastoral caregiver of any faith tradition can help clients from other faith traditions in matters of concern—except those concerns that are related to the client's specific tradition, theology, history, jurisprudence, or culture. At least, the pastoral caregiver can, when necessary, connect the client with members or leaders of his/her own faith tradition and culture.

In Islam, visiting the sick and helping those who are in need is strongly emphasized as a religious duty, essential to one's relation to the Divine and as a required community act. "On the Day of Judgment God Almighty will say, 'O son of Adam! I was sick but you did not visit me.' The person will respond, 'O Lord! How could I visit you and you are the Lord of the Worlds?' He will say, 'Did you not know that my servant so and so was ill, but you did not visit him? Did you not know that if you visited him, then you would have found me with Him?" (Sahih Muslim Hadith #6232). Mercy, compassion, and support are strongly emphasized in both Islam and in Muslim communities. When a Muslim is hospitalized, it is very common to see extended family and community members visiting him/her in such numbers that it might seem strange and even annoying to people of other faith traditions.

In order to achieve multicultural competency, the model of standards developed by Derald Wing Sue, Patricia Arredondo, and Roderick McDavis (1992) seems adequate. This model includes a "3 x 3" matrix—three Characteristics times three Dimensions—in which most cultural understandings can be organized or developed. For example, the characteristics—(a) counselor awareness of his/her own assumptions, values, and biases; (b) understanding of the worldview of the culturally different; and (c) developing appropriate strategies and techniques—would each be described as having three dimensions: (a) beliefs and attitudes, (b) knowledge, and (c) skills. Thus, a total of nine competency areas are identified.

Although this model was developed for counselors, pastoral caregivers are no different. In attempting to understand one's own view of Islam, the professional must examine the accuracy of his/her sources of information on Islam. Most available sources for non-Muslim Americans on Islam, including family, schools, religious institutions, media, and political events, do not allow for a fair, let alone favorable, view.

Bias against Islam and Muslims is commonplace. Ironically, these biases may have had religious origin through the unfair and uninformed indoctrination and programs offered in various religious institutions. Most of these institutions see Islam as a rival or as a historic enemy. In documented reports and studies, many religious institutions present Islam as a force of evil that is incompatible with modernity, democracy, and the West.

Media is another source of stereotyping and misinformation in addition to political institutions. Edward Said explains this problem eloquently:

> The orthodox coverage of Islam that we find in the academy, in the government, and in the media is all interrelated and has been more diffused, has seemed more persuasive and influential in the West than any other "coverage" or interpretation. The success of this coverage can be attributed to the political influence of those people and institutions producing it rather than necessarily truth or accuracy. . . . It had given consumers of news the sense that they have understood Islam without at the same time intimating to them that a great deal in this energetic coverage is based on far from objective material. In many instances "Islam" has licensed out only patent inaccuracy but also expressions of under-strained ethnocentrism, cultural and even racial hatred, deep yet paradoxically free-floating hostility. (Said 1981, 64)

Other concerns that Muslims have about pastoral care can be dealt with through education and programs among Muslims and in Islamic centers, making clear its functions and the assurances that institutions can give of neutrality, professionalism, and access for Muslim leaders to serve and minister to clients of their own faith. Muslim clerics must be invited to attend seminars and training sessions on counseling and other pastoral care areas.

Another model that I would recommend for professionals in order to enhance their sensitivity to people of other cultures, in this case Muslims, is the Intercultural Model (Lartey 2003). Norman Sundberg and David Sue state:

"Intercultural counseling is enhanced by the knowledge of the client's degree of identification with the relevant cultures and the use of cultural reference group members who are most important in their lives" (1989, 351). In this model, every human being is considered in some respect to be:

1. Like all others:
   Taking this into consideration will allow the professional to:
   a. Affirm the humanity of all
   b. Acknowledge the worth, value, and dignity of all
   c. Be aware of the humanity shared by all
   d. Provide recognition, respect, and advoca[cy] for the oppressed
   e. Understand power dynamics in intercultural encounters

Muslims have more shared commonalities and values with other "People of the Book" (i.e., Jews and Christians) than many people imagine. During my many interfaith encounters, I have heard assertions from both Jewish and Christian leaders that the more they learn about Islam, the more they become convinced that it is closer to their faith than Christianity, in the case of Jews, or Judaism in the case of Christians. To illustrate, Jews find Muslims' belief in the absolute oneness of God and the rejection of the divinity of Jesus draws them closer to Islam. One Jewish elder told me once that if he were not a Jew, he would choose Islam as a religion. On the other hand, Muslims revere Jesus and his mother Mary, which is not the case in Judaism. Several Christian congregations I have met with have been pleasantly surprised to know that the Qur'an includes a chapter named after Mary, and that Muslims love and revere Jesus.

In support of this, Margaret Miles states: "It is time to notice that people of different religions have more in common with one another than they do with people who claim no religious orientation. But sibling rivalry lingers, and it can be a very powerful form of conflict, as anyone who grew up in a family can attest." (1999).

2. Like some others:
   The professional caregiver will understand that every group has unique characteristics. This will allow him/her to understand:
   a. Groups are affected by history, experience, and what happens to other groups
   b. Group identity and influence
   c. Groups are similar and different from others
   d. The ways and dynamics of power

3. Like no other:
Regardless of the cultural origin of an individual, they are shaped
by various factors that make a person unique and different from
his/her dominant culture. If caregivers bear this in mind, they
will be able to avoid stigmatizing or offending any individual, and
consequently every individual is able to have the advantages offered
by the caregiver. It will also enable us to observe that:
a. Individuals are unique
b. Individuals form unique experiences and make their own choices
c. Clients are helped to exercise appropriate choices
d. Clients are encouraged to see, judge, and act for themselves
e. Pastoral caregivers focus on clients

Muslims value certain characteristics in caregivers, and feel encouraged
when they meet them. These include:

- Respect for Muslims' cultural and religious identity;
- Experience and effectiveness in dealing with Muslims or with
situations similar to those faced by Muslims;
- Empathy;
- Understanding of Islam unless the issue at hand is of religious nature,
in which case, Muslim clients require that the caregiver be a Muslim;
- Honoring the confidentiality of counseling sessions and not espousing
political opinion antagonistic to Muslims (Kobeisy 2004).[2]

Providing sensitivity training that includes information and skills on values,
principles, cultures, and practices of Muslims are essential elements in the
education and professional development of pastoral care students and providers
in various institutions.

Islam and Muslims

The word *Islam* has both religious and linguistic roots. In Arabic, it may mean
"peace" and "purity." In religion, it means submission to the will of the One
God, the Creator, Allah. Many Americans and Westerners err when they
describe Allah as the "Muslim God." In fact, Arab Christians and Jews use the
same name, "Allah," to describe God. During my interfaith travel to Turkey with
the Hendricks Chapel at Syracuse University, I have seen and heard priests and

rabbis who used the word *Allah* for God and have met Jews and Christians who are named as "Abd Allah," which means "servant of God" in Arabic. This usage can also be found in Iran among people of non-Muslim faith.

The word *Muslim* identifies every adult male or female who consciously and publicly announces that "there is no god but the One God and Muhammad is the Prophet of God." Strictly speaking, fulfillment of this simple requirement is all that is needed to call oneself a "Muslim." While the word *Islam* describes the religion, the word *Islamic* describes the principles, values, scriptures, sites, and institutions of Islam, and does not describe people. It is ironic for many public officials, reporters, and pseudo-experts to link the term *Islamic* to negative characterizations of people and practices (e.g., Islamic extremism, fascism, terrorism, terrorists, etc.). There is no religion in the world that is linked directly with negative practices of some of its members in the way Islam is. Al Faruqi defines Islam as: "The ideals to which all Muslims strive and by which they would and should be defined. Hence, true objectivity demands that Islam be distinguished from Muslim history and instead be regarded as its essence, its criterion and its measure" (1984, xiii).

Islam began in the seventh century and has become the second largest of the world's religions. To Muslims, Islam is more than just a set of beliefs and practices. It is, rather, a system that encompasses the relationships of Muslims to each other and to their society from birth until death (Altareb 1996; Farah 1994; Carter and El-Hindi n.d.). The main teachings, laws, principles, and values of Islam are derived from the divine and final revelation, called the Qur'an, and the example of Prophet Muhammad, called "the Sunnah."

Some people call the above-mentioned conceptualization of Islam as "Scriptural Islam," which many Muslims aspire to achieve but are not always able to attain. Wormser states: "Scriptural Islam is more than a religion. It is a detailed guide to human conduct, providing precise instruction in areas including personal hygiene, diet, dress, marriage, divorce, inheritance, taxation, and others. Particularly in the case of family law, the demands of the text often clash with long established cultural patterns" (1995, 337).

The Islamic Worldview

Islamic worldview consists of the following elements:

(a) Innate goodness of human beings, (b) Moral absolutism, (c) Unitary concept of Creator, (d) Brotherhood based on faith, (e) Women as mothers of civilization, (f) Domination of the earth is for Allah (God), and (g) Unity of knowledge (Rashid 1990, 19).

Islamic Beliefs and Practices

Islam as a religion refers to regulations pertaining to piety, ethics, beliefs, and practices of worship. These spiritual aspects of worship are called *ibadat* (Esposito 1995). This aspect includes the "roots" or foundations of the faith, for instance, Allah's uniqueness, the final prophecy of Prophet Muhammad, prayer, almsgiving, fasting, and the pilgrimage to Mecca. The other aspect of Islam is called *muamalat*, which refers to the ideas and practices of Muslims in the context of changing social, economic, and political circumstances (ibid.).

Articles of Faith. Islam indicates three levels of faith. They include: (1) *Islam* (the practical manifestation of religious requirements); (2) *Iman* (the beliefs or convictions of the faith); and (3) *Ihsan* (excellence in all aspects of human life). While every Muslim must aspire to achieve *Ihsan*, it is mandatory to maintain the first two levels of faith. The articles of faith are six:

1. *The oneness, uniqueness, and unity of God.* This article is called *Tawhid.* Islam does not attribute any physical form by which Allah is to be known or identified; rather, Allah is described through His most high attributes and with the most expressive and beautiful names. Muslims often cite the ninety-nine names and attributes of Allah, including The Most Merciful, Most Compassionate, The Creator, The Sustainer, The Peace, The Light, The All-Knowing, All-Wise, and so forth.

2. *Angels.* Angels are created from light in a variety of shapes and with unimaginable power given to them by God in order to perform the tasks entrusted to them. Angels do not have free will. Angels, therefore, cannot disobey God. Muslims revere the angels. Their presence is sought through reading the Qur'an, by remembering Allah, and in doing righteous deeds. The angels are also present during times of illness and at the time of death.

3. *The scriptures.* Islam believes that Allah has given to humankind specific scriptures and messages. Muslims accept all original scriptures in their pure and undistorted forms. Jews and Christians are also called "People of the Book" by the Qur'an—accepting the

truthfulness of their original scriptures. The Qur'an represents to Muslims the last testament and revelation from God to humanity.

4. *The messengers and prophets.* As one of the essential elements of faith in Islam, Muslims believe in all the messengers and prophets before Prophet Muhammad. One frequently hears Muslims repeating in Arabic, *Salla Allahu alaihi wa sallam,* which means "peace be upon him," whenever the name of any prophet or messenger is mentioned. Furthermore, a Muslim would not enjoy watching any of these figures impersonated on the stage or screen. Moreover, in Islam, it is forbidden to joke about or mock any prophet or religion. Muslims believe that the most revered messengers of God are Noah, Abraham, Moses, Jesus, and Muhammad, the last messenger of God.

5. *Life after death.* Islam teaches that death is only a transition from this life to the next. In the life to come, everyone will be answerable to Allah for his/her deeds. This underlines the importance of accountability and responsibility in Islam.

The Practices of Islam. There are five essential practices called the Pillars of Islam. They are expected of every adult Muslim, male or female. These are (a) *Shahadah* (the profession of faith); (b) *Salat* (Prayer); (c) *Zakat* (almsgiving); (d) *Sawm* (fasting); and (e) *Hajj* (pilgrimage).

a. *Shahadah* (profession of faith) identifies the belief that there is no god but the one and only God, and that Muhammad is His last Messenger. This declaration is repeated frequently, during prayers and during times of both stress and joy. Muslims like to affirm this cardinal belief at the time of death. They want to recite this belief or have it recited to them as they approach the end of their lives.

b. *Salat* (prayer) is the second pillar of Islam and the supreme act of worship. The term *salat* means, literally, "connection" and "gift," and that is the positive context in which Muslims perceive prayer. There are five daily prescribed prayers: at dawn, midday, afternoon, after sunset, and at night. These prayers are short and require bowing and prostration. Prayer requires a quiet, clean place (a prayer rug or a clean towel) and should be said in the direction of Makkah (Mecca, in English) in Saudi Arabia and its holy shrine the Ka'bah. There should be no idols, statues, pictures, or persons to distract the praying individual. No one is allowed to walk in front of another person who is praying. It is very common for devout Muslims to pray additional voluntary prayers. Prayer can be a source of strength, support, and inner peace. Daily prayers are said individually, or in congregation for those who are able to arrange it. Congregational prayer makes *Salat* a powerful, unifying element for the whole community. *Wudu* (ablution) is a process of ritual cleanliness required of Muslims before prayer, and should be repeated if their prayer is broken or interrupted by responding to bodily needs, by sleep, by losing consciousness, or by profuse bleeding. A complete bath without soap (i.e., *ghusl*) is required of women after menstruation, after childbirth, and after intercourse. Symbolic dry wash can substitute for the above when the patient is too ill to use water, is wounded, or there is simply no water available. During prayer, individuals may speak or recite loudly but they may not speak to others while praying.

c. *Zakat* (charity or almsgiving) is an act of both worship and of community. This pillar helps the rich to show their compassion and, at the same time, rids the poor of resentment of those who are better off. According to Abdulaziz Sachedina: "In a number of poor Muslim countries this benevolence provided by wealthy individuals has underwritten badly needed social services for those who can not afford them" (1997, 32). Rich Muslims pay 2.5 percent of their accumulated wealth annually to the poor and needy.

d. *Sawm* (fasting) takes place during the month of Ramadan, which is the ninth month of the Islamic lunar calendar. It rotates every year because the Islamic calendar is eleven days shorter than the Gregorian calendar. During fasting, adult, healthy, and nontraveling Muslims are required to abstain from food, drink, and sensual pleasure from dawn until sunset each day. After sunset, all these restrictions are removed until dawn of the next day. Elders and terminally ill persons are exempt. People who are ill, travelers, and pregnant or breast-feeding women do not have to fast, but are required to make it up later on when they are able. Fasting may require special arrangements for meals or medication. Oral medicine, I.V. hydration, and nutrition break the fast. Eye- and eardrops, inhalers, injected medicines, rectal enemas and suppositories, blood tests, and endoscopies do not break the fast. The end of Ramadan is marked by one of the two most important holidays for Muslims called *Eidul-fitr*.

e. *Hajj* (pilgrimage) is the fifth religious duty of the Muslim and is a pilgrimage to the sacred monuments of Makkah (Mecca), at least once in a lifetime for those who are physically and financially able. Pilgrimage takes place during the first thirteen days of the twelfth month of the Islamic calendar year. Approximately three million Muslims attend pilgrimage every year. Sachedina states: "The pilgrimage brings together Muslims of diverse cultures and nationalities to achieve a purity of existence and a communion with God that will exalt the pilgrims for the rest of their lives" (1997, 33). Muslims who are not present at Makkah at the time of pilgrimage are emotionally and spiritually connected to its rituals, watch them on satellite TV, talk about them, and increase their own worship practices. The culmination of Hajj rituals is called *Eidul Adha*, and is celebrated as the second of the two most important holidays for Muslims.

Islamic Holy Texts and Sources. The Qur'an is the first and most important source of understanding and legislation in Islam. The Qur'an was revealed to Prophet Muhammad piecemeal, over a period of twenty-two years. For Muslims, the Qur'an is used for prayer and as a guide for social and economic life. The goal for most Muslims is to commit the Qur'an to memory. The Qur'an is recited in homes for blessings, for strength in crisis, and during times of joy. During illness, many Muslims prefer reading from the Qur'an and/or having it recited to them in hopes of a cure.

The second source of understanding and legislation in Islam is the Sunnah (tradition) of the Prophet. This includes the Prophet's statements, actions, and tacit approval. It is recorded in several texts and has been authenticated, eliminating inauthentic readings.

Islamic Holidays. In addition to the two major holidays mentioned above—namely *Eidul Fitr* and *Eidul Adha*—various Muslim communities may celebrate other holidays in various ways. These holidays include the *Maulid* (birthday of the Prophet), *A'ashura* (the tenth day of the Muharram (a day of mourning observed by Shi'a and Sunni Muslims), *Isra,* and *Mi'raj* (the Night Journey of the Prophet)—among others. Because the Islamic calendar is lunar, I have not included any specific dates for these holidays.

The Muslim Community

The American Muslim community, like that of Muslim communities worldwide, is made up of two main groups—(1) the Sunnis, who represent the majority of Muslims (85–90 percent of the total Muslim population), and (2) the Shiites, who account for 10 to 15 percent. The Sunnis can be subdivided into four main schools of thought, while the Shiites can be subdivided into a number of sects. The split into these two main communities occurred early in Islamic history in a contention over the succession to the leadership role of the Prophet Muhammad after his death. While the Sunnis believed that the succession should be open for all according to a selection process, the Shiites insisted that it remain within the family of the Prophet. Extremists have transformed the conflict into a theological, practical, and doctrinal division. While the subdivisions in the Sunni community are not seen as contradictory, different Shiite sects are seriously alienated from one another.

In cities where Shiites have significant numbers of followers, they build their own houses of worship, institutions, and school systems. In cities where they are a minority, they join the Sunnis in their worship and celebration of holidays, and they seek religious services from the Islamic institution nearest to them—which is the case here in the United States. Only a few centers in the United States (e.g., Los Angeles and Detroit) are built by local Shiites. In other places in the United States, Shiites meet their religious needs through the services of local Sunni Islamic centers and send their children to Sunni schools.

American Muslims

The Muslims of North America can be divided into two distinct groups: immigrant Muslims and indigenous Muslims. As for the non-African immigration of Muslims to the United States, there are indications that it might have started in the late nineteenth or twentieth centuries, and occurred in waves. The first wave occurred in the late nineteenth century, and was mainly Arabs from greater Syria. Most of these were poor and working-class people who accepted unskilled work and menial jobs. They took American spouses and assimilated into American society. This wave continued until World War I, after which a second wave continued through the 1930s, ending with World War II (Denny 1995; Haddad 1991).

A third wave of Muslim immigration after World War II included many people from the elite of Middle Eastern and South Asian countries seeking education and professional advancement. Although many returned to their home countries, a large number remained, kept their Islamic identity, and assimilated into American life. The emigration patterns reflected changes in American immigration policies as well as sociopolitical and economic upheavals overseas.

The majority of indigenous American Muslims, mainly African Americans who constitute 30.2 percent of the total Muslim population in the United States (Stone 1991), identify themselves with mainstream Sunni Islam, while the rest constitute the membership of the American Muslim Mission led by Imam W. D. Muhammad. Muhammad diverged from his father Elijah Muhammad's Nation of Islam and instructed his followers to integrate their community into the country's mainstream Muslim community (Ahmed 1991, 20).

While most Muslims identify themselves as Sunni, there is an Iranian Shiite group, fourteen strains of black Muslims, and other offshoots, including mystical Sufism (Marquand and Andoni 1996). Although the Nation of Islam is considered a religious offshoot by other Muslims, some feel that the Nation was a necessary transitional stage toward the group joining mainstream Islam. Furthermore, many of the African American Muslims owe their affiliation with Islam to the Nation. According to other Sunni Muslim officials, there is reason to believe that the Nation is indeed moving gradually toward the mainstream (Wormser 1994, 103).

According to Stone (1991), Muslims are already America's second-largest religious group. News alerts issued regularly by the Council of American Islamic Relations (CAIR) estimate the number of Muslims in the United States at eight million. While Muslims in any single Islamic country can be regarded, to some extent, to be culturally as well as religiously homogeneous, Muslim minorities in North America, particularly in the United States, are as diverse as the various world Muslim communities. Each group, in addition to ethnic, cultural, and religious differences, comes with different educational, historic, economic, and political experiences and aspirations.

When dealing with American Muslims, the complex makeup of identity must be acknowledged in order to deliver services to them effectively. Many caregivers err by assuming that one set of information on Islam can be of help to or accepted by all Muslims.

In order for pastoral care professionals to deliver services to Muslims effectively, they must incorporate Islamic ideological beliefs, cultural traditions, family support systems, and personal preferences into that care. Understanding must also include the cultural conflicts that may not even be recognized by the clients themselves.

It is advisable that pastoral caregivers keep handy in their offices some guides to the Islamic rules about care and the interaction of caregivers and those to whom they minister. At the same time, it would be helpful to keep a directory of the local or national Islamic organizations that could help in the counseling process or in answering the counselor's questions.

Muslims' Social and Family Structure

Living in large and extended families is the norm in most Muslim cultures. For Muslims who come from these cultures, nuclear families exist mainly because of economic pressures and/or reasons related to immigration policies. Islam in general advocates for the elderly. The adult children are expected to take care of their aging parents. There are no nursing homes in Muslim countries. In a study by Yvonne Yazbeck Haddad and Adair Lummis, American Muslims were asked, "If it is too difficult or expensive to care for elderly parents at home, should a good care facility be found?" (1987, 88). Almost half the respondents disagreed, yet slightly less than a fourth agreed and slightly more than a fourth had mixed feelings. Decisions about health care, end of life, do-not-resuscitate orders, and major treatment strategies can be multigenerational. In most Muslim cultures, families tend to hide illnesses, particularly serious ones, from the patient. The purpose is to protect the patient from any feeling of despair or hopelessness. It would be appropriate, if it is determined that the patient should know the facts of his or her condition, that the caregiver explain the situation gently and in the presence of his or her approved relative. In the case of translating when the patient or client doesn't understand English, the translator must commit to translating the facts without altering them. The translator may use the culturally appropriate language, but must communicate the same facts.

Gender Roles

Because gender roles in Islam and in Muslim cultures are little understood, people in the West attribute exoticism to the subject and often rely for their understanding on fiction or conjecture. In widely distributed sensitivity training material developed by a reputable U.S. academic institution, the false idea is set forth that a Muslim man cannot shake his own daughter's hand because of strict Islamic rules against touching between the sexes. In fact, the restrictions are intended only for opposite sexes if they are *not* close relatives or members of the immediate family. So, there is no restriction on contact between fathers and children, siblings with each other, nephews and nieces with their uncles and aunts, nor for grandparents and their grandchildren. And, in fact, not all Muslims adhere to such restrictions or consider them as necessary.

The implications for gender roles in Islam in a pastoral and health-care context are as follows:

- Some Muslim women dress in ethnic or "covering" clothes.
- Some women wear head cover (*hijab*) or face cover (*niqab* or *burqa*). This is intended to keep a woman's body covered in the presence of strange and unrelated men.
- Private parts must not be uncovered except by necessity in medical emergency.
- Showering must be done behind a barrier if others are present.
- Preference is for same-gender care providers if possible, especially for intimate care (OB/GYN).
- Knock before entering a Muslim woman's room (and this rule would apply to X-ray technicians, PT staff, and RNs, as well as pastoral caregivers).
- Unnecessary touching of opposite gender (e.g., patting, hugging, hand shaking) should be avoided.
- It is important to assign a same-gender patient's room. A woman patient may be uncomfortable staying alone with the opposite gender.
- Some women patients may avoid direct eye contact out of respect and modesty.

Muslims' Diet

The Muslim diet is called *Halal*, which means religiously lawful (it is analogous to the Jewish kosher diet). Muslims are allowed to eat only meat that is slaughtered by Muslims or Christians or Jews. Conservative Muslims may insist on meat that is slaughtered solely by Muslims, called *Zabiha*. Most Muslims do not eat rare meat. Some Muslims may ask for vegetarian or seafood diets in hospital or other health-care facilities.

Forbidden substances for Muslims include:

- Alcohol and all intoxicants
- All food containing pork or pork by-products
- Pure blood
- Gelatin, lecithin, glycerides from pig
- Lard

View of Health and Illness

Life with all of its aspects is considered a test from God. The goodness of an individual is expressed by how a person reacts to both health and illness. In health, a Muslim is expected to be grateful to Allah for his grace and mercy and to utilize such health in leading a righteous life. In illness, a Muslim is expected to be grateful to Allah for what he or she has, patient in facing difficulty, and hopeful in Allah's mercy. Illness is seen as expiation from sins and, sometimes, as punishment for previous sins. A skilled pastoral caregiver can reduce the burden of a Muslim patient by assuring him or her of Allah's mercy and forgiveness and in assuring the patient, when appropriate, of the possibility of healing. Islam maintains that there is no illness that does not, at least potentially, have a cure. The cure, however, may not yet be known. The only exceptions to this concept are the terminal issues of old age. Seeking treatment is encouraged in Islam and it sometimes is a religious obligation.

In Islamic religion as well as in Islamic culture, the soul, mind, and body are seen as interconnected and, therefore, influence one another in health as well as in illness. Illness, mental or physical, is seen as a lack of harmony between the inner and outer self. Symptoms of mental dysfunction may be neglected or denied for a long time, thus resulting in worsening the client's condition. In physical illness, unquestioned authority may be given to the professional as a result of a cultural respect for authority.

It is possible that negative feelings and emotions may accompany illness among Muslims. These feelings include guilt and shame. The reasons for such feelings are partly religious and partly cultural. The religious reason is based on the assumption that someone might be undergoing punishment from God for sins and bad deeds. This can be dealt with by simply emphasizing Allah's attributes of mercy, forgiveness, and Ultimate Wisdom. Other reasons for shame and guilt can occur as a result of losing autonomy—feeling controlled, intimidated, and afraid (Kobeisy 2004b).

Below are some general principles/rules regarding Muslims in pastoral and health care:

- Islam makes it obligatory to help others. The Qur'an declares, "Saving a single soul is like saving all of humanity" (Qur'an 5:32).
- When two values are in conflict, the Islamic principle calls for "Doing good without inviting harm." If this absolute goal is not possible, Islam calls for "reaching the most beneficial with the least possible harm."

- Religious obligation can be delayed, modified, or even dismissed in times of necessity or danger.
- Emergency treatments must be given.

Medicine.[3] In addition to the prohibition of pork or pork by-products in food, they are also prohibited or discouraged in drugs and compounds used in medical treatment. The only time they are allowed in treatment is when there is a medical emergency and there is no religiously lawful substitute. Items that may include pork or pork by-products include Insulin, Heparin, and porcine grafts used in some heart surgery.

Furthermore, items containing alcohol should also be avoided unless absolutely necessary. Such items include Ethyl alcohol (a.k.a. ethanol), which is an intoxicant and forbidden; medicines containing ethyl alcohol should be avoided—for instance, some cough syrups and mouthwashes. Other chemicals in the general category of "alcohol" are not intoxicants and may be used as medical solvents (i.e., benzyl alcohol, glycerol).

Birth Control, Abortion, and Fertility Treatment. Birth control is allowed, particularly when it is not permanent (as in the case of sterilization)—unless the mother's health condition warrants it. A stillborn baby after four months must have a name and be given full Muslim burial rites.

Abortion is prohibited except when the mother's life is endangered. Some Muslim schools of thought disallow it after the first forty days, unless the pregnancy is expected to be unusually difficult and threatening to the life of either the mother or the child.

Fertility treatment is allowed if it is hormonal or involves insemination with the husband's sperm.

Post-Childbirth and Postnatal Care.

1. Female caregivers are preferred for prenatal and postnatal care
2. Keep the patient covered
3. Limit the number of individuals in the delivery room
4. It is common to announce the "call to prayer" to the newborn
5. Circumcision is mandated for male babies
6. Mothers are encouraged to nurse
7. Mothers may nurse for up to two years
8. It is common to shave the head of the newborn after birth

Organ Donation and Transplant. Organ procurement is, in general, allowed with certain required conditions for both donors and recipients. These requirements include:

- *Living donor.* Must be adult, sane, a willing volunteer who will not be harmed physically, aside from the dangers of the surgical procedure; the donor must not gain financially. The organ must not be essential for the donor's continuing life.
- *Deceased donor.* In this case, a prior consent or the consent of the next of kin (e.g., legal guardian, trustee, or representative) is necessary. Furthermore, the organ must be used for saving the life of another. No organ should be removed from a person unless that person's death has been certified. If an organ was obtained but not used for any reason, it must be properly buried unless this is not allowed locally for legal or for medical reasons.

End-of-Life Issues.

- Euthanasia and assisted suicide are forbidden
- Decision-making capacity can be multigenerational
- Blood transfusion is allowed
- Life support is allowed
- Brain death criteria are accepted to define death
- A patient in vegetative state is considered alive
- Terminal withdrawal of life support from a living patient is not allowed
- Withholding hydration and nutrition from a living patient is not allowed

Steps to Take before Death.

- Contact family
- Allow family members to be present at the time of death, if possible
- Common to have many visitors
- Qur'anic recitation is desirable; audiotapes may be used if necessary
- Offer visit of hospital chaplain

- Reaffirmation of cardinal beliefs
- Pain relief with narcotics is allowed; some may refuse narcotics

Hospice Care.

- Patient and family may ask to remove pictures, statues, or other religious symbols
- The patient may become extrareligious
- There may be supplications and recitation of Qur'an
- Large number of visitors is expected

After Death.

- Close the eyes and cover the body
- Face body towards Mecca if possible
- Autopsy is not allowed unless absolutely necessary
- The body is washed and wrapped in white cloth
- Quick burial
- No cremation; no embalming

Conclusion

In this time and age of increasing diversity and rapid globalization, there is no excuse for not properly, accurately, and sensitively understanding and serving each other with dignity.

It is imperative for Muslims to understand the realities of American culture and take part in that cultural exchange, thus enriching the American culture and the world. One of the areas that Muslims need to understand, participate in, enrich, and benefit from is pastoral care. Muslim communities and leaders must facilitate the interaction and exchange with, and act as resource for, pastoral care professionals and providers. Muslim spiritual leaders should be trained in providing pastoral care for their members and for members of other faiths as well.

On the other hand, it is imperative for pastoral care professionals to understand the Islamic religion and Muslim cultures and be sensitive to the needs of Muslims. Furthermore, they must advocate changes in public policies and practices that are not fair to minority populations, including Muslims.

The rule of thumb for developing sensitivity is not to assume anything about any Muslim and only to plan services for them according to the expressed needs of that patient and his or her family. It is essential to build trust, rapport, and positive regard for the client from the first encounter. Assure the Muslim client of your neutrality and willingness to serve. The Muslim family and community structures and values can be of great support to the healing process without violating confidentiality laws or personal expectations.

The most important task of a pastoral care worker is to take the fear and anxiety away from the Muslim patient and to provide them with the help they need or ask for. Although religious rules and guidelines must be observed, the patient needs to be informed that in the case of emergency, religious requirements can be delayed, waived, or even suspended in order to save his or her life. One of the most important goals and objectives of Islam is the protection of life.

Most importantly, pastoral care professionals must seek professional development in dealing with Muslims and to approach this chapter as a beginning, rather than with a "mission accomplished" mentality.

NINE

Developing a Buddhist Approach to Pastoral Care: A Peacemaker's View

Mikel Monnett

As the United States becomes a more multicultural and multireligious society, the ranks of health-care chaplains are no longer being limited solely to Judeo-Christian clerics. In an effort to increase interfaith understanding and ecumenical awareness, I present here one model of health-care chaplaincy that derives itself from a Buddhist perspective and show how I use it in my daily work at one of the top ten hospitals in the United States.

It has often been said by great Buddhist sages that the essence of the Buddha's teachings can be summed up in the first sermon that he gave in Benares. That sermon centered on what Buddhists call The Four Noble Truths: that to exist is to suffer; that our suffering is caused by our attachment to what is transient; that since our suffering has a cause, it must have a remedy; and that the remedy is to follow the Eightfold Path of the Buddha. This Eightfold Path is a series of disciplines that, if properly and diligently practiced, will free one from the path of suffering and allow one to realize one's true nature or Buddhahood.[1]

Chief among these eight practices is the concept of *right livelihood*. Most forms of Buddhism express a reverence for all life and stress the duty of a devout Buddhist to work for the benefit of all sentient beings. So many Buddhists are often found working in so-called helping professions, such as social work, nursing, addiction recovery, counseling, and so forth. In the United States, that sometimes includes hospital or hospice chaplaincy.

The Mahayana Way

Buddhism is often dismissed by theists as not being a "true" religion because it is based not so much on a belief system in a Supreme Being as on a series of realizations through mental practices, chief among which is meditation (*dhyana*) and moral conduct (*sila*). Indeed, those of us who are Buddhist often refer to our practices as *mind training*: we do these things in order to clear away obscurations like ego clinging that inhibit us from seeing the nature of this world as it truly is. In essence, we are seeking to see the world without the prism of ego distortion. There are a variety of techniques to do this but Mahayana Buddhists have found one of the most effective is the development of compassion by working for the benefit of others rather than oneself. The effect of this is to loosen our concerns for our "self" (which is an illusionary mental concept born out of ignorance and selfishness) and instead to develop an empathetic understanding with other beings and compassion for them (*bodhicitta*). This is one of the core practices of the Mahayana tradition.

How this is expressed depends upon the time, place, culture, and level of the individual practitioner's understanding and commitment. To some, this might involve becoming a forest monk, a wandering ascetic who lives in the wilderness and does austere yogic practices, dedicating the merit to all sentient beings. To another, it might entail giving up family life and entering a monastery with other monastics, while to still another it might entail living in a small temple on the edge of a Japanese village and conducting rituals for the people there. All of these have been shown by Buddhist traditions throughout history to be effective ways of overcoming one's sense of self and to benefit others.

In the early 1960s, another way of expression came about when Thich Nhat Hanh created the School for Social Service in Vietnam, and began to teach what he called *Engaged Buddhism*.[2] In Engaged Buddhism, the practitioner does not withdraw from the world and practice the Buddha's teachings in solitude or with a small group of like-minded individuals; instead, the practitioner remains engaged with the world and attempts to deepen his or her understanding of Buddhadharma through that engagement. The interaction with others and with their society becomes a part of the practice, just as much as meditation, studying liturgical texts, or performing rituals.

The impact of this new expression was felt not only throughout Vietnam, but quickly spread to other Asian Buddhist countries as well. It can be seen in the works of Sulak Sivaraksa in Thailand, Aung San Suu Kyi in Burma, and the Dalai Lama of Tibet. It has reinvigorated the Buddhist traditions of those countries, given hope to their various peoples, and provided a spiritual basis for enlightened social action and protest.[3] In the United States, the civil rights movement, the antiwar movement, and the feminist movement led many people to become actively involved in changing their culture. Influenced by Mahatma Gandhi and Martin Luther King Jr., many also sought a spiritual discipline within which to frame their work and beliefs. Buddhism, with its emphasis on individual development and experiential knowledge, seemed to fill the bill for some of these people. Engaged Buddhism allowed them to see that what they were already doing could be a part of their spiritual practice.

One of those people was Bernie Glassman, an American priest of the Soto Zen school of Buddhism. Glassman felt that Buddhism without engagement was a mere intellectual exercise, while engagement without discipline was doomed ultimately to failure. Glassman and his wife and fellow priest, Sandra Jiko Holmes, envisioned a religious order that would embrace the Four Foundations of the Parliament of World Religions and be based on the Zen concepts of not knowing, bearing witness, and healing. The new order would include both clergy and laypersons who would be united by their dedication to the practice of engaging with the societies of which they were a part.[4] This could entail finding innovative ways to work with the homeless (such as the Greyston Mandala Project in New York) or helping health-care professionals to cope with the demise of their terminally ill patients (like Joan Halifax's Project on Being with Dying in New Mexico).

Hospice and hospital work seemed especially suitable for this type of engagement, for both deal with the suffering of sentient beings during a crisis stage of life and also provide a daily arena in which to deal with the complex issues of bioethics, economic injustice, health-care systems, and other social dilemmas of our modern society. As the hospital was a microcosm reflecting the problems of our society, the Engaged Buddhist practitioners would find themselves immediately interacting with some of their society's toughest issues.

Interfaith Chaplaincy as an Expression of the Mahayana Way

Although many hospitals were originally founded by spiritual orders to care for the poor and indigent, today's hospitals are more secular institutions striving to meet the diverse needs of a multicultural population. Still, the predominant faith of the people of the United States is traditionally proclaimed to be Christian. The question can therefore be asked, "How can a Buddhist chaplain serving in an interfaith capacity possibly minister to the predominantly Christian populace of most hospitals when he or she themselves are not Christians?"

The person asking such a question misunderstands the role of the chaplain. For the role of the professional chaplain is not to proselytize a particular dogma *but to stand with the patient where they are at and to help the patient utilize their own spiritual views and beliefs as a resource for their own healing.* Today's hospital chaplain is part of a team, a health-care professional with a post-graduate degree who has often done an internship and a residency in clinical pastoral education in order to qualify for his or her position. And today's multicultural and multifaith society requires that they have a working knowledge of other faith traditions and practices if they are to be of service to a good number of patients. Depending on where they are located, they might find themselves ministering to a Wiccan, a Muslim, or practicing traditional spirituality, as well as to a Christian. Having some knowledge of the basic tenets of each of these traditions is a necessary prerequisite helping the patient to utilize their own resources in the healing process, whatever the chaplain's own personal beliefs might be. But being able to stand with the patient (and/or their family) where they are is absolutely essential.

Having said that, it is true that a chaplain's personal beliefs do influence how they view their hospital ministry and their individual *style* of pastoral care. So it is fair to ask, "Where does a Buddhist style of pastoral care originate?" I cannot speak for all Buddhists, but for myself I fall back on Three Tenets of the Peacemaker Order.

First, *not knowing*. Not knowing entails the ability to walk into a situation without a preset agenda. This means that you walk into the patient's room with what we call *empty mind* (as opposed to a blank mind): you bring with you everything that you have learned, everything that you have experienced, and everything that you are. But you do not plan on what you're going to do until you take a look at the situation as it presents itself.

To understand how this works, consider this analogy. Each week, one of the local TV stations in the area where I live does a random drawing in which a chef goes to a person's house and cooks them lunch. *But the rule is that the chef may only use those ingredients and those devices that are available in that person's kitchen.* The chef enters with empty hands and must decide what he or she is going to do only after seeing what's available. Such is the Peacemaker way of not knowing: you decide what you're going to do based on the situation as it presents itself in that particular moment.

By *bearing witness*, we mean to see clearly the situation that's there, no matter how painful. Many medical professionals build a wall between themselves and their patients to protect themselves from the misery of their patients' suffering. Often they do this because they are afraid that, were they to be touched by every patient's suffering, their own already overburdened hearts would break and they would no longer be able to do the work that they need to do. So they develop a veneer of professionalism that supposedly protects them from being overcome by the suffering they see every day.[5]

I believe this is an incredibly bad idea and is the cause of much of the burnout, suicide, and substance abuse that we see among health-care providers. In reality, if they would only allow their hearts to break—to fully experience the misery and suffering of their patients with them—they would find that an astonishing thing happens: your heart can break and you can go on. By acknowledging your pain rather than running away from it, you find that what you feared was unbearable can indeed be borne. More importantly, there is a joy that comes from being fully a part of the process of illness and healing with a patient and their family, rather than being one step removed from it. This is how we bear witness.

Finally, *healing action*. Arthur Klienman has written that modern physicians "diagnose and treat *diseases* (abnormalities in the structure and function of body organs and systems), whereas patients suffer *illnesses* (experiences of this value change in states of being and social function: the human experience of sickness)" (Kleinman et al. 1978, 251). It is the function of the health-care chaplain to help the individual patient and their family to work through this process of change, not to proselytize their own particular creed or dogma.

So, a Buddhist chaplain who enters a patient's room would not be there to serve his or her own egoistical needs, but to serve the patient's spiritual needs, whatever they may be. Drawing from my own experience, this may include reading from the Bible, leading a family in prayer, or simply holding the hand of someone facing an operation, who is incredibly frightened. It may include standing with a doctor who has to give a patient a terminal prognosis or serving as an ethical consultant with a treatment team who have to inform parents that their child is now brain-dead and should be taken off life support. The point is that I am not there to proselytize but to give support to the patients, staff, and families. *And it is through this interaction that I am expressing Buddhadharma, just as a minister in an Abrahamic tradition might feel that through the same interaction she or he was expressing God's love.*

And obviously I am more able to help in that process by learning as much as I can about other faiths and other traditions, including Christianity. It has been my experience that in times of crisis people seek solace in their religious traditions and that the more familiar I am with those traditions, the more effective I am in helping them to use their beliefs in their own healing process. I am often astounded by the fact that so many clergy know so little about faiths (or even denominations) outside their own. If you did not know about how the Navaho view the dead, for instance, you might misinterpret a Navaho family's reluctance to view the dead body of a loved one. The more information you have, the more accurately you are able to see the true situation and to respond accordingly. And the better able you are to help in the individual's healing process.

But in adhering to the Three Tenets of the Peacemaker Order as a means of ministering to patients, does this mean I reject other methods? Of course not: it just means that the Tenets provide the ground from which I operate and from which my ministry originates. I also incorporate into my approach Rogerian empathetic listening, family systems theory, and object-relations theory, as well as some of the psycho-systems theory of Graham (1992), the Five Families approach of Wegela (1996), and the remarkable Barnes-Jewish Discipline for Pastoral Caregiving (2001), about which much has been written elsewhere. Just as a doctor may select a particular medicine for a specific patient, so will I use the means that I feel is appropriate to the situation or to the individual. But the Three Tenets are always at the core of what I do.

Concluding Thoughts

As the United States continues to become more multicultural, we are also becoming more multireligious. And as many of the representatives of those other religious traditions strive to be of service to others, they will begin to seek out positions within the community now predominantly occupied by Christian clerics. I believe that it is possible for people of other faith traditions (such as myself) to serve in these roles while maintaining the high standards of competency and professionalism that have evolved over the years and that people have come to expect. Our qualifications and titles may be different, but I believe that our approaches can be just as effective in dealing with the problems facing our society.

As our society becomes more diverse, so should the ranks of health-care chaplains.

PART TWO

OPPRESSION-SENSITIVE PASTORAL PRACTICE

TEN

The Tasks of Oppression-Sensitive Pastoral Caregiving and Counseling

Donald M. Chinula

Counseling is the process of enabling a distressed person or group of persons to overcome the symptoms of their distress and achieve wellness or healing. As a general rule, counseling is employed when the distressing factor is believed to be predominantly emotional and psychological in nature. Effective counseling might alleviate the distress but not necessarily cure its underlying cause.

Pastoral care and counseling is caregiving that draws on the symptom bearer's spiritual resources in symptom management. It is premised on the belief that the Christian faith has efficacious resources to inform and enrich the management of the problem at hand and empower the symptom bearer toward restoration or transformation. In this process, symbols or metaphors of divinity become central sources of empowerment.

While the term *pastoral* might imply that the helper must be an ordained officer of the church, the vocation of pastoral care and counseling is not limited to church officers. It includes lay professionals who, through academic study and clinical training, are certified to have achieved a notable integration of the theological and psychological disciplines in their preparation for the vocation of pastoral caregiving.

Historically, the counseling vocation has been undergirded by depth philosophies and psychologies. A predominant number of the latter have been the intrapsychic psychologies of the psychoanalytic movement. This movement has largely sought to explain human psychological and personality development in terms of intrapsychic conflicts and their resolution. It understands emotional, psychological, and spiritual perplexity as etiologically rooted in deep-seated and unconscious psychic traumas and conflicts. It has developed intervention strategies consistent with this philosophical and theoretical disposition.

The natural child of the intrapsychic orientation to psychotherapy are the hyper-individualized, one-on-one intervention modalities, wherein distressed individuals or groups seek help in private offices of trained professionals. These professionals assess and diagnose presented problems and propose or prescribe management plans. The agreed-upon plans are often developed between the presented and afflicted individuals (if adults) and the professional caregiver. This is a hyper-individualistic model that many pastoral counselors today practice.

Hyper-individualistic caregiving focuses on the individual sufferer in its assessment and diagnosis of the presented symptom and in its management. This is done on a case-by-case basis, often in private counseling offices. Even where a family is the presented unit of analysis, hyper-individualistic pastoral caregiving focuses on its idiosyncratic characteristics and individualizes its distress as unique to it.

Because of its primary focus on the individual, the hyper-individualistic model lacks serious critical social theory and analysis to inform its praxis. The opportunity for an ultra-systemic approach to assessment, diagnosis, and intervention is missed. Also lacking in the hyper-individualistic model are serious justice, peace, and empowerment motifs. Each of these motifs is central to the Christian gospel as the oppressed hear it, and potentially useful for working with the oppressed or marginalized of any community.

Another flaw of hyper-individualistic pastoral caregiving is that it lacks an earthly evocative symbol to shape and guide its vocation. The focus has been on the individual sufferer. Pervasively, hyper-individualistic pastoral caregivers employ the traditional or "classical" methods of helping the afflicted; these methods are *guiding, healing, sustaining,* and *reconciling*—and their variants.

The therapeutic assumption is that attention to the guiding, healing, sustaining, and reconciling tasks will alleviate the symptoms and enable the bearer of those symptoms to become functional and productive once again. It has seemed unimportant to address the question of the social forces that conspire to precipitate the symptoms in the first place and how these forces prohibit or diminish optimal functioning and productive living. In short, the question of how the pervasive sociocultural forces might provoke and reproduce symptomatology is not a central concern of the hyper-individualistic model of pastoral caregiving as shaped by the perspectives of pastoral theologians Seward Hiltner, William Clebsch, and Charles Jaekle. The work and writing of Howard Clinebell has, since the 1970s, been devoted to correcting this shortcoming.

In addition to Clinebell, feminist, ethnic, and non-Western psychologists and social critics helpfully address this question.

I have argued in my book, *Building King's Beloved Community: Foundations for Pastoral Care and Counseling with the Oppressed* (1997), that a clearly articulated, earthly, evocative symbol is critical for an effective practice of oppression-sensitive pastoral caregiving, and, drawing upon Dr. Martin Luther King Jr.'s unique articulation of the *beloved community*, I have proposed it as intensely heuristic. The beloved community rigorously engages and focuses the practitioner on a transcendent social order as the penultimate task of effective pastoral caregiving. It furnishes a compelling vision of a society rid of social leprosy, a society that creates and promotes an environment in which individual personalities can best prosper.

The root metaphors of peace, justice, and love furnish the essential catalysts for healing and eternal wellness; that is, the beloved community is a transformed society committed to justice, peace, and love. Its citizens are transformed persons, passionate about peacemaking, justice seeking, and loving. The soul of such a society is healed by its passion for justice and peace and is kept healthy by its passion for love of life in all its forms. The psyches of its citizens are likewise transformed and nurtured by the fact that they thrive and are nurtured by peacemaking and justice seeking. It is this transformative power that commends the beloved community as an evocative symbol of oppression-sensitive pastoral caregiving.

The common understanding of peace is the absence of war or strife. It is the absence of riots, social unrest, revolution, civil war, terrorist attacks, international war, or general upheaval. Strifeless peace is false peace or negative peace, in that it depends on the acquiescence of the oppressed to the forces of evil. It thrives on repression or suppression; for example, women's acquiescence to discrimination in this society in order to keep the peace or not rock the boat is not peace. It is *contained violence*. Such peace obscures and shields obscene oppression, exploitation, and dehumanization. It is ungodly and contributes to unspeakable pain, suffering, and sorrow. This kind of peace corrodes and corrupts the social fiber at the same time that it twists and torments the human psyche. It is insufferable, diabolical, and intolerable.

Oppression-sensitive pastoral caregivers must employ at least four tasks, among others, in their caregiving vocation. These are: *reclamation, conciliation, transformation*, and *transcendence*.

Reclamation as a task of oppression-sensitive pastoral caregiving aims at reclaiming by the oppressed and marginalized their "lost legacies" at the same time that it promotes healing. In individualistic pastoral caregiving and counseling, healing performs a remedial and restorative role. It has a reparative function. Its principal utility is the treatment of the symptom.

Groups oppressed on account of sex, race, class, and other repressive syndromes overwhelmingly exhibit a loss of divinely bequeathed self-worth and human value. A rigorous engagement with the transformative evocative symbol, the beloved community, in the vocation of pastoral caregiving empowers the caregiver to empower the symptom bearer to reclaim the sense of "somebodiness" that issues from being a copy of God's own image and personality. Such prophetic pastoral caregiving aids the sufferer to achieve more than remedial, restorative, or reparative relief. It aids and supports a deeper adventure to reclaim God-valued, God-allied, God-dignified, and God-bequeathed personhood, psyche, and personality that has been shackled, twisted, and crippled by oppressive syndromes.

Conciliation is another powerful task of oppression-sensitive pastoral caregiving in that it goes beyond the traditional task of reconciliation to embrace the therapeutic stance of overcoming the hostility of the oppressor or oppressive syndrome. It seeks to win over or secure the friendship of the opponent, not simply to repair a broken relationship. It employs itself as a tool of community formation by dissolving enmity and forging interpersonal and intergroup fellowship. It is not sufficient for pastoral caregiving to merely *reconcile* the symptom bearer to others and to God. It is necessary that the symptom bearer *conciliate* himself to himself and to others. Conciliation empowers her to befriend the worst in herself and others.

Transformation: Individualistic pastoral caregiving does not list or discuss *transformation* as one of its tasks, but the art and task of oppression-sensitive pastoral caregiving requires it. As conceived here, transformation refers to changing the condition, nature, or character of persons and society so that the old is replaced by the new. It is the bringing about of a new order that may incorporate some aspects of the old but whose predominant quality is novelty.

Oppression-sensitive pastoral caregiving achieves this transformative goal if it transforms the oppressed from being objects into being subjects of their history; from being nobodies into being somebodies. This requires a progressive, not static, view of God. God cannot always be seen as a changeless or change-hating deity who loves the status quo. The doctrine of transformation I espouse here requires that we conceive God as a hater of life-denying and health-destroying status quo and a lover of life-affirming and health-promoting change. God loves life, affirms health, and promotes biophilic and salugenic (health-giving) communities. God will not sit impassively and dispassionately in the face of death-dealing status quo. Emotional, psychological, and spiritual deaths are equally displeasing to God. In the face of these diabolical forces, God becomes not changeless but a change agent for the good and for health.

Of course, in order to accommodate this new human creature, society also must undergo transformation from violence, hatred, exploitation, and abuse of people, to justice, love, peace, and equality. Transformation of persons must be accompanied by the transformation of society and its institutions. Oppression-sensitive pastoral caregiving mandates the transformative healing of both human and societal psyches. The healing of one without the other is meaningless, since the untransformed will continue to be a source of psychic toxicity.

Transcendence is another essential task of oppression-sensitive pastoral caregiving. Hyper-individualistic pastoral caregiving does not recognize *transcendence* as a task of pastoral caregiving. *Transcendence* is the doctrine of classical theology used analogically to refer to the otherness or out-there-ness of God. Divine reality is conceived as a being that stands over against the world and finite beings. God hovers beyond the created order. This is usually contrasted with the doctrine of divine immanence, which refers to the presence, nearness, or indwelling of God in the created order.

In employing the theological doctrine of *transcendence*, oppression-sensitive pastoral caregiving focuses on the inexhaustibility of divine reality, which infuses the human *spirit*. That is, as *imago Dei*, the human capacity for self-transformation and actualization cannot be limited by any humanly imposed standard. No human norm can be the measure of wellness, of excellence-in-being, because human norms are limited, exhausted, and evacuated by sin. The sinful oppressor cannot be allowed to become the norm for the oppressed.

Only the transcendence of God can provide the norm for the self in its quest for healing and meaningful living. God's transcendence inspires and enables the oppressed to surmount humanly imposed limitations in the path to life at the same time that divine immanence is experienced as a friend and companion who understands. With God as the inexhaustible transcendental reality and motive force, the oppression-sensitive pastoral caregiver empowers oppressed humanity to tap into reservoirs of both *divine transcendence* and *divine immanence* in its claim to the fullness of life.

It is critical that oppression-sensitive pastoral caregivers keep constantly in mind that oppression is a syndrome. It is more helpful to speak of *oppressive syndromes* rather than merely *oppression*. Like psychiatric syndromes, oppressive syndromes are multilayered and multifaceted and are almost always present in persons who present as the afflicted. Our society evolved from the syndrome of violence, and against the powerless. That violence has morphed into complex syndromes that oppress, distress, repress, and dehumanize.

For those of us in the pastoral caregiving vocation, it would be hugely prophetic if we could found an organization such as the "International Association of Anti-oppression Caregivers" (IAAC), or something similar, whose purpose would be to expose the oppressive syndromes that contribute immeasurably to disabling societal and human psyches, and challenge all our institutions to engage in self-examination for the purpose of declaring themselves anti-oppressive. Specific outcomes sought would be to challenge all our social institutions to examine themselves for the purpose of publicly declaring themselves antisexist, antiracist, antihomophobic, and anti- whatever else we can identify and demonstrate as a force in the oppressive syndromes that debilitate the emotional and spiritual wellness of the human ecology.

ELEVEN

Never at Ease:
Black, Gay, and Christian

Cheryl Giles

More than a decade after the historic Clinton-era legislation produced the watery "don't ask, don't tell" compromise, gay men and lesbian women continue to serve in the military, though only under a cloak of silence. These men and women give their energy, time, and sometimes their lives to a system that encourages them to "be all they can be," as long as they "don't tell" who they are.

Outside the military, gays and lesbians across mainstream America are demanding the rights and privileges afforded to heterosexuals, despite the ongoing morality debate fueled by political forces whose agenda appeals to conservatives and the religious right. Polls show a growing trend toward acceptance, even in the military, with increasing numbers of Americans showing support for the rights of openly gay people to serve in the nation's armed forces.

A CNN/*USA Today*/Gallup poll conducted nationally a few weeks after the 2004 presidential election (November 10–21, 2004) asked 1,015 adults, aged 18 and older, "Do you favor or oppose allowing openly gay men and lesbian women to serve in the military?" Polling results indicated that 63 percent of Americans favored allowing openly gay and lesbian persons to serve in the military, with 32 percent opposed. A similar poll conducted in 1993 produced significantly different results, with only 40 percent favoring openly gay and lesbian persons serving in the military with 52 percent opposed (Kiefer 2004). These findings certainly support a growing acceptance of gays and lesbians in a sector that has been historically prohibitive. This juxtaposition of public tolerance and institutional conservatism is not new and may indeed be a harbinger of change. But for psychologists, psychiatrists, and other caregivers, it poses troubling questions about effects on the gay men and lesbian women who try to maintain a focused outlook in the face of mixed messages and impossible choices. Is the shame and dishonor inflicted on some of the most dedicated members of the military worth the price of service to country?

The impact of the "don't ask, don't tell" policy on enlisted gay and lesbian soldiers has enormous consequences and calls into question the overall ability of the military to "treat the whole" person. In a recent presentation of the PBS television documentary series *Frontline*, "The Soldier's Heart," U.S. Army Col. Thomas Burke, Director of Mental Health Policy for the Department of Defense, discussed the goals of the military:

> We are always trying to [improve] our understanding of the soldiers' problems: physical, mental health problems. We're always trying to make the system better, more responsive, to make sure that there's going to be enough resources and capacity in the system to take care of whatever problems the soldiers have during deployment, after deployment and after they leave the service.[1]

Despite these goals, the culture of military service has been difficult to change. The impact of combat stress and the stigma associated with seeking help to deal with combat stress is still regarded by many as a sign of weakness. Burke acknowledged the shortcomings of mental health services in a climate that is hostile to those who seek help:

> There is a stigma attached to having mental health problems and seeking help . . . but it's not limited to the military. It exists in our society as a whole. Now, the military culture is unique, and there is a certain perceived stigma on the part of the soldiers that they are not going to get promoted; they won't need mental health services.[2]

Clearly, reluctance to acknowledge and seek help with mental and emotional problems is not new, even when help is available. Add to this reluctance a need to keep the core of one's very identity secret, and the result can take an overwhelming toll with spiraling consequences. In the military, even if help is forthcoming in dealing with issues of trauma, anxiety, guilt, and other symptoms of combat stress, that help is not likely to address the need to maintain a secret identity to avoid dishonorable discharge. The one who is helping can't ask and the one who needs help can't tell, and the likelihood of establishing any kind of trust is nil.

The resistance to supporting soldiers faced with the dual stress of combat and hiding their sexual identity to avoid discharge can erode their psychological well-being. And so, most gay and lesbian soldiers continue to suffer silently as they compromise their integrity to fight for the freedom abroad that, ironically, they are denied at home (SLDN 2004).

Sometimes these men and women decide the price of secrecy is too high. They may acknowledge their sexuality to a superior or to a fellow soldier. Perhaps their intention is to share the secret with one person just to relieve the emotional pressure. Or maybe they decide to take up the battle and go public with the fact they are gay or lesbian. The entertainment industry, which some consider a bellwether of national thought, has produced dramatic reenactments that chronicle the life and death of a gay or lesbian soldier's military career.

Freddie's Story

Freddie's story is one such tale. While it never appeared in the newspaper, or in any other public media, his is a story of devastating emotional pain, isolation, and loneliness fostered by a conviction that he lived in a world that did not welcome him, even though he was willing to give his life for that world, and confirmed by an establishment willing to accept him only if he pretended to be someone he was not.

As an African American gay man, Freddie was no stranger to feelings of not belonging. His family loved him but could not accept that he was gay. Probably he should not have joined the military, but he was used to hiding who he was and never gave it a thought.

Freddie was handsome: six feet tall, trimly built, with clear, honey-colored skin, dark wavy hair, and a captivating smile that framed brilliant white teeth. At nineteen years old, he looked like someone on a magazine cover. Freddie was bright, articulate, and poised, with an outgoing manner and a quiet confidence that belied the uncertainty and fear he held close to his heart. Raised to be thoughtful and honest by parents who valued faith, love of God, and integrity as the cornerstones of family life, his relationship with his mother and father was both trusting and trusted. But the single most troubling issue disarmed Freddie in his young life: He could not tell his parents he was gay.

Freddie's story begins in the pastoral counselor's office, where he sits comfortably—not a hint of anxiety while he listens to his mother and father speaking. His father is tall and striking, clearly the model for Freddie's good looks. His wrinkled forehead and the circles under his eyes reveal the anxiety that robs him of sleep. His mother, slim and attractive, is normally warm and outgoing. She takes charge of the meeting and, like her husband, shows signs of worry and loss of sleep.

Yes, this is their first time in counseling together. In the past, they brought issues of concern to their pastor for discussion and advice. Now, they are overwhelmed with the complexity of their son's problems and feel they need more help than the minister can offer. Yes, they feel a bit uncomfortable, but they understand the process and are ready to proceed. They have requested this consultation with the goal of beginning family therapy following the dishonorable discharge of their son from the Army. They want help.

During the interview, Freddie's mother gives a history of the family, while Freddie and his father remain silent. She is forty-five years old, and her husband is fifty. Freddie is their only child. The family is middle class and lives in the suburbs. Both parents graduated from college, earned master's degrees, and are highly respected professionals. She is a loan officer for a community credit union. Her husband is an IT professional and was in the Army Reserves for many years before retiring just prior to the Gulf War. Both parents are actively involved in their church and local community, where they hold leadership positions in a variety of charitable and civic organizations.

His mother describes Freddie's early childhood as "ordinary." He was a "normal," "quiet," and "well-adjusted" child who did not cause any problems when he was growing up. They had close contact with their numerous extended-family members and Freddie had many cousins and friends whom he played with growing up. She acknowledged that she and her husband had wanted a large family, but gave up trying to get pregnant after she miscarried when Freddie was two years old. This event had been particularly painful for both of them, but they had never really talked about it or sought help for the sadness and disappointment that had never quite left them. No question was too personal. She explained that the decision not to have more children "just became one of those things that we avoided talking about until it was a nonissue."

As Freddie grew older, his parents focused all their attention on his enjoyment of learning and discovering new things. Freddie was a good student in school and received mostly As and only a few Bs on his report card. He participated in after-school activities that included taking piano lessons and playing on an intramural soccer team that his father coached. The family went to church every Sunday, and Freddie sang in the youth choir. During high school, Freddie kept himself busy playing video games, reading, and building computers. He spent time "hanging out" with his friends and going to the movies but never had a girlfriend. In fact, when the time came to attend his senior prom, Freddie attended with a neighbor's daughter who could not find a date. People who knew Freddie considered him to be generous with his time—and always happy. He graduated from the local high school with a "Most Likely to Succeed" award and a plan to study computer science at college and start his own business. After high school, he decided to stay in the area close to family and friends and enrolled in a small liberal arts college not far from home.

Unbeknownst to his parents, he had been dating his best friend, a junior in high school, for the past year. This was Freddie's first relationship with a boy, and he wanted to keep it quiet. As time passed, he began to feel the need to share this part of himself with his parents but could not muster the courage to approach them. When the relationship ended abruptly just before he started college, the need to talk with his parents became less immediate.

During his first few months in college, Freddie reported liking his courses but struggling with the social atmosphere on campus. "I feel like I don't fit in there," he would tell his mother, "When I meet new people, my heart races and my stomach churns."

At home for Thanksgiving break, Freddie told his mother he felt isolated and lonely at school. Still grieving, he missed his "boyfriend" and the comfort of their relationship. In what Freddie later called "an impulsive act," he announced that he would not return to school. He wanted to join the Army and serve in Iraq. His parents were disappointed, but felt he should make his own decision. While they hoped he would complete college, they trusted this was the best decision for him and he would complete college when he returned home after the war.

Freddie enrolled in the Army and was sent to basic training. During this time, he kept in frequent contact with his parents. He reported liking the challenge of physical activity in the Army; he had made several new friends. His mother recalled that it was the first time since before he dropped out of college that he seemed happy with his life. Shortly after basic training, however, Freddie was sent to active duty in Iraq, and the excitement of military life and making new friends soon faded.

Once deployed, Freddie found it difficult to adapt to the ongoing stress of combat and the potential danger of terrorism. Despite the support of his new friends, he began to isolate himself from the group. He refused to talk to them about what was bothering him and rejected their suggestion that he seek help. Further adding to his feelings of isolation and inability to communicate with his fellow soldiers was the growing feeling of fraud and dishonesty: he could not tell them he was gay. In a letter written to his mother, he wrote about the lack of safety he felt and the stress of seeing so many soldiers wounded in combat. He worried that he was unable to sleep, eat, and had difficulty paying attention most of the time. As his isolation grew, Freddie began to feel that he could not trust anyone around him. Although he wanted relief from the anxiety and stress that he experienced, he absolutely refused to get help and the depression became worse. By now, not only his peers but also his squad leader were aware of his problem:

> It's the vast majority of the soldiers that have adjustment problems. They're having trouble sleeping; they're having anxieties; they have mild to moderate depression. We can work with those soldiers and get them the care that they need and get them back to work. It's just a matter of overcoming the initial fear, that reluctance to seek help, to talk about it. But we encourage them . . . a lot of the issues that soldiers are dealing with . . . Relationship problems, financial problems, legal problems are problems [of the] late-teenage, early-20's group. That's part of growing up.[3]

Like most enlisted young men and women his age, Freddie's development was forced into high gear without the guidance that was necessary to help him understand all the changes that were taking place. He was removed from his squad and placed in a mobile mental health unit where he met with a psychiatrist who evaluated him for combat stress and depression. He was calm but reluctant to speak honestly, even though his misery was overwhelming him. During the interview, Freddie answered many questions about his feelings and the symptoms that he was experiencing. On a sudden impulse, he "came out" as a gay man to the psychiatrist, whose immediate response was that he would have to include this information in his evaluation report as part of the "don't ask, don't tell" policy. Freddie was shocked. He had somehow naïvely believed the psychiatrist would understand that he needed help.

Freddie tried so hard to explain the burden of keeping silent about his true identity when he was already struggling with the stress of combat and the sight of people dying. He needed to talk, to feel safe, and to be accepted. The psychiatrist told Freddie he was really sorry, but rules were rules. Freddie had already felt that he had compromised his own integrity by not coming out sooner, and now he felt betrayed by the army. One week after the meeting with the psychiatrist, Freddie received a dishonorable discharge with a strong recommendation that he continue to receive weekly counseling and medication for depression.

In less than six months, Freddie had ended the relationship with his boyfriend, started college, dropped out, joined the Army, and received a dishonorable discharge. He returned home to live with his parents, scared and wondering what he could do to repair the mess he had made of his life.

As Freddie's mother talks about the days before his discharge and return home, she recounts to the pastoral counselor how she and her husband left for work each morning praying for his safety and returned home at night with their son foremost in their thoughts, hoping no one was waiting for them with unthinkable news. Quiet and introspective, they shared dinner and conversation over the day's events, read or watched television, and retired, the peace of their dreams punctuated with worry that often woke them in the middle of the night. One day, they arrived home to find their son sitting in the living room waiting for them.

They were shocked and surprised but so happy to see their beloved son that any suspicion of something being wrong dissipated with his assurance that he was not hurt and had been granted an unexpected leave. Suddenly there was joy in the household, and while his mother prepared dinner she continually stole looks at him, thrilled to have her son home whatever the reason.

Freddie was withdrawn over dinner, saying less and less and finally ending all attempts at conversation, saying he was tired and hungry, even though he ate little. He promised his parents a full update after dinner. The parents glanced at each other, both sensing something wrong with their son, but let it be because they were so glad to see him and because he seemed so exhausted. Even lifting his fork appeared to be an effort almost beyond him. Finally, dinner was over, and Freddie, followed by his parents, went into the living room and sat down. They waited.

Freddie sat for a few minutes. Several times he seemed about to say something but hesitated. Then he took the letter out of his pocket and handed it to his mother, who read the letter and began to cry quietly as she passed it to her husband. His father read the letter, shook his head in shocked disbelief, and, barely able to talk, said one word to his son: "Why?" Freddie, looking more and more exhausted with each passing minute, stared at his feet, held his breath, and said, "Because, Dad, I'm gay." His father rose without a word, turned and left the room, walked into his bedroom and quietly shut the door. His mother sat crying for a while, then looked at him in a way that made him feel more miserable than he believed possible. "I don't understand," she said. "We are people of faith. We believe in God and his teachings. This goes against everything we believe in." "I'm sorry, Ma," was all Freddie could manage.

Although he had wanted to avoid "coming out" to his parents "until the right time," he knew, looking at his parents over dinner, that this was not an option. He could not hide the fact that he had been dishonorably discharged on the grounds he was openly gay. Now he felt he had no choice but to confront his fear and the prospect of rejection by his parents, extended family, and church.

After a while, his mother rose and walked over to her son. She took his face in her hands and kissed his forehead. "I don't know what to do," she told him, "but I know that we love you and I know that God will show us what to do. We need to pray for his guidance." With that she went into her bedroom and closed the door.

In the days following his discharge, Freddie continued to struggle with depression. He was having recurring nightmares about wounded soldiers and experiencing panic attacks in public places. He stayed in his room most of the time, refusing to come out except for an occasional meal, but his mother heard him thrashing, crying, and sometimes screaming in his sleep.

His father went to work every day, came home at night, ate his dinner, then went into his bedroom and sat quietly, saying nothing, doing nothing, until he dropped into an exhausted sleep.

Freddie's mother was scared and worried, fearing for the emotional and physical health of both her husband and son. Something had to be done. After several days, she did the only thing she knew how to do in troubled times. She went to church.

She sat quietly for a while in church, praying and enjoying the quiet feeling it gave her, even though she knew it could not last. Then she went to the minister's study and knocked on his door. An hour later she left, unburdened of the events of the past days but without the usual comfort and relief that she had come to expect from speaking with her pastor. The pastor had listened quietly, barely reacting to the woman's admission that her son was gay. His reaction surprised her. She did not know what to expect, but certainly it was not what he told her.

In the counselor's office, where she has gone at the insistence of her pastor, Freddie's mother takes a deep breath, sighs, and then continues, speaking of her session with the pastor: "He just sat there shaking his head, saying, 'This is not good. Oh, this is not good.' He said he would pray for us. He said God would help us through this. And he said he thought Freddie needed help that was beyond what he could give us. Then he gave me your card and said I should call."

Discussion

Freddie's story raises challenging issues for the pastoral counselor. Three major themes warrant attention: (1) Freddie's mental health, (2) the role and function of secrets, and (3) the impact of homophobia in the black church.

The most immediate concern is Freddie's mental health. In the past, he has had no obvious mental health problems, but since his discharge from the military and return home he is having symptoms of depression and trauma: recurrent nightmares, crying, withdrawal, and isolation. The disappointments and losses of the past six months leave him feeling stressed, anxious, and alone. His recent difficulties with school and the military culminate with his "coming out" as a gay man in a family that is actively involved in the black church, where gay and lesbian people who do not maintain secrecy are ostracized. Freddie's choices from this point on, particularly with regard to the church, will have serious implications for the entire family.

In *The New Gay Teenager*, psychologist and researcher Ritch C. Savin-Williams notes a paradigm shift in the way that gay teenagers view themselves. "They have same-sex desires and attractions but, unlike earlier generations, new gay teens have much less interest in naming these feelings or behaviors as gay" (2005, 1). In the past, researchers have paid scant attention to what sustains healthy gay adolescence and young adulthood based on the lived experience of these young people. Consequently, the complexity of race, class, and social location has been minimized in these discussions. Savin-Williams identifies the shortcomings in this approach and its negative projections on teens:

> Without minimizing the experience of those in distress, I wanted to suggest that there was another side of being young and gay. Not all such adolescents were suicidal. I wanted to argue against a problem-centered approach and for a perspective that celebrates the promise and diversity of gay teens. . . . If they listened to us experts, I feared they'd be apt to give up, reach the conclusion that their life was inevitably distraught, and perhaps even eventually kill themselves. (Ibid., 62)

The "new gay teenager" goes beyond sexual identity as the defining characteristic of self. Rather, these teenagers have come to understand their sexuality as fluid and evolving, part of their ongoing development toward healthy adulthood. Savin-Williams advocates moving away from the "clinicalization" of gay youth—that is, diagnosing the behavior of gay youth in clinical rather than normative terms. He tells us that more than thirty years after the American Psychiatric Association removed homosexuality from the list of mental disorders (in the Diagnostic and Statistical Manual of Mental Disorders [DSM]), "scientists and clinicians alike have actually *re-pathologized* homosexuality by portraying gay teenagers as exceptionally vulnerable, leading high-risk lives" (ibid., 183). Savin-Williams is telling us that a gay teen may face social problems like rejection and peer cruelty, behaviors that often leave a teen vulnerable to high-risk behaviors as a mechanism of escape or rebellion. However, this is the response of adolescence and not solely the realm of gay adolescence. So being gay and being mentally ill are not necessarily synonymous, and certainly not all youth who come out as gay or lesbian have mental health problems.

Over the past two decades, volumes have been written about what is wrong in the lives of gay and lesbian youth. The discussions are often problem centered when they should focus on examining adolescent development over time.

All families have secrets, and the ways in which they choose to keep or reveal them can have far-reaching effects for every member of the family, particularly for the children. Freddie's family holds two distinct secrets—his mother's miscarriage when he was two years old and his identification as a gay man. As it turns out, these secrets have stifled communication and forged a barrier that none of them even suspected until now. "The stories that people tell about themselves and their family histories must be listened to carefully—both for what they tell and for what they omit" (McGoldrick 1995, 49). In Freddie's family very little is known about the relationship between his parents at the time of his mother's failed pregnancy. As his mother tells it, they never talked about the loss or the end to the larger family they had planned or even whose decision it was not to try again; and they never sought counseling help. They have always appeared to be loving and open, but their inability to acknowledge their pain and grief to each other and to take the necessary steps to heal has shut down communication between them. Without ever intending to, they have passed this inability to communicate to Freddie. Now the agony that finally leads Freddie to blurt out his own long-held secret disrupts the status quo in more ways than the family can yet grapple with:

> A secret may be a source of power, binding together those who share it, though it may also create shame and guilt because of its rule of silence. Because they create covert splits in the family, secrets also have a mystifying power. . . . To understand secrets, it is important to assess who is protected and who is excluded by the secret. (Ibid., 180)

Healthy families are able to communicate and resolve conflicts. They disagree, argue, talk, accept their differences, and move on. This process frees them to love and support each other as family members and still maintain a healthy interest in themselves as individuals. They develop an abiding trust that individual and group conflicts can be resolved through communication—talking things out. In his memoir, *What Becomes of the Brokenhearted*, E. Lynn Harris, a popular gay writer and frequent guest speaker, reflects on being closeted while growing up in the South and the difficulty of "coming out" as a gay man and embracing his talent for writing:

> One night while talking to my Aunt Gee, I mentioned that I was becoming comfortable with spending my life alone since I was a gay man. As I have said before, my aunt has always been supportive of me, no matter what, but during this talk, she said something that hurt me deeply. "Baby, if I raised you, I don't think you would have been gay." . . . I said No Aunt Gee, you're wrong. I might have learned to love myself sooner, but I still would have been gay. I knew she didn't mean any harm, nor did she understand that she was implying that my being gay was a product of my environment. (Harris 2003, 238)

Freddie, an accepted and privileged member of one of his church's most exemplary families, is threatened with becoming an outcast. Peter Gomes, minister in The Memorial Church and Plummer Professor of Christian Morals at Harvard, reflects thoughtfully on the aversion to homosexuality for religious people:

> Nearly every such person who acknowledges an aversion to homosexuality does so on the basis of what he or she believes the Bible to say and in their minds there is no doubt whatsoever about what the Bible says, and what the Bible means. The argument goes something like this: Homosexuality is an abomination, and the homosexual is a sinner. . . . Therefore, if we are to be faithful to the clear teachings of the scripture, we too must condemn homosexuality; it is the last moral absolute, and we compromise it at our own peril. (1996, 145)

Religious dogma is often used to justify what would otherwise be blind prejudice against gays and lesbians, a prejudice that has and can become a sacred sanction for violent acts and oppression by seemingly faithful people:

> . . . the tragic dimensions of this biblically sanctioned prejudice among the most devout and sincere people of religious conviction are all the greater because no credible case against homosexuality or homosexuals can be made from the Bible unless one chooses to read scripture in a

way that simply sustains the existing prejudice against homosexuality and homosexuals. The combination of ignorance and prejudice under the guise of morality makes the religious community and its abuse of scripture in this regard, itself morally culpable. (Ibid., 147)

So, where does this leave Freddie, a young man who has grown up in the black church and is one of the faithful? He has attended weekly services all his life, sung in the choir, worked with the youth minister, and been a loyal member of the congregation. By virtue of his honesty in disclosing his homosexuality, he faces moral conviction that he is an abomination to God and no longer welcome in this community. Freddie suddenly finds himself dispensable and alienated from the church that he has known and loved his entire life.

Kelly Brown Douglas, author of the pioneering work *Sexuality and the Black Church: A Womanist Perspective,* is one of the leading voices in calling the black church to action against homophobia and toward greater dialogue on a sexual discourse of resistance. This discourse moves beyond the dualism of the sacred and secular by embracing wholeness in our lives (1999, 131–32). Like Gomes, Brown Douglas challenges the long-held position that homosexuality is sinful to God, arguing that fostering homophobia against black gays and lesbians is an act of oppression by blacks against blacks. She writes that oppression has historically been used by the white culture against black people. But black people who hold that homosexuality is an abomination to God and that it threatens the black family are using oppression against their own.

It is perhaps in revealing that homophobia is actually *contrary* to the well-being of Black life that Black people might arrive at a more liberating view of biblical tradition in matters of sexuality. It might allow the Black community to lift the sacred canopy that it has placed over homophobia. To reiterate, the authority of scripture is in large measure determined by whether or not a text supports the life and freedom of the black community. A sexual discourse of resistance should clarify that homophobia is antithetical to black life and freedom and thus disrupt the terrorizing manner in which Black people have used biblical texts in regard to sexuality. . . . The Black community's sexual discourse against homosexuality does not save lives, but rather helps White culture to destroy them. (Ibid., 107)

The Role of the Pastoral Counselor

The pastoral counselor's first and most urgent priority is to address Freddie's recent behavior. Freddie's apparent mental and behavioral issues may, indeed, be a sign of illness, but they may also be the result of too many years of carrying a burden of secrecy. The pastoral counselor must make this determination early on and seek a medical or psychiatric evaluation for Freddie, if necessary.

Once the stability of Freddie's mental health is determined, the counselor can begin to work with the family on the impact of secrets in their lives. The loss of their second child was more traumatic for Freddie's parents than they ever realized. The task of the pastoral counselor is to help the family understand what is triggered by a loss of this magnitude and what is at stake in burying the secret. In a family where there are expectations for success, this loss may be seen as a failure, particularly on the part of the mother whose traditional success is linked to giving birth and perpetuating the family.

Perhaps Freddie's mother chose to protect herself from future failure and disappointment by refusing to get pregnant again. Her husband remains silent. Perhaps his love for her forces him to agree with her choice, but silence is often a mask for anger and disappointment. This couple has expended so much energy in playing out their roles of secrecy.

The task of the pastoral counselor is to help this family repair the breach of trust that has resulted from their inability to confront their secrets and gain an understanding of each other by listening and learning to let go of deeply held assumptions. The pastoral counselor is further challenged to build support for Freddie by encouraging each family member to untangle his or her feelings of loss, anger, sadness, disappointment, and frustration, so they can identify what gets in the way of their acceptance of him, and Freddie's acceptance of himself, as a gay man.

Once they move beyond their own emotional discord, they can seek ways to support him as he seeks his place in the church. Also, Freddie's parents must consider their own position as respected members of the congregation, whether or not he remains in their church.

Freddie's quandary is that he may be at risk of losing his membership in the black church, which has nurtured and embraced him, but coming out could free him to embrace fully his talents and abilities, knowing that confronting his greatest fear is behind him. The task of the pastoral counselor is to help Freddie and his family identify their strengths and resources as they confront this dilemma.

In Freddie's case, the pastoral counselor begins with the knowledge that Freddie has had loving parents, a solid religious background, and a supportive extended family. The family must be encouraged to consider his sexual behavior far less important than how he feels about being gay in the context of his faith and every other area of his life. The counselor can help the family conversation by helping the parents realize that a narrow focus on sex, which reinforces widespread homophobia—especially in the church where any discussion of sexual activity outside of marriage, but especially homosexual sex—may trigger moral absolutes. By encouraging resistance to this way of thinking rather than fostering a stigma of deviance, the pastoral counselor can help the family build on their strong foundation.

These opportunities for an open dialogue may benefit Freddie and his family. The counselor observes that Freddie and his mother seem ready for the honesty and hard work that can lead to healing, but Freddie's father may be more reluctant to give up his silence. The church and its members may not be willing or able to fully embrace Freddie in spite of their views on homosexuality. Pastoral counseling promises no absolutes and offers no guarantees. It simply aims to bring mental and spiritual comfort to the troubled.

TWELVE

Addiction, Power, and the Question of Powerlessness

Joel Glenn Wixson

In an effort to move the question of addiction out of the moral realm, the originators of Alcoholics Anonymous (AA) worked to have addiction considered a disease. Consistent with what has come to be called the "disease model"[1] of addiction, it is an "equal opportunity disease" said to affect people from "all walks of life." An unintended byproduct of this shift has been the tendency to conceive of addiction as something that similarly affects everyone.

Sadly, this conceptualization ignores the implications of sociopolitical power,[2] culture, race, sexual orientation, religion, sociopolitical demographic, and other differences as they relate to an individual's experience of addiction. This essay critiques the disease model with regard to its marginalization of the experience of difference in struggling with the problems of addiction. AA and its use of the concept of powerlessness is thought of as an example of how a central tenet of AA, intended to support healing, can have the opposite effect. Reflexive and narrative practices are suggested as alternative approaches that allow people struggling with addiction to access some elements of self-help models (i.e., the social support component) while reflexively considering and perhaps rejecting others (i.e., the notion of powerlessness).

Alcoholics Anonymous: A Step in the Right Direction

It would be futile to attempt to present a comprehensive history of AA in this short discussion. AA has existed since 1935, and in the intervening years, many stories of its origins have emerged. These accounts range from tracing its roots to the Oxford Group, through detailing the lives of its founders Bill Wilson and Dr. Bob. Rather than attempt to replicate these stories here, I will present a brief oral history of AA.

I am suggesting the idea of an oral history with the intention of conveying the somewhat amorphous nature of AA. In this context, the history is not one of citations and "facts," but one of a movement conveyed and perpetuated by involvement and participation. A formal history would tell a story of something static, rather than something constantly in motion. I believe the latter more accurately expresses the nature of AA.

AA is a singular entity, intentionally without organization or hierarchy. It took this form in its inception in an effort to uphold the commitment to being by, for, and about any individual who had a "sincere desire" not to drink. AA was designed to be an entity rooted in people, not institutions.

I probably first heard about AA on TV or on the radio. As a child, it meant little to me, except that I knew my father, an American Baptist Minister, would tell people they should go to meetings. He thought it would help.

I imagine there are lots of people who have a similar understanding of what AA is, based on the experiences of others—perhaps twice removed. Having worked in the field of substance abuse treatment now for some years, my experience and knowledge of what AA is has changed quite a bit. Along with attending meetings myself, I have worked with many people who have had long-term relationships with AA. These experiences draw me to consider AA as an entity that can be at the same time lifesaving and oppressing, supportive and problematic.

AA is also referred to as "the program," or "the fellowship." I have seen people's lives saved by what the program offers. I have also seen people turn from its doors and run, hopeless, back to the streets. I have experienced the vast differences that manifest as the "program," across meetings, through stories told about meetings, and articulated by colleagues in the field. In my experience, AA is as vast and complex as its membership, affecting each participant differently.

In this way, AA is not a discrete entity to critique, but a movement carried in the hearts and minds of its participants. AA was to be something available to anyone who wished to participate, not something that one had to join through initiation. However, a culture of "earning one's seat" has developed along the way. "Earning one's seat" refers to what a person has had to go through in order to "hit rock bottom" and "be ready to let go and let God," in the vernacular of AA.

An outgrowth of the idea of earning one's seat is the suggestion of insider-/outsider-ness. If you have not earned your seat you are considered an outsider.

You would not be excluded from attending meetings, but you would be expected only to attend "open meetings." In AA, open meetings are for anyone who might be interested in attending an AA meeting, problems with alcohol or not. Closed meetings are reserved only for those who have acknowledged a problem with alcohol. In an effort to protect the anonymous nature of the process, this dichotomy has been established.

As I am a person who does not consider myself a member or someone who has "earned my seat," I am cast as an outsider. As an outsider, I can support insiders in their desire to stop drinking, but I cannot "identify"[3] with them. I am not critiquing AA as someone who has used AA for personal reasons, though I believe I do have a personal relationship with AA, having worked in the field of addiction as long as I have. My outsider status makes me an observer, and rather than allow for any question around this issue, I would situate myself as such. I am a person who has known hundreds of people whose lives have been touched by AA in many ways. I have appreciated the basic tenets of AA and have applied them to situations in my own life, but I have not "earned my seat."

This point is relevant as it relates to the possibility of what persons can indeed understand of the fellowship from the "outsider" perspective. It has been my experience that challenging critiques of AA are often met with concerns about understanding. It is typically suggested that a lack of belief in the value of AA is rooted in a lack of understanding of its nature or "how it works."

This issue could be related to the insider/outsider dichotomy, or to the sublime power of the positive effect the program can have on individuals for whom it does work. From the perspective of someone who considers AA the thing that saved their life, it would seem odd indeed to hear that another might have concerns about it, especially someone who is an outsider. Additionally, it would be reasonable to consider the perspective of an outsider somewhat limited.

Although I acknowledge these concerns, I believe that AA cannot move forward without a careful consideration, not only of the lives of those who have benefited from what AA is, but also from attention to the effects it has had on those who have not benefited. I would point to my experience of having worked with people whose lives were adversely affected by their involvement in the program, and my desire to bear witness to these experiences in an effort to support this critique. I do not mean to suggest that this makes me an expert; I simply offer it as the basis for my knowledge.

It is for these reasons that my critique must be rooted not in response to documentation of a historical entity, but in response to something that is moving and changing; a critique based on AA as it is reflected in its participants, those saved and those cast out. AA is not like a car that either starts or does not; AA is more analogous to the tides. Although they predictably sweep in and out, they are reflexive of the beaches they meet. High tide does not land on the same sand that low tide left in the previous cycle. Time has changed AA, but more than time, people reconfigure it from moment to moment. Insiders and outsiders, AA lovers and haters alike, carry the story of AA. It is this account of AA that I will reflect on, on this day, from this perspective, from this beach. I leave it to the reader to determine which grains of sand are useful and which should be left for someone else to ponder.

The "Disease" Approach to Understanding Addiction

Prior to AA's inception, problems with alcohol were popularly considered to be a reflection of the moral weakness of the person consuming the substance. In this way, the contribution of AA in the form of conceptualizing these problems as a disease was groundbreaking. In an effort to bolster this idea it has been suggested that AA's founders, Bill Wilson and Dr. Bob, worked with the American Medical Association to establish the formal diagnosis of "alcoholism."

Currently, though, the text most often referred to in the diagnosis of such disorders does not contain the term alcoholism. The current edition of the American Psychiatric Association's Diagnostic and Statistical Manual Text Revision refers only to the categories of alcohol abuse, dependence, and withdrawal. This not withstanding, AA literature contains many references to "the disease of alcoholism," and uses the term alcoholic to describe the people who would benefit from participation in the program.

Over the seventy years since AA's inception, many treatment continua have been established in the United States. Many adhere to the principal that problems with alcohol are most usefully described as being related to a "disease of alcoholism." In general these programs consider AA to be a vital, if not primary, component of their treatment.

Utilization of AA in these programs can range from the requirement of attending a certain number of meetings per week, to an almost total immersion in AA. Examples of these two extremes in the treatment system in the United States include outpatient counseling programs that suggest participants go to several meetings during the course of the counseling, to halfway houses that offer no other services and require that residents go to up to three meetings per day.

In order to understand how AA might be applied in the treatment context, it is necessary to understand the basic building blocks upon which it is based. They are the Twelve Steps and the Twelve Traditions (AA 1976). For practical purposes it is the Twelve Steps that are most relevant here.

Widely considered to have been a version of a program developed by the Oxford Group, an evangelical Christian movement of the 1920s, the Twelve Steps are intended to guide the alcoholic through a process of "recovery" from the disease of addiction. They are as follows:

- Step one: We admitted we were powerless over alcohol, that our lives had become unmanageable.
- Step two: Came to believe that a Power greater than ourselves could restore us to sanity.
- Step three: Made a decision to turn our will and our lives over to the care of God as we understood Him.
- Step four: Made a searching and fearless moral inventory of ourselves.
- Step five: Admitted to God, to ourselves, and to another human being the exact nature of our wrongs.
- Step six: Were entirely ready to have God remove all these defects of character.
- Step seven: Humbly asked Him to remove our shortcomings.
- Step eight: Made a list of all persons we had harmed, and became willing to make amends to them all.
- Step nine: Made direct amends to such people wherever possible, except when to do so would injure them or others.
- Step ten: Continued to take personal inventory and when we were wrong promptly admitted it.
- Step eleven: Sought through prayer and meditation to improve our conscious contact with God as we understood Him, praying only for knowledge of His will for us and the power to carry that out.
- Step twelve: Having had a spiritual awakening as the result of these steps, we tried to carry this message to alcoholics, and to practice these principles in all our affairs. (Ibid., 59)

The adherence to the notion that problems with alcohol constitute a disease, and that the disease could be treated with these Twelve Steps, led to the development of programs with a specific set of components. Traditionally, group meetings were thought to be useful as they provided participants with the experience of becoming familiar with others who have the disease. Additionally, these contexts provided opportunities for participants to be confronted with various symptoms of the disease.

One of the symptoms traditionally associated with the disease of alcoholism is "denial."[4] Much has been written about the causes and effects of denial in the disease process (see Clancy 1961; DiCicco et al. 1978; Moore & Murphy 1961). It is widely accepted that denial is one of the main tools alcoholics use to attempt to maintain control over their alcoholism. Furthermore, it is widely accepted that the process of "breaking down" the denial of the alcoholic is essential if they are to succeed.

The notion that problems with alcohol could be understood as a "disease" and that problems with drinking could be described as "alcoholism," brought with it the suggestion that anyone could "catch" it. This way of thinking, in combination with the growing belief that AA was a treatment for the disease, led to the homogenization of the problem. This in turn led to a homogenization of the response. As with other entities characterized as diseases, the cure is the same regardless of who you are.

Groups are used to allow participants to confront their denial and other symptoms through hearing accounts of others' experiences, and as opportunities for other group participants to challenge directly conclusions individuals may be making about their lives and their experiences. Groups were constructed around themes thought to be generically associated with the disease of addiction, rather than driven by the specific needs of individual participants.

AA tradition has referred to the experience of individuals assumed to be under the influence of denial as having, among other things, "stinking thinking," or "doing the same thing and expecting different results." The group context of confrontation reflects the conclusion that the disease of alcoholism must be challenged for it to be overcome. It further reflects the conclusion that success can only be achieved if the alcoholic admits that he or she has the disease and, more importantly, accepts his or her powerlessness over its effects. This is reflected in the First Step of the process.

The notion of accepting powerlessness, its homogeneous application, and the effects of this stance constitute the basis of my critique. It has been my experience that powerlessness is not an idea similarly understood across diverse groups. This constitutes my bias in this discussion. The notion of powerlessness is inherently connected to sociopolitical power, and therefore the utility of accepting one's powerlessness is intertwined with the amount of power to which one has access in the first place.

I have known individuals for whom the experience of accepting powerlessness has been useful. Contrasted with this situation are accounts of persons I have known whose lives afforded them little power to begin with, and for whom a further diminution of power presented a life-threatening struggle. For the purposes of this discussion, I will present the example of an individual who, by virtue of her profession, has access to sociopolitical power, but by virtue of her gender has little power. I have done this in an effort to present the complexity of issues associated with power and addiction.

"Something for Me"—Betty's Story[5]

"I need to find something for me," she said, as the tears began to flow. Sitting in my office, Betty reached for the tissue box. This was our first meeting. Betty had been struggling for about six months with the role alcohol played in her life.

Betty had come in at the request of her family. They had grown concerned because she seemed to be spending more and more time drinking. From her own account, she would sometimes drink a whole bottle of wine in an afternoon. She would do this while she was home alone, waiting for her husband to get home from work, or her sons to return from school.

We were trying to understand how it was that alcohol had begun to exert such a powerful influence on her life. "Can you tell me what the tears are about?" I asked.

"The boys don't need me anymore, and Tom is always working. He doesn't need me," she replied.

"You said you wanted something for you," I responded. "I am curious about what you meant by that." From this query grew a recounting of a life in which Betty had been a leader. She had been the first in her family to move away from home. Alone, she had supported herself though college, and continued on to finish medical school. Prior to meeting her husband, she had been working at a family health clinic in Harlem, New York, part of a new program in which health-care providers went out into the city to care for those in need.

In our conversations, she recounted her experiences of going out into the housing projects attempting to care for those who lived there. Her experience of the conditions in which people lived had affected her profoundly. She saw, at first hand, the difficulties with which many people had to contend in living their lives. She felt a strong commitment to caring for these people, even though she knew the work entailed a relatively high amount of risk. These experiences contributed to her strong sense that caring and connection were things she should stand for in her life.

After meeting her husband, Tom, they moved away from the city to follow the direction of his career. Soon after leaving the city, her first son was born. Betty adopted the role of caregiver and let go of her work in medicine. It was at this time that she started to feel pressured to change from the path she had taken as a leader, someone who stood outside of what was expected, and to adopt a more traditional role as a mother and wife. The pressure came from her family, who expressed their belief that this course of action was the most appropriate for her.

Eighteen months after their first son was born, she gave birth to her second son. Tom continued to develop his career, and began to spend more and more time at the office. Betty found herself taking care of the boys, the house, and the other associated chores. For the most part, she enjoyed watching them grow up, and, for a while, didn't miss her career.

When we started meeting, the boys were in their mid-teens and spending more time with friends, doing homework, and engaged in their own lives. Tom's career took up much of his time, leaving little time for him to spend with Betty. Betty was left with taking care of the house, doing the boys' laundry, playing golf with her friends, and talking on the phone. She wanted to do something more stimulating but found herself wondering how she could do anything without making herself unavailable to her sons if they needed her.

She found herself drinking while waiting for the boys to get home from school, or waiting for Tom to come home after work. It was during this time that Betty began to experience alcohol as her "only companion." She found it comforting and drinking helped her deal with her boredom.

It was in this context that we began to explore her desire to have "something for her." In talking about what this might be, she connected back to her experiences in the clinic and the work she had done in the city. She said she had given all that up for her husband's career and for the boys. She said that she felt like much of her life had been given over to her family's needs, and taking care of their home. She said that she needed something that she would find different, something she would find satisfying.

Betty and I had encountered many roadblocks in our attempts to describe something that would be for her. Betty felt a strong commitment to her sons' needs, and didn't see how she could commit to an activity that might make her unavailable to them. Her husband's work was somewhat unpredictable, making it difficult for her to know when his family responsibilities would be transferred to her.

Alcohol had helped her forget about her desire to find something in her life that would give her a sense of purpose. She found this assistance quite seductive. She struggled to conceive of a life without this support.

"I just have to admit that I'm powerless over alcohol," Betty eventually said, as the tears started to well up in her eyes. Over the course of several stays in Twelve Step-oriented detoxification facilities, she came to understand that powerlessness over alcohol was the essence of taking her life back. She was being invited to believe that the only way for her to change her relationship with alcohol was to admit that she could not control her drinking.

But how was she to experience this invitation in the context of a life already dominated by things she had given up? How was she to experience an invitation to powerlessness in the context of having so little control of the direction of her life? How was she to experience the suggestion that she give up alcohol in the context of a life where the only solace she believed she had from her memories of commitments she'd made and lost touch with, was in a drink?

Difference and Addiction

Betty's story represents an example illustrative of the experiences of many people with whom I have worked. Traditional modes of treatment based on the Twelve Steps don't adequately account for the differences in power experienced by many of the people who attempt to access recovery through these programs. The idea that someone might already be in a "one down" position because of culture, race, sexual orientation, religion, sociopolitical demographic, and other differences is not considered.

The First Step of AA assumes homogeneity of sociocultural power in relation to the abdication of power over one's relationship to alcohol. As it is written, it ignores the impact the requested admission might have in the life of a person whose existence is already characterized by the absence of power. It seems to minimize the implications of making such a request in such lives, and the difficulties and honest resistance that might occur in response to such a suggestion.

Betty had a great deal of trouble complying with this step. She experienced the idea of admitting powerlessness over her drinking as simply another instance of her having to give up something that was important to her. For her, alcohol was the last thing she had to hang on to. It was something that allowed her a brief respite from the pain that resulted from her having ended up in a life that seemed so far removed from the life she set out to lead while she was in medical school.

Although the context of the powerlessness invitation set out in the First Step is intended to free the person from the turmoil of repeated attempts to control one's drinking, for Betty, and many others, it is experienced as yet another loss of power. It is seen as another piece of one's identity being removed. Betty experienced the possibility of admitting powerlessness as another aspect of her character being taken away from her.

Although the substance abuse treatment system in the United States has had success in identifying the importance of groups and the utility of AA in its ability to fight against loneliness and isolation (both issues experienced by many as central in reclaiming their lives), it has fallen short in a critique of its ability to discern differences in the individual's relation to power in our culture. At best, AA assumes that power is equally distributed across the lives of program participants; at worst, it completely ignores the existence of sociocultural power and the role it plays in participants' experience of their lives.

This lack of critique might be traced back to a unique element of the substance abuse treatment system. This uniqueness sets substance abuse treatment apart from any other mental or physical health-care system in this country. This element is the prevalence of individuals whose personal experience is the primary credential they carry for doing their work.

The presence of what are known as paraprofessionals leads to an assumption that the power relations between participants and staff are equilateral. "We're all the same in the game" is an expression commonly used in an effort to assure participants that they are among equals, and that their lives are being understood in the context of people who have "been there" and share a common set of experiences. Being an insider among insiders is intended to have a positive effect on those seeking treatment.

The intention of this practice may be to diminish the possibility that participants will have a basis to believe they are being judged. Additionally, it is hoped that sharing a common experience may lend credibility to the position of the person attempting to counsel the participant. It is also suggested that the presence of paraprofessionals will aid those seeking help in hanging on to the hope that they, too, may yet be able to reclaim their life from their relationship with substances.[6]

Whatever the reason, the lack of awareness of differences in the experience of sociopolitical power in substance abuse treatment settings and philosophies is detrimental to the successful recovery of many people. I have worked with many individuals who are members of marginalized groups who experience the AA invitation to powerlessness as a final step they are unwilling to take. Like Betty, they understand the suggestion that admitting powerlessness over alcohol is the only way to reclaim one's future as a replication of the very stressors that made the experiences offered by substance use so seductive in the first place. In their experience, admitting powerlessness amounts to a surrender of a different kind than the one envisioned by the founders of AA. It is tantamount to the acceptance of a life in slavery. It is not experienced as an invitation to move forward, but one to continue to slide into an abyss of domination and subjugation.

The suggestion that alcohol is "all I have left" will not sound unusual to many treatment providers. The ability of substances like alcohol to move into a place of cherished partnership is one of the great hazards of addiction. Once a person begins to hold this belief, others can begin to look like the enemy. Establishing trust with someone who may be predisposed to consider you an enemy is very difficult. For this reason many people who work in substance abuse treatment experience these types of statements as a tactic in service of the substance trying to keep people from taking their lives back.

In the context of levels of sociopolitical power, though, the issue becomes how to make the distinction between a tactic intended to keep people stuck, and a lifeline people have been hanging onto in the face of fighting against a paradigm of subjugation and marginalization. The former represents a position in which power is available but is being interrupted by excessive consumption. The latter represents the experience of oppression being mediated by consumption.

This is not to suggest that alcohol's intentions for Betty's life revolved around support. In fact Betty was herself growing more and more concerned about the way her relationship with alcohol was developing. She saw her reliance on alcohol's ability to soothe or buffer her growth in awareness of life problems, and she witnessed the effects that her drinking was having on her sons and on her relationship with her husband. None of this awareness made her happy.

What I am proposing is the necessity of a system of practice that acknowledges the differences in peoples' experience associated with differences in cultural background, race, sexual orientation, religion, sociopolitical demographic, and so on. What is needed is a treatment system that will allow those concerned to discern the distinction between invitations that are in support of new directions and those that are replications of past oppression. What is needed is a way to engage people struggling with addiction in conversations that consider their unique experience of living in relation to sociopolitical power and the role played by their relationships with substances. This represents a fundamental shift from an approach to treatment of problems with substances that advocates for a single path to recovery, to one that acknowledges the differences people experience in relation to this form of cultural power. Below I will outline such a system.

Changing the Discourse

Adopting a perspective on substance abuse treatment that includes a critique of sociopolitical power relations requires a fundamental shift in the way substance abuse is understood. Traditional models view substance abuse from the disease perspective, placing the disorder inside the person. The traditional view holds that substance use disorders must be treated in the context of this frame, and that abdication of one's ability to control them is essential.

This view is squarely rooted in modernist assumptions about humanity.[7] From this viewpoint diseases are entities that inhabit the bodies of individuals. Individuals suffer from these diseases until they are cured or the diseases are otherwise removed from the body.

Proponents of this perspective readily compare addiction to cancer, diabetes, and even allergies, and see their treatment as parallel to treatments for other similar disorders. From this perspective, the disease model is not a metaphor, but a description of the true nature of an individual's relationship to substances. The link, then, to forms of treatment informed by modernist thinking is a foregone conclusion.

An alternative perspective is to consider problems with substances as something that exists in our culture. The unique manifestation of cultural problems exists in the unique effects each has on the affected individual or community. From this perspective, a critique of the cultural implications of power on the affected individual can be included in the process of treatment. In fact this kind of exploration is an essential element of the process.

This alternative perspective to dealing with alcoholism has been discussed at length by various writers (see Epston and White 1990; Freedman and Combs 1996; Dickerson and Zimmerman 1996) in discussing the use of narrative therapy. The application of narrative therapy in the context of problems with substances, however, is less widely discussed (see Winslade and Smith 1997; Glenn Wixson 2000). A full description of the process of narrative therapy is beyond the scope of this chapter, but I will address some of the specifics as it relates to problems with substances generally and invitations to powerlessness specifically.

Addiction and Narrative Therapy

The practice of narrative therapy exists in a context of a specific stance in relation to problems. In this context, people are not the problem; problems are the problem. Briefly, therapy progresses as the history of problem effects are traced through people's accounts of their lives. As the effects of problems are described, elements that stand outside of what one would expect, given the intentions of the problem, come to light. These unexpected elements often provide doorways to other unexpected elements that describe beliefs and practices that stand in resistance to the influence of the problem.

These beliefs and practices usually lead to more beliefs and practices. An accounting of these practices becomes an outline of preferences that people hold for their lives. As these preferred identities (White and Epston 1994) become more fully described, they provide resources to individuals seeking to reform their relationships to problems. Additionally, they provide a useful contrast between the preferred identity and the one associated with the problem and its effects.

In the context of Betty's invitation to express her powerlessness over alcohol, I attempted to consider the effects this decision might have in her life. In an effort to avoid assuming I could understand what effects this decision might have, I asked Betty if she would be interested in telling me what she meant by "admitting she was powerless over alcohol." Her response was, "It means I can never drink again." Again the tears began to flow.

"And what would it mean for you to never drink again?" I asked.

"It would mean that I couldn't be with friends," she began. "It would mean that I couldn't be comfortable when I go out to eat, that everyone will be looking at me and wondering what is going on. I mean—I've always had a drink. It's never been something that I didn't do. People will wonder what is going on with me."

Traditional treatment models would suggest that I identify these statements as part of her process of self-pity. They would suggest that she is rationalizing her use by connecting it to socializing. Traditional models of treatment would suggest that she is minimizing the danger of ongoing use by suggesting it is just part of what she does.

Narrative ideas, on the other hand, encourage me to consider her statements in the context of an implied preferred way of being. Her preferred identity is reflected in the choices she makes, in the beliefs she has, and in her hopes and desires for her life. Betty is expressing hers in her statements as she describes her concerns about losing her connection to practices that connect her to people that matter to her. Rather than dismiss her statements only as manifestations of the intentions of the problem, I can consider how they might connect to aspects of her experience that matter a great deal to her. I can consider with her the possibility that they might, in fact, connect to still other elements of her experience she will find useful in renegotiating her relationship to substances. Additionally, I can further explore whether these elements of her experience reconnect her to relationships that matter to her.

I asked Betty if she would be interested in telling me why being with friends and not feeling like everyone else, and of other people wondering what was wrong with her, mattered so much to her. From this beginning point, over the course of several meetings, we began to explore her experience of relationship in her life. For Betty, caring and support were things she valued greatly. We discovered that these were things she, as a young woman, had been able to cultivate in a relationship with one special friend. She was able to do this in the absence of being able to find care and support in the context of her parents and brothers and sisters.

In this way, my curiosity about her response to my questions regarding her intentions relating to powerlessness, and my stance of considering these statements from the narrative perspective, allowed us to connect to meanings that were not consistent with those I would have been invited into through traditional treatment. Rather than being connected to some hidden desire Betty has to continue to drink, these statements were more usefully associated with her desire to stay connected to people. Moreover, tracing the origins of this desire led us to a commitment she had to caring and support.

I subsequently became interested in more fully describing this commitment. I did this by exploring with her the origins of this commitment, and wondered if there weren't people or traditions or experiences in her life that were supportive of it. This practice was intended to more richly describe elements of her life that were connected to her life preferences.

In engaging in this practice we resisted the invitation to ascribe assumptions that are based on naturalistic conclusions about people's motivations.[8] In so doing, we were more likely to discover valued elements of her life that could connect her to cherished memories and experiential resources that might be valuable in her migration away from substance use.

I hoped that by exploring the origins of her commitments to caring and attention, we would be able to identify resources she could use in her efforts to stay in connection to people she cared about without continuing down a road we both were concerned about. Furthermore, I hoped the process would offer us an alternative to the invitation to powerlessness that had started us on our journey. To further elaborate the origins of her commitment to care and support, I sent her the following letter:[9]

Betty,

At our last meeting you talked about spending time with your friend and that that was how you saw how other families lived. You also said that those experiences made you wonder why you weren't getting from your family what your friend got from his. You talked about wanting your parents to show up and support you at recitals and other events in your life and that you wanted, and still want, them to be involved. Was it being with your friend that got you thinking that your parents should be supportive of you in your life? If it was, how did this happen? If not, how did you find out about support and caring?

You said you wanted support from them and that that is part of what you are missing from Tom and your family now. I was wondering how it has been that you have not given up on wanting support up until this point? How is it that you have been able to stay with your desire to have your family care about you and your boys? What does it say about you that you have been able to hang on to the desire for support and caring until this point? How was it that you were able to reach out to others as a way to get that support and care? Was there something that happened in your life that got you to think it was worth hanging on to? Did reaching out to others let you know that there were ways to get support and caring?

I'm wondering what your family has missed out on by not showing interest in your life and your family. I'm also wondering about ways you have stood up for showing caring and interest with your sons. How is it that you have shown interest and support for your sons up to this point? What does it say about you that you have hung on to the position that caring and support matter, and made sure you show caring and support with them? What would they say about that? How do you think they would react to the fact that this is something you have been unwilling to give up in your relationships with them?

What do you think it says about your commitment to them that you have been unwilling to replicate your family's lifestyle with your sons? What do you think they would say about your ability to create your own lifestyle to stand up to how your family was?

In Partnership, Joel

This letter represents my attempt to connect Betty's commitment to caring and support throughout the events of her life. First, I address her commitments in the context of their origins in her young life. I am situating my questions in the context of her learning about what she now experiences as missing in her life. I am tracing the origins of the development of this sense of something missing. I am asking questions intended to trace the roots of her ability to discern the absence of caring and support in her current relationships.

In the second section I am attempting to encourage her to describe more fully what it is that has assisted her in staying connected to her commitments. These questions are intended to elaborate connection between her commitments and her efforts to live consistently with those commitments. They are also intended to find connections between her commitments and what it is that sustains those commitments.

In the third section I am exploring whether specific events in her life are examples of her living consistently with her commitments. I am wondering if things she shared with me about her actions are connected to experiences she had with people in her life. I am also inviting her to consider their voice in supporting her in her actions now. Questions that invite the evocation of voices of people in her life in this section and in others are examples of a practice intended to repopulate persons' lives with the presence of individuals who have supported or are supporting them in the living out of their preferred identity (White 2000).

By inviting people to consider who it is that would not be surprised by their attempts to hang on to their hopes and goals, or their intentions, and inviting them to consider how they would respond in witnessing their present actions or intentions that are consistent with those intentions, we create the possibility for people to add individuals to their resources from the past and present who support their ongoing efforts. In this way we were beginning the process of repopulating Betty's life and developing a community of concern shaped by her commitments to caring and support. Communities shaped around these specific commitments can be very powerful and useful to people as they face the intentions of the problem. This process can be extended in a variety of ways.

It is the recognition of the importance of developing a system of allies that correlates most closely to what traditional forms of treatment have to offer. AA offers a social context for the reclamation of lives from the problems of addiction. It is in the elaboration of the narrative and traditional modes of creating these networks of allies that a powerful collaborative melding of the two exists.

Narrative Therapy and AA:
A Collaborative Approach

It is now commonly accepted that the most useful aspect of therapy is the relationship created by the therapist and the client. In my experience this is paralleled in AA. Many of the people I have worked with have pointed to the relationships they build in the AA community as being the most important aspect of the program. Their home groups, their sponsor, and those with whom they go on commitments become the communities of concern within which they develop a life of sobriety. The Twelve Steps, the lore, the sayings and propaganda, then, become the grist in which these relationships churn.

As I have stated, narrative practice recognizes the necessity and importance of communities of concern. These communities are centered on the telling and retelling of preferred identities as people and groups reclaim their identities from the grasp of problems. These communities may spring from the desire of a couple to redefine their relationship around the needs of their children rather than traditional constructs of marriage. They may arise from an individual's regaining his connection to his sense of core values. Or, as in Betty's case, a community of concern may be created around her establishment of closer ties to her commitment to caring and concern.

Additionally, communities of concern can be made up of a variety of individuals. Family members may be invited in to witness an interview with an individual, in which the individual expresses his or her commitments to strongly held values. A group of third graders might convene to proclaim their intentions to take their school back from bullying, or a group of "addicts" might invite close friends to a meeting to have their friends witness their conversations about their efforts to reclaim their lives from addiction, and the steps they have taken to do so.

Whatever their genesis and membership, these communities reflect what is commonly valued about the structure of AA. AA and other communities of concern share a commitment to the belief that a group's recognition of an individual's commitments and values is powerful. They share the understanding that reconnection with groups of people stands up against the insidious nature of addiction. They share a commitment to upholding the dignity of the people who participate in the resulting conversations. Additionally, and perhaps most importantly, they share the belief that the people who populate these gatherings hold the knowledge and resources necessary to reclaim their lives from the devastation wrought by addiction.

It is in this shared set of beliefs that the power for a melding of these seemingly disparate philosophies lies. The readily available community offered by local AA meetings can be lifesaving for individuals struggling with problems with addiction. Being able to, in most U.S. cities and on most nights of the week,[10] find open group meetings in which one can participate is an invaluable resource for millions. These meetings offer an alternative to the loneliness and isolation that confront many people attempting to take their lives back from addiction.

Combining this resource with narrative practices creates a union in which individuals may participate with others attempting to migrate toward a different kind of relationship with substances, while reclaiming preferred identities along the way. The support offered by the AA community, combined with the reclamation of values, goals, hopes, and dreams, may well provide a stable platform upon which to reclaim lives, families, communities, and entire cultures. This melding of approaches creates almost limitless possibilities for the future development of approaches to treatment that address the needs created by the growing cultural complexity of our society.

The primary contribution of narrative practices, in the context of problems with substances, is the ability to situate the reclaiming of preferred identities within the context of cultural forces and a critique of the influences these forces have had on the individual. While preferred identities are reclaimed from the margins of an individual's existence, the forces that supported that marginalization are exposed. These exposures are then explored to establish the tactics used in the process of marginalization.

In the telling and retelling process of the communities of concern, the marginalization and tactics used to do so are further exposed, creating the possibility for the critique to have even greater ripples into the community. This process allows for the effects of the critique to enter the community, situated within the context of its effects. In this way, it is less likely that any one group will be further stigmatized as the purveyor of the problem.

In Betty's situation the telling and retelling of her commitment to caring and concern had the effect of situating her experience as a child within the context of her commitment to creating a caring environment for her family and her community as an adult. Connected to this caring environment were many lessons she wanted to teach her sons about parenting and about responsibility and community. As the telling progressed, her sons were able to witness the ideas and invitations Betty received that tried to convince her that her commitments to specific ideas about parenting and community weren't legitimate or important. They discovered the connection she experienced between her desire to take care of them, the sacrifices she had to make regarding her career, and the way those sacrifices led her to believe she had "given up on the community" and therefore had "no right to have a voice in what would be useful in the community."

This delegitimization of Betty's perspective led to the marginalization of the values she associated with that perspective. Continuing the process of marginalization, Betty struggled with her desire to become more active in the community, spending less time with her sons. With this came an invitation for her to consider herself a "less than perfect mom," a person who "selfishly focused on her own needs, rather than those of her children." These invitations served to further separate her from her commitments to caring and connection.

A critique of the origins of these invitations creates the opportunity to explore their tactics in engaging Betty's life. A telling and retelling process allows for the potential for these tactics to be known more broadly in the community. The knowing of these tactics, and the agendas they represent, create the possibility for others in the community to consider their existence in the lives of other families.

It is in this way that this process moves beyond the traditional constructs of therapy, those based on disorders in individuals, and into a process where critiques of sociopolitical power relations as articulated in the invitations members of oppressed groups receive from the society at large become the focus. It is in this context that the process of therapy becomes an active part of the process of social change, which constitutes the moral responsibility of the counselor (Hoshmand 2001).

By taking this step away from the "disorder vision" of addiction, narrative practices add an essential element to the process of addiction treatment. Additionally, these practices provide a revitalized platform for one of AA's original goals—that of moving the discourse of addiction away from that of a moral failing. In fact, as Betty's story exemplifies and my experience affirms, it is the strong commitment to a moral foundation and the invitations that delegitimize those moral passions that most often fuel the power of addiction. Narrative practice's ability to undercut this power by opening up possibilities to reconnect with those passions is what I have witnessed to be the most powerful aspect of this practice.

Conclusion

Alcoholics Anonymous is an entity with a seventy-year history of assisting people in taking their lives back from addiction. However, in the course of this history

AA has failed to provide a context in which the differences in sociopolitical power expressed in the lives of its participants can be critiqued with regard to their experience of the Twelve Steps. I have attempted to provide an invitation to that critique that recognizes the individual manifestations of the power relations it attempts to expose.

Additionally, I have offered narrative practice as a platform upon which an active, ongoing critique may be engaged in that might allow for the community aspects of AA to continue to be utilized, while the existence and effects of unequal sociopolitical power may be explored and acted against. It is my hope that by so doing, a melding of the two practices may provide those suffering with the effects of addiction a place where they can reconnect with their preferences for their lives, their moral commitments, and their passion for creating a better world. In so doing we can begin the process of working together in creating a better world for all of us.

THIRTEEN

Flowers and Songs:
A Liturgical Approach to Pastoral Care

Eric H. F. Law

In 2002 the Roman Catholic Church canonized Juan Diego, the first Native American saint. It took almost five hundred years after the event in which he encountered the divine revelation through the Lady of Guadalupe at Tepeyac before the church recognized the significance of Juan Diego's role in the life of the church in the Americas. One of the reasons why it took so long was that there were disputes as to whether Juan Diego actually existed; perhaps he was just a legend. But one cannot ignore the impact of Our Lady of Guadalupe in the Americas. The story of Juan Diego is worth retelling here for the benefit of those readers who do not know the story. The summary below is based on Virgil Elizondo's extensive work on the Guadalupe event in his book *Guadalupe: Mother of the New Creation*.[1]

In 1531, ten years after the conquest of Mexico by Spain, "Everywhere the inhabitants of the lake and the mountain had surrendered" (ibid., 5). The church had worked diligently to convert the Indians to Christianity. But under this political backdrop, any transference of the faith was colored by the emancipation of the native way of life. Nevertheless, Juan Diego had been faithful in following the teaching of the church. On a Saturday night, he was on his way to Mexico City to receive his instructions from the priest. When he reached the foot of a small hill named Tepeyac, "He heard singing on the summit of the hill: as if different precious birds were singing and their songs would alternate as if the hill was answering them" (ibid., 6). When the song ceased, he heard someone calling him. He followed the voice and saw a lady whose clothing "appeared like the sun, and it gave forth rays." She asked him, "Where are you going?" (ibid.,

7). He explained that he was going to Mexico City to receive instructions from the priest. There she gave her first instruction:

> I very much want and ardently desire that my hermitage be erected in this place. In it I will show and give to all people all my love, my compassion, my help, and my protection, because I am your merciful mother and the mother of all the nations that live on this earth who would love me, who would speak with me, who would search for me, and who would place their confidence in me. There I will hear their laments and remedy and cure all their miseries, misfortunes, and sorrows.

> And for this merciful wish of mine to be realized, go there to the palace of the bishop of Mexico, and you will tell him in what way I have sent you as a messenger, so that you may make known to him how I very much desire that he build me a home right here, that he may erect my temple on the plain. (Ibid., 8)

He readily accepted the mission and went to the palace to seek the ear of the bishop—Don Fray Juan de Zumárraga. With some difficulty, he finally got to see and to tell the bishop what he had "admired, seen and heard." But the bishop answered him, "My son, you will have to come another time; I will calmly listen to you at another time. I still have to see, to examine carefully from the very beginning, the reason you have come, and your will and your wish" (ibid., 9).

Juan Diego left knowing he had not accomplished his mission. On the same day, he returned to Tepeyac and the lady appeared to him once more. He asked the lady to send "one of the more valuable nobles, a well-known person, one who is respected and esteemed" to be the messenger (ibid., 10). But the lady insisted that he was the one. So, the next day, Sunday, Juan Diego again went to the palace to see the bishop. This time, the bishop told him that he could not act on the lady's wishes solely on the basis of his word and message. A sign from the lady would be necessary for the bishop to believe that Juan Diego was indeed sent by the Lady from Heaven. Juan Diego left once again without accomplishing his mission.

When Juan Diego returned home, he discovered that one of his uncles, Juan Bernardino, had caught smallpox and was nearing death. Through the night, his uncle begged Juan Diego to find a priest to hear his confession before he died. The next day, Juan Diego took another path in order to avoid meeting the lady whom he thought would delay him from getting a priest to his uncle before he died. Yet, the lady came down from the top of the hill and blocked his path, and standing in front of him, said, "Where are you going?" (ibid., 14).

Juan Diego explained the situation with his uncle. The lady assured him that his uncle was already healed and not to be worried. She then instructed him to climb to the top of the hill where he had seen her before, and cut and gather flowers he would find there and bring them to her. He did as she instructed and was surprised to find all kinds of exquisite flowers from Castile, because it was December in Mexico, not a time for any kind of flowers. He gathered them and placed them in the hollow of his mantle. He took the flowers to the lady who said, "These different flowers are the proof, the sign, that you will take to the bishop" (ibid., 17).

Juan Diego took the flowers to the palace and again, with great difficulty he finally got to see the bishop. He told the bishop everything that had happened and that he did bring a sign, as the bishop had demanded. "He unfolded his white mantle. . . and at that instant the flowers from Castile fell to the ground. And in that very moment she painted herself; the precious image of the Ever-Virgin Holy Mary, Mother of God Teotl, appeared suddenly, just as she is depicted today and is kept in her precious home, in her hermitage of Tepeyac, which is called Guadalupe" (ibid., 20).

When the bishop saw her, he and all who accompanied him fell to their knees and were greatly astonished. The bishop prayed to her and begged her to forgive him for not having believed her will, her heart, and her word. He immediately started the building of her temple. When Juan Diego returned home, he discovered that the lady had indeed appeared to his uncle and healed him.

The first time I read the whole story, I imagined Juan Diego, doing what he was told, walking back and forth every week from his home to the church in the city to receive his instructions—a prescribed way of life according to the conquerors of his people. And on that December evening, he was interrupted by the appearance of the Lady of Guadalupe. He was invited to take a sabbath, which began with following the songs of the birds and later the signs of the flowers. Through his encounter with the Lady of Guadalupe, he was raised up from a lowly poor Indian into the messenger of the divine, delivering a message that would change the history of the Americas. In the Náhuatl tradition, "Flower and song" represents the truth.

The Náhuatl theologians stated: "It may be that no one on earth can tell the truth, except through flower and song." Rational discourse clarifies yet limits the mind, while flowers and song stimulate the imagination to ponder the infinite. For the Náhuatl, it was only through poetic communication and beauty that the heart of human beings could enter into communion and communication with the divine—both individually and collectively. For the Náhuatl, truth was expressed through the suggestive harmony of the seen and heard. Through the beauty of the image (flowers) and the melodious sounds (poetic word), the divine could be gradually experienced, and one could gradually come to share in the divine wisdom. (Elizondo 1997, 34–35)

In this story, Juan Diego and his uncle Juan Bernardino represent a people who were conquered and oppressed. The "traditional" pastoral care imposed by the Christian leaders was unhelpful, to say the least. The Christian "instructions" were actually harmful to the self-esteem of this conquered people and reinforced the oppressive reality created by the powerful conquerors. The interruption of the divine appearance was an invitation for the oppressed people to take a sabbath, to listen to songs and gather flowers. To enter into sabbath is to enter a liturgy in which the historically powerless learn and experience the truth—the truth about their blessedness in God's eyes and the truth that their experience of oppression was not part of God's plan for humanity. This truth disputes the incomplete reality projected by the historically powerful in society. Through songs and flowers, Juan Diego learned the truth that he was beloved by God, even though he and his people were conquered and powerless and were on the verge of dying spiritually, as symbolized by the figure of his dying uncle.

The story of Juan Diego reveals key steps for pastoral care of the oppressed:

1. Interrupt the unhelpful rituals that reinforce the power of the dominant group.
2. Invite the oppressed community to take sabbath.
3. During sabbath, invite the community to participate in a liturgy that:
   a. Affirms their blessedness
   b. Enables them to speak the truth of their experiences
   c. Correlates their experiences with the Word of God, and
   d. Empowers them to act in ways to transform their oppressive situation.

In 1983, I was a seminarian in charge of a congregation that consisted of mostly refugees from Vietnam and Cambodia, with a few retired, educated, old-time Episcopalians. I was put in charge of this community because the very experienced priest who had started the ministry a few years previously was called to start a new church on the other coast. I was a seminarian doing my field-education study at this ministry at the time the experienced priest moved away. The bishop's committee asked me to stay with the ministry until they called a new priest. After all the farewell parties and goodbyes for the priest and his family, I faced the daunting task of coordinating and facilitating the liturgical and pastoral needs of this community as a second-year student in seminary, who could only work fifteen hours a week.

Here were some of my observations of this community as I was trying to determine how to go about providing pastoral care for them with all my limitations. The individualistic models and skills for pastoral care that I learned from seminary were of little use in this situation. Between my limited time availability, and the church members' working schedules, we had very few opportunities for one-on-one conversations. The Sunday morning liturgy was not well attended because many of the church members had to work on Sunday. The form of the liturgy was the standard Episcopal Eucharist translated into Chinese. Since I was not ordained, I had invited a European American priest to preside at the Eucharist. I had taught and coached him to say the liturgy in Cantonese. He was eager to learn. Due to the difficulty of learning to pronounce words in a language that has eight tones, he struggled through the words each Sunday morning while the congregation tolerated and appreciated his effort. I was not much better in my delivery of the sermon, because my Chinese language skill was that of a ninth grader from Hong Kong. The hymns we sang were all European hymn tunes with translated lyrics, which often were ill fitted to the melodies and had little meaning as we struggled through them. The reading of lessons from Holy Scripture was done by the few members who could read, most of whom were educated, upper-class Chinese Episcopalians, while some struggled to locate the page where the lessons were in their Chinese Bible and the others pretended that they were reading from their Bibles.

As this European American priest and I struggled through the liturgy each Sunday, I soon realized that the liturgy was not nurturing the congregation as it should. The liturgy was simply an imitation of a worship process that had worked in another culture in another time. Personally, I was uncomfortable, as their spiritual guide, with all the cultural and historical religious power connotations.

I decided to focus my energy and time on creating another kind of gathering that would truly serve this community pastorally and liturgically. I started a monthly gathering at different church members' homes. I established a regular format—a liturgy—for each gathering. Our liturgy included:

1. Meeting at the church member's home and preparing the food. Informal conversation would take place.
2. Opening prayer and grace offered by the pastor.
3. We eat. More conversation.
4. We gather around to listen to the Gospel for the upcoming Sunday. We would listen to the lesson three times and after each reading, each member of the group was invited to share their reflections on our shared liturgy. Because some of the participants could not read, it was necessary that they learn to retell the biblical story by heart before we began sharing.
5. A time to share individual concerns.
6. A time of prayer led by the pastor.
7. More informal conversation and storytelling.

Every month, excitement built as we prepared to gather at another church member's house. Group members prepared the food and packed it for travel. They made arrangements for everyone's transportation. One month, we would be eating, singing, and praying in an expensive condo in Cambridge. The next month, we would be laughing and praying in a one-room apartment in a low-income housing project, sitting on chairs made out of cardboard boxes and crates. The location was not important as long as we had storytelling, laughter, food, and genuine concern for each individual and family.

The people shared their experiences escaping their war-torn home countries. They shared their hopes and struggles in raising their children in this new country, while working long hours with little quality time actually to spend with their families. They shared their struggles to survive in an environment that did not affirm their language and their life experiences. They reminisced about the "good old days." They shared their experiences of conversion to the Christian faith. The scriptural sharing always revealed something significant for them, sometimes challenging them to take up power to do something about their oppressive situations, sometimes affirming their experiences and their realization that they were blessed, no matter what happened to them and their families.

I remembered fondly many moments at these gatherings where I sat back and silently thanked God for this time where the people of this community came to care for each other.

Once a month, we interrupted the ritual of life and work and took a side trip. Like Juan Diego, we entered into a sabbath to listen to songs and to gather flowers. We entered a liturgy that enabled us to speak the truth about our experiences and how God challenges and affirms and moves us out into the world again with renewed energy and vision. Instead of conforming to society's imposed roles, we regained our self-esteem through this community of mutual nourishment. We became messengers of the truth out in the world.

I was forever grateful to have stumbled onto this liturgical community approach to pastoral care so early in my ministry. When I was working on my first book, *The Wolf Shall Dwell With the Lamb* (Law 1993), my research in the field of cultural anthropology confirmed that this approach worked especially well for the historically oppressed communities. Later, I discovered that this approach could also work well with communities in which both the powerful and the powerless were present.

Over the years, I have consulted with many church communities at the invitation of denominational leaders. A recurring request has been for me to work with a church community in which a small group of powerful people dominate the decision-making process, while the majority quietly suffer and sometimes are not conscious of the power dynamic that surrounds them, believing that it is normal. Recurring patterns of stress upon the formal leadership and consistent decline of the community are always the presenting symptoms of this unhealthy power dynamic. I always approach these consultations, which often evolve into pastoral relationships, liturgically.

The first thing I ask is that the community set aside time for the consultation process—to take a side trip, to honor sabbath. In most cases, I ask for a monthly gathering of at least four hours for a six- to twelve-month period. I develop the same "liturgical" pattern for each gathering. The following is a typical pattern:

1. Opening song: I use the same song for all the gatherings because this provides a level of safety and familiarity once the community has learned the song by heart.
2. Opening prayers: After the first two gatherings, I usually invite a member of the community to offer prayers.
3. Community Bible study:[2] I divide the group into smaller groups of six to eight, and move them through this process in no more than half an hour. I always study one of the lessons from the upcoming Sunday lectionary. The process involves reading the same text three

times and inviting each participant to share his/her reflection using the Mutual Invitation[3] process.

4. A dialogue on a major topic: This is a carefully designed process enabling the community to dialogue on a major topic concerning their community life. These topics may include: celebrating their past, examining their present, looking toward the future, and so forth. I take great care in ensuring that the voices of the "powerless" are heard, while the "powerful" are invited to listen.

5. Sharing of learning: I then invite the community members to share what they have learned.

6. Prayers of the people: The sharing of learning naturally leads to offering of prayers for self, others, and the community.

7. Holy Communion: When appropriate, the liturgy of the Eucharist is celebrated.

8. Commissioning and dismissal: The members of the group then commission each other to go forth, taking what they have learned, both skills and knowledge, to continue to support their community.

Over time, the liturgical style of gathering becomes a gracious and sacred time and space in which the powerless in the community are affirmed and empowered to speak the truth, while the powerful, if they are willing to listen, realize that they have been misusing their power and eventually retreat and support the yearning and movement of the people in the community. If the powerful of the group are not ready to listen, they will probably be absent from these gatherings and continue to exercise their power outside.

The mutual pastoral support of these gatherings will, in due course, empower the people to challenge the powerful, bringing the community back to where God is calling it to be.

This process will take time. The story of Juan Diego teaches us that the powerful often will not listen until the powerless persist in making themselves known. After the second rejection by the bishop, Juan Diego, under the pressure of a dying uncle, almost gave up his empowered state and returned to the submissive, conquered state of being. He was doing what he was told by the powerful again—to go find a priest to give the last rites to his dying uncle. He even tried to avoid meeting the Lady of Guadalupe. He was avoiding sabbath.

But she once again intervened and found Juan Diego. She insisted that he take his sabbath and collect flowers for her—the truth—instead of going to find a priest to prepare for his uncle's death. Honoring sabbath is about finding truth and life, and not death. The sabbatical detour that Juan Diego took gave him the courage to confront the powerful with the truth again, even though the powerful were not ready to hear him. His persistence was based on his empowerment in knowing the truth: that he was beloved by God.

Therefore, the invitation to sabbath must be consistent, because there will be the tendency to give up or to return to the old ritual prescribed by the powerful. The consistent interruption of this unhealthful ritual is essential if the liturgical community approach to pastoral care is to work. The regularity of these sabbatical liturgies helps build the relationship and trust through which the people can regain their self-esteem and courage. Through the liturgy, the flowers and songs, the truth emerges. The truth will empower the powerless to act. They are the messengers of the good news. The truth will confront and silence the powerful. Together, the powerful and the powerless work together to realign their community to conform to God's desire for humanity.

FOURTEEN

The Politics of Tears:
Lamentation as Justice Making

William Blaine-Wallace

No! First we grieve and then we march.—Glenda Hope *(Thornton 2002, 188)*

A couple of years ago, I attended a conference that hosted a few of the foundational voices in family therapy. I was drawn to the work of one of the speakers. I'll call her Ann. She presented a brief video clip of her work.

Six persons—three men, two women, and an adolescent boy, representing three generations of one family—sit with their therapist. The therapist had arranged for Ann to consult with them for a session. The therapist tells Ann before the session that his work with the family is stuck, that there has been no movement over the last couple of sessions.

Ann enters the counseling room to the sounds of loud chatter. She sits among the family. The racket increases, particularly the giggles of the youngest, the thirteen-year-old grandson of the quietest person in the room, the grandfather, who is seated to Ann's right.

Ann sits still and silent amid the clamor for what seems like a long time. Eventually, Ann says, almost in a whisper, "There is much noise." The decibels increase, especially the sniggers of the adolescent.

Ann waits for a while longer and then softly says, "I wonder, if noise could speak, what would noise have to say to us?"

In a few moments, the grandfather speaks: "Noise would say that we need to speak." A nervous laughter escapes the grandson. The grandfather continues: "There is much to talk about that is hard to talk about but needs to be talked about." Air is let out of noise like a pinpricked balloon. An uncomfortable silence remains.

Ann, looking around the semicircle of family members, says, "Is this too hard to bring to words now? What do you think? Shall we talk or not?"

The grandfather responds, "We must talk about my cancer. We can't avoid it any longer. Yes, it is very hard for me. I've been independent for as long as I can remember, able to be strong for others. Now, I am going to be dependent. I don't know how. We must talk."

The air of relation gushes into the room like a breeze embracing us through a just-opened window on an early spring morning.

Sorrow over the losses of everyday life has a way of rendering us mute. Being mute is more than deadly silence. Sometimes it is noise. Whatever the manifestation, it is an inarticulate (literally, disconnected) wailing. Occasionally there is a place or time when we can express our anguish during times of loss, for example, like the death of a child, or the devastation of an earthquake. More often we cannot and are stuck leaving the anguish unvoiced but present, like the clamor of six kinfolk not yet connected to the cancer of their patriarch.

Unattached voiced wailing whips around in silent despair manifested in day-in-and-day-out busyness and boredom. When the whipping and lashing and flogging of such unattached wailing is left unheard, like the six members of the yet-to-be heard family, we become stuck. We move through our days with agility. However, at day's end, when I am bold enough to pray honestly and ardently, I discover a forgotten sadness stored in the top bin of my spirit's icebox. My depression is a frozen grief. I am not alone, I cannot escape it.

Our stolid sorrow is epidemic. A nation "zones out" in front of American Idol while Washington makes illegitimate war and maneuvers coffins invisibly through Delaware, as the Pentagon radically underreports Iraqi and Afghani deaths, both military and civilian. The arm of Pennsylvania Avenue has its hand in the cookie jar of our future, eyeing Supplemental Security Income (SSI) checks that my grandmother both counted on and was proud of after decades of standing in front of a cotton loom in Saffie Mill. And we are mostly curious about the Super Bowl—if not the game, the commercials.

Depression requires the thin oxygen of isolation. Sorrow seeks the fresh air of communion. That the United States has forgotten how to grieve, to its great sorrow, is a sad testimony to a culture that has made the individual sacrosanct, self-sufficiency an eschatological aim.

Who has the presence of heart to establish community for broken and bound-up hearts? Who hears our wailing waiting to be voiced? For instance, who is there to say to us, at the death of a friend, the loss of a job, the abandonment by a partner, "If your tears could speak what would they say?" Is it your priest? Is it a kindly acquaintance at work? Is it the companion with whom you walk around the reservoir three days a week? Is it a friend at coffee hour?

Harder questions prejudice my diagnosis that society has calcified sadness, leaving us as the living dead: Who is there to say to us, "If your slumping shoulders wrote you a letter, what would be in it?" Or, "What would be the last will and testimony of your sixty-hour work week?" Or, "If your rage could write a song, what would the lyrics be?" Or, "If your numbness thawed out, what would it say?" Would it be your therapist? Your journal? Your prayer shawl? To whom do you dare speak? Who is your Ann?

My questions are formed from a specific orientation to the sacred. And, here, I give voice to the evolution of my experience of praying to God, a progression among and through the community of the brokenhearted, over the course of almost three decades—it evolves from He to She to Relationship. Grace, more than the serendipitous breaking in of love, is a grounded character of love that is both commonplace and continuous in the communion of the brokenhearted. Broken hearts, pieces shared, are hearts broken open by the love they make (Palmer 2005, 2). From hearts cracked open through shared suffering flows a surplus of love. The community of the brokenhearted has a habit, in which history gives witness and richly distributes the excesses of the love they conjure. Love that spills over the lip of the communion of the brokenhearted is the energy of and for justice making. God, for me of late, rather than mediated through grace, is Grace, "the resilient, fragile, healing power of finitude itself" (Welch 2000, 178).

The richest soil for God, then, is the ground of our absence and emptiness, the places where we are mute, the experiences about which we are at a loss for words. At times of devastation, beyond all security of language and identity, where calculation withers, love, in the particularity of the neighbor, rushes in and permeates the void (Lane 1998, 73). Love, contingent upon alterity, the presence of the other resolutely remaining other (Lévinas 1999, ix–xiii), attends to our stammering, determined not to quiet or console, but to witness. What love attends is at times obvious—the howling of the little boy who has just lost a sister to the tsunami, the animal-like murmurs of the middle-aged man who has recovered memories of child sexual abuse. More often love is required to witness sighs, groans, and embodied gestures of violation of unconscious or undisclosed origin like the increasingly vacant eyes of the underemployed Haitian health-care workers at the nursing home, the emergent irritability of the otherwise swimmingly sufficient church treasurer whose records are being audited, the strange tic of a millworker who has been groped from behind by her foreman for thirty years (Thornton 2002, 101). Love witnesses our incomprehensible wailing, in all its manifestations.

Godly lovers, then, are those who have an uncanny capacity to watch impotently and wait helplessly. They stand beside and among stuck tongues and empty but open hands, not presuming to understand, know, cure, or heal. Godly loving is not so much learned as passed on. Those who witness the broken tend to be those whose brokenness has been witnessed and attended. They are the mute among the mute.

Out of the community of incomprehensible wailing—a community in which the identity of witness and mourner has become indistinguishable through a mutuality of brokenness—comes a resonant song, what Dorothee Soelle called lamentation (1975). Soelle recognized lamentation as incomprehensible wailing that, when witnessed, is transposed into an articulate voice. Lamentation is incomprehensible wailing that has found a song to sing, and someone with whom to sing it. Such singing, she believed, is "psalmic language," not because it reflects a particular literary genre, but, rather, contains the elements of "lament, petition, expression of hope" (ibid., 72). "I call upon thee, O LORD, make haste to me. Give ear to my voice, when I call to thee! Let my prayer be counted as incense before thee, and the lifting of my hands as an evening sacrifice" (Ps. 141:1-2, RSV). A choir of lamentation makes a mysteriously joyful noise unto the Lord through a convivial envisioning of a future born out of solidarity—St. Paul's "seeing through the glass dimly." Listen to the gospel group The Blind Boys of Alabama before they hit the big time. Shared suffering is doxological (Thornton 2002, 159–63).

I remember a period in my life when I spent days among those dying ghastly deaths, in the poorest part of a city, and nights with the supposedly living, in a corridor of a wealthy suburb. My friends wondered how I possibly could do such work, day in and day out. I wondered how I could do such living night in and night out. Among the dying, I learned to distinguish deep joy from shallow happiness.

Doxology, cries of joy birthed from the tears of shared suffering, is eucharistic. Body broken in community time after time, for us again and again, is news, good news, before and after it is sound doctrine. Eucharist keeps open a wound that offends the senses and manners of a church and society in which sufficiency is sacrosanct, a wound from which the hopes of and for the insufficient spring (Thornton 2002, 197).

Eucharist, as convivial drama in three acts—wailing, lamenting, rejoicing—is dangerous to the powers and principalities who count on a dissonant, numbed constituency of the complacent singing sanguine praise songs to a cocksure God. I'm reminded of Annie Dillard's notion that if Christians in the pews realized what they were participating in through Eucharist, they would wear crash helmets to church. Doxology is the point at which grief becomes political.

I grew up in Albany, Georgia, during the civil rights movement. My father had a clothing store on Broad Avenue, scene of extreme violence against the emboldened and untiring protestors. I would stand on the corner and watch in horror. Also, on weeknights, I would ride with my mother to "colored town" to take our "maid" home. On many a night, as we drove down either a dusty or muddy road past a dilapidated, white clapboard church, I would hear undulating, unnerving, exhilarating, destabilizing, jubilant song so energized as to almost break down the walls and raise the roof.

I sensed then and believe now that there was an unbreakable bond between what happened between those walls, under that roof, and on Broad Avenue. Martin Luther King Jr., Andrew Young, Julian Bond, Jesse Jackson, and John Edwards led the marches past my father's store. Those behind them embodied the uncontainable passion.

Some forty years later, two Februarys ago, at the beginning of Black Awareness Month, I received an e-mail about a campaign to get the TV documentary series *Eyes On The Prize*, the most celebrated history of the civil rights movement, back on air after over a decade in the archives. The documentary had been imprisoned by copyright restrictions that on the surface seem bureaucratic, but, when scratched, smell of what Walter Brueggemann calls Royal Consciousness, economics of affluence, politics of oppression, and religion of immanence (2001, 30). Civil rights leader Lawrence Guyot said that the restrictions are analogous to the books of Martin Luther King Jr. and Malcolm X being banned. He continued, "If people had stuck to the law, black people wouldn't have the right to use restaurants and hotels."

If not by fine print and legalese, the regnant dominion drowns out *Eyes On The Prize* by reciting its official doctrine, optimism (Hall 1996, 463), to the middle majority, lulled into dreams of gated communities by the illusion of a prosperous present. The regnant dominion keeps trying to hum the citizenry to sleep, fearing that the strangely joyous lament of the grieving and aggrieved community of the marginalized will be heard. The outsiders' strident hope for the future threatens the insiders' obsessive concern for the present, and has compromised the future. The evidence can be found in the Bush administration's willingness to hand down to our children an almost unimaginable debt and an increasingly pillaged environment in the service of the moment.

In spite of what church has mostly become in the United States—pathos coopted by patriotism—the Judeo-Christian witness is rooted in grief. The ministry of Jesus, and of those who came before him—Moses, Jeremiah, Isaiah, Amos, Micah—codified the stories of incomprehensible wailing of the abandoned into songs of lamentation among the dispossessed, creating joyous solidarity dangerous to the prosperity of temple and town.

I believe the principle task of the church in the present-day United States is to reclaim and restore our Judeo-Christian pathos, a tradition of grieving that both encourages and equips us to embrace our present experiences of suffering and death toward freeing engagement in and for a world groaning in travail. We have a rich tradition to draw from, what Johann Baptist Metz calls a "dangerous memory" that loosens the grip of dominant claims about life (Thornton 2002, 133): "Memory has a fundamental theological importance as what may be termed anamnetic solidarity or solidarity in memory with the dead and the conquered which breaks the grip of history as a history of triumph and conquest interpreted dialectically or as evolution" (Metz 1980, 184).

Anamnesis solidarity plays a powerful role in worship, such as at the services of Watts Street Baptist Church in Durham, North Carolina. The congregation begins services with "Psalms of Lament," what they call "the public processing of pain." They take their processed pain to the streets, holding prayer vigils at the site of each violent death in Durham (Brueggemann 2001, 122).

The Gospel Is "Grief Work" Gone Public

Public grief offers more than the road to freedom for the oppressed. Public grief creates the strongest possibility for more genuine reconciliation between perpetrators of violence, tyranny, power abuses, and their victims. The Christ of God illumined through the eighth-century prophets and Jesus yearns for a cosmos throughout which all that is estranged is reconciled. Reconciliation worth its salt begins with the victims' public expression of grief and, if at all possible, in the presence of their perpetrators.

Many processes of reconciliation fail because the victims are decentered. Extraneous recipes for reconciliation are imposed on victims by those who either pretend, or presume, to act on their behalf. The voices of the victims are patronized and, at worst, silenced. When the voices of victims are at the center of the reconciliation process, and effectively heard, their first and strongest voice is the story of their pain and loss told in as much detail as possible to those who have hurt them.

Archbishop Desmond Tutu, after the first public hearings of the Truth and Reconciliation Commission in South Africa, received a poem from a radio listener who heard the broadcast testimonies of several victims:

The world is wept. Blood and pain seep into our listening; into our wounded souls. The sound of your sobbing is my own weeping; your wet handkerchief my pillow for a past so exhausted it cannot rest—not yet. Speak, weep, look, listen for us all. Oh, people of the silent hidden past, let your stories scatter seeds into our lonely frightened winds. Sow more, until the stillness of this land can soften, can dare to hope and smile and sing; until the ghosts can dance unshackled, until our lives can know your sorrows and be healed. (1999, 119)

The most startling finding of the Truth and Reconciliation Commission was how much of the work was accomplished in the simple yet excruciating recollection by the victims of their experiences, the grief brought to light and life through the sharing of memory, and the possibility for forgiveness that emerged from the sharing of sorrows. While forgiveness and reconciliation do not always follow from public and publicized grief, very rarely do they occur when communal and communicated mourning is overlooked or bypassed.

Public grief also creates the strongest possibility for more genuine reconciliation between nations in conflict. Conflict resolution expert Olga Botcharova has worked tirelessly and effectively in Bosnia, Serbia, and Croatia. She writes that violated nations move to knee-jerk positions of invincibility that exacerbate further violence because they do not take the necessary time to grieve losses and attend to suffering (2001, 279–304). Botcharova has found that through an intentional, timely, and persistent sharing of the pain caused by violation, space is opened for options other than retaliation; solutions are found that are broader than the thin détente that most often exists.

What if, as writer David Grossman suggested in the February 8, 2005, issue of the *Los Angeles Times*, the peace talks between Israel and Palestine began with the acknowledgment and sharing of the suffering each had caused the other? Possibly a passage toward peace would begin with confession: "We're sorry." Such a beginning would augur for a resolution stronger than that built on hostility and suspicion, the kind of solution that extends one hand in peace and withholds another hand so as to keep a firm grip on the guns.

What if America had mourned 9/11 for more than the proverbial three days? Possibly we would have been less complacent about and compliant with the then-administration's Armageddon-like response of big and bigger bombs first in Afghanistan and second in Iraq. What nation is next?

I'll say it again, this time more emphatically, given the church's penchant to present herself, for sufficiency's sake, as a loudspeaker for current American cultural idealism and imperial political agendas and initiatives: Public and publicized grief is the ecclesiology most faithful to our Judeo-Christian heritage, central to distinguishing our faith communities from the power and principalities that hold this eon captive by insidious stun guns of prosperity that numb the populace into complacency. It is also essential for waging a nonviolent revolt against regal consciousness, thus elemental for prospering the reign of God. The construction and heralding of narratives of grief in the pastor's study, at adult forums, during Eucharist and other liturgies of loss, beside the water cooler, from the vestry meetings, among those eating lunch at the soup kitchen, through choir rehearsal, break open the deadness of spirit that imprisons our compassionate hearts. "The beginning of noticed pain," says Walter Brueggemann, "signals a social revolution" (2001, 91).

Faith communities are both assumed and summoned to be the stewards of public and publicized grief. What follows are a foundation for and five pieces of sacramental gear that faith communities may steward in the work of overseeing the faith community's building and proclaiming of grief narratives. More recently, I have come to pray the foundation. Over the years, I have come to trust the application of the five elements across the spectrum of the classical pastoral functions (Thornton 2002, 3)—guiding, healing, sustaining, and reconciling—and within the many contexts of pastoral presence—conversation, visitation, preaching, liturgy, teaching, facilitation of meetings, conflict resolution, evangelism, supervision, discernment, social and political action.

Grounded for and by a Howling God

Then Jesus gave a loud cry and breathed his last. And the curtain of the temple was torn in two, from top to bottom. (Mark 15:37-38)

And the earth shook and the rocks split. (Matt. 27:51)

In the story of the crucifixion, at the moment of Jesus' death, God exposed God's own self—not revealed, exposed. The burning bush and backside of Yahweh are displaced by a full frontal (Brown and Miller 2005, 59). In *Preaching Mark in Two Voices*, by Brian K. Blount and Gary W. Charles, Charles writes that "the passive voice of the verb, schizo, indicates that this rendering is the divine response to the death of Jesus; the tense and meaning of this verb suggest a violent, completed, and decisive action. As God rends the veil (katapetasma) of the sanctuary (naos), that which divided the holy from the profane is removed" (2002, 240). God's unattached wailing violently, aggressively, uncontrollably crosses the boundaries of the acceptable and sane, the predictable and containable. God is out there, as parents are when the incomprehensible abyss that is the death of a child severs oneself in two, shakes one loose from the sturdiest bearings, splits one's world wide open, leaving one wholly exposed.

When I pray, as I often do when called across thresholds of relative order into the chaos of broken persons and communities, and, when I try to grab hold amidst my own world's tremors and terrors, I find myself grounded by the image of the God of Abraham and his children wrenched loose and left open by utter loss. Besides the comfort of good company—Emmanuel: God with us—proximate others oftentimes are transposed into Other: "Is not the face of one's fellow [sister or brother] the original locus in which transcendence calls an authority with a silent voice in which God comes to mind?" (Lévinas 1999, 5). When others become Other, good pastoral presence as action and goal becomes blasphemous. The pastoral response of "Say more about that" and "If your scream could write a letter, what would the first sentence be?" might melt both message and messenger. Who dares to speak? Might the offering of a tongue rendered mute be enough and plenty?

Silence

Ann, the consulting psychiatrist, entered the noisy room of the six family members and therapist who were mired in an incomprehensible wailing that had yet to be voiced. She could have cleared her throat, and said, as I probably would have said, "Okay, good morning, let's get started, who wants to begin?" Instead, she sat silently for a while.

Ann's silence was, I believe, more respectful than strategic. Respect for those who suffer imposes a silence (Soelle 1975, 69). Pastoral theologian Sharon Thornton writes that the pastoral caregiver's place of silence at the feet of those who are grieving and aggrieved, when shed of professional trappings and contrivances, and grounded in an open heart, is best described as a sacramental-like act of beholding (2002, 204). Beholding is the beginning place of relation, prior to description and resistant to explanation, by which ordinary time is transposed into sacred moment. It is like the time, during Eucharist, when I as celebrant break the bread of God's broken body, hold the severed remains in two hands, and lift the pieces for the congregation to behold. The rubric in *The Book of Common Prayer* reads, "A period of silence is kept." I rather think an experience of silence is created.

Howard Thurman, in discussing the woman brought before Jesus for adultery (1981, 105–06), writes, "Jesus raised his eyes and beheld the woman." Jesus' initial silence was not a "Rogerian notion of unconditional positive regard" (Thornton 2002, 201). Rather, Jesus' silence was an act of absolute respect that involves a commitment to the deep humanness of others (ibid.). Jesus did not "accept" the woman "in spite" of her adultery, a "liberal" position that is implicitly judgmental; he honored the gift of her being. The woman's sex life was irrelevant.

Listening

Silence as respectful attention is not the beginning of a linear process of pastoral talk, the hush before the rush of dialogue. Rather, silence is the spring from which those who are beheld find the fresh water of words to communicate their experience. Hence, silence is a listening that watches and waits and receives what the others are able and willing to share.

Ann's silence among the six family members and therapist enabled her to eventually name no more or less than that which those around her offered, incomprehensible wailing, respectfully received: "There is much noise." Ann's simple and sublime naming is rich with insights critical to the dynamic that moves incomprehensible wailing to convivial lamentation, toward joyful solidarity that liberates.

The late and greatly beloved family therapist Harry Goolishian once said, "Listen to what they really say, and not to what they really mean" (Andersen 2002, 18). Goolishian's psychology was spiced with Ludwig Wittgenstein's philosophy, "The aspects of things that are most important for us are hidden because of their simplicity and familiarity. One is unable to notice something because it is always before our eyes" (1953, 129). Expressions are not gleanings from internal constructs; they are social contributions, gifts for participating in bonds with others. Expressions bewitch understanding, not vice versa (Andersen 2002, 8).

As pastoral caregivers, we usually feel compelled to get at and understand what someone means, as if our task is the deliverance of meaning. How often I have said things to the sorrowful and traumatized because I believed I needed to say anything that counted for something. The pastoral vocation is, first and last, about relation, not deliverance. Furthermore, the meaning, hope, freedom, and healing born of relation does not need to be legitimatized "from above" as an "in-breaking," a grace we give thanks for, participate in, and yearn for more of. Relation is good enough.

So, good news: grief work requires no experts. The words the grieving and aggrieved share with us are not to be adroitly mined but valued, cherished, treasured, qualities born of an innate, "naïve" curiosity (Monk et al. 1997, 302). To assume that the words have hidden meaning requiring our excavation is to cross beyond the boundary of that which is offered, which is a violation of the others' spirit. Words are gifts, not clues.

Gifts are to be opened. Ann says, "I wonder, if noise could speak, what would noise have to say to us?" The grandfather answers, "Noise would say that we need to speak." The grandfather continues, "There is much to talk about that needs to be talked about but is hard to talk about." Ann respectfully checks with the family to see if it's okay to continue to open the gift, "Is this too hard to bring to words now? What do you think? Should we talk or not?" The grandfather concludes, "We must talk about my cancer."

The grandfather, I believe, did not come to the session or wait for a time in the session to say, "We must talk about my cancer." The grandfather did not know what he was going to say before he said it (Monk et al. 1997, 6), as if the "unsaid" already exists, waiting for its time, waiting to be noticed, discovered, or "unearthed" by the craft of the therapist (Freedman and Combs 1996, 44–45). The initially silent Ann, paying respectful attention to the noise of incomprehensible wailing, allowed those in the room to name the not yet known, and through such naming, be heard to be a voice of lamentation. The voice of lamentation was a new, previously unstoried narrative, co-constructed by therapists and family (ibid., 46) in solidarity, awakening a previously unimagined future ripe with fresh possibility.

The Reverend Glenda Hope talks about a "life stance of thankfulness" that waits for God's guidance in silence (Thornton 2002, 201)—what her friend, Sharon Thornton, suggested "we might call contemplative listening, a disciplined kind of listening in which we attempt to disregard any of our preconceived notions, theories, and hunches about someone and their experiences" (ibid.).

Contemplative listening cautions us to take a careful position in respect to the heretofore crown jewel of pastoral caring—empathy (ibid.). Empathy presumes the possibility of knowing the other, and privileges the act of knowing the other. The assumption that we share an understanding with another as result of a resonant connection may violate the space or particularity of the other. Contemplative listening "brackets empathy with a 'hermeneutic of suspicion'" and invites us to participate with the grieving and aggrieved in cocreating the not yet known, an imaginative enterprise of restoring "dignity, freedom and hope" (ibid.).

Charting Absence

When the women went to the tomb to anoint Jesus, he was absent. Mary Magdalene's anxious cry is a collect over their desperation: "They have taken away my Lord and I do not know where they have laid him" (John 20:13).

Public grief work begins with companions walking toward an empty tomb, a labyrinth circling to a center of absence, where together we stand and cry for ourselves and for our loved ones. One of Chile's women said: "Every time I see a madman or a hobo in the street I think it may be my husband, or that he might be somewhere in a similar situation" (Schreiter 1998, 33). The one request of a woman who lost a son to apartheid was that South Africa provide a tombstone for a body never found. A survivor of child sexual abuse prays for memories, as painful as they may be, from which to orient her horror.

I spent ten years among people dying from AIDS during the first wave of the pandemic. Those who died were young and, for the most part, healthy prior to onset of the disease. One of the most remarkable dimensions of their dying was the horrific wasting and disfigurement of their bodies. I remember the fevered passion with which we created squares for the AIDS quilt that sought to recapture and reconfigure the profiles of their once sufficient and embodied lives. And we relished every chance to join the squares together on the mall between the White House and the Capitol.

Our relation to those who have died or disappeared doesn't end; it changes. Yet, change demands a touchstone from which to depart. Marking death and disappearance in concrete and material ways is the beginning of the journey. Ritual and liturgy are our instruments of peace. We have the aforementioned Judeo-Christian tradition of "dangerous memories." We have the voices of present victims, who, when their voices are heard, can collaborate with the stewards of ritual and liturgy to mark the tombstones of their sorrow and anguish. As we gather around the victims and their cocreated tombstones, their memories become the community's memory. The community's memory is dangerous to the stasis that preserves ecclesial and political dominance.

Reiteration

On the road to Emmaus, two disciples are fleeing the pain of Jesus' execution and the city in which it happened. A stranger approaches and accompanies them along the way. A dialogue ensues over the afternoon and evening that transposes an oppressive story into a redemptive one.

The grieving and aggrieved need a predictable and consistent audience for telling and retelling their stories, over and over again (ibid., 43, 46). The purpose of repetition is not to talk ourselves away from the past, to forget the past, but to remember the past in a new way. At the time of loss and trauma, the words shared don't necessarily convey the meaning desired. The narrative that will conquer the pain, stave off the abyss of nothingness, transform the memory, enable us to move ahead is a cacophony of words slowly but surely co-constructed into a liberative language in and from which a preferred future is cocreated. A liberative story is built by sharing old and new word arrangements over and over again. There is no telling how often stories of sorrow and tragedy need repeating in order for a new perspective, a glimpse of meaning, an unforeseen path, a previously unimaginable forgiveness, a once-closed future to open. Such openings are not outcomes. Again, they are moments of grace (ibid., 46). Public grief work as narrative construction is an anticipatory and active waiting.

Hospitality

The atmosphere in which pastoral caregivers wait with the grieving and aggrieved in repetitive conversation needs to be carefully considered. When Jesus cooked breakfast on the seashore for his bereaved disciples, fishermen, he prepared fish: not his fish, their fish (ibid., 89).

When building our AIDS hospice, we collaborated with the finest interior designers in the Northeast to create spaces that were extravagantly welcoming—Mapplethorpe prints, one ceiling painted as clouds, another as a trellis entwined with grapevines. Our guests mostly were unimpressed. We had prepared deathbeds at the Ritz. They desired deathbeds that reflected the spirit and tastes of the homes they had to leave.

I'm reminded of an experience in a Rwandan refugee camp. Children were given crayons so that they could draw their experiences of loss, their feelings of trauma. The children ate the crayons. They were hungry and had never seen crayons before (ibid., 107).

With hands carrying carefully prepared recipes of compassion, we are apt to trip over the rug of our cultural biases and power advantage, spilling our impotent good will in the laps of our guests. Godly hospitality is a moveable feast, one that moves from our hearths to the hearths of our neighbors. Hospitality that empowers those dislocated by loss and trauma decenters the host and centers the guest. As decentered hosts, we will feel awkward, disempowered, the ones interpreted rather than the ones interpreting, those beheld in uncomfortable ways by the beneficiaries of our regard. Our own disorientation possibly is the strongest connection we may have to the disoriented ones to whom we attend. We become more like than unlike them. The distance between caregiver and cared for closes; the distinction between server and served is lost. Mutuality is established.

A Conclusion

Faith communities that dare to embark on an ecclesiology of public and publicized grief most likely will suffer, particularly in a time when the dominant religious discourse is about triumph. Triumphalism not only infuses the conservative churches that, say, march into worship to "The Star-Spangled Banner." Triumphalism permeates progressive churches as well. More progressive denominations and parishes assume that they are compelled to focus on growth in numbers of persons and dollars to account for loss in membership and expensive buildings handed down from a previous era of prosperity and power.

Faith communities that drink from the "dangerous memory" that is a Judeo-Christian heritage purified of its historical equivocation to temple and town, that feast off the redeemed memories and restored future of the broken, are likely to fail the imposed and/or presumed indicators of survival and success, which, it seems, are finally about accommodation. Those left unaccommodated by the transposition of wailing, lamentation, and solidarity—often those with deeper pockets and more connections—probably will leave. Budgets will hemorrhage. Buildings will leak and crack. Endowments will shrink. Pews will offer more than the eighteen inches between people that the church growth experts suggest.

What's left of daring churches that more richly develop the wailing–lamentation–solidarity dynamic may be a post-Christian community that resembles the pre-Christian community that witnessed Jesus' execution—his mother, the beloved disciple, an aunt, and a cherished friend. I believe that the faithful who remain steadfast in these "failing" churches most likely will hear the faint promise of a new, unorthodox, organic, dependent, fragile community: "When Jesus saw his mother and the disciple whom he loved standing beside her, he said to his mother, 'Woman, here is your son.' Then he said to the disciple, 'Here is your mother.' And from that hour the disciple took her into his own home" (John 19:26). From house church such as this, heaven is made.

The post-Christian house church does not necessarily need to exist in opposition to, and define itself against, mainline church. The house church of the grieving and the aggrieved, if heard as a principal voice amidst the other voices in and of denominational and parish life, can infuse and, over time, revive a dying institution.

Age old choruses of hope-filled hallelujahs ring through the Judeo-Christian tradition, beginning with Genesis 1:1-2, when the Spirit moved over chaos and emptiness, and stretching through time to a once-widowed parishioner embracing a just-widowed parishioner, after Eucharist, in the narthex, last Sunday, with other parishioners gathering around to shelter. Each day, "Amens!" such as these repoint the crumbling mortar between a few more bricks on the tired façade of Christendom. When and as we privilege these "Amens!" in the daily life of our faith communities, the restoration of our tradition progresses more swiftly.

FIFTEEN

Pastoral Care with Persons Living with HIV/AIDS

Altagracia Perez

When Jesus was at table in the house, many bad characters—tax-gatherers and others—were seated with him and his disciples. The Pharisees noticed this, and said to his disciples, "Why is it that your master eats with tax-gatherers and sinners?" Jesus heard it and said, "It is not the healthy that need a doctor, but the sick. Go and learn what that text means, 'I require mercy, not sacrifice.' I did not come to invite virtuous people, but sinners."
(Matt. 9:10-13, NEB)

Many times throughout the Gospels Jesus was painfully clear that he was at odds with the values of the religious establishment of his time. His good news message was focused on salvation for all who were lost. He preached, he healed, and he forgave whether the person was considered "good" or "bad" in the eyes of the religious. The pious and the virtuous were at a loss because this was not their understanding of God's righteousness.

In the mid-1980s many righteous and religious people were again faced with a confusing gospel reality. A mysterious disease was infecting a segment of the population that was seen as living in sin. Gay men were dying and no one knew why. It seemed mysterious—like an act of God. There were others dying, too—without notice. Intravenous drug users were dying of the same mysterious virus. They, too, seemed to be reaping the consequences of sin.

In the midst of this human tragedy many in the religious establishment were clear that this disease and death were a consequence of sinful behavior. Very few churches, but among them some Episcopal churches, saw it as an opportunity to preach love, offer forgiveness, and heal. As the years passed and the few deaths became an epidemic it became clear that the virus was not selective. Now women and children, heterosexuals and persons who required transfusions, all were susceptible to infection. There was a full-blown epidemic at hand and all of the righteous establishments created for the good of the people—government, churches, and schools—were pretending that it did not exist, and refused to serve the people affected by it.

More than twenty years into the HIV pandemic many things have changed. What has not changed is the seemingly unique ability of this virus to cause all of us to examine what we expect of human community, what the institutions we have created have done to improve or worsen individual quality of life, and how we will talk about government, religion, and all other social institutions in the face of this pandemic.

The quality of the challenge of this pandemic is such that any person interested in any aspect of human services could work on it in the AIDS field. The HIV/AIDS pandemic has had an impact on every area of life: nutrition, housing, medical benefits, employment, politics, academia, religion, sexuality, addiction, mental health, and, of course, physical health. Every social structure created to assist in living has been challenged, and taxed.

It is for this reason that those who are on the underside of history, those who because of prejudice and injustice are not privy to a full life equal to those with means, power, and privilege, are disproportionately affected by this disease and by this pandemic. They have not had equal access to social institutions and their benefits. Those whose life vocation is to serve people in need, whatever the field, must understand the complex socioeconomic, political, and spiritual impacts this disease has on people. It is a prime case study for the complexities of service and ministry, and a good teacher of the truth that there is always more to do than can be done. Yet what we do and the sensitivity and care with which we approach our work can make a great difference in the quality of many people's lives.

What Is HIV/AIDS?

The precise origin of the human immunodeficiency virus (HIV) is not known. Although it is similar to viruses found among animals, there is no way of knowing how the virus came to be introduced into the human population. Because the virus mutates rapidly, it is possible that it sat dormant for many years and only recently has mutated to the current virus with its devastating impact on the human immune system and the complex of symptoms known as AIDS.

The HIV virus attaches itself to human immune cells and through replication takes their place, depleting the body of the immune cells that fight diseases. The weakened immune system leaves the body vulnerable to certain cancers and opportunistic infections, which could not have taken hold in a body with a healthy immune system. AIDS—Acquired Immunodeficiency Syndrome—is a complex of symptoms, diseases, and infections that occur when the immune system is completely compromised because of the advanced stage of HIV infection.

The virus is transmitted through unprotected sexual contact, and through use of infected needles. The vaginal and seminal fluids and blood of infected persons, if introduced into the body, will transmit the virus. In order to prevent infection persons should use prophylactics (condoms and dental dams) during sexual intercourse in order to prevent contact with their partner's body fluids. Injection drug users must use clean needles; they should not share needles or should clean their needles, syringes, and other paraphernalia with a 10 percent bleach solution for disinfection.

There is no vaccine for HIV. Treatment for this infection consists of medications that slow down the replication of the virus, thus conserving the immune system, and treatment for the opportunistic infections. The medication therapy is expensive, often costing as much as $12,000 a year, and usually there is need for treatment of serious side effects as well as infections, which add to the cost for treatment. Persons have been known to live with compromised immune systems for a long time, but until there is a cure or a vaccine HIV/AIDS is a chronic fatal illness.

What Does the HIV/AIDS Infected Population Look Like?

When HIV was first identified it was primarily discovered among white, homosexual men. There were cases of infection among injection drug users, but this was not widely known. The greatest numbers of infected persons in the 1990s were from these two populations and their sexual partners. As the decades passed, the face of HIV/AIDS infection changed. Increasingly new infections were among women and people of color. Disproportionately the communities most affected are communities of color. In 2003 African Americans accounted for 49 percent of diagnoses, Latinos 20 percent, and whites (non-Hispanic) 28 percent. These numbers are all the more shocking when we remember the percentages of these communities in the population of the United States. Of the estimated 290,809,777 people in the United States in 2003, 14 percent are African American, 14 percent are Latino, and 69 percent are white, non-Hispanic. The numbers are staggering. The increase in infections among women is also a cause for concern. The Center for Disease Control says that in 1986 women accounted for 7 percent of new AIDS cases. In 2001 that number was up to 25 percent. Of these new cases among women, 64 percent were African American women and 17 percent were Latinas. Again these numbers are disproportionate to their numbers in the general population and the rate of increase continues to rise.

The ways in which persons become infected is also important in understanding the complexities of this disease. It is estimated that 75 percent of infections among women are from heterosexual contact, with the rest coming from injection drug use. For men, sexual contact with other men continues to be the number one method of transmission. The second most common method is injection drug use with a combination of both of these modes being the third most reported method of transmission. Issues of sexuality and drug use are taboo in most, if not all, U.S. communities. Add to this the stigma already suffered by communities of color and women—who through oppression (racism and sexism) have already been highly sexualized. People of color and women are often described as especially "physical" and sexual by nature. This in turn has led to sensitivity and defensiveness in these communities when issues of homosexuality or promiscuity or substance use are raised. It is a challenge to overcome this barrier in HIV/AIDS prevention education, and there is a need to take this into account when addressing this topic among these oppressed communities.

Injustice's Consequences for the HIV/AIDS Pandemic

This disease has always been a social issue. Although many in an earlier generation would whisper about cancer, it never had the social stigma of HIV/AIDS. The community first identified with this disease was one that had been condemned by the dominant culture as the epitome of evil. The prejudice against homosexuals only fueled the fear of this unknown disease. In the incredible book by Randy Shilts, *And the Band Played On*, the author chronicles the beginning of the disease in 1976 when all the world came to the greatest party of the century in New York, and the almost ten years that it took before the public was made fully aware that there was a serious problem in their midst. The death of Rock Hudson was the first awareness for most people about the numbers of persons infected. Some of the most influential establishments in our society, including the medical, political, and media leaders, evaded and delayed while thousands of people became infected and died across the country. Scientists seemed to be working at odds with each other instead of working to end the health crisis. Politicians totally ignored the severity of the crisis, with communities outraged at President Reagan's unwillingness to even acknowledge that there was a crisis. The media worked at scandal and scary headlines, but failed to cover the news of what was really happening. Were it not for the social acceptability of homophobia and heterosexist norms, this could not have happened. The fact that the gay community was perceived as expendable allowed the virus to spread wildly without the public awareness, research, and basic public health responses that were required (Shilts 1987).

The next communities to be identified at risk were injection drug users and Haitians. These communities were also seen as an unfair burden on U.S. society. The fact that for many years Haitians and other racial/ethnic groups were identified as high risk for this disease exacerbated the lack of knowledge and understanding about transmission. It took years for advocates and activists to insist that classification of risk be made based not on racial/ethnic group identity but upon behavior and modes of transmission. Again the communities identified as infected allowed the majority of people to assume that this virus was something that did not affect them and that reinforced racial/ethnic prejudices already present in the society.

The groups that became identified with the virus in what came to be known as the second wave of the epidemic also lacked the economic resources to respond to the epidemic. Communities with little or no access to health care because of their immigration and/or economic status did not seek medical treatment at the first symptoms of the disease, as was happening in the gay community, which became much better educated and organized to respond to early symptoms.

The whole evolution of this pandemic has been marked from the beginning with the social stigma and prejudice held against minority populations within the United States. This was only complicated when low-income and indigent persons were diagnosed as being at high risk. As women become the newest face of AIDS, they bring the challenges that women continue to face in a male-dominated culture.

Women and children present different challenges to methods of diagnosis, treatment, and service. The symptoms women presented in the early stages of infection were not those that medical personnel were trained to identify. Studies conducted primarily among men did not provide the information necessary to diagnose and treat women. The medications that were beginning to prove effective for men were not working for women, and this presented a whole new set of concerns. Women who were pregnant were at risk of transmitting the virus to their newborns during the birth process and while breast-feeding. All of these conditions were not the ones under which medical trials were conducted. Advocates have worked to increase the numbers of women included in clinical trials for the medications being developed.

This approach, however, is only partly responsive to the challenges that women face. The Joint United Nations Programme on HIV/AIDS (UNAIDS) presents the following as some of the reasons why the infection rate among women is increasing:

- sexual subordination (in many countries men control the sexual relationships between men and women);
- economic subordination (in almost every society, women face discrimination in education, employment, and social status); and
- female biological vulnerability to HIV (women are more likely to get sexually transmitted diseases [STDs] and/or transmit them to their unborn babies).

Although the status of women in the United States is better than that of women in the developing world, these challenges continue to be true for U.S. women and are especially true for women of color and poor women. Prevention is a challenge because women who are at higher risk for poor health outcomes are also, by extension, at higher risk for HIV infection. Women in abusive relationships are less able to insist on protected sex for fear of battery (emotional and physical). Younger women in relationships with older men are also at a disadvantage in negotiating safer sex. All of these add to the complexities of responding to the spread of the virus. Unlike the gay community, which through education and awareness was able to decrease the number of new infections, the oppression of women diminishes their power to respond in similar lifesaving ways.

Women and children also present a challenge to service providers. The ability to comply and to participate in all the necessary appointments with doctors, caseworkers, and therapists is a challenge for women with children. Service providers have had to make provision for childcare, transportation, and other ancillary and supportive services that make it possible for women to receive treatment and care.

Until now we have discussed the social challenges to the minority communities who suffer with the virus under conditions already made difficult through discrimination and poverty. Also at play is the psychological impact of oppression on these communities. The Surgeon General's 2001 report, "Mental Health: Culture, Race and Ethnicity," describes the impact of the recent terrorist attacks on marginalized communities: "Ethnic and racial groups face socioeconomic inequality that makes them disproportionately vulnerable to violence, discrimination, and poor health." These factors exacerbate mental health problems, and, like terrorism, any major stressor will have more debilitating consequences for these groups. Many studies have made the connection between discrimination and mental well-being. Feelings of frustration, repressed anger, depression, and despair are all common among people who suffer discrimination. When the stigma of HIV/AIDS is added to a community already living under siege, the ability to respond is negatively affected. It is difficult to make life-saving/life-giving choices when in a state of chronic depression. It is difficult to deal with added financial pressures in a family that is already struggling with poverty.

In the black community distrust of the public health system led many to disbelieve prevention and treatment messages. The Tuskegee experiments that took place from 1932 to 1972, where black men were purposely infected with syphilis, has made it very difficult for government agencies to credibly disseminate prevention and treatment information. The sterilization abuse suffered by women of color has also led to a distrust of medical institutions. In Puerto Rico from 1930 to 1970 women were routinely sterilized through coercion, deceit, or without consent. In 1975, ten Chicana women filed a lawsuit against Los Angeles County Hospital for the same reasons. The communal knowledge that public health systems have often been coconspirators in the oppression of communities of color makes them unlikely sources of trustworthy intervention and prevention for HIV/AIDS. When we add concerns about immigration status and the impact that has on willingness to engage the authorities, we can see that there are many reasons why people from oppressed minority communities have a difficult time going to public institutions for help.

Death rates due to HIV/AIDS paint an all-too-clear picture of the consequences of these barriers to health access in minority communities. While new medications have caused the rate of death due to AIDS to drop among whites, it has continued to rise in communities of color. A U.S. Department of Health and Human Services fact sheet summarizing the need to eliminate disparities in health outcomes among minority communities describes the problem this way: "African Americans are ten times more likely to die of AIDS than Whites. AIDS is the leading cause of death in African American women aged 25–34 and the third leading cause of death in African American men in the same age group. . . . Hispanics were also almost three times more likely to die of AIDS than their White counterparts in 2001."

In racial/ethnic minority communities the infection and death rate are related to a lack of good information, access to timely medical treatment, and complications from other issues of discrimination and oppression. But even in the white gay community there has recently been an increase in the number of infections, especially among young men. This has been attributed in part to a misunderstanding about the medications available to treat people with HIV/AIDS. The fact that there is medicine that prolongs life has led some to think that there is a cure, that this disease can be managed like other serious illness such as diabetes, hypertension, and so forth. The message that emphasizes the need to be safe when engaging in risky behaviors is not being communicated as clearly or as often as it was in the 1980s and '90s.

To seek to respond with care and compassion to the communities being devastated by the HIV/AIDS pandemic without taking into account the disparities that exist among the different communities infected is difficult at best. This is not just another health concern that can be dealt with by supplying information and medication. Being able to provide what is needed in a way that will be received requires an understanding of the barriers that exist, why there is distrust, and what seems like a lack of response to a disease that is so obviously devastating the community.

A Response of Faith

The challenges for those dealing with this pandemic on a daily basis at times seem insurmountable. The seeming intractability of the disparity in infection and death rates is depressing. The despair of the families that continue to suffer with this disease in silence is terrible. For those communities that have had success in the past educating and protecting the community there is a renewed commitment to take care of business and not rely on government support to take care of the problem in the community. But for those communities that have never seen a significant drop in infection rates, strategies have to be developed, designed, and implemented to make a real difference in this battle.

As people are faced with the reality that the stigma around HIV/AIDS has not diminished in communities of color, and that "silence = death" (as the 1980s slogan said), it is important that the word begin to be spread that there are ways of protecting the community from the devastating effects of this disease. The epidemic is pervasive and in any given neighborhood, everyone knows someone who is being affected by it. What is important, then, is to get the message out to everyone, especially to those who are obviously at risk due to their behaviors. But increasingly information needs to get to those who are at home and are unaware that they might be at risk.

Many think that churches are critical to this message getting to those most in need of hearing it. There are many efforts, funded in part with government funds, to bring the religious community to the table, to design messages that can be shared in the context of the congregation, to have congregation-based testing campaigns and information and referral programs to help connect people with culturally sensitive programs that provide comprehensive services. However, too many churches in minority communities still have not taken their place as part of the team working against this pandemic. Charles Wilson from the People of Color Against AIDS Network, a Seattle-based nonprofit, expresses what many across the country feel: "they [congregations] don't believe it's necessary. . . . They say if you're not engaging in a sinful act, then you don't have to worry about HIV." This argument, still used by many churches to avoid involvement in this epidemic, is simply not true. As we have seen, the largest increase is among women who are engaging in heterosexual activity, often with partners with whom they believe they are in monogamous relationships or whose drug use is unknown to them. Besides the clear fallaciousness of this argument, there is the challenge of Jesus' own words, with which we began.

The church is in the business of offering love, forgiveness, and health to all for whom Christ died. This message is universal, as we are reminded in 1 John 1:8: "If we say that we have no sin, we deceive ourselves, and the truth is not in us." Some churches have begun to live into this, moved by the devastating effects of the epidemic in their local congregations. There are now networks and resources being created in most major cities, established by churches to work together with community organizations to end this epidemic, especially in communities of color. In southern California, religious leaders have partnered with the county health departments and local groups to create a resource book with basic facts, strategies, and sermon ideas that can be used by black churches to begin to address this issue in their congregations. This guidebook, entitled *Healing Begins Here: A Pastor's Guidebook for HIV/AIDS Ministry through the Church*, is sensitive to the challenges faced by some churches, and offers a way to craft a message that can be helpful without churches violating their own teachings or principles. Resources like these are being created for the Latino community as well, so as to work with those churches that have not traditionally engaged in community education projects, such as conservative evangelicals and Pentecostals.

It is important that churches be challenged both from within and without with their true mission. What is sad is that it doesn't take much to make a big difference. The primary goal is to increase and positively affect the messages about HIV/AIDS within the community.

Sermons that discuss the reality of the pandemic using local statistics and stories and that call for a compassionate and caring response from the Christian community are one way to begin to create an atmosphere of openness around this infection. Having the leadership take a nonjudgmental posture, using language of forgiveness and service, will set the tone for discussions within the congregation. Having pastors' forums and workshops for different age groups that emphasize prevention and the available community resources are other ways of increasing the sharing of positive messages. Congregations that feel it is against church teaching to discuss condoms, or to seem to accept extramarital sex and drug use, can still invite a health professional to share basic public health information, with the pastor introducing the presenter with a few words about church teaching and the reason why it has become critical that these workshops be offered in the church for the whole community. Clarifying that the information is meant to empower community members to share lifesaving information in the community as part of the good news that they are called to share in every area of life is another way to get around discomfort among church leadership.

The truth is that even if the congregation's leadership does not feel comfortable sponsoring workshops, having them allow health/community groups to come to the church to set up tables with information and resources designed for the community goes a long way toward creating an atmosphere of openness and emphasizing the importance of intervening in the continued growth of infection in the community.

Many denominations also have resources that have been designed specifically for use with youth groups and Bible study groups. These can be adopted for minority communities, taking into account the historical factors of discrimination and prejudice that affect those communities.

Counseling also needs to be done with sensitivity to the situation and the reality that people have lived with for generations. The despair, guilt, and suffering experienced by people living with HIV/AIDS needs to be addressed with a message of hope, the hope of the resurrection, always remembering that God's message of unconditional love and forgiveness is for just such as these. It is important for church leadership to learn basic facts about HIV/AIDS and have some knowledge of local community resources available for referral. Pastoral counseling will play an important role in giving hope and strength to persons who are themselves infected, or whose lives are being affected through the presence of the disease among family members and other loved ones. It is important to remember that in many ways the impact is similar to that of persons who have suffered a deep trauma. Depression and post-traumatic stress disorder are likely reactions to the devastating news of one's own infection or that of a loved one.

Many congregations have been creative in the ways they have incorporated HIV/AIDS education and care in the church's ministries. Some have developed whole ministries with this focus; others have incorporated them into health fairs that deal with the many diseases that impact the local community.

Whatever the strategy, the importance of church involvement at this point in the epidemic cannot be underestimated. It is critical that churches become centers of life, giving information and access to services that will improve the quality of life of the families suffering in silence.

There will always be those within the congregation that resist this ministry. They will be like the Pharisees of Jesus' time, people who have dedicated their whole lives to living righteously and that are very wedded to the law of God without much connection to God's mercy. Information and awareness will help to get many in the congregation to understand the importance of this ministry. Also very helpful is having an experienced HIV/AIDS educator/advocate, preferably someone who is personally living with the disease and who understands the importance of the church's involvement, to share their journey with this disease. Personal stories of people whose lives have been transformed from despair to hope, from depression to productivity, can be very inspiring for those who seek God's glory through the ministries of the church. What church leadership must be sure to do is to identify persons within the congregation who do understand the importance of nonjudgmental compassion to provide the leadership of the ministry.

God's People the Prophets

Some among the congregation's leadership will be moved to go beyond basic education and ministries. Some will be called to share the reality of life within their community with the wider community and especially with decision makers who can make an impact on the quantity and quality of resources available in communities that are already suffering from lack of health resources. Keeping informed of important budget hearings, legislation, and policy changes that affect the services provided in the community is important. This information will be shared gladly by community organizations that need the church's support. Having the church, a respected, long-standing community institution, advocate for the importance of increases in funding and policies that protect vulnerable people is important. Although in most big cities the constituencies infected by HIV/AIDS are no longer ignored, there are many midsized and small towns and cities that still need to have respected leaders stand up for those who are not respected or valued in society. The church, its leaders, and its programs can play an important role in modeling compassion and justice in towns where stigma still silences too many who are too vulnerable to speak up for themselves.

What Would Jesus Do?

The question made popular on bracelets and key chains challenges us today who face a devastating health crisis that affects the lives of thousands throughout the nation. Jesus throughout the Gospels stood with and ministered to the needs of those on the margins of society. The church is called to follow in his footsteps and not to fall into the idolatry of self-righteousness. To know that God alone is called to judge, and yet God chooses to show mercy, sends a clear message about the role of the church in this pandemic. The same urgency that churches experience in the face of natural disasters, marshalling their resources to respond to those who are suffering, is the response we need to stem the tide of this epidemic. If we bring to bear all the gifts that God has given us, we will indeed be continuing to do what Jesus did: to "bring good news to the poor . . . proclaim release to the captives and recovery of sight to the blind; to let the oppressed go free, to proclaim the year of the Lord's favor" (Luke 4:18-19).

SIXTEEN

Ableism: The Face of Oppression as Experienced by People with Disabilities

Carolyn Thompson

"Ableism" names a subtle and pervasive bias that assumes nondisabled people (people with no physical, sensory, or mental impairments) are "normal" and that people with disabilities represent an undesirable deviation from this norm. The disability is seen as a personal dilemma to be privately endured, and we have placed the responsibility to adapt on the individual with the disability. The person's flaws are to be hidden or overcome or fixed. We have let a biblical emphasis on healing become a fixation on "cure," so that the medical diagnosis becomes the defining factor and the person with a disability is always the patient in need of corrective treatment. This approach usually translates into trying to make people with disabilities look and function like the majority regardless of the cost in terms of time, money, medical procedures, or pain that they must endure.

Ableism defines a person in terms of his or her appearance, impairments, and limitations and uses them as a prejudicial measure of the person's acceptability and worth. These descriptions are often paired with their opposites (healthy or sick, broken or whole, smart or stupid, beautiful or ugly, strong or weak, helpless or productive, useful or burdensome, compliant or obstinate). These dualistic classifications leave no room for the ambiguity, fluctuation, and unpredictability that frequently characterize the lives of people with disabilities. People are reduced to stereotypes that carry the burden of stigma. In our literature and entertainment, media people with disabilities are often cast in narrowly prescribed roles of angelic innocent, inspirational hero, naïve dupe, tragic victim, comic sidekick, or evil villain. Then we laugh at them, condemn them, feel sorry for them, or venerate what we interpret as "their terrible suffering."

These myths and labels perpetuate images of disability as pathetic, tragic, or shameful, outside the realm of normal life experience. They box people in, imprison their potential, and wall out freedom and possibility; they deny people the choice of being uniquely themselves. We set up standards for participation that frequently are unattainable by people with disabilities, such as climbing stairs, reading twelve-point type, learning algebra, or enunciating clearly, and then we hold people in bondage to these expectations. We ignore, reject, pity, ridicule, or punish all who cannot meet these rigid able-bodied criteria. As Walter Brueggemann says, these "intimate patterns of unforgivenness produce a living death" (Brueggemann 2006, x). This is oppression.

Oppression Related to Groups of People

Disability is so often left out of the discourse about justice where race, class, and gender are givens. I believe that people in general have a hard time seeing disability as a factor in social justice issues. The mainstream hears about the medical search for a cure, the religious prayers for the suffering, and charity pleas for donations to help the poor handicapped. The stories are not framed in the context of justice issues. For this reason I am going to use a concept developed by Iris Marion Young in her book, *Justice and the Politics of Difference*, to talk about the ways people with disabilities, as a group, experience the injustice of "ableism," what she calls the "Five Faces of Oppression" (see also Adams et al. 2000, 35–49). She says that oppression is characterized by cultural imperialism, marginalization, powerlessness, exploitation, and violence, and that the presence of any one of these five conditions is sufficient for calling a group oppressed. In giving some examples, Young says that people with physical and mental disabilities are usually oppressed by marginalization and cultural imperialism. I will expand on that to show how people with disabilities, as a group, frequently experience all five types of oppression to some degree, at one time or another.

Young's theory is that by applying these five criteria to the situation of various groups it is possible to compare oppressions without reducing them to a common essence or claiming that one is more fundamental than another. This is important because there has been a tendency for some groups that have historically been recognized as oppressed to refuse to acknowledge the oppression of brothers and sisters in another type of group.

We have a tendency to think of oppression as the exercise of domination by a political power, such as the subjugation of the Jewish people by the Romans in Jesus' time, the repression of black South Africans under apartheid, or the persecution by individual rulers such as Hitler in Germany or Mao in Communist China. In these situations, the oppression is clearly an evil perpetrated by a singular tyrant. We are loath to admit that oppression might be something in which we ourselves unknowingly participate, a structural system of constraints on certain groups of people. The causes of the oppression are embedded in unquestioned norms, habits, myths, assumptions, and language underlying institutional rules and the collective consequences of following those rules. In this structural sense, oppression refers to the vast and deep injustices suffered by some groups as a consequence of these unexamined attitudes, cultural stereotypes, reactions, and behaviors of the media, bureaucracies, and well-meaning people in ordinary interactions.

In her analysis, Young says that oppression refers to a structural phenomenon that limits or diminishes a group of people, so we need to understand in sociological language how she is using the term *group* to define a particular way of belonging. She says a social group is a collective of individuals that exists in relation to at least one other group; that is, a group's identity arises out of its relation to another group. A group is different from an aggregate of individuals or an association. An aggregate is a combination of people, such as everyone who lives on a certain street, or everyone who drives a particular make of car. An association is a formally organized institution like a club that has a form defined by established rules, positions, and offices. There is a process by which an individual voluntarily joins an association such as registering or being voted upon by the current members. These two models of belonging are made up of individual people who already have a developed sense of their own identities before they become part of the aggregate or association; the individual self exists prior to the collective self. Such patterns of belonging fit with the individualistic Cartesian concept of the self as entirely autonomous, unified, and standing apart from history and affiliations. This self is an unencumbered agent, free to make all his or her own choices about life.

But Martin Heidegger talks about how one sometimes finds oneself in a particular group, something he calls "thrownness" (Heidegger 2008 [1962], 58). The individual is thrown into a particular group whether he chooses to be or not. When you reach a certain age, you become a teenager or a senior citizen. The group imparts an identity to the individual; it constitutes the individual. Groups may come into being but they are never "founded." Group differences cut across individual lives in a multiplicity of ways that can entail privilege and oppression for the same person in different respects or settings. Groups are fluid, shifting, and overlapping. In complex societies like our own, all individuals have multiple group identities even though they do not freely choose to be part of any particular one.

I believe that Young's theory about oppression as it relates to groups of people is particularly relevant to the experience of people with disabilities. In one sense, society has tended to see the struggles of someone who is disabled as a personal, individual problem based primarily on the limitations attributed to his or her physical, mental, or sensory impairments. It would also see the resolution of the problem as a private challenge to be dealt with by that individual. Like others in this society, however, people with disabilities are not entirely free, autonomous individuals. Over and over, people with disabilities find themselves thrown into a stereotyped group where they have to deal with an identity not of their own choosing. They get defined by a medical diagnosis, a special education label, an insurance category, or by how they look, move, talk, see, or learn. By being identified as part of one of these groups, they cannot easily escape the oppressive web of constraints that surround the group.

The Five Faces of Oppression

Below are the five faces of oppression (cultural imperialism, marginalization, powerlessness, exploitation, and violence) as described by Iris Young. For each one I have listed the particular ways it is manifest in the lives of people with disabilities.

Cultural imperialism involves the paradox of experiencing oneself as invisible at the same time that one is marked out as different. The dominant (read: "nondisabled") meanings of a society render the particular perspective of people's disabilities as invisible, while at the same time stereotyping them and marking them out as "other." People with disabilities are erased from the landscape. The dominant group projects its own experience as representative of all humanity and the differences of others become reconstructed as deviance and inferiority. Groups that are culturally imperialized become stamped with an essence, a nature that is in some way attached to their bodies, and thus not easily denied. This inferior image must in some ways be internalized by the subjugated group in order for them to survive, thus the experience that W. E. B. Du Bois called "double consciousness," the sense of always looking at oneself through the eyes of others, measuring oneself by a standard "of a world that looks on in amused contempt and pity" (Du Bois 2005 [1903], 2). For people with disabilities this cultural imperialism means:

- Not seeing people like themselves on TV, in the news, in advertising, in movies.

- Lack of access to buildings, transportation, communication, the Internet because it never occurred to the nondisabled dominant majority that the built environment could or should be designed to be more usable by a wider variety of people.
- Lack of appropriate education and health care because no one knows or can imagine how to deal with something outside their dominant frame of reference.
- Putting a constant effort into not being invisible, while at the same time trying not to appear any stranger than the dominant culture already thinks one is.

Marginalization. Young says that this is perhaps the most dangerous form of oppression, for a whole category of people is expelled from useful participation in social life and thus potentially subjected to severe material deprivation and even extermination. They are seen as outside the norm. A person pushed to the margin has only a meager share of what is important to those in the middle. The welfare system itself produces new injustices by depriving those dependent on it of rights and freedoms that others are guaranteed as part of their citizenship. Those dependent on bureaucratic institutions are often subject to patronizing, demeaning, intrusive, arbitrary, and sometimes punitive treatment. Being dependent in our society implies a sufficient warrant to have one's basic rights to privacy, respect, and individual choice suspended. Professional social workers, doctors, educators, lawyers make decisions based on what they think will be good for the disabled person with no regard for the person's self-knowledge or the personal expertise of others living in similar circumstances. Marginalization involves the deprivation of cultural, practical, and institutional conditions for exercising one's capacity in a context of recognition and interaction. For people with disabilities, this marginalization translates into:

- Not being able to participate in elections or community meetings because they are held at inaccessible locations, the information and materials are not in an accessible format, or there is no public address system or other accommodation for people who are deaf or hard of hearing.
- Being excused from weekly attendance at worship because it is difficult to get into the church. Rather than the faith community dealing with the lack of access so they could welcome the participation of everyone, they just tell the disabled person who uses a wheelchair

that she can watch the service on TV.

- Being excluded from social events and celebrations because they are held in inaccessible locations.
- Having to deal with demeaning comments and intrusion of one's personal, bodily space.
- Being called rude, selfish, or lazy when they request reasonable accommodations, such as having a class moved to a wheelchair-accessible classroom.
- Facing discrimination in employment situations.
- Being referred to with a label such as, "The Patient," "Bed #7," "The Case," "The Blind," "The Epileptic," instead of being called by one's name.
- Being perceived as outside the norm, as unclean (like women in patriarchal culture). (Disabled people in subsidized housing tell of having to endure more frequent intrusive inspections of their apartments than nondisabled people and being held to higher standards of order and cleanliness.)

Powerlessness. Powerlessness designates a position in the labor force, school, and society that allows a person little opportunity to develop and exercise his or her skills, to take advantage of opportunities for advancement. There is an inhibition in the development of one's capacities, a lack of decision-making power, and exposure to disrespectful treatment because of the status one occupies. One is not seen as respectable or worthy of attention. It means being invisible in many ways, being ignored, not having one's voice heard. Some of the powerlessness comes from internalizing the negative messages that society sends to and about disabled people. Disabled people who are powerless:

- Wait on lists for years to get the services to which they are entitled.
- Are not told about educational or employment opportunities.
- Are not included at the table when decisions are being made about their future.
- Watch the education, employment, housing, and social service programs they need be the first cut from school, state, and federal budgets.
- Exist on monthly incomes way below the Federal Poverty Level. The limits on assets a person can have in order to qualify for Supplemental Security Income (SSI) or Social Security Disability Insurance (SSDI)

have not changed since the SSI law was enacted more than thirty years ago. In other words, a meager $2000 for individuals or $3000 for couples is allowed to cover emergencies.

- Get treated like children regardless of their age in years.
- Get yelled at and chastised if they do not understand a verbal explanation or ask for it in writing or a more legible format.
- Are not seen as a whole person; they exist as an assemblage of parts to get divided up among the medical specialties.
- Endure countless rounds of medical treatments and procedures that leave their bodies trampled like the ravaged countryside around a battle site.
- Are often examined or treated in medical settings with no respect for their personal modesty. Many have told of being stripped nearly naked, laid out on a gurney, or told to walk/move this way—and that in an amphitheater filled with medical students and interns.

Exploitation occurs through a steady process that transfers the results of one social group's labor or circumstances to benefit another; it is about using other people for one's own gain where there is an unreciprocated transfer of power. The disadvantaged group may have to perform tasks for someone on whom they are dependent. This work is often menial and repetitious, and the members of the oppressed group are put in a servile position lacking autonomy and subject to taking orders. The status, power, freedom, and self-realization of the person or organization using them is possible precisely because an exploited group of people works for them. Disabled people who are exploited:

- Are given only menial jobs doing custodial work like cleaning toilets.
- May be kept in a sheltered workshop when they have mastered the tasks and might be ready to advance to more challenging, more interesting work.
- Have been labeled as "freaks" and used in sideshow entertainment as objects of morbid curiosity.
- Are often taken advantage of sexually; they may be seen and used only as a sex object, a novelty. Many who spent time in hospitals as children tell of being fondled or sexually abused by medical staff. In one recent memoir by a woman with a spinal-cord injury, the author recounts how the physiatrist who was to make her back brace came to the rehab hospital late in the evening when few nurses were

around and kept trying to fondle her breasts as he supposedly took her measurements. She tells of going for a job interview several years later after getting her degree and having the headmaster move around next to her wheelchair and start caressing her thighs (Linton 2005).

- Are used by religious leaders as models of inspiration and noble suffering.
- Become the bearers of demonic traits as in the character of Darth Vader in Star Wars or the Joker in the Batman movies. People who have a psychiatric disability (mental illness) or disfigurement are in particular jeopardy of being perceived as dangerous.
- Have their disabling conditions and impairments used to represent character faults, lack of faith, brokenness and sin. One example is the popular hymn "Amazing Grace." It could be just as meaningful if it read:

Amazing grace how sweet the sound	*Amazing grace how sweet the sound*
That saves a wretch like me	*That saves and strengthens me,*
I once was lost but now am found,	*I once was lost but now am found,*
Was blind but now I see	*Was bound but now am free.*

- Are taken advantage of by doctors and researchers for medical studies and experiments that do not directly benefit the patient; they may end up as someone's Ph.D. project. For instance, residents of Fernald State School in Waltham, Massachusetts, were used for radiation experiments without appropriate informed consent.

Violence includes severe assault, injury, and death, but also incidents of harassment, intimidation, or ridicule simply for the purpose of degrading, humiliating, or stigmatizing group members. Violence is systemic because it is directed at members of a group simply because they are members of that group. Violence is oppressive not only in direct victimization, but in the daily knowledge shared by all members of the oppressed group that they also are liable to being violated because of their group identity; violence hangs as a constant threat on the horizon. What makes violence a face of oppression is less the particular acts, though these are often utterly horrible, but the social context surrounding them that makes them possible and even acceptable. Violence often involves insecurities on the part of the perpetrators; their hatred of some groups may be bound up with their own fear of identity loss. For them to acknowledge the cultural reality of the other "deviant" group may put the lie to the dominant group's implicit claim to universality. Disabled people suffer violence when they:

- Become the objects of pranks, assaults, and rape.
- Are portrayed as not human and therefore not worthy of care, sustenance, medical treatment, or lifesaving procedures.
- Are subject to forced sterilizations, to painful, damaging, sometimes fatal, scientific experiments, and extermination as in the Holocaust.
- Are caused to undergo abusive discipline and religious "cleansings" because of their disability.
- Are locked in solitary confinement and given only cabbage and bread to eat for days on end.
- Become the victims of "mercy" killings. For example, in 1993, Tracy Latimer, a Canadian twelve-year-old, was murdered by her father. She had severe cerebral palsy and needed a lot of care, but she could eat out of a spoon, was happy most of the time, and went to school every day. He father said he killed her because he did not want to see her suffer any more. The courts are still wrestling with this case, which many call an act of "compassionate homicide."
- They see their kind devalued and threatened with extinction through increased prenatal testing and abortion.
- They are told they have a "life not worth living," and society allows as how it is not a bad idea for them to seek a physician-assisted suicide. Most of the people, predominantly women, whom Jack Kevorkian aided in taking their own lives were not "terminally ill." They were depressed but not getting appropriate psychiatric treatment.

Some Truths about Life with Disability

These five patterns of oppression paint an awfully grim picture of life with disability. Is that all there is? There must be other ways we can look at the experience that bear some truth but are not so laden with negativity. Let us consider some of the realities, which, though they may be hard to face, are not inherently evil.

Disability is about difference; it is one of the characteristics that contribute to the diversity, the plurality of life. Physical, sensory, and mental impairments cause the body to look, move, sound, feel, talk, think, behave in different ways. Disability does not fit into neat, orderly categories; it is not one of those journeys we can arrange on our own terms, like a trip to Disneyworld or a tour of Italy. The adventure with disability will likely be full of paradox and ambiguity and fluctuation. The person may feel great one day and have terrible symptoms the next, without any predictable signs or explanations. There may be some things the body cannot do at all and others it does surprisingly well. A disease or disability can manifest itself differently in each person, and some people have more than one disability. It may be readily obvious or "hidden." Because of the varied circumstances (social, cultural, economic, religious) that affect how people deal with life, two individuals with the same diagnosis may have very different attitudes, approaches, and outcomes relating to the same disability.

Disability is a contingency of being human in a less-than-perfect world. Life has risks. We do not have control over all the circumstances that can result in disability, and as advances in medicine, science, and technology continue to reduce the death rate from infection, injuries, and chronic illness, we are more likely to survive events that would have killed us ten to thirty years ago. People will continue to live longer but with some level of disability. The 2000 U.S. Census revealed that about 20 percent of the population has significant disabilities. Nearly all of us will eventually be touched by disability in some way or other. Disability is a natural, ordinary occurrence in life.

Encountering disability can feel like having one's life turned upside down. The unexpected arrives in a devastating diagnosis, a traumatic injury, the birth of a child with congenital anomalies, or the chance encounter with a disabled person. One has to reassess a world where nothing is the same as it used to be. Anger, guilt, and blame are not uncommon reactions. There may be losses to mourn—loss of some function, loss of an earlier identity, or loss of a cherished image about how life was supposed to be—and fears to confess. Learning to negotiate a terrain where nothing is familiar can feel like culture shock. In some ways life will slow down; a person may need more rest, more time, more patience, and more endurance.

While some conditions are progressive, degenerative, and may cause pain, many are not, or at least not all the time. Most people who have been disabled for some time acknowledge that they had to learn how to integrate the disability into their lives, to live with it, not "overcome" it. At some point, they realize that the disability is most likely not going to disappear, and that they could end up on the sidelines of life if they put all their energy into looking for a cure. One needs to learn the difference between acceptance and giving up. The physical or mental impairment a person has does not need to be her whole identity; it is just a part of who the person is. It is not something to ignore or pretend we do not notice; that response can make a person feel invisible. The disability is one attribute among the many that makes this person unique.

Countering Oppression

Is there any escape from this web of injustice, from being stereotyped in negative ways, figuratively erased, pushed to the margins of life, rendered powerless, exploited, and abused by the individuals and institutions of the dominant culture? How does a disabled person confront such oppression? Can our belief systems and faith communities respond in ways that are affirming and life-giving rather than compounding the problem?

Part of dealing with cultural imperialism is becoming aware that it exists and realizing how people with disabilities, like everyone else, have internalized its precepts. We may still have to function in that world of the dominant culture, but we can be conscious of what it is we are doing and find ways to be less entrapped. As Christians, we are called to be in the world but not of the world; we have a different way of belonging that runs counter to much of what the dominant culture prescribes. We believe that Jesus Christ came to tear down the walls that divide people and that the church represents a new kind of community where everyone belongs. It is a corporate image, a community made up of many members where each brings different yet complementary gifts. We are all interdependent. "To each is given the manifestation of the Spirit for the common good" (1 Cor. 17:7).

The welcome participation of people with disabilities is not an option for the church; it is a defining characteristic. The familiarity and friendship that can grow within a church where there is respect and mutuality among the members is one of the best antidotes to the cultural imperialism that would render anyone who is different as inferior and deviant. More specifically, as people with disabilities we can name ourselves with descriptors that emphasize that we are people, first, who have some disabilities, and we can take back the words others are using in a derogatory way, such as "crip" or "gimp," and use them with pride. We can refute the negative stereotyped labels and refuse to be made invisible. When the characters in a movie script include disabled individuals, we can insist that the producer hire actors with those disabilities and not nondisabled actors. We can quit hiding in the background, embarrassed that our appearance will offend someone. We can help society think through the ways to make the built environment accessible to all.

Marginalization expels people with disabilities from the center of society where most of the jobs and opportunities occur, where the vitality and power reside. Sometimes it can feel like one is clinging to the bare edges of life with nothing beyond. However, maybe living on the margins of life, as some of us do, has its own possibilities. Perhaps we are not on the edge of nothing, but on the border of something new, something on the other side. The person on the margin may be in a unique position to see what is out of view for the people in the center of the circle. This position provides its own advantage for political analysis and mediating between the accepted way and a different world.

Jesus had to negotiate life from the margin. He lived on a:

- Theological edge: He was steeped in Jewish teaching but did not fit in to the scheme of things.
- Geographic edge: "Can anything good come from Galilee?"
- Social edge: His best friends had no class, no social standing.
- Edge of common understanding: His closest followers misunderstood him. (Taylor 2000)

And yet he changed the world. We need to remember that he had his own solid center; his identity was anchored in the knowledge that he was God's beloved Son. And we, too, are beloved sons and daughters of God.

While people with disabilities may be able to reap something positive from a vantage point on the margin, there is still a need for this group to be a more integral part of society. A theology of healing and wholeness may be helpful here. There are many accounts in Hebrew and Christian Scripture about people being healed, and the way these accounts are told puts the focus on the cure or eradication of the condition. I want to suggest that healing is not so much about having something fixed or corrected as it is about becoming whole and being restored to one's rightful place in the community. This wholeness happens when all the parts of our individual and corporate lives that have been left out, neglected, or excluded are brought together in love. Sometimes we are guilty of "marginalizing" that part of our body that is not working, to be angry at it, to demean and relegate it the edge of our consciousness. It can be difficult to acknowledge that impaired part as worthy of our care and respect, and to recognize it as a part of us. This task of integration is challenging work both for the individual and for the church and wider society as we try to create a space where everyone can participate and feel valued. This is where wholeness becomes holy.

We know that to name some thing or some being is to have power over it. Names have a lot of power, and life, to a large extent, is controlled by how we name it and are named by it. Being named to a group that is not given any respect can make one feel powerless. Even words like "poor, pitiful, afflicted, suffering" paint a picture of something that is hopelessly distasteful, unsatisfactory, cursed, and pathetic. "There is an arrogance to such pity. It does not presume equality, but rather conveys the condescending implication of helplessness and inferiority" (Gold 2002, 19). How do people with disabilities get out from under the unjust myths and labels that others have applied to them?

As a young girl I endured name calling and taunts about how I looked. I pretended not to hear. The adults around me said, "Just ignore them; they don't know what they are talking about." And I did not know any other way to respond. Years later, as an adult, I was walking through a parking lot near a university campus and some frat boys hollered insults about my appearance. It did not occur so often, but it did still happen. I felt assaulted and vulnerable. The incident gnawed at me, not so much because of what they had said but because I did not know how to respond in a way that maintained my own integrity, that was empowering to me.

Then I recalled a wonderful scene in the movie *Roxanne* where Steve Martin takes on a rude fellow who is taunting him about his long nose. For every derisive comment the guy throws, Steve Martin tosses something right back that is even more outrageous. Soon the whole bar crowd is laughing and cheering Martin. I started thinking how I might rebuff the offensive comments aimed at me with something humorous.

- "Hey, you look like you have a shrunken head."—"Yeah, I stood under a hot shower too long."
- "Your face is on crooked."—"I know. I was in a hurry with my make-up this morning and have not had time to straighten it out."
- "Why are you still wearing your Halloween mask?"—"Oh, I accidentally used superglue instead of face lotion and now I can't get it off."

Honestly, I have not had the occasion to use one of these retorts, but I am no longer fearful of encountering a foul-mouthed bully.

Jesus had a way of telling stories that began with an ordinary setting but then took an unexpected twist or turn, and he often responded to questions with an answer that sounded absurd. What he says disrupts the usual way of looking at life, makes a connection with the listener and causes a reaction. He was a gentle man with few earthly possessions, but he was not powerless. He was not afraid to upset the usual order of things. For people with disabilities who feel trapped in the powerlessness of their lot, one of the biggest hurdles is to risk disturbing the status quo. It is hard to confront the dominant culture alone, and a single person is easy to ignore or throw out. But a committee of five, a group of forty, or a crowd of seven hundred has to be recognized. People with all types of disabilities, their families, and friends who join together for advocacy work will not be invisible. Remember that Jesus also said, "Where two or three are gathered together in my name, I will be with you" (Matt. 18:20).

The victims of exploitation are the groups of people a society does not respect. They may be people who are seen as inferior or who have never been given a voice in matters. It is harder to exploit someone seen as an equal. We need to challenge the theologies of guilt, shame, brokenness, and pity that contribute to the exploitation of people with disabilities. The story in Genesis tells us that humankind was created in God's image, "according to God's likeness" (Gen. 1:26), so that each person reflects part of that divine mystery; together we make up the beautiful mosaic that God intends. If we truly believed that God imbued each person with dignity and worth and gifts to share, I think it would be harder to exploit our fellow humans. If all life is a gift from God and there is integrity to this creation, then every human being is innately gifted and has something to offer that others need. We need one another for our gifts to be revealed. And disabled people have gifts to share that have emerged precisely from the experience of living with disability.

If disabled individuals are perceived as less than human, as only the carriers of impairments, they are more likely to become victims of violence, even the acts of violence that purport to be for their own benefit. An object may be easier to dispose of than a sentient being. One way to contend with the violence against people with disabilities is to help people come to terms with the fears they have about disease and disability, to recognize their own feelings of insecurity and vulnerability that they are projecting onto the people with disabilities.

For disabled individuals who have been the victims of violence, the most caring response may be gentle, patient listening. Some will have stories they have carried alone for decades. They may have cried out or tried to tell someone long ago about what was being done to them, but no one could hear. They may have been too busy just surviving and getting on with life to ponder the effect the abuse or violence had on their bodies and souls. For many it has been in the process of writing memoirs that the incidents of old have come to the surface and begged an audience. Bodies remember what the mind can try to forget, and sometimes an unexpected event will trigger an old memory. The perpetrators may be long gone and the parents may be too old or mentally frail to understand what happened to their child fifty years ago. But like the victims of atrocities during apartheid in South Africa, or the witnesses to the slaughter of Jews in the Ukraine during World War II, the stories need to be heard for there to be peace in the victim's soul.

The Way Forward

Given that people with disabilities as a group cannot totally escape this oppression—cultural imperialism, marginalization, powerlessness, exploitation, and violence—it is going to have some bearing on their lives. In a pastoral care setting, they will need someone who can listen without displaying revulsion at certain physical/medical details. Nor will they appreciate a lot of questions about the pathology of the impairment; those facts are probably not that relevant to the social/cultural/psychological/spiritual issues anyway. People with disabilities do not want pity, sainthood, or getting off easy because someone feels sorry for them. Someone who has been in denial about the presence of disability in her life may need help acknowledging and accepting the reality. People need to know that they are not in this alone. There are support groups for people with the same chronic illness or condition, there are online groups, there are cross-disability groups and advocacy organizations, and there are Web sites for specific diseases and disabilities. There are all kinds of books and studies about the whole phenomena of disability itself. Life with disability means:

- Loving a rambunctious five-year-old boy who does not talk or want to be hugged.
- Playing basketball or rugby or dancing when you can't walk.
- Coming back to work after being hospitalized for a mental illness.
- Creating a national, Web-based, up-to-the-minute exchange of disability information from one's bed, with a computer mounted overhead.
- Shifting roles and responsibilities when a disabled family member can no longer do certain tasks.

- Getting a college degree when you are blind.
- Surprising people around you with the unexpected.

Help people to know that besides the oppression, disability is about patience, persistence, endurance, and possibility. It is about acceptance and not being perfect. It is about learning to trust and learning to ask. Disability is about resilience, being flexible, using one's imagination and creativity and being adaptable. It is about life—even this life—being worth living. It is about hope and the integrity of creation. It is about becoming whole and loving all the different parts of yourself. Disability is about being who you are—and not being ashamed of it.

SEVENTEEN

Pastoral Care
with Transgender People

Sarah Gibb Millspaugh

Pastors are community caregivers. True community care must be based in an understanding of one's own community. Within every religious community of every religious faith, there are transgender people. It may not be evident to the pastor; fear and shame keep many silent. Transgender identities may be visible or invisible within a congregation, but they are there just the same. We are called in communities of faith to serve all of God's children. We are called to seek justice, to work for radical inclusiveness. This kind of work calls us and challenges us to stand with the oppressed, to examine oppressive structures, and always to remain open to learning and reflection on the journey. Pastors are called, in the spirit of Jesus, to confront the life-denying fallacies of our culture that serve the powerful and punish the powerless.

We learn from this dominant culture that people come in two biological sexes, male and female, and that this biology naturally corresponds with two genders, man and woman. Males express themselves as men, females as women, we are taught. But the reality of transgender people's lives stands as a testament against the universality of male and female, and a system that upholds this universality is, ultimately, life denying.

The goals of this analysis of transgender pastoral care are threefold: to familiarize pastors with characteristics of transgender people and communities; to address and critique the prevalent models of pastoral care that transgender people experience; and to construct a healing and freeing model of pastoral care with transgender people.

Transgender is an umbrella term, encompassing multiple modes of gender identity and expression. The Unitarian Universalist Association Office of Bisexual, Gay, Lesbian, and Transgender Concerns identifies four communities within the transgender movement: crossdressers, transsexuals, third-gender people, and intersexuals (Greve and Kron 2000, 1–2). The definitions within these communities continue to evolve as the diverse transgender community grows in awareness and visibility. Because of the evolving definitions and people's own evolving self-knowledge, it's important as a pastor to respect and accept the self-definition of each transgender person, whether that definition fits within the following categories or not.

Crossdressers, also known as transvestites, dress in the clothing style of the "opposite" gender, either fully or partially, for pleasure, relaxation, or entertainment purposes. The majority of crossdressers are heterosexual men who do so in secrecy (ibid., 1).

Transsexuals are, generally, people whose internally felt gender is different from the gender typically associated with their biological sex at birth. For example, a female-to-male transsexual person can be born in the body of a female and identify as male. Transsexual identity may or may not cause one to seek out sexual reassignment surgery (SRS). Some transsexual people undergo hormone treatment or plastic surgery either in conjunction with, or separate from, SRS.

Third-gender people understand that their gender transcends the categories "male" and "female"—their identity lies beyond these categories. Third-gender people often prefer the term transgender to third gender (ibid.).

Intersexuals are people whose biological sex at birth transcends the categories "male" and "female." The genitalia of intersexual people are considered "ambiguous" by medical professionals, and/or an intersexual individual may have some female and some male reproductive organs. Intersexuals have historically been known as hermaphrodites. Often medical professionals and parents elect to perform surgery on intersexual newborns to "assign" them a female or male sex.

The 1990s saw the emergence of a new spirit of community building, organizing, and activism among transgender people. Although transgender organizations exist across America, a transgender individual may or may not be connected with a supportive organization of others who share that individual's self-definition. In fact, because of fear and shame, many transgender people remain in the closet.

The people and subcommunities that comprise the transgender umbrella share some issues with lesbian, gay, and bisexual people. Some people who identify as transgender also identify as lesbian, gay, or bisexual, so the separation is not that clear cut. Other transgender people identify as heterosexual. Gender identity and sexual orientation are two separate continua—contrary to popular assumption, transgender identity does not always resolve in heterosexuality. For example, a male-to-female transsexual can be happily married to a woman both before and after SRS. People don't "change their sex" to become heterosexual, they change it to become outwardly who they are internally.

Transgender people share some oppressions with gay, bisexual, and lesbian people, and that is why they often work in conjunction for recognition and rights.

> Gays, lesbians, and bisexuals are stigmatized and oppressed because they violate social standards for acceptable sex behavior; transsexuals because they violate standards for sex identity. Intersexuals are punished for violating social standards of acceptable sex anatomy. But our oppressions stem from the same source: rigid cultural definitions of sex categories, whether in terms of behavior, identity, or anatomy. (Feinberg 1993, 98)

While transgender, bisexual, lesbian, and gay people also share threats of physical violence, verbal abuse, harassment, and rejection by family and faith community, there are some oppressions that transgender people face in a significantly different way. Transgender people face enormous barriers to even the most basic health care. Harassment, misunderstanding, and even refusal of care by health-care workers are all too common.

> I remember late one night in December my lover and I arrived at a hospital emergency room during a snowstorm. My fever was 104 degrees and rising. My blood pressure was pounding dangerously high. . . . The doctor in charge began physically examining me. When he determined that my anatomy was female, he flashed me a mean-spirited smirk. . . . He told me to get dressed and then he stormed out of the room. . . . The doctor returned after I was dressed. He ordered me to leave the hospital and never return. (Ibid., 2)

Transgender people face the stress of living in a world that denies and punishes their existence, both implicitly and explicitly, both actively and passively. Simple acts such as filling out forms can become painful. Leslie Feinberg describes the dilemma posed by the everyday: signs such as "Gentlemen" and "Ladies," checkboxes such as "F" and "M:"

Because it is legally mandated that all our lives must fit into one of those two tiny boxes, many of us actually face imprisonment or institutionalization merely because we don't. We live under the constant threat of horrifying violence. We have to worry about what bathroom to use when our bladders are aching. We are forced to consider whether we'll be dragged out of a bathroom and arrested or face a fistfight while our bladders are still aching. It's an everyday reality for us. Human beings must use toilets. (Ibid., 68)

Marginalization and denial do not only come from the straight, nontransgender community: they also come from gay, lesbian, bisexual, and allied people and organizations. Existing within a power structure that punishes difference in sexual orientation and identity, organizations working to promote gay rights have often sought to downplay or ignore variances in gender within the community, seeking to focus on presenting the most "palatable" face to a homophobic and transphobic nation. In the past fifteen years the transgender community has come to be mentioned in the movement by name (gay, lesbian, bisexual, and transgender, or GLBT, has become common parlance) but more rarely in spirit. Transgender speakers and organizations were all but invisible at the 2000 Millennium March on Washington.

It is important to remember that transgender oppression does not exist in isolation. The nature of the oppression differs for individuals and communities, and is interlaced with many factors, including geography, class, religion, race, sexual orientation, and ethnicity. Transgender oppression's lived reality cannot be separated from the homophobia, racism, sexism, and classism that also play out in the daily lives of transgender people.

Transgender people who are attracted to people of their same biological (or in the case of intersexuals, assigned) sex often come out as gay, lesbian, or bisexual before coming out as transgender. In this way identification as a bisexual, gay, or lesbian person can serve as a means to, and not an end of, acceptance and self-definition. Sometimes when a previously identified gay or lesbian person comes out as transsexual, they no longer identify as gay or lesbian; they identify as transsexual and straight.

Of the ministers engaging in pastoral care with openly transgender people, various degrees of knowledge and acceptance are demonstrated, from absolute intolerance and denial to confident affirmation and empowerment.

Caregiver as Gardener

Margaret Kornfeld's gardener model of the pastoral caregiver is particularly applicable to pastoral care with transgender persons (1998, 10). Her gardener's task is twofold: to tend to the ground (the community) and to the plants in the ground (the people). Therefore gardener pastoral caregivers are not only concerned with the individual problems and pathologies of those for whom they care. They perceive the ways that plants' concerns are affected by the ground of the community and with society at large. Thus, they tend to the person who presents a need for care and to the system that creates the need for care. Further, the gardener's job is not to make the plants grow—Kornfeld makes clear that God does that—but to nurture them into healthy growth. The gardener holds the big picture, tending, nurturing, fostering positive change in persons and in communities at large.

In the pastoral care of transgender people, Kornfeld's description of the gardener fits to an extent. But gardeners, in general, are only positive and nurturing to the plants they think are supposed to grow in their garden. Gardeners weed. Transgender plants, not mentioned in any gardening guide the gardeners have ever seen, don't fit in with their rows of pink and blue petunias. Gardeners don't know what to do with them. A transgender divinity school classmate (who chooses to remain anonymous) describes the experience of seeking pastoral care from such well-intentioned gardeners—chaplains at a Southern Baptist college:

> These Southern Baptists loved me. They convinced me that God loved me too, and that the only reason I was questioning my gender and my sexual orientation was because I had been abused. For four years, they tried to convert me to the doctrine of heterosexuality, but no matter how much they loved me, it never quite took. I guess someone forgot to mention to them that GLBT people are born and not made.

A second kind of gardener recognizes, indeed, that transgender people are "born and not made." These gardeners cultivate the ground, the community, to help every plant in their garden thrive. And if the soil doesn't have the right composition for a transgender plant, the gardener adds compost, mulch, and water. This gardener appreciates the uniqueness and integrity of each plant, valuing the abundance of life above some preordained vision of garden design. Barb Greve has had affirming experiences with his ministers in the church he has attended all his life:

As I have gone through my own coming out journey and shared it with my ministers, some of the most powerful things, particularly in this last phase of pronoun switching and my expressing myself more outwardly, have been my ministers' understanding that this is part of a journey and their acknowledgment that they're honored to share pieces of it with me. Their recognition that this isn't just "something that I'm doing," but rather that this is a serious matter, and something that we're sharing together, has been incredibly pastorally positive.

Both variations of the gardener model have drawbacks as well as advantages for work with transgender people. A rigid gardener model, though often well intentioned, is harmful, for it denies the identity and the very life of transgender people. A pastoral caregiver can easily fall into the trap of trying to help a transgender person conform to the gender that society believes fits them. But in so doing, the caregiver denies the courage, the reality, and the life-seeking impulses of the transgender community member. The more accepting, nurturing gardener model has many advantages, in that it provides holistic, attentive care that honors the dignity of transgender people. It bears witness to the pain and suffering of transgender people while also witnessing—and seeking to change—the society that created the pain. It involves work with the community to help transgender persons in a quest for wholeness. A limitation of this model is that the caregiver, while respecting the transgender person, may still not understand the person (since transgender people are rarely, if ever mentioned in pastoral care guides) and may come to regard this person as an exotic novelty, thus furthering the transgender objectification and "thingifying" the person.

Transgender persons are not the only ones who can grow in gardener-style pastoral care. Immense growth can await a pastoral caregiver by working with and learning from transgender people. United Methodist clergywoman Maurine Waun describes a moment when visiting a male-to-female transgender parishioner in the hospital. The nurse had just brought in a male urinal.

In the course of my ministry over the previous several years I had stood up for Larry, marched in the Pride Parade, stuck my neck out with colleagues and church people and learned to be particularly sensitive to people's issues, but never did I feel a deeper act of compassion for someone's most private and personal secret than I did with Dawn in that split second. (1999, 86–87)

The pastor learned and grew from the encounter, deepening her understanding and resolve.

Countering Oppression

In *Building King's Beloved Community: Foundations for Pastoral Care and Counseling with the Oppressed*, Donald M. Chinula presents a model for pastoral care that counters the "thingifying" effects of oppression. He identifies four tasks for pastoral caregiving based on Martin Luther King Jr.'s constructive thought: reclamation, conciliation, transformation, and transcendence (1997, 56).

The goal of reclamation is the healing of the diminished self-esteem and the fractured self-concept of the self, both direct results of systemic oppression. Central to this healing, for Chinula, is the revelation that we are all created in God's image. This particular revelation is tricky for transgender people, as the very text from which it is drawn, Genesis 1:27, has been invoked to deny transgender people's legitimacy: "So God created humankind in his image, in the image of God he created them; male and female he created them." Oddly, this text has also been used to deny intersexual people's legitimacy, justifying plastic surgery on newborns with "mixed" genitalia, as if their genitalia were somehow outside of God's creation (Gross 2000, 1).

The key to unlocking this text and using it for liberation rather than subjugation lies in both debunking the assumptions behind oppressive interpretations and reconstructing an image of God. Helping to demonstrate how this God-ordained "naturalness" of the social norm was human created, not God created, is a first step in liberating God from oppressive interpretation. But in reimaging lies the more powerful message. God, in whose image both male and female are made, is beyond gender or comprises aspects of female and male. God, in this sense, is transgender. Imaging God as transgender is both biblically accurate and theologically sound. People who are transgender are, then, created in God's image, just as much as nontransgender males and females.

A great potential ally for pastoral caregivers in the healing of the fractured self-concept and diminished self-esteem of transgender people is professional therapy. Therapy, for those transgender people who can afford it, can be profoundly helpful in the courageous journey to healing and self-acceptance. The presence or absence of professional therapy in the life of a transgender person can influence the type of pastoral care a caregiver is called upon for.

We see pastors on a short-term basis, either a flare-up in our lives or some major personal crisis. Be it good or bad we turn to religion, to pastors, at these times. Therapists are more of a long-term help to fix life problems that a transgender identity compounds. In a therapeutic setting, there's more time to struggle through the trans identity, both as a personal issue and as a relationship issue. On the pastoral care side, we don't have time to deal with that. The pastoral care setting is not about the identity, it's about whatever's going on in life, but because all of our identities impact everything in our lives, transgender identity is part of the equation.

As pastoral caregivers it is also important to recognize that, by nature of beginning the coming-out process, or by nature of requesting pastoral care, transgender-identified people are already on the path to healing self-concept and self-esteem. The burden is not on the caregiver to initiate this process—it becomes the caregiver's job to help it along.

Connection with transgender support and liberation movements is another valuable step toward healing. The experience of meeting other people with similar gender identities is deeply affirming. A feeling of isolation transforms into a feeling of inclusion. "We need each other. We each know what it's like to fight back alone. We need each other's strength as allies. And we know what it's like to feel like the only one who's different. When 'difference' suddenly comes into focus as diversity it's a healing experience" (Feinberg 1998, 55). Pastoral caregivers can help connect isolated transgender people with resources for peer support.

The second task Chinula identifies is conciliation. Conciliation aims to reach out to the opponent and secure a friendship. It goes beyond patching up a broken relationship; it involves transcending anger, however justified, to reach out in love. Martin Luther King Jr. exemplified conciliation in his persistent, loving, nonviolent activism. Conciliation, for the transgender, is very difficult, as it is with all oppressed groups, due to the vast and personal nature of "the opponent." If the opponents are those who denied your humanity, your integrity, your reality, then one must reach out in conciliation to nearly every cultural institution: the government, religion, the media, schools, the English language, as well as those who have, however unwittingly, caused or enabled transgender suffering: family, friends, abusers, harassers, perfect strangers. The opponent in this case can seem very overwhelming. But perhaps the opponent is a philosophy, or a dogma, that drives the oppression and causes people to act as they do: a bi-gendered worldview, sexism, or heterosexism. Relocation of the opponent from "everyone" to a philosophy can open up doors for conciliation.

It's not that people are all bad, it's that we've all been inculcated with a poisonous philosophy. The philosophy can be unlearned.

It is no small task to reach out to the opponent in friendship. It is, ultimately, a spiritual task that takes great courage. But it is necessary for survival. Conciliation, rather than the sublimation of anger, can be viewed as an outcome of truly recognizing and addressing one's anger. While fully acknowledging this anger, one can choose to reach out in conciliation, not for the benefit of the opponent, but for one's own benefit. Anger, especially anger at such formidable opponents as the transgender have, can be all-consuming if one lets it get to that point. Conciliation, making peace, securing friendship can both create peace and advance the causes for which one is fighting. Conciliation does not end the struggle for recognition, respect, and rights. Just the opposite—conciliation counters despair, conciliation fuels hope, conciliation empowers work for justice. Conciliation fuels the next of Chinula's steps: transformation.

Transformation, in Chinula's definition, is twofold: it involves transformation of the self and transformation of society. The vocation of pastor is uniquely equipped to foster both. Central to self-transformation, for Chinula, is understanding of history. Moving from object of history to subject of history is essential in the journey from feeling "thingifyed" to feeling fully human. The choice to begin, and continue, the coming-out process is also a choice to affirm one's place as subject rather than object of one's own personal history. Leslie Feinberg's book *Transgender Warriors: Making History from Joan of Arc to Dennis Rodman* (1996) moves the transgender, as a movement, from object to subject, placing the personal struggle within a historical context of struggle.

In conjunction with the nurturance of personal transformation, pastors can use their positions of authority to transform society. They can also empower transgender and other members of their communities to become agents for social change. Starting from the assumption that none of us are free if some of us are oppressed, pastors can preach sermons, lead Bible study groups, and lead prayer groups that foster empathy and solidarity with all who are oppressed, whether by gender identity, sexual orientation, race, class, religion—the list goes on. However, specific education on particular oppressions is necessary.

Just because an individual is drawn into the vortex of a movement, it doesn't mean that person will automatically be enlightened on every aspect of other peoples' oppressions—particularly that which they do not directly experience. Each individual sill needs to overcome the bigotry that has been instilled in us from an early age. A gay man does not necessarily see the need to fight sexism automatically; a white transperson doesn't automatically see the need to fight racism. But the progressive momentum inherent in movements offers a greater potential for individuals to gain an understanding of the struggles of others. . . . (Feinberg 1996, 51)

A second key factor in transformation is truly making the congregation welcoming of the "T" as well as of the "GLB" in "GLBT." Too often in our welcoming-church movements, "transgender" is just a politically correct add-on to "gay, lesbian, and bisexual." A 2000 survey I did of Web sites of Protestant welcoming-church movements revealed that, while the majority included transgender welcoming in their mission statement, the programs were essentially about welcoming diverse sexual orientations rather than gender identities. The Unitarian Universalist Association's Welcoming Congregation Web site was the exception.

Transformation unfolds from a nonstatic view of God, a view in which God is "a hater of life-denying and health-destroying status quo and a lover of life affirming and health promoting change" (Chinula 1997, 57–58). God also leads us into Chinula's fourth step, transcendence. As people created in the image of God, our capacities for transformation cannot be limited by a humanly imposed system of oppression. The pastoral caregiver's job is to nurture in the transgender person the power to transcend the oppressor's categories of gender, and the power to transcend the oppressor's unearned right to define transgender reality. Personhood transcends categories. In Chinula's framework, we are all part of a divine reality that is greater than the sum of the parts of this world. This divine reality is within us and it transcends us. It can help us rise above oppression. Spiritual practices that tap into this transcendent spirit, such as prayer, singing, bodywork, and meditation, can call us into transcendence not only in our spiritual lives, but in our whole lives.

The process of reclamation, conciliation, transformation, and transcendence is a particularly potent spiritual path, leading the way from brokenness to wholeness, "nobodiness" to "somebodiness." In traveling this path with transgender people, the pastor is not alone. Traveling the path alongside will be the transgender person's friends and loved ones, community of support, therapist, coworkers, and religious community. The loving support of a pastor through this journey can be healing in and of itself. It is challenging work, but the rewards are deep. And it brings us that much closer to truly embodying King's vision of beloved community.

EIGHTEEN

Problems or Partners?
Senior Adults and a
New Story for Pastoral Care

Janet Ramsey

Guard against self-deception, each of you. If someone among you thinks he is wise in this age, let him become foolish so that he can become wise. For the wisdom of this age is foolishness with God.—1 Cor. 3:18-19

I have often chosen to go into unfamiliar settings in spite of the discomfort involved, gaining a sense of perspective. . . . Arriving in a new place, you start from an acknowledgment of strangeness, a disciplined use of discomfort and surprise. (Bateson 2001, 27).

Discomfort and Surprise

As a seminary professor I have found that a first course in aging and pastoral care can be a strange and uncomfortable experience, especially for younger students. They are entering a world that differs greatly from the youth-oriented environment around them. I try to find ways to increase their discomfort so that they won't ignore or deny it, so that we will all have a beginner's mind. Unlike the predominantly youthful images they see on campus or in the media, the faces they now see come from a variety of locations on the life span. Instead of only listening to jokes about aging and old people, students begin to hear older people talking about their struggles, their victories, their times of doubt and questioning—stories reflecting the entire range of human experience. It is gratifying to see attitudes changing—typically, the students begin to look forward to this aspect of their future vocations. Some of them become vocal advocates for aging persons, and, as they face their own anxieties and misconceptions about growing old, they move on to a more balanced view of the later years. But Bateson and Saint Paul were both right—when arriving at a new place, when wishing to gain a wiser and wider perspective, we must begin by acknowledging our discomfort. We must take the risk to look a little foolish.

I have even more fun providing the element of surprise (see Bateson above). Seminary students who sign up for an aging class are quite confident they do not hold ageist attitudes or assumptions, but I know that is impossible—ageism comes with simply living in our society; no one can totally escape this malady. So to help us all become more wise, and to move us toward resisting the real foolishness of this age, I tell them a story.

Heidi, 78, came to my office for pastoral counseling several years after having done successful marital work with her husband, Hank, 80. She was alone this time. When I had first met the couple, I'd been impressed by the goal they brought to their work: they wanted to increase the intimacy in their relationship. I knew that Hank had great difficulties expressing emotions (he told about being orphaned at an early age and raised by cold, domineering aunts) and that connecting to Heidi on a deep level frightened him, but they both worked hard, began sharing both negative and positive feelings, forgave each other a bit, and appeared slowly to be creating a new story for their relationship. Now, suddenly, Heidi reappeared. I was shocked by her appearance—she was using a walker and had gained at least fifty pounds. She told me she had been hospitalized during the past year for congestive heart failure, suffered from occasional incontinence, and was often short of breath. But Heidi didn't come to talk about her declining health—she launched into a vehement description of how upset she was about her marriage. She now had a one-sided, highly negative narrative about her current life with Hank, and she obviously had been telling herself this story more than once. It was difficult to remember the former Heidi, who had so patiently and lovingly encouraged her husband's growth. As she finished her unhappy tale, she hung her head and expressed guilt about her angry feelings: "I know, as a Christian, I should not feel this way," she said. "But he just disgusts me, especially his personal habits. I have lost all desire to be with him."

At this point, I always stop and ask my students what questions they would want to ask Heidi. Each year they respond with a variety of interesting suggestions, such as probing the possible effects of cardiac-related symptoms, or wondering about the impact of her declining health on their relationship. No student has ever suggested one of the questions I did, in fact, ask that day—"Is there another man in your life?" Heidi answered in the affirmative.

My students look stunned—not only that I would ask this question of a seventy-eight-year-old great-grandmother, but even more so by her response. Heidi acknowledged that she had a serious "crush" on a man she'd met at church, saying, "He makes me feel wonderful. We are really soul mates." After many years of working with older adults, I responded to Heidi as a woman first and as an older woman second." It did not particularly surprise me that, like anyone in the midst of either an emotional or physical affair, she had started noticing the negative aspects of her spouse's personality and behavior, ignoring his positive traits. Her emotional affair was the key that unlocked her secret of her strange behavior; age-related maladies were only secondary to what she was experiencing interpersonally.

As the case study ends, students realize that they have overlooked something fundamental—older persons have powerful emotional needs similar to those of all people, at any age. They recognize that their unconscious stereotypes have blinded them to Heidi's basic humanity, making it impossible for them to hear her story as one of God's whole (and romantic and sexual!) creatures, a woman who experiences a full range of normal needs, including the need to be close to another person.

Homogeneity: False Narratives of Simplicity

As Heidi and Hank's story shows, working with older adults not only takes us into a strange and surprising world—it also increases our appreciation for life's complexities, surprises, and nuances. But not all of this discomfort is caused by age-related differences. Whenever we attempt to understand human beings more deeply, whenever we try to fill in the picture of someone's life, we are brought face to face with endless varieties in shadow, color, and detail. In the case of older adults, this diversity is extensive and occurs in many domains, including educational background, class, personality, economic standing, and race. To state what should be obvious, every older adult is a unique individual with a unique personal history.

Against ageism, which, like all prejudices, attempts to homogenize people, telling the same false and simplistic story for all persons in a group, gerontologists have long emphasized that persons who are old are more different from each other than at any other time of life—they have had more time to get that way. This pluralism requires that we constantly redefine what it means to be "old," and that our ongoing revisions be both internal (the ways we talk to ourselves about aging) and external (the ways we interpret stories to others).

When I met Heidi I had been working with senior adults for many years, but I write here confessionally, as someone who has certainly made her own foolish errors. I first discovered my love for working with old people as I sat on the front porch of a woman who lived across the street from my house in a small Pennsylvania town. For years, she was my model for "old women"—kind, sweet, and happy to stay in her home, a literal milk-and-cookies kind of grandma. But twenty years later, when I began working as a pastoral counselor specializing in gerontology, I had to revise my assumptions—for example, that older women were all staying home living calm, quiet lives. Instead, I found most of them to be too busy with their careers or with raising their grandchildren to even consider sitting and rocking on the porch.

These changes are not all historically based, of course—cohort group effect, as it is called in gerontology, is only one factor among many that must be kept in mind. To complicate things even further, there are also identifiable patterns of thought and behavior among elders. These similarities, recognizable by culture, ethnic group, and religious denomination, do not so much modify diversity as help us find our way through it. One researcher recently confirmed that what constitutes "successful aging" varies by ethnic group, along with the language we use to describe it. Certainly for all of us who are congregational caregivers, one-dimensional, culturally limited expectations simply will not do.

Small wonder, in the face of this great diversity, that we feel some degree of discomfort and surprise when we hear a story like Heidi's, for it dawns on us that there is no one group called old people, and that our own lives have been permeated by many oppressive and limited attitudes about aging that we learned in our own families. Thus, as we will see, there can be no one-size-fits-all program for senior adult ministry, no single "script" for how a congregation responds to the needs of its seniors, no uniform way to encourage all older persons to redefine their post-retirement vocations.

Narratives of Scarcity

> The disciples said to him, "Where can we get enough bread in this desolate place to satisfy so great a crowd?" Jesus said to them, "How many loaves do you have?" They replied, "Seven—and a few small fish. After instructing the crowd to sit down on the ground, he took the seven loaves and the fish, and after giving thanks, he broke them and began giving them to the disciples, who then gave them to the crowds. They all ate and were satisfied, and they picked up the broken pieces left over, seven baskets full. (Matt. 15:33-37)

A respect for the diversity of each person's story leads us to a basic question concerning the very rationale for including this chapter in a book about pastoral care and oppression: Is there a fit? Most of the people we meet in our religious places of worship do not appear to be oppressed. We think of the so-called young-old who are affluent, traveling or spending their days on the golf course, or we consider the enormous amount our country spends each day on health care for our seniors, and we may ask, "What's so oppressive about growing old? Why a chapter on aging, pastoral care, and oppression?"

Again, we must keep in mind diversity, this time economic. Although the poverty rate for older adults as a group is lower than in years past, and although this rate is now lower among those over sixty-five than in the general population, using this one (statistical) finding to justify disregard for those who are old and poor would be shameful. We know that, on one hand, many of our older citizens do enjoy great material advantage; they have accumulated, over the years and often through their own efforts, significant financial recourses. But, on the other hand, far too many older people live in abject poverty and must make untenable choices every day—for example, between purchasing the medications they need or heating their homes adequately. Since many of these impoverished elderly can no longer attend worship services regularly, they become easy to overlook when we come together for worship in our comfortable pews. For many denominations of European Americans in particular, congregations are economically and racially homogeneous, and it is far too easy to form opinions about aging and resources without real awareness of those older Americans who struggle to get by. Ironically, many of these elder poor live in the very communities that surround our churches and synagogues.

Demographics also reveal economic diversity by age status, gender, and race. Older women (12 percent) were more likely than older men (8 percent) to live in poverty in 2002, and people age sixty-five to seventy-four had a poverty rate of 9 percent, compared with 12 percent of those persons age seventy-five and over. Perhaps the most glaring contrast is by race—in 2001, the median net worth of older white households ($205,000) was five times larger than that of older black households ($41,000).

Oppression has many names and can, of course, exist in prosperous households as well, since elder abuse knows no economic boundaries. Furthermore, both intuitive sense and research confirm that happiness cannot be equated with financial success (see Kasser and Ryan 1996); certainly not all wealthy older adults are happy, particularly in Western culture. Having bought into a lifestyle that values individual power, autonomy, and achievement, some persons over sixty-five are ill-equipped for the interdependence, mutuality, and cooperation that will be required in their later years. These are the older men and women who, when they serve on our congregational committees, behave more like CEOs than like servants of the gospel, demonstrating their needy greatness. Like Shakespeare's old King Lear, they are "as full of grief as age, wretched in both."

Lack of understanding about economic diversity can also lead to a kind of generation war, which is, for the impoverished old, a cruel joke. As the costs for health care and other necessary commodities rise, and as people live longer and longer, the voices of pastoral caregivers must be informed, balanced, and realistic. In the future, we may be the only voice of reason and calm in the midst of a resource-anxious world. For we have a decidedly different point of view—Christians and Jews have been taught, out of our prophetic tradition, to love justice and honor one's parents, and caring about economic justice for the poor and the old brings both of these commandments together. Furthermore, Christians are also called to witness to the abundance that Jesus made real the day he fed five thousand with a few loaves and fishes—we believe that, if the world can learn to share, there will be plenty, not scarcity. What a privilege it is for all of us in the Judeo-Christian tradition to play this prophetic role—to speak out for those who have no voice, to advocate for the poor and the old, not only in our congregations but in our global community. We are called to remember the poor (see Patton 2005), with both our words and deeds. This is pastoral care that takes oppression seriously; this is pastoral care that matters.

Finally, we must remember too that not only do individual members of each congregation differ, but also congregations themselves are dissimilar—culturally, economically, and geographically. No one vision for an older adults' ministry can be handed down from churchwide offices and expected to fit all. Since I write some of these materials myself, I find that I must constantly remind myself of this diversity. As soon as I make a generalization about "older adults" or about "ministry with older adults," I must qualify my own generalizations. Pastoral care with older adults, in whatever form, must begin with attending to diversity.

Ageism: Narratives of Division

> Is not the cup of blessing that we bless a sharing in the blood of Christ? Is not the bread that we break a sharing in the body of Christ? Because there is one bread, we who are many are one body, for we all share the one bread. (1 Cor. 10:16-17)

June had tears in her eyes, as she thanked me, after my presentation at her church, for making her feel better about being old. She went on to tell me that last year, when a new pastor came to her church, she was asked to discontinue her ministry as a Sunday school teacher, with no explanation other than a reference to her age, and with no expressions of appreciation. "The pastor just came in my classroom one Sunday morning after the children were gone and told me it was time to 'step down' and 'give some younger person a chance.' I taught that class for twenty-five years, and just like that, I was cast aside."

Against the belief that we are all part of the body of Christ, as we share the same cup of blessing, stands the harsh fact that not every person is valued, either in our society or in our congregations. Tragically, the story of June is not unusual—there is overwhelming evidence that age-based discrimination is widespread. This includes our legal system (Eglit 2005, 52), medicine (Yoong and Heyman 2005), the media (Davis 1984), educational systems (Wasserman 2003, 83), and the business world (Hayhurst 2002, 9). Although we tend to automatically group people by their race, sex, and age in our social life, one of the unfortunate results of this categorizing is what has been labeled ageism— prejudice and discrimination against older people based on the belief that aging itself makes people less attractive, intelligent, sexual, and productive (Butler 1969). Ageism can be either explicit (as in "firing" June), resulting in obvious and visible acts of discrimination, or implicit, resulting in attitudes, thoughts and comments with ageist content (e.g., she's too old to be teaching our young people). In all cases, narratives of deficiency, incompetence, and unattractiveness lurk beneath the surface of our conscious lives, causing immeasurable damage to older adults' self-esteem and to their ability to maintain courage and hope in a demanding world. When one has experienced years of combined explicit and implicit ageism, it is difficult to take risks, to seek justice for discrimination, to live each day with optimism and dignity, to challenge your pastor's decision. No, surprisingly, older people themselves often make the most ageist comments; they have internalized years of these cultural perceptions. But ageism in any form stands in total contrast to Christ's vision of the reign of God. It can have no part in our life together—neither as we gather around to drink from one cup, nor as we go out to serve the world.

What is remarkable is that, unlike racism and sexism, ageist practices and attitudes often go socially unpunished and personally unnoticed. June, for example, felt she had no one to whom she could speak; she was afraid of being seen as a foolish old person who just couldn't let go. Strangely, the same people who would never make racist or sexist comments fear no embarrassment and feel no compunction after making a joke about "a foolish little old woman." It would appear that our internal dialogues are formed so early that later we fail to recognize the need to edit them. Ageism is the only prejudice that we create for ourselves; we will all experience it if we live long enough.

The causes of this phenomenon are complex. Some psychologists believe that human beings lack the capacity to see past our own level of development, therefore decreasing our empathy for others (Golub et al. 2002). We also fear death inordinately in Western society—older people remind us that we will all grow old and die—and dependency even more so (see M. Baltes 1996). But these years are not necessarily sad and lonely times, filled with depression and despair. Although early research in social gerontology emphasized losses and decline, more recently psychology has shown a balance of gains and losses as we move through the life span (P. Baltes and M. Baltes 1990). What is seldom obvious in our ways of thinking or acting, what we do not easily understand, is that we Americans have largely "invented" our own experience of aging (see Maddox 1991). These factors combine with others, such as our emphasis on productivity at the marketplace, to form deeply entrenched, discriminatory beliefs and practices toward older adults. I passionately believe that naming and speaking out against the attitudes and practices of ageism is a core responsibility for all pastoral caregivers.

I have found one persistent sign of ageism in the language we use: so much of it is youthcentric. Reminiscent of feminists who discovered androcentric language and noted that women are referenced primarily when their behavior presents a problem or when they are exceptional in some way (when compared to a male norm; see Schussler Fiorenza 1983), pastoral caregivers must resist the tendency to describe older persons as "problems to be solved." It is common to refer to older people in positive terms only when they appear to transcend the limits of physical aging—"He still jogs every day; he's so young for his age!" Or, "Isn't she attractive for a seventy-year-old woman!" The point of reference for these comments is, of course, younger persons—not the intrinsic worth of maturity and wisdom, qualities that senior adults themselves have developed.

Theologically, the language of Miroslav Volf is helpful—he helps us understand that when we exclude those whom we perceive as different, we make them into "Others," into nonhuman objects whom we can treat without respect. Instead, Christians are called to a way of life in which those who are different are just another part of the neighborhood, part of the community formed at the foot of the cross. We are those for whom Christ died (we do not exclude our neighbors; we embrace them). Volf recognizes that not only our fear of death and strangeness, but also our inordinate fear of suffering, distracts us from our oneness as human beings and keeps us from embracing those whom we fear and misunderstand. This insight is particularly applicable to older persons, whose physical suffering is often quite visible. Consider, first, the foundation of Christian community, the cross. Christ unites different "bodies" into one body, not simply in virtue of the singleness of his person ("one leader—one people") or of his vision ("one principle or law—one community"), but above all through his suffering. The cross, then, becomes the theological center under which persons of all ages stand together in an essential oneness. This unity enables our victory over all "isms" and is the ultimate vision for pastoral care with all people.

Scripture also abounds with stories affirming the benefits (especially for our religious communities) of human wisdom—and here the social sciences combine with theology to form another powerful argument against ageism. For wisdom, unlike knowledge, develops only as people live long years. Robert Kegan, a developmental psychologist at Harvard, described cognitive and emotional development (his version of what we call wisdom) in terms of "orders" of consciousness. At early levels, we are conscious, we understand the world, and we can communicate clearly; we have a sense of self. By the fourth and fifth orders, however, our perspectives have expanded and multiple points of view are possible. A person now can be said to write and edit (interpret) the story of his own life. There is no longer the need to change "you" into being more like "me." However, these orders of consciousness and emotion can only occur as our self evolves, as we are transformed, and that requires years of lived and interpreted experience (Kegan 1998). In other words, one must live long and think deeply and well.

I am convinced that this form of wisdom, this wider and more empathetic perspective, is precisely what the world needs now. While conducting my own research on spiritual resiliency, I had the honor of meeting numerous older adults who appear to think and feel at the fourth or fifth order; they are particularly able at interpreting their lives in the light of their spiritual faith, at reframing the challenges and losses that came to them. As I learned of their strength and resiliency, their rich gifts for ministry, and their wise insight, my own ageism decreased. What a contrast spiritually strong elders in our congregations present to the stereotypes that so infect our culture!

The Context for Care

Everyone knows it is happening—our congregations are aging. Along with the rest of our nation, members of churches and synagogues consist more and more of persons past sixty-five. In the years to come, this will increase rapidly. This has not led to increased attention to ministry with older adults, a fact that may seem strange unless one considers the predominantly negative narratives about aging and older people described above. Neither seminaries nor the leadership and governing boards of our religious institutions have committed to proactive, imaginative, and appropriate pastoral care with, by, and for older adults. We have ignored both the needs and the gifts of senior adults in our congregations and in the communities that surround them. At best, we are reactive and worried—worried that we might become a "dying congregation," the pejorative phrase frequently muttered when pews are filled with grey and white heads. Of course we all want young people to come to church, but is not the missio Dei intended for people of all ages, young and old?

Avoidance, denial, ageist assumptions, insensitive language, and inadequate congregational structures have too often led, albeit by default, to precisely the phenomenon this text wishes to address—oppression of the marginalized. In the following section, I will briefly describe an approach to ministry that celebrates the partnerships we can have with older persons, an approach that avoids a problem-saturated approach to pastoral care.

Reactive Ministries for Partnership with Older Adults

Steve is a newly retired member of a large Lutheran church in downtown Minneapolis. A former businessman, he has been active in his congregation all his life, participating in a soup kitchen, the men's group, as an usher, and as chair of several committees. A bright and articulate man who reads his Bible daily and has a disciplined prayer life, Steve recently had a minor stroke. He finds his energy level decreased and he has to prioritize his activities to get through the day. But Steve is determined to find ways to continue to serve his congregation. He thinks he might like to become more involved with young people, including his children and grandchildren. "What does vocation mean to me now?" He wonders. "Shall I call and ask about the mentoring program being organized for confirmands. . . ?"

Rebecca, a ninety-two-year-old widow living alone, is not only homebound but largely confined to her chair. Legally blind, almost deaf, and disabled from a stroke and a broken hip, she remains a very busy person. "Do you realize how many people I must pray for each day?" she asks her lay visitors. "There is my pastor (he really needs my prayers!), the people who are sick (there's quite a list this week), my niece and grandnephew, those who are hungry around the world, the seminaries and the churchwide staff. . . ." Rebecca's church celebrates this prayer warrior and takes her vocation very seriously, bringing her, each week, a list of persons in the congregation who need her intercessions. By Sunday night, she knows what her work will be for the coming week, and she does it, with joy.

What a wonderful resource God has provided in our older members. Their gifts are varied and their faith is strong. In congregations where there is intentional ministry with, by, and for older members, there is a richness of intergenerational activity and mentoring that serves everyone well. People come together to consider how faith and life might intersect at all stages of the life span. Suffering and joy are both acknowledged, and, through mutual conversation and consolation, young and old live and work together, reading, studying and worshiping—trying to discern what it means to be a child of God in an ambiguous, complex world.

This is both my vision and, to a limited extent, a reality, derived from my visits with numerous congregations. Wonderful programs for pastoral care already exist, and I have gathered up, through the years, some helpful strategies for intergenerational partnerships. I list them here in order of importance, but there are many others that diversity demands.

Proactive Model

Context: Youth-Oriented Culture
Demographic "Emergency"
Unpreparedness in Congregations and Seminaries

TRUST	CARE	COMPASSION
Embrace	Involvement	Ministry as celebration
Enough for everyone	Intentionality	Elders as resources
Elders as neighbors	Flexibility	and partners in ministry
Genuine humor	Elders as models	Joy as motivation
Wise perspective	Truth-telling	Hopeful, encouraging,
Ability to risk	Face to face	energizing & creative
Language of mutuality	Collaborations and	Deeply theological
Shared power	partnerships	Enters the suffering of others
Intergenerational		Ministry to, with, and by older
"You are my brother!"	"I am with you"	adults
"You are my sister!"		"We will live, work, and pray together."

Reactive Model

Context: Youth-Oriented Culture
Demographic "Emergency"
Unpreparedness in Congregations and Seminaries

FEAR/ANXIETY	APATHY	CHARITY & GOOD INTENTIONS
Exclusion	Neglect	Problematizing
Resource battles	Inaction	Elders as "objects of care"
Aged as the "other"	Rigidity	Guilt as motivation
"Humor" at expense of	Invisible elders	Despair, discouragement,
older adults	Denial	boredom, & burn-out
Resistance to change	Turning away	Solution by committee
Language of scarcity	Highly	Political correctness
Power games	individualistic	Ministry *to* older adults
Generational segregation	"Maybe this will	Clergy-lead ministries
"You are different!"	go away!"	Superficial spiritualizes
		"I will take care of you."

1. Use a proactive, rather than a reactive, approach (see charts one and two, below). When a congregation wants to use the gifts that older adults have, and plans in advance, they find that trust, care, and compassion replace fear, apathy, and charity. All persons are embraced, there is enough for everyone, and intergenerational activities are appreciated. Involvement in planning and implementing education, worship, and service activities is widespread and flexible so that elders can mentor and model their faith for younger members and, in turn, be energized by them. When pastoral care is organized proactively, "We will live, work, and pray together" replaces "I will take care of you."

2. Begin by listening to senior adults themselves. What do they wish to do? What do they need? What are they unhappy about and what more could be done to help them grow in their faith? Any committee formed to explore pastoral care or ministry with senior adults should largely consist of senior adults, but should also include congregational leaders, who must have an investment in the process so that resources will be found to fund it.

3. Consistently avoid problem-saturated and ageist language in sermons, bulletins, reports, and informal conversations. If the congregation is declining it is unlikely that this is because of its old members. Externalize the issue appropriately by asking, for example, "How relevant is this congregation's mission for the surrounding community?"

4. Emphasize community, deeply and theologically understood, over mere "social get-togethers." Research shows that spiritual community is a multifaceted, crucial resource for resiliency in older adults. They can assist us in understanding its riches, through the stories of their lives (see Ramsey and Blieszner 1999), and they need to experience it to remain strong, personally and spiritually.

5. Remember those who can no longer come to church, including the cognitively impaired and the very old and frail, and keep them in the community's heart. It is a tragic misconception that persons with dementia no longer have spiritual needs, as anyone who has read Psalm 23 to a person with early Alzheimer's knows. Often able senior members who know these folks best will be their best caregivers, but all lay visitors need education and training, for example, on communicating and on the appropriate use of ritual. The most rapidly growing group among the elderly are the so-called old-old, and many of them (though certainly not all!) are frail and homebound, no longer able to speak for themselves.

They need our attention and our advocacy with policymakers. This, too, is pastoral care.

6. Replace old patterns of obligation and necessity with the metaphor of holy friendship when considering pastoral care with homebound seniors (see Ramsey 2006). Nourish such a ministry in the congregation, not only for the clergy, but also for lay caregivers, and constantly evaluate its effectiveness and respectfulness.

7. Always think intergenerationally, and plan most educational and social service activities by topic and need, rather than by age group. It can be insulting to older adults to expect them to go to "dumbed-down" classes for seniors (ibid., 263). From time to time, offer topics "meaty" enough to capture the attention of those facing death, dying, or caregiving responsibilities (and provide respite care during class for the latter!). The work of gerontologist and pastoral caregiver Mel Kimble has taught us how important issues of meaning are for older persons, especially at the time when death approaches (see Kimble 2003). We must include them, as part of our pastoral care programs.

8. Do not assume that older members are all conservative and will not be open to change; like anyone else, they need education and understanding before accepting new ideas.

9. Use often the language of vocation. Help newly retired adults to redefine and rediscover their own vocations by encouraging specific ministries (e.g., Rebecca's prayer list, Steve's mentoring program). Retirement does not have to be all about leisure; nowhere in Scripture are we told that discipleship ends at sixty-five. We need the care and service our older adults are willing to give!

Conclusion

We have become far too at home with old stories of old people. Pastoral caregivers, like many other helpers in Western culture, have often settled for demeaning and restricted narratives of aging persons, narratives that reinforce the dull and destructive myths of a youth-oriented culture. Lacking peripheral vision and denying the many ways in which we construct our own realities, we have told each other, "That's just the way it is when you get old!"

Pastoral care, in partnership with senior members, need not be boring, dull, or unimaginative. There are many empowering stories available to us as pastoral caregivers, not only in Scripture but in the real lives of our people. With God's help, and with a wisdom not our own, we can move from learned fear to narratives of community, compassion, and interdependency. We can partner with the spiritually strong persons in our midst who have lived lives rich in faith, resiliency, and wisdom—precisely the qualities sorely needed in our confused and broken world.

NINETEEN

Pastoral Care and Gay Men: The Amazing True Story of the Life and Death of One Good Man

Christopher Medeiros

There were many "homes" for young Doug Carty. There was the "home" Doug came from, one he maintained by his relationship with his family. People as good and decent as Doug Carty don't just appear out of nowhere, they come from love. Anyone who knew Doug at all knew his deep love for his family. Perhaps his own personal demons kept him from sharing parts of his life with those he loved, but in no way did that ever alter the depth and commitment of his love for his family. From his family, Doug developed his hard-working nature, integrity, strength of character, and generosity. All of these things enabled Doug to draw wonderful people around him for his entire life.

The other major home for Doug was his family of friends, especially Gene and Wolf. We gather around this amazing place today that they have built with love and friendship, the grounds and view that Doug literally helped build with his own two hands, a place that has become home, in so many ways, to many of us. All of Doug's friends helped him, through the simple, but profound, act of friendship, to come to love and accept himself more and more.
—Excerpt from Doug's memorial service

---

*Details of this story, including Doug's name, have been changed to protect the privacy of his friends and family.

This is the amazing and ordinary true story of the life and death of one good man.

Doug Carty was fifty years old when he died unexpectedly, doing what he loved most—camping. If Doug fit any stereotype it was that of a strong, quiet man with a heart of gold who is such a popular figure in American culture. Doug kept his emotions in check, although he had a hearty laugh and a sad movie on TV would bring a tear to his eye.

Doug served his country in the military for thirty years. He loved the outdoors. He could be found camping in his tent when weather permitted, and he loved hunting and fishing.

He loved and was dedicated to his family. He was the middle child of five children. He grew up in a loving, working-class Irish Roman Catholic family in semi-rural suburbs in Maine. He was the son who always checked on his parents. Doug was the one who went to sporting events with his father and took his mother to medical appointments. Even when he lived a two-hour drive from his parents, he was the one who would drive to their house after snowstorms to be sure the driveway, roof, and walkways were clear. At the holidays he loved all the family traditions. He took great pride in helping the family cook and prepare things for Christmas, Thanksgiving, family birthdays, and many other events.

Doug was the kind of man you know you would call if you needed a ride somewhere or a favor. Every year he would help his best friends organize camping events; he would go down to the camping site days before to help clear the land and set up tents. One year, he organized a group and spent days clearing away trees on a friend's land to help them save money.

He was a very private person. Although Doug loved his family and his friends deeply, he was the kind of person who kept many of his feelings to himself. Like all of us, he had personal demons, but during his all-too-short life he believed he had to protect those he loved from the complexity of his world. Every once in a while, he seemed to drink a little more heavily than usual when he was with his friends; but he never drank in front of his family. When he did drink with his friends he seemed to drink only a little more than everyone else—and most people never noticed.

Although Doug was surrounded with love from his family and friends, he kept so many things private that even those who knew him well knew that there were things about Doug they didn't know. Doug grew up with love and faith, but he grew up in a world and a church that told him being gay was a bad thing. Doug knew he was gay and kept the world of his family and the world of his gay friends separate to protect, he thought, all of them and himself.

Besides the battle between the gay and straight worlds in which Doug lived, he also never seemed to fit comfortably in the gay world. Much of the way gay life evolved in the United States in Doug's time didn't seem to have much to do with Doug's own lifestyle. He preferred trees, lakes, and valleys over the urban gay neighborhoods of the cities. His idea of fashion was clean work clothes and casual wear. He drank beer, not cocktails. He was ruggedly handsome, with hands made strong from chopping down trees—but he didn't know much about facials and manicures. Being gay in a homophobic culture can be extremely difficult; and finding you don't fit into the subculture you are supposed to be part of can add even more pain and isolation.

In his forties, Doug discovered another man like himself who fit into a gay subculture called "the bears"—gay men who wear flannel shirts and jeans, not designer clothes, and have bellies, not washboard abs. Bears would more likely be found camping in the woods than going to after-hours clubs in the cities.

Doug made friends, good friends, among "the bears." He even dated a bit, although because he kept his worlds so separate, it was nearly impossible to have someone too special or too close in his life, someone who by his very existence might loosen the boundaries Doug had built so carefully.

The last weekend of his life was beautiful. It was late summer in the mountains; there was warm sunshine and leaves were just starting to change. Doug was on a campout with about thirty other gay friends on the land of his two closest friends, Gene and Wolf. They all attended a local country fair together, laughed, talked, drank, and played music. Doug even reconnected with an old flame, John. Life was good. On Sunday, at noon, they all ate a hearty brunch and said goodbye, making plans to see one another again soon.

That night, at midnight, doing what he loved most, camping with a friend, Doug died.

Death has a way of breaking boundaries and uncovering long-hidden truths. When Doug died, the police called his family, telling Doug's brothers that there were "items of an alternative lifestyle" found in his tent. Doug, in fact, had a flyer from a gay film festival and his collection of teddy bear pins—souvenirs that many of the gay "bears" wore or collected as namesakes. At first, both the police and Doug's brothers thought the pins had some strange sexual significance in his life and were connected, somehow, with his death. They would later come to understand that they were simply a collection, symbols important to a man who was finding a small corner of the world where he could be himself. The initial misunderstanding, however, led his brothers to decide to burn everything in Doug's tent before the rest of his family or friends could see his last possessions—

perhaps thinking they were protecting their family, perhaps not knowing how to handle finding out their brother was gay.

With Doug's death his family suddenly had information about their son that Doug had worked hard to keep from them during his lifetime. They called everyone they could think of to tell them of Doug's death, but his family didn't know how to contact people they had never met. Doug's biological family simply did not know his very real gay family. They were not even sure that Doug had gay friends. Fortunately, one of Doug's sisters knew how much Doug loved camping and also knew the areas where he usually went camping, so she made sure that the newspapers in those areas carried his obituary—hoping that somehow Doug's friends would find out about his death.

That small gesture did finally let his friends know, two days after his death, that he was gone. His gay friends from all over New England and Canada gathered back at Gene and Wolf's house as soon as they heard—the same place they had been laughing and camping with Doug just days before. His death was a mystery. They didn't know how to contact his family to offer their sympathy, and didn't know how to explain who they were to Doug. They simply didn't know what to do; so they sat together that night, the night before his funeral, and cried, held one another, and told stories of their friend. There was sadness, confusion, and isolation. Just a few miles away, Doug's biological family and family of friends grieved apart, separated from one another by a wall of ignorance.

Finally, John, who had been reunited with Doug only a few days before, felt he had to find out something. John knew that he and Doug's other friends had to find a way to say goodbye to someone who had been woven so closely into their lives and their hearts. That night he called the church where the funeral was to be held the next day to ask the priest how Doug had died. Father Paul told John that he had been meeting with the family and that the cause of death was unknown, but Doug had been found dead in his tent by the man with whom he was camping. John told the priest that Doug's friends did not know the family but they would come to the funeral and sit in the back, wanting to pay their respects but not cause any trouble. Without any explicit words, it became clear that the priest knew from the family that Doug was gay; now he was aware that Doug's gay friends had contacted him. Father Paul found a way to be pastoral and comforting to both of Doug's families, talking to both, giving information and lending a listening ear.

At the funeral, John greeted the priest and thanked him for the help he had given to Doug's friends the night before. In the course of the funeral, Father Paul made sure to mention both family and friends several times in his sermon. It was subtle, but profound, and not lost on Doug's gay friends. At the end of the liturgy the coffin was brought to the back of the church to have the pall, the bright white sheet with a cross on it that had draped the coffin during the liturgy, replaced by the American flag that traditionally drapes the coffins of those who have served in the military, the flag that would later be presented to his mother. In a gesture that seemed so matter of fact, as though he were simply randomly asking a favor of someone who was sitting at the back of the church, Father Paul asked John (and in so doing Doug's whole gay family) to help remove the pall and place the flag on the coffin. In that moment, Father Paul brought together, for the first time ever, the two families that loved Doug Carty. The walls that had kept all of the people that loved Doug separate had begun to crumble; love and death making all boundaries melt away.

After the funeral, there was a military gun salute outside and all who had loved Doug Carty clung to one another. They watched as the family members and friends from Doug's straight life headed into the church hall. These gay men didn't know if they would be welcome, and the very idea that they might make Doug's family—whom he had loved and protected so fiercely—uncomfortable was an impossibility in their minds. They would do nothing to upset the family.

Then Ellen, one of Doug's sisters, and her female partner walked up to them, just before they got in their cars to leave. Ellen said she had figured out who they were. She was also gay, but the walls Doug built kept her and Doug from ever talking about it.

Weeks after the funeral, Gene and Wolf held their own memorial with his friends and his two sisters at their house, the last place Doug had smiled and laughed. Together they all laughed, cried, prayed, told stories, read poetry, and broke bread together. All those who loved Doug held and supported each other in a way Doug never would have thought could be possible.

A moving part of the memorial was the prose poem written and read by Doug's friend John:

The End of Summer

The end of summer approaches.

The days grow shorter, the air cooler.

The bears know the long winter is coming, and they play in the

September sun, relishing in the dwindling days of sunlight, celebrating
the sheer joy of time with friends before the long winter's sleep.

The leaves know too, they explode with their brightest and most beautiful faces before they brown and they fall away.

The September clouds grow and cover more and more of the once summer, now fall, indigo sky.

We celebrated the last gasp of summer together, never imagining . . .

I knew about the shorter days, the cooler air, bright falling leaves, and the growing clouds, but I didn't know how much the fall wind would take.

Winter is not yet here, yet there seems no warmth anywhere, The nights are cold.

In mourning, even thickest wool blankets feel threadbare against my skin.

Winter will come and be colder without you. It is so hard to believe there will ever be spring, and yet, spring will come.

As the calendar marches on and the winter clouds will thin and float away.

When the spring sun melts the ice and warms the cold earth and I will remember how you could melt my blues and grays away with a look, a smile, a hug.

When I feel the warm breeze I will remember your open heart.

I will feel spring again.

I will remember you.

I will smile.

But in my heart,

Even when I see the clearest spring sky,

It will never be as blue as your eyes.

In the months that followed, the sadness of grieving continued, but the legacy of love continued, too. Doug's sisters and later his mother would stay in touch, e-mailing, calling, and meeting for dinners and brunch—brought together by the simple love of one good man. At Christmas, they all gathered together, Doug's two sisters and their families, and his mother, to celebrate the holiday, remember Doug's life, and share stories the others never knew about the man they all loved.

The mystery of Doug's death took a few months for the medical examiner to report officially, and although a single cause of death will probably never be found or understood, one contributing factor in Doug's death was probably the very high level of alcohol in his blood.

In the world we live in today, LGBT (lesbian, gay, bisexual, transgender) people have made great advances. This is most true in the United States and other Western countries. LGBT people are no longer labeled as "disordered" by the medical or psychiatric communities. Openly gay people are beginning to be depicted positively on television and in films. They also serve as senators and congressional representatives. Gay people have become a political presence; civil unions and legal marriages now exist in various states and countries. In the religious debate in the United States, gay people are beginning to have a voice. The debate regarding sexuality in the Anglican Communion, and the election in New Hampshire of an openly gay bishop to the episcopate, the Rt. Rev. Gene Robinson, make it clear that in many ways the world has changed. However, the change is, so far, relatively small and far from uniform.

As you consider Doug Carty's story, it is important to remember that Doug's deeply closeted existence existed only a short drive from the possibility of legal marriage in Massachusetts, and just a few miles from where Bishop Gene Robinson leads the diocese of New Hampshire.

The life experience of the out, urban, affluent openly gay man is only one small part of the spectrum of the LBGT community. Still, today, many working-class gay men live and die in suburban and rural areas, in the two-thirds world, in conservative religious households and societies where the closet is the only thing that protects them from loss of their families, friends, jobs, and even their physical safety. Being gay is still a criminal offense in many places around the world, with punishments ranging from prison to torture to death.

Doug had a long and honorable career in the U.S. military, which could have been taken away in an instant, depending on how the "don't ask, don't tell" policy was enforced. He lived in fear that society, his family, and his straight friends would never accept him, or would, at worst, reject him "if they knew."

Doug had never fit into even the limited roles our society has chosen to recognize for gay men. Even today, although gay men may be accepted as actors or hairdressers, many in the United States still believe in legally barring them from openly serving in the military, marrying, or adopting children. There are few openly gay men playing professional sports in this country for fear their teammates, coaches, and fans would never accept them.

This story is meant to be a kind of literary icon, a symbol or window into looking at many different issues, especially those affecting gay men. A list of questions for reflection on this story follows. They are meant to help focus and give shape to a discussion or reflection on the pastoral care of gay men. How might you answer them?

- What other questions occur to you when reflecting on Doug's story? How can you, in your setting, foster a discussion on some of the issues raised here?
- What are some of the differences in pastoral issues with "out" gay men as opposed to "closeted" gay men?
- When and how is it important to see someone as a member of a marginalized group? When is understanding someone in that light important and when is it less relevant? What things are common among marginalized groups, and what are important ways people vary within a group of which they are a part?
- What are the differences between stereotypes and legitimate differences between gay men and the general population?
- What are some of the specific things about gay men that may make them differ from the general population? Suicide rates? Alcoholism?
- How does the phenomenon of the "closet" and "coming out" make LGBT people different from the general population?
- What are some of the concrete costs for a person, in the world they live in, to coming out and to not coming out?
- When we are operating in pastoral settings, do we realize that often people may have "membership" in minorities of various kinds of which we are not aware? Are there ways to reach out to these people? How?
- How do we understand when people's identities fit multiple categories? How might such issues as race, ethnic group, educational level, social class, rural vs. suburban vs. urban culture, and sexual orientation operate together in one person?

- When thinking about how conflict may arise among families, friends, and partners on the death of a person significant to them all, what ways can you help dialogue and discussion to happen? When is it important to help foster dialogue and when is it important not to be involved?
- How familiar are you with issues around problem drinking/binge drinking/alcoholism issues in general?
- When thinking about families, how much do we take into account the different ways all people, but gay people in particular, construct families? Do we allow people to define families or do we compare all to the yardstick of biologically related, nuclear-based families of traditional white, straight American culture? What is the value of friendship? Do we allow the strength of people's relationships define who is family or do we easily allow traditional definitions to influence how we view someone's family?
- How do we handle major revelations about people that only come with their death? How can we be pastoral in those cases? How do we deal with situations where secrecy, privacy, and death are intertwined? Does someone's death change the nature of such information? Do we, or should we, protect the privacy of the dead in the same way we would protect the privacy of the living?
- How could the way in which we think about the circumstances of a person's death radically change the way they are remembered by the people who have been part of their lives?
- Are the rituals of death, such as wakes and funerals, more for the living? How do we incorporate people into those rites as part of the grieving process?

TWENTY

The Time of No Room:
Changing Patterns in Responses
to Homelessness in Britain

Kenneth Leech

My local newspaper, the *East London Advertiser*, contained three, apparently unrelated, stories on February 13, 2003. One reported that the battle to save Spitalfields Market, one of our most historic and best-loved sites, had been lost to the property developers. "The battle is over" was the headline. It ended with a quotation from a representative of the campaigning group SMUT (Spitalfields Market Under Threat): "We just wanted to show the Corporation of London that it can't trample all over the people of the East End and get away with it." But that was precisely what it had done. The second story described the proposed Minerva Tower, another huge office block that, if it goes ahead, will dominate the landscape around Aldgate, the eastern edge of the financial district, putting both St. Botolph's Church and the local residents into its Babel-like shade. The third celebrated a police sweep on young commercial sex workers in the Commercial Street area.

Each of these stories related to districts very close to where I lived, and to each other. They bring home the fact that it is now—and I think this was always the case, but it has become more visibly obvious in recent years—virtually impossible to compartmentalize or to speak coherently about homelessness without a sense of connectedness. We cannot speak of homelessness without speaking of drugs, mental health, health care generally, redundancies, migration patterns, affordable housing, government housing policy, wars internal and external, gentrification, and so on. The onward thrust of the financial district into the East End, the attempt in "development-speak" and in real estate rhetoric; to abolish the East End; and replace it by "city fringe"; the encouragement of gentrification and therefore the pushing out of homeless people and prostitutes, as well as poor, working-class people and those in the middle-income groups—all this is part of a connected process. It will be all too familiar to comrades in the U.S. and elsewhere. Sociologists such as John Eade in London and Chris Mele in New York have been busy examining parallels and contrasts (Eade and Mele 2002; Mele 2000). Pastoral workers in British and American cities need also to maintain and strengthen links.

As a student in East London at the end of the 1960s, in this very same neighborhood, I got involved with several organizations that were working with older homeless men, including methylated spirit drinkers. Later, as a priest in Soho in 1969, I founded Centrepoint, the first all-night shelter for homeless young people and now one of the biggest organizations in this field in western Europe. For the last few years I have chaired UNLEASH (United London Ecumenical Action with the Single Homeless), which has, for twenty-five years, sought to be a voice from the churches to the politicians and the public, as well as an educational resource for Christian and other groups (Logan 2002).

It is said, in our postmodern jargon, that we cannot see "the big picture," but only fragments. But this, too, has always been so. Nevertheless, while—as I realized forty years ago—geographical proximity to problems and needs is no guarantee of accuracy of vision, it should be remembered that people who are most involved in local issues may see the "big picture" more accurately than national figures, who may see a broad but illusory one.

Homelessness is increasingly global, affected by changes in the global economy, patterns of migration, and so on. The sociologist Saskia Sassen speaks (slightly misleadingly) of a "sudden growth in homelessness" (Sassen 1991). UNICEF estimated in 1995 that there were one hundred million children living in city streets, of whom half were in Latin America and the Caribbean. Many commentators have warned of the likelihood of millions of displaced persons as a result of the war against Iraq. And who knows where the next victims of the permanent war economy will be found?

In the U.S., it is estimated that on any night in the city of Atlanta there are eleven to sixteen thousand homeless persons. Yet the pattern here is changing. In Philadelphia, in 1960, 75 percent of homeless people were over 45 years old, and 87 percent were white. By 1988, 86 percent were under 45, and 87 percent were black or ethnic minorities. In the U.S. as a whole, it is estimated that there are between one and three million teenagers living on the streets.

I want, against this global background, to focus on Britain, and on Inner London specifically. At the risk of the very compartmentalizing that I have criticized, I shall isolate five areas: the changing character and composition of the population of homeless people; the questions around geography, "regeneration," and property; the questions about the "hidden homeless" and "rough sleepers"; some issues about co-option and mergers; and the questions emerging from the existence of "sacred" and "secular" agencies. Arising out of this, I want to leave with you the question about whether specifically Christian organizations are still needed.

The Changing Character of Homelessness

First, the changing character of homelessness. I have lived and worked in the East End of London, close to the point where the financial district ends and an area of acute poverty begins, for the largest part of my adult life. When I first came to St. Botolph's Church, Aldgate, in 1958, the homeless people in this area were almost entirely male, white, often Scottish or Irish, aged over forty, generally with alcohol problems, with a subsection who lived on bombed sites, derelict buildings, and open spaces (of which "Itchy Park" in Whitechapel Road, where I lived from 1993 to 2004, was a classic example). Since those days, homeless people have included women, younger people, black people, middle-class professional people, and so on. All this is well known. Some of the shifts go back thirty or more years; some of them are more recent. Let me refer to three particular changes.

The racial composition of the homeless population has both shifted and become more visible. White-led projects often claimed that there were no black homeless, when in fact the truth was that black homeless did not come to white-led projects. At the same time, black people were not visible as homeless. This has now changed. The pattern here has been different from that in American cities, and this has been partly because of the different relationships between poverty, race, and class. In my neighborhood, for example, where the majority of the population is Bangladeshi, the problem of homelessness has been family focused, in contrast to the older white single male pattern.

The appearance of crack cocaine needs more detailed attention than I can give here. Chris Jencks has documented this in great detail in relation to Chicago and other North American cities (Jencks 1994), while Kevin Flemen of Release in the UK estimated several years ago that 49 percent of homeless people in London were injecting drugs. (In the general population the figure is 1 percent.) Certainly, in street work with young sex workers in this neighborhood, the use of crack cocaine has outpaced amphetamines and heroin in recent years.

The numbers of homeless people from middle class and professional backgrounds has increased, and the year 1991 was a turning point. In that year there was an increase in repossession of homes because of mortgage arrears. According to government data, homeless families increased by 30 percent in that year as a result of building society repossession—in earlier years a very unusual practice. Repossessions grew from about two thousand in 1979 to twenty-three thousand in 1987. In addition, a study in 1996 claimed that one in ten young homeless persons were graduates. Instability and insecurity is now embracing a wide spectrum of groups.

Geography, "Regeneration," and Property

Second, the geography of homelessness. In current property development jargon, the East End of London, as it was once seen as beginning at Aldgate, no longer exists. We are now "city fringe," one of the many products of the relentless eastward push of the City of London, the financial district within which profits matter more than persons. This itself raises urgent issues. So much work in the field of homelessness is concerned with caring for poor people. Yet we need to remember the words of R. H. Tawney, that what thoughtful rich people call the problem of poverty, thoughtful poor people call the problem of riches. On the "city fringe" we are daily experiencing what is called, sometimes obscenely, "regeneration," sometimes a euphemism for the displacement of the people. We are being told, from time to time, of the importance of "affordable housing," but affordable by whom? The "shrinking stock" of affordable rented housing was noted as long ago as 1962 in the London County Council's Committee of Inquiry into Homelessness, but the position has deteriorated dramatically since those early years. A study in May 2003 by the Joseph Rowntree Foundation has confirmed what most people in the field knew—the increasing difficulty of access to affordable housing in Britain. Yet many people still look at homelessness in terms of personal pathology or mental illness, neglecting the wider issues of access to housing.

Let me give an interesting example of the shifts in geography. For the past eleven years I have lived on the corner of Altab Ali Park, formerly known as St Mary's Churchyard, Whitechapel. Since the early nineteenth century the park was known as "Itchy Park" because of the numbers of homeless people—mostly vagrant alcoholics, often methylated spirit and crude spirit drinkers—who slept there. I look out onto this park all the time and, by day and night, I can see exactly who sleeps there and what goes on there. It is a long time since I have seen any homeless person sleeping there at night. On the corner of the park, in the rooms below me, are the former offices of St. Botolph's Project, and a few seconds across the road are the offices of Centrepoint (which I founded in 1969). A few minutes away is the office of Crisis. About ten minute's walk to the south are the offices of Thames Reach Bondway, the National Housing Foundation, and Turning Point. Five minutes east are a Salvation Army hostel—almost on the site where the Salvation Army was founded—and the Whitechapel (Methodist) Mission. I guess that together, even allowing for the collapse of St. Botolph's Project, these organizations employ around six hundred people. So there are more paid workers in the field of homelessness in this small area than there are homeless people! I draw no particular conclusions from this except the significance of geographical shifts in the access to and use of territory.

Rough Sleepers and "Hidden Homeless"

Third, the issues around rough sleepers and the "hidden homeless." It is clear that "rough sleepers"—people who sleep in the streets—are a tiny percentage of the homeless population, although much attention has been focused on them,and the original government initiative was the Rough Sleepers Unit. In January 1997, Tony Blair, before he was Prime Minister, spoke of the importance of being "intolerant of homeless people on the streets." This was the beginning of an attitude that has persisted and become more unpleasant and oppressive. Interestingly, those who objected to it at the time were accused of being alarmist, of having overreacted, misunderstood, and so on.

Much attention has been on beggars. In Britain, this was a political issue for "New Labour" before it came to power. "Clear beggars from streets says Blair" was a headline in *The Times* on January 7, 1997. Six years later, as the courts in Manchester were arguing the case to make begging an imprisonable offense, groups in California were arguing for criminalization not only of begging but of giving to beggars. Journalists here believe that the Manchester case could lead to a "national ban on beggars" (*The Independent,* August 22, 2003; in Weaver 2003). Research on begging is full of uncertainty combined with intense conviction on the part of some of the researchers. A study in 1994 by the London-based project Crisis suggested that 80 percent of beggars were homeless, and that most of the money was spent on food.

There have been many street counts, although they have not included people in squats or derelict buildings. They have omitted people who were not, literally, asleep. Of course, the numbers have gone down. This was, after all, the point of the exercise. But what is the point of the approach? Is it about visibility, or about focusing on such a small group in order to give the impression that "something is being done?" And does it mean that even this small group of "rough sleepers" has diminished or that it has simply been pushed on elsewhere, or moved into inaccessible places? To have reduced the numbers of the visible homeless is very convenient to local authorities. According to a report to the board of St. Botolph's Project on July 8, 2002, the London Boroughs of Tower Hamlets and Hackney had no policies on homelessness because their recorded numbers of rough sleepers were less than ten!

There are, however, not surprisingly, some oddities here. In the London Borough of Newham in 1999 there were, allegedly, only eleven rough sleepers, yet the Department of the Environment was funding an outreach worker to work with young homeless, expecting him to take on two hundred cases per year!

The issue of "hidden homeless," highlighted by the late Carolyn Ye-Myint in 1992 long before it became part of jargon, has recently been stressed by a writer in New York (Ye-Myint 1992; Bernstein 2001). Mary Kneafsey, formerly of St. Botolph's Project, suggested that, with the growth of a new government plan called "Supporting Persons," getting funding for individuals will get harder. Once benefits can only come via a post office account (April 2003), what happens to people with no identification? No identification, no money, no housing benefit, no accommodation. When we get to asylum seekers and refugees, the situation gets worse.

Co-options and Mergers

Fourth, the issues around co-options and mergers are different, but connected. Alasdair MacIntyre, in *After Virtue* (1981), rewrote Lord Acton's famous dictum. "All power co-opts," claimed MacIntyre, "Absolute power co-opts absolutely." The history of New Labour has been marked, in the area of social policy, by a series of co-options of workers from the voluntary sector or from other nongovernmental organizations, some of whom have been given senior and powerful posts within government, while others have been placed in positions of significant influence. As this has occurred, much of their earlier critical thought seems to have dissipated, and they have toed an uncritical and subservient line to New Labour policies and ideology. Fortunately, some have resigned, or been pushed out, and in some cases their critical abilities have returned!

The recent British government White Paper *Winning Back Our Communities* (White Paper 2003) is yet another example of the clumsy authoritarian style of the present government, and of its apparent determination to follow North American policies in all the areas where they have most conspicuously failed. Homeless people are among the most vulnerable members of our society, precisely the people who always suffer greatly at times of economic recession and of overseas war. But military approaches are not peculiar to the approach to Iraq. There has been, for some time, what the New York sociologist Herbert Gans called a "war against the poor" (Gans 1995) and the current proposals seem to be part of this war.

The government could go further along the North American road, and instruct the police to move homeless people from central cities to inhospitable suburbs, a common practice from California to Connecticut. Or they could follow a suggestion from Atlanta and make "urban camping" illegal—as if being homeless was a holiday. There are moves in California to make not only begging, but giving to beggars, a criminal offense. Parts of Britain, such as Manchester, may well follow. The tragedy is that some members of the present government were among the sternest critics of this kind of approach when it came from Conservative spokespersons. But this kind of turn around is hardly new, and it will lead to the worsening of situations, something which, at one time, they saw clearly.

The issue of mergers is linked to survival. My former colleague John Downie gave me permission to quote some comments that he made that have proved depressingly correct. He pointed out that agencies of the St. Botolph's Project size—sixty to eighty employees—were finding things difficult financially. (Since then the Project has collapsed.) Questions such as quality indicators, levels of accountability, the increasing cost of services, and so on, were leading such agencies to look to possible mergers. But whom then do they serve? Projects may merge, get statutory funding, and then become subcontractors for government. Downie commented:

> The choice seems to be one of either becoming a large, not for profit, subcontractor for government, or revitalising our charitable roots with a somewhat reduced service portfolio. The former would allow us to do more overall, and the latter would allow us to meet unmet need, and tackle it in the way we wanted. . . . It is not just a rational matter: it strikes at our very reason for being.

Sacred and Secular

Finally, the issues arising from "sacred" and "secular" agencies. There is a long history of Christian (and other religious) groups working in this field. Alongside them, and sometimes arising out of them, are groups that are seen as secular. This is well known. Recently, however, there have been a number of developments. There has been an interest in, and promotion of, what the U.S. and British governments now call "faith communities." These are probably still mainly Christian, but there are others. The New York Zen Center, for example, has been active in the field for some time.

Common, too, are church-founded projects that have moved in a secular direction, severing any explicitly Christian links. Sometimes the local church maintains a nominal connection even though most of the workers are not Christians, and there is no interest in Christian theology in the way the project functions. My sense is that there is a good deal of confusion, mystification, and ambiguity here. In their different ways, St. Botolph's Project and Centrepoint are examples of groups that once had close church links and no longer do so, though there are differences between them. There is often a reluctance to confront these issues.

There are also examples where churches once provided space and support and then ceased to do so, as in the case of the relationship between St. Mary the Virgin in New York City and the Safe Space project.

There is a great deal to be said on this area, but I feel that the loss of a Christian theological dimension and sociopolitical critique rooted in theology is a serious matter. Without this, church-based projects can become little more than social work agencies with a vaguely religious tint, or effectively secular agencies over which churches try (usually unsuccessfully) to exercise some control. Something crucial has been lost.

Take the begging issue, for example. Almsgiving is a spiritual obligation in Judaism, Islam, and, arguably, Christianity. If a government makes such an obligation impossible to fulfill, what are the religious communities to do? If Christians have a duty to share their wealth with the poor, and some of the poor are forbidden by secular law to tell us of their needs, where is the Christian community to go? These issues go right to the heart of the faith. Yet few church-based groups raise issues about this for fear that their funding might be affected.

My final question therefore is, Are Christian groups still needed in this field of work? If my comments in the preceding paragraph are correct, then the answer is clearly, yes. With a strengthened and courageous Christian prophetic movement, something crucial could be regained. What might this be?

The Time of No Room

I want to begin a response to this question by remembering my dear friend David Brandon, who died in 2001. David was the only British academic to be involved continuously with the study of homelessness for over forty years. It all began because he was homeless himself, having run away from a violent father, and he slept in doorways near St. Botolph's. We met in 1964, by which time he was working with a project for homeless people in central London. David was a deeply spiritual person, with an equally deep distrust of "spirituality," and he moved from the Society of Friends to Zen Buddhism. As I reflect on our long friendship, four areas seem important: the dignity of the person, the inevitablity of darkness, the necessity of struggle, and the vision of the future. I guess that we shared most, though not all, of these.

David combined a fierce confrontational public style with a profound respect and care for individuals. Though he did not believe in the doctrine, he was a practitioner of what I (though not he) call incarnational theology. It is often said that incarnational theology is the central feature of the social tradition within Anglicanism. I believe that this is true, but we need to recognize some problems. A high view of human nature and potential, rooted in the idea of the image of God in all persons, can degenerate into an idealistic and naïvely optimistic liberalism that bypasses conflict, struggle, and the fall of humankind. This was a point that William Stringfellow often made. It is also easy to assume that those who know the doctrine are thereby led to do the work. The gospel suggests otherwise: it is those who seek to do the work who will know the doctrine (John 7:17). If we take this seriously, close cooperation between Christians and those of other faiths or none becomes not simply acceptable but obligatory and creative.

But then, second, comes the darkness, the *via negativa* that must affect all who work theologically in this field. Much of what David and I shared, in working with people who had hit rock bottom, was a sense of paralysis, hopelessness, a sense of being brought down by it all. Of course, I do not wish to convey the impression that everything in these areas of work is dark and dismal. There were, and are, many shafts of hope, points of ecstasy, rays of light, moments of fun, times of refreshment. Yet increasingly, after forty-five years of working in inner-city neighborhoods, I realize how central is the symbol of darkness.

This is evident at an obvious level, historically and politically. The East End of London, in particular, is linked historically with images of the dark, from William Booth's "darkest England" and Jack London's "people of the abyss" to the present day. Much of the time, communities, interest groups, subcultures, even whole populations are literally "in the dark" about what the "principalities and powers" are up to in their schemes of "regeneration" and "renewal." The experience of being on the receiving end of other people's decisions, linked to the facade of "consultation," is common, if not universal, in inner cities. It is combined with a sense, historically rooted and apparently verified, that there is "nothing that we can do," and that those in power—the property developers, central government, transnational companies, or the local state with its "hangers-on"—will get their way. There is a sense of paralysis rather than apathy—the fruit, in many cases, of years of struggle, of banging one's head against a brick wall.

Let me return to my own experience as a priest in the East End, working with homeless people, drug users, people with "mental health problems"—an experience common to us all, yet experienced most intensely and most painfully by some of us to whom are given such labels as "psychotic" and "manic depressive." The work of priesthood, here as everywhere, is one primarily of presence rather than of skill and function, and at the heart of Christian priesthood is the encounter with darkness, specifically the dying of Christ and his descent into hell, those events that must precede resurrection. Here again, there is a vital role for theologically rooted Christian people. Darkness is the necessary prelude to resurrection, and between them is the descent into hell. We must never seek to evade the darkness with all its confusion and uncertainty.

In pastoral care in dark times, silence is critical. If we are to be genuine carers, we need to slow down and absorb situations, to learn how to be passive and receptive. It is true that the Greek word from which the words *passion* and *passionate* derive means "suffer," but its root is related to passivity. It is the opposite of active. To be active is to do something; to be passive is to do nothing, to receive. Of course I realize that without a context these sentences can be dangerous and wrong. There are times when drastic action is called for. There are times to speak loudly, times to "rage against the dying of the light." I am not recommending silence and passivity as universal postures. I am myself a lifelong activist and much of my energy still goes into campaigns and struggles for justice. All I am trying to do is correct a distorted emphasis in speech and action and to stress that silence and receptiveness are important parts of being human, and of being loving instruments of care.

We need to lose our fear of silence, as of darkness and solitude, and this can only come through patient and disciplined practice. I once said, at a meeting of my support group, "I don't think I have got the balance right between the active side of me and the contemplative." A woman who has known me for a long time commented, "By introducing the word *balance* you have confused the discussion. It is not a question of balance. What you need to learn is how to integrate, to do the things you do in a more contemplative, reflective way. You may end up doing more, not less, but it will be done in a more reflective way."

I am sure she was right. One of the most serious dangers confronting those who minister in the city is that their lives come to be built on frenzy and compulsive busyness. This usually leads to a lack of focus, a tendency to accumulate more and more things, a collapse of reflection, and the cultivation of a personal culture of obligatory tiredness. This personal culture then becomes socially infectious so that one may communicate little to others other than one's own exhaustion—not a very kind gift to people who may already have enough problems of their own. The practice of silence and solitude, including the cultivation of inner stillness and inner peace, is a vital component of an urban spirituality.

Third, Christian social tradition includes also the struggle with the regions of death and slavery, of oppression and captivity. This is often described as the "prophetic dimension" in pastoral ministry, but prophecy is not a dimension, rather one description of the whole nature of ministry. If this prophetic sense is lost, Christians may minister to "the homeless," bind up wounds, feed the hungry, cope with crises, but never engage the system, never confront the powers, never challenge the way things are. The older I get, the more important it seems to me that the prophetic moves into the center of Christian work. But the forces against it are formidable, the forces that seek to coopt the churches as religious arms of the secular power.

In his obituary of David Brandon, published in *The Guardian* on December 13, 2001, the psychiatrist Phil Barker brought out the uncomfortable nature of his prophetic style:

David Brandon was the most difficult man I ever met. Our every meeting left me unsettled and ill at ease. . . . To the surprise of the pompous, he never forecast his challenges. Sidling up to us, he whipped out his remarkable wit and intelligence, like a Socratic razor, which often cut him as much as any foe. Twenty years ago, at my request, he paralysed a dour Scots audience, unleashing a torrent of abuse upon those who merely spun the fantasy of health care, rather than caring for people. When they tried to defend themselves, he feigned resignation. 'I see. . . . You're the kind of people who would wallpaper the gas chambers.' (Barker 2001)

Amos would have been proud.

Finally, the hope and vision of God's kingdom, the social fruit of the resurrection, is the regulative principle of all good theology. I do not see how any movement of Christian social action can survive unless it is rooted in this vision. It was Thomas Merton who said that "the time of the end is the time of no room": the time beyond the end must be the time of divine community where all are valued and loved.

This essay was developed from a paper given in 2003 to UNLEASH, United London Ecumenical Action with the Single Homeless, founded in 1981. For the history, see Logan 2002.

TWENTY-ONE

Loss, Death, and Dying from a Hospice Perspective

Webb Brown

According to the dictionary, a hospice is "a shelter or lodging for travelers, children or the destitute, often maintained by a monastic order." In the Middle Ages, pilgrims could find welcome and hospitality with the monks and nuns whose religious houses provided the medieval version of today's bed-and-breakfast accommodations. When guests became ill, the brothers and sisters would care for them until they recovered or departed this life. For the terminally ill, therefore, hospices were places in which they could receive end-of-life care in a loving, supportive environment.

In 1967 Dame Cicely Saunders, a registered nurse, opened the first modern hospice, St. Christopher's, in London. St. Christopher's was created to provide palliative (or comfort) care to terminally ill and dying persons in a supportive environment; for many, this kind of care offered an attractive alternative to the institutional care provided by modern hospitals with their focus on curing disease. In the short period of time since St. Christopher's opened its doors, hospice has grown dramatically. Today, individuals and organizations associated with the hospice movement offer end-of-life care to people around the world.

Hospice's philosophy, articulated beautifully by Dame Cicely, is simple and profound: "You matter to the last moment of your life, and we will do all we can, not only to help you die in peace, but also to live until you die." For hospice caregivers, this means walking side by side with patients and their families—neither ahead of them, nor behind them—as they experience the complex interrelationship of the dance of life and the dance of death. It also means helping patients free themselves from pain of every kind: not only the physical pain of illness but also the emotional and spiritual pain created by old hurts and wrongs of every sort. As a result, true hospice pastoral care has to be liberating. It must include efforts to break the bonds of oppressive social structures and institutions, and to heal whatever wounds those structures may have caused in the life of the patient and his or her family.

The Hospice Model of Care

No one wants to die in pain, and almost no one wants to die alone. Hospice care is grounded in these basic truths of the human condition, and as caregivers we make every effort to address them. Clients can receive hospice care in their own homes or at dedicated residences, which offer care for terminally ill patients who do not have a primary caregiver in their home or for whom a nursing home or hospital would be the alternative. Hospice care may continue for months, or it may be a matter of weeks or even days; but whatever its duration, the decision to enter hospice is made by the patient and family; and all care-related decisions thereafter (whether these relate to medication and the medical interventions of palliative care or to other issues) involve, insofar as possible, the patient and his or her family.

Hospice care acknowledges that pain wears many faces, and that physical pain is often entwined with (and intensified by) the hurt resulting from spiritual, emotional, and/or psychosocial issues. To address this reality, caregivers work in interdisciplinary teams composed of nurses, social workers, chaplains, volunteers, and administrators. Patient and family are at the center of this circle of care; and in the fundamentally feminist model described here, no member of the team is more important than the others. Whatever our individual skills and expertise, each of us is attentive to the variety of issues that may require intervention and support. This includes the spiritual dimension of our patients' lives as well as, in some cases, the religious dimension.

I want to pause and underscore this last point, because understanding that chaplains (and clergy in general) do not exercise exclusive rights with respect to pastoral care is one of the most important lessons I have learned in hospice ministry. Reflecting the nature of the work that we do, hospice is—and needs to be—a nonhierarchical "team ministry." As caregivers we are, metaphorically, "midwifing" death, and our collective task is to assist the patient's transition from this reality to the next (however that may be defined in his or her belief system). As such, all hospice work has a deeply spiritual dimension. The chaplain is responsible for coordinating the various aspects of formal pastoral and spiritual care; but she or he is hardly alone in providing such care. In fact, the person who is present when a patient's most critically important spiritual or religious experience occurs is just as likely to be the nurse, or social worker, or a volunteer.

Consider Walter, a patient at Chilton House, the first hospice residence in Massachusetts, which opened on December 31, 1991. Walter was referred to Chilton House by a clinic at Cambridge City Hospital, which offers free medical services for the homeless. Walter was a quiet, gentle, middle-aged white man living with AIDS who had, as he put it, "fallen through the cracks" and ended up on the street. Our agency chose to offer Walter free care, which meant that we would follow him throughout the course of his illness and provide a burial site and services when the time came.

Walter accepted services for his medical needs gladly, and he greatly enjoyed talking with staff and volunteers about science fiction, which was not just his hobby but his true spiritual home. Before becoming homeless, he had spent most of his free time in local libraries, reading sci-fi; and so coordinating Walter's spiritual care involved not only pastoral counseling to discuss the questions he posed, such as "What happens when you die?" but also locating hospice volunteers who would share his interest and check out library books that they could read and discuss together. Later, when I planned the memorial service for the interment of Walter's ashes, three of the volunteers, who had become quite fond of him, asked to participate by reading selections from some of his favorite science fiction works.

Was this liberating pastoral care, and did it enable Walter to live as fully as possible with friendly companions, who saw no stigma in his homelessness or diagnosis of AIDS? Did our awareness of his condition, and our consciousness of the pain it undoubtedly had caused him, enable us to approach him with love, in solidarity? I cannot know. I do know that Walter wished to have a hospitable place to spend his last weeks of life, a place in which he felt safe and where he was treated with dignity. He told us that hospice made this possible.

Opportunities for Liberating Pastoral Care Around and Within Us

Hospice care is not about "doing charity" or being "better than." It is about being in solidarity with patients and families, and walking with them as they make their journeys through the valley of the shadow of death. Pastoral interactions seldom occur on a truly level playing field, however, and this is certainly the case in hospice, since our clients have lost control of their health and wellness, whereas we, their caregivers, have the privilege of good health. But if this imbalance is irreparable (at least in the near term), other "imbalances" are not: that is why hospice pastoral care demands that we be keenly aware of issues of social location, and how our own social location might be interpreted and experienced as oppressive, or liberating, by the patients and families we seek to serve. Whether it is the host of institutionalized "isms" that divide our society, or the economic and religious power structures that separate haves and have-nots so sharply, we need to understand how these forces have played out—and can continue to play out—in our clients' lives and in our own. To illustrate, let me use my own social location as an example.

I, the caregiver, am an upper-middle-class white woman who has always had ready access to a privileged position in American society. My social location can get in the way of my efforts to offer compassionate and loving pastoral care, or it can support them if I remain aware of it and adjust my behavior accordingly. As an example, let me describe my brief encounter with Mrs. Gloria and her family, and with Charlie and Susannah.

Mrs. Gloria, a seventy-two-year-old African American woman, was receiving care at home with several family members as her primary caregivers. On a Wednesday morning, I received a call from Kate, the hospice nurse caring for Mrs. Gloria, who told me that her patient was actively dying. Mrs. Gloria's own minister, the priest from the African American Episcopal Church where she worshiped and with whom she was close was out of town; the family wished the hospice chaplain to attend her.

When I arrived at her house about fifteen minutes later and walked into the bedroom, Mrs. Gloria was lying comfortably in bed, nonresponsive and breathing ever so slowly. Kate and I were the only white people present, and while Mrs. Gloria's family knew and trusted Kate because she had cared for Mrs. Gloria for more than a month, none of them had ever met me.

As a hospice chaplain, you are always walking a fine line by offering care while simultaneously enabling the sources of healing within the patient and her family to be liberated. This balance was particularly important here, given how oppressive white hegemony often is for people of color in American society. Rather than act like a bull in a china shop, therefore, I chose to say softly that I felt honored and privileged to be a guest in Mrs. Gloria's home and to join with them at this time in their circle of love. I explained that I did not wish to impose myself or my beliefs on them, and that with their permission I would offer prayers for her and Prayers for the Dying from the *Book of Common Prayer*.

I also asked what prayers and petitions they would like offered and learned that one of her sons, an active member of his faith community in Texas, wished to offer prayers as well. I knelt by Mrs. Gloria, placed my hands on hers, and encouraged everyone who wished to join in laying on hands and invoking God's love and blessing on her and all of her family, present and absent.

Mrs. Gloria died peacefully as we were praying for her transition from this life to the next. Kate and I sat with the family, offering a ministry of presence to help hold their grief and sorrow. After an hour or so, I offered to call Mrs. Gloria's church, leave a message about her death, and ask her rector to contact the family as soon as he was able. I also asked if there was further care I might offer, at that time or later on. The daughter, who was taking charge, had already planned to contact the funeral home and felt confident about receiving care from their rector when he returned the next day. While I hope my presence with Mrs. Gloria and her family during this sacred time was perceived as liberating, I shall never know for sure. As is often the case in hospice work, the most I can do is to hold the question.

Charlie. In hospice chaplaincy it's not uncommon to find opportunities for liberation within yourself as well as in others. In this respect, Charlie, a sixty-one-year-old, white, working-class guy who was dying of colon cancer, was one of my greatest teachers.

Charlie's cancer had been diagnosed several months earlier, and he was being treated in the local Veterans' Administration hospital, when he learned there was nothing more that could be done medically. Given the prognosis of a week or so to live, he had decided, with the support of his family and doctor, to return home and receive hospice care. Now at home, he was requesting a visit from the hospice chaplain, because he was experiencing great spiritual anxiety.

When his nurse, my colleague Arlene, told me about his request, she also explained that while Charlie was still at the VA hospital, he had met with the Roman Catholic chaplain, but that the visit had not gone well. When Charlie had voiced his fear of death, the priest had told him that the only way he could get to heaven was to repent of his sins and ask forgiveness of God. Apparently Charlie became livid, sent the priest out of his room, and swore he would never see a priest again.

Arriving at Charlie's house, I noticed a huge Harley motorcycle on the porch. When I was shown into the bedroom, I found Charlie sitting on the side of the bed, dressed in Harley overalls—with two long earrings dangling from his left ear. My heart skipped a beat, and I became aware that if I were to have any hope of being present with Charlie and his wife I would need to put aside my own long-held, stereotypical views of bikers.

As Charlie began to speak, my stereotypes dissolved. I later learned that he had been the leader of the local community's bikers and that they, like many other biker groups, did amazing works of outreach and charity. Even without such knowledge, however, his warm personality and kind eyes smiling though his pain spoke volumes.

Charlie's story was moving. When his two sons were quite young, his first wife had abandoned him and the children, and he had raised the boys on his own. His sons had been active as acolytes in their local Roman Catholic parish, and although they, like Charlie, had drifted away from the church over time, they were honest, contributing members of the community. Charlie himself had saved the lives of three people, including a badly wounded Army buddy, and he was joyful that he had made it through Vietnam without ever killing anyone. He had tried to lead a good and loving life, and he did not understand what sins he had to confess and ask forgiveness for so that he could enter heaven. Nevertheless, he was anxiously concerned about his meeting with the VA chaplain, and he wanted pastoral help in understanding what be needed to do to make sure he would go to heaven.

One way to help Charlie address his spiritual anxiety was to help him look at his image of God. For many of us, moving from an image of God as a punitive judge, demanding confession of "non-sins," to an image of God abounding in steadfast love, full of compassion and mercy, is a lifetime journey. Charlie and I had one visit to try to do that work. I prayed silently for the grace of God to enable me to explain to Charlie that I was not a Roman Catholic, but that I wanted to share my own experience with him.

I described how my childhood understanding of God as a Being who rewards us when we are good and helps us when we are bad had become broader, deeper, and more complex as I grew older. I suggested that sometimes dogma can be used as a weapon to prevent people from asking questions that are difficult to answer, and that rules are often the way to keep people in line. When the rules become what we worship, the essence of God's love is lost. To embrace a God who is overflowing in steadfast love, forgiveness, and mercy enables us to know that when we die, we will go to a place—heaven in Charlie's construct—of safety and love.

Charlie and I engaged in dialogue, and I attempted to draw from him examples of times in his life when he had experienced God's boundless love and compassion. We also talked about his fears in an effort to discern what other issues might be involved besides his desire to go to heaven. With his permission, we prayed together, and I offered blessings for his healing from his fears and anxiety.

Did Charlie work through his fears and embrace God's love for him? I hope and pray so; but I shall never know for certain. He died at home, three days later, with his family by him, offering their love for his passage from this life to the next. At their request, I officiated at his funeral, which was held at the local funeral home chapel, because Charlie had not wished to be buried from the church next door. It was a sacred privilege to work with the family to create a liturgy honoring and celebrating Charlie's life, naming its meaning, and lifting up the numerous ways in which he touched the lives of so many others. More than a hundred bikers came in their leathers to pay tribute to their friend and hero.

Why was Charlie one of my greatest teachers? First, he broke the bonds of my negative stereotypes about bikers. Additionally, I learned yet again about the courage it takes to ask difficult questions about God and love and afterlife. I pray that before he died Charlie was liberated from the abusive interpretation of church dogma, that played on his fears. Whatever happened, I do know this: Charlie is teaching others in heaven about the joys and goodness of compassion—and biking.

Susannah. The invitation to enter into another person's life journey is one of the greatest privileges of hospice work. Susannah, a beautiful, feisty young woman, extended just such an invitation to our team when she decided to forego further experimental treatment for her terminal breast cancer.

Susannah was born and raised in Colombia, in South America, in a traditional family where her father, the patriarch, was "in charge" of her mother, her two brothers, herself, and the servants. She was intellectually gifted and had been well educated in Roman Catholic schools, including university, in her native country. She came to the United States in her twenties, settled in Boston to earn a degree in physical therapy, and established what turned out to be a thriving practice. At twenty-eight she married a man who was a nonpracticing Jew and became close with his extended family. At the same time, Susannah remained a devout Roman Catholic who attended church regularly, and when she was first diagnosed with breast cancer, at the age of thirty, she joined a healing prayer group in her local parish. She also chose radical treatment, including a mastectomy and reconstructive surgery, and was in remission for more than a year. During that time, she and her husband conceived a child, which she miscarried before term.

Then the cancer returned with a vengeance. It had metastasized into her lungs, and soon after learning this alarming news Susannah decided to forego more curative treatment. With wisdom far beyond her thirty-four years, she chose to bring hospice care into her life while she was still healthy—a young woman who had been at the top of her form professionally when she was diagnosed. She wanted us to look at her as a whole person, not a patient; and she was willing to put denial behind her, so that she could live as fully as possible in the face of her illness. Such behavior takes great courage, and the example of her courage was one of many precious lessons the team and I would learn from Susannah as we cared for her over the next six months.

I felt an immediate bond with Susannah on my first visit. She exuded a zest for life and was articulate about the fact she did not want to die. She felt it was unfair that her life was being cut short, when she and her husband had so much to offer to make this a better world. She also felt that her faith was being tested, because her church teachings made it difficult for her to hold God and cancer in the same frame. She had left the healing prayer group when her cancer returned, and she was no longer attending church. If God was all-powerful and loving, why didn't God give her the miraculous cure for which she prayed? Sadly, Susannah's mother, who had come from Colombia to be her primary caregiver, was contributing to the oppressive and abusive interpretation of church dogma that was causing Susannah so much anxiety. Reminding her daughter that a cousin who had been diagnosed with cancer had prayed for a miracle and had been cured, she said Susannah must not be worthy because her prayers were not being answered.

When Susannah called in hospice, she requested that the full team be involved—nurse, social worker, chaplain, and volunteers. In separate counseling sessions, both the social worker and I learned that Susannah and her brothers had been abused in childhood by their father. This revelation helped to uncover the connection between her image of Father God, the all-powerful patriarch who would not grant Susannah a cure, and her experience of her all-powerful birth father, who had abused her in childhood. Susannah's images and experiences of Father God and earthly father were painfully enmeshed. She felt huge rage toward her father. She felt rage against God yet never lost her faith in God. And she struggled mightily to find justice in all of this.

The manifestation of these conflicts emerged in anxiety, which gripped her almost daily and regularly interrupted her sleep. She knew she was going to die, and she worked hard to reconcile with her father before her death; not necessarily to forgive but to reconcile. (Her father did come to visit Susannah two weeks before she died; but we have no information about the content of those visits.) She also asked the Roman Catholic nuns from a nearby convent to bring the Eucharist each morning to her and her mother (who was also visited regularly by a Spanish-speaking priest that I had contacted).

Our team employed a range of interventions in an effort to enable Susannah to untie the oppressive bonds of patriarchy that bound her. To heal Susannah's anxiety, Leah, the social worker, used a variety of techniques including Reiki (noninvasive energy work), hypnosis for imagery transformation, and meditation. She also encouraged Susannah to focus on images from her homeland in Colombia, such as its lush countryside and intense fragrances, in order to nourish her rich dream imagery.

Susannah's English was excellent, but I have often wondered whether our work with her might have been more effective if Leah and I had been able to speak Spanish. The barrier of culture meant Susannah was never really at home, and it was a great gift that she was able, nonetheless, to be in touch with her deepest self as she strove to move through her experiences of abuse and anxiety.

To address Susannah's spiritual pain, she and I formed what we called our "Feminist Theology Book Club." We met every two weeks and discussed various readings from such sources as Theresa of Avila's *Interior Castle*, Carol Christ and Judith Plaskow's *Womanspirit Rising*, Marilyn Sewell's *Cries of the Spirit*, and Jane Hirshfield's *Women in Praise of the Sacred*. The rich imagery in these sources, combined with the colorful metaphors in the psalms, many of which were favorites of Susannah's, and the wisdom writings in the Hebrew Scriptures, enabled her to identify experiences in her own life of a loving, merciful God, overflowing with compassion.

Susannah and I prayed together. We engaged in theological reflection about "unanswered prayer" and questions about life after death. Susannah's interior life was rich and deep, and this gave her wonderful access to her faith in God, even as she demanded justice from God on issues she felt were unfair. Living with the questions is indeed a spiritual challenge. I hope I was able to assist Susannah in embracing the propositions that life is not necessarily about answering questions, but questioning answers; that love is about embracing the questions; and that faith is about providing the means to live with the questions.

Before her illness, Susannah had been a successful professional, helping many patients regain their health, and her sense of herself as a competent woman who could care for others as well as herself was an important part of her self-image. We arranged for her to volunteer in her local public library, which she was able to do several times before her strength declined and she became too ill to manage. When her relationship with her husband began to show signs of stress, we encouraged her to have a "last fling" by joining him on a business trip to Florida. Her adorable white poodle, Sebastian, was the child she longed for and never had. I assisted her in deciding that she would give Sebastian to her mother-in-law, as she felt her husband would be too absent-minded to care for him properly.

Did our pastoral care and support help Susannah achieve liberation from the abuses she had experienced? Would she have been able to heal her spiritual angst and anger without the team's collaborative efforts to care for her as a whole person? Were the spiritual interventions on the part of the hospice team helpful as well as supportive? Living with these questions is part of being a hospice chaplain.

Susannah lapsed into a coma several days before she died. Her mother, husband, and one of her brothers surrounded her with loving care as she made the transition from the dance of life to the dance of death and being reborn with God. The Roman Catholic chaplain from the hospital where Susannah had been treated, who was a spiritual friend of hers, said at her funeral Mass that he was sure not a day would pass that she wouldn't corner God in heaven, shaking her fist and demanding that a cure for cancer be found, so that others might be able to have longer lives to contribute to the betterment of humankind. I am convinced he was right; hardly a day passes that I am not aware of the precious gift I was given by being allowed into Susannah's life.

Celebrating Life and Honoring Grief

"During the 1960s, my parents, well, actually, my mother was an active member of the mostly white Episcopal church in Harvard Square. I remember hiding in the bell tower during Sunday school, when my mother was teaching the younger kids. Even though I don't attend any church now, and my parents stopped going to that church in the 1970s, I wonder if they could be buried from there?"

Alice raised the question of her parents' burial with me in the second pastoral care session we had while her father was a patient at Chilton House. Her mother had died almost a year before, and Alice had been saving her mother's ashes until her father's death so that she could have a funeral for them at the same time. Mr. Purdy, 74, had been an invalid for some years and now was terminally ill with chronic heart failure. He was part Native American and part African American, while Mrs. Purdy, an African American, had been born and raised in Canada. She and her husband had spent their adult married lives in Cambridge, and Alice had become her father's primary caregiver after her mother's death. Concerned that his declining condition required more care than she could provide given the demands of her job, they had decided to bring him to Chilton House, so that she could spend quality time with him instead of exhausting herself trying to tend to his personal care.

Mr. Purdy spent nine days at Chilton House. While he was alive, I offered pastoral support to him and to Alice, including, at their request, prayers for spiritual encouragement and comfort. Alice and her dad had enjoyed a close, loving relationship through the years, and although she was expecting his death, I knew that her loss would be intensified by the fact that he was her remaining parent. (When our first parent dies, the veil between us and our own mortality is rent. When our second parent dies, the veil is ripped off as we realize, consciously or unconsciously, that we have no parents to keep us from being "the next ones in line.") I had assured Alice that I would do whatever was necessary to manage her parents' burial from her church of choice in Harvard Square.

The morning that Mr. Purdy died I happened to be at Chilton House, and with Alice's permission I phoned the assistant priest at the church in Harvard Square, and asked him to come to offer prayers over her father's body. Using the lens of social location, I asked the assistant, Mark, to join in me in pastoral ministry, rather than calling the rector, because Mark, like Mr. Purdy, is a person of color.

Mark and I spent several sessions with Alice and her best friend planning the joint service for the Purdys. We discussed the Scripture readings, the choice of music, which included hymns that were favorites of Alice's parents, and ways to include her estranged brother in the service that wouldn't require Alice to spend time with him. (The complicated issues between Alice and her brother simply were not going to be healed by one service of celebration of their parents' lives.)

These planning sessions were a time for Alice to reflect on her life and the lives of her parents, and she spoke quite a bit about the years during the civil rights movement when her mother had been the director of the church's Sunday school. The then-rector had intentionally asked Mrs. Purdy to serve in that capacity in the liberal, mostly white church. Alice remembered in particular several white women who worked closely with her mother, and she was hopeful that they might attend the service and come to the reception afterwards in the parish hall.

Aware that race was an issue here, I found myself walking a narrow path between my own thoughts about how the service should go and Alice's needs in her time of grief and loss. Because of our shared experience of pastoral ministry, Alice asked me to take the "lead" in the service for her parents, but I demurred, feeling it was important that the church's assistant Mark conduct the liturgy, and that I, as a white chaplain, play a lesser role. As in any funeral or memorial service at which I am asked to officiate, however, I wanted to be certain that the liturgy would be structured around three goals: (1) to praise God and to give thanks for all of creation; (2) to give thanks for the life of the deceased and to name how his or her life made a difference; and (3) to support the gathered community in their sorrow and grief.

Alice wished to have the ashes of both her parents at the service. I suggested that the liturgy include a time of presentation of the urns—one to her brother and one to her. Mr. Purdy was a veteran and an American flag had been given to the family. Alice decided she wished me to present the flag to her brother during the service. Together we developed a liturgy based on the Rite for Burial in the Book of Common Prayer but expanded to include specific elements intended to heal broken relationships and to lift up happy memories about her parents' life in that church some forty-five years earlier.

As it turned out, the service was also an opportunity for Alice to do grief work and to begin to heal from the loss of both of her parents in a year's time. The reception, with its seasonal decorations and personally chosen foods, gave her a tangible way to honor and pay tribute to her parents. About 150 people attended the funeral, and many of them told touching stories about her parents and their life among the nearby African American community in the 1960s and 1970s—including the fact that any number of young people considered the Purdys "second parents." For Alice, this afforded an opportunity for "meaning making" and for naming the value of her parents' lives, an important component of the grief process. Whether her brother was also able to experience healing from the service and reception, I will never know, as we on the hospice team met him only at the funeral; but I pray that this was possible for him.

For several months, Alice chose to attend the hospice-sponsored bereavement group that I lead. She was an active and receptive participant in the group, which helped her to learn about the grieving process as well as to be with others who were also grieving the death of a loved one and coping with loss and sorrow. Those who attend bereavement groups learn that, as Rabbi Earl Grollman has taught us, grief is nature's way of healing a broken heart. It is our body's emotional response to loss—as natural a response as eating when you are hungry, bleeding when you cut your finger, and yelling "ouch" when you crash your elbow against a wall. At the same time, you can play an active role in the healing process by talking about the pain of your loss, which bereavement groups encourage participants to do. As one bereavement group member told us, "Grief feels like parachuting into a foreign land: you don't know the language, or the landscape, nor where your resources immediately are located."

There is no blueprint that can provide a roadmap or serve as a guide through the grief process. Grief is deeply personal, and how any one of us experiences it will depend on our relationship with the deceased, our personality, our social location, and our attitude toward life and ability to cope in times of crisis. Nevertheless, there are "tasks of grief" that are common to everyone who is experiencing "normal" grief.[1]

- *Accepting the loss of your loved one.* Funeral or memorial services are helpful for this task, but it is a process that takes varying lengths of time. Alice, for example, said that the funeral planning was helpful for her in accepting her dad's death, but that for weeks after her mother died, she kept picking up the phone to call her, only to remember, again, that her mother had died.

- *Feeling some or all of the feelings of loss and grief such as sorrow, sadness, anger, relief (that your loved one is no longer suffering), guilt, loneliness, and despair.* Alice articulated clearly that she was very sad and missed her father deeply; but at the same time, she was relieved that he was no longer trapped in his body, which hadn't worked for several years.

- *Adjusting to the environment without your loved one.* For Alice, this adjustment included living into the fact that she no longer needed to provide constant physical care to her father or, in the last few days of his life, to visit him at Chilton House in every spare moment of her day and evening. She was also aware that she needed to find friends with whom she could share the stories that she and her father had become accustomed to discussing. In other cases, this adjustment means adapting to new roles that the deceased had previously fulfilled, such as paying the bills, tending to repairs, or shopping for groceries and cooking. Many a hospice client who has lost a spouse or partner has voiced the pain of feeling that they must "invent a whole new life for themselves," particularly since our society tends to be so couples oriented.

- *Transforming the image of your loved one and doing some ritual work.* This step is especially important when a loved one has died with a debilitating disease, or one that left him or her wasting away, and your memories are stuck there. This task involves transforming your memory of your loved one into an image of how he or she looked in the fullness of life. Making a scrapbook of photos taken before your loved one became ill, choosing a favorite photograph and putting a fresh flower beside it regularly, writing about active and happy times with your loved one, talking with family and friends who remember the deceased in the fullness of life: all these are ways to assist in this task.

Many hospice clients tell me that they talk regularly to their loved one. They are aware, of course, that the loved one is dead; but they feel close to the spirit of the deceased and talking keeps the connection. Alice made a picture board honoring her parents, which she brought to share with the bereavement group. It was a wonderful memory trip for her and also gave her the freedom to allow herself to reconnect with life in ways she had had to give up when she was devoting all her energy to caring for her father.

For many people, making an effort to find meaning in their sadness and sorrow is an important component of the grief process. When we approach the loss of a loved one with a cup-half-full attitude, we have an opportunity to make meaning of our loss, to examine the changes that have occurred, and to explore ways to make a new beginning. We never fill the hole made by the loss of a loved one, and yet the pain lessens over time and we are able to reconnect in new ways. For some, it is helpful to envision grief as a cut finger, an injury sustained while cutting onions or tomatoes. The wound bleeds, hurts, and needs to be tenderly cared for to begin healing. The bandage may fall off several times—while the wound reopens or the scab gets scratched away—but eventually the healing process is complete. Although the scar is always there, the pain surrounding the scar is gone, and you have the use of your finger once again.

Sometimes You Have to Break the Rules

Toni, an intelligent and personable seventy-year-old white woman who was living with terminal leukemia, had been a hospice patient—served by our team of nurse, social worker, and chaplain—for several weeks. Toni and I had established a wonderful working relationship as we met every other week for pastoral counseling. Her years as a teacher of math and computer skills served her well in analyzing her life and current situation. She had requested help in sorting out her feelings about such things as family relationships, the meaning in her life, and how she could be sure that her husband would be all right after her death. While she did not believe in an afterlife, she became enthusiastic about the notion that, like all matter, she was part of the cycle of life. An avid gardener, she could embrace the prospect that at death she would become like compost and somehow be recycled into the fabric of all life.

I am ahead of myself, however. After four weeks of hospice care, Toni decided to seek blood transfusions to increase her energy. In the world of insurance companies, transfusions constitute "curative care" (not "palliative care"), which results in denial of hospice benefits. So over our team's protests, Toni was taken off our hospice client list because the agency would no longer receive reimbursements for social work and chaplaincy visits.

We at hospice have petitioned—so far unsuccessfully—against this policy. But the institutionalization of hospice, via Medicare, Medicaid, and insurance reimbursements, often creates a catch-22 situation that interrupts the flow of patient-centered care. For example, the price of a medication often determines whether it can be used; while the insurance company, not the needs of the patient and family, will determine how many reimbursable visits from a social worker are allowed. Such practices are extremely frustrating for hospice teams attempting to offer the best possible care, and they mean that patients sometimes become disenfranchised by the health-care system even when their caregivers have their best interests at heart.

Could I abandon Toni and the sacred work of life review we were doing: Naming the meaning and purpose of her accomplishments, such as the grassroots company she had started some years earlier to offer computer training to school children in many large American cities? Reviewing her relationships with family and friends to come to as clear and open a place as possible (including who would get what "stuff" from her apartment) and to heal any old hurts with her four adult children? Helping her to exercise as much control as possible in her daily life so that she could maintain the dignity she deserved? Working through issues of transcendence, how she would be remembered? If pastoral care truly is linked to justice and compassion, the only plausible answer was "No." I chose to continue my visits with Toni on a pro bono basis.

Toni became another of my greatest teachers. We met regularly for four months and I learned about her courage; her ease in meeting difficult moments with grace (she once fell while her four-year-old granddaughter was visiting, so she asked her granddaughter to help her figure out how to get herself up from the floor); her ability to stay in and enjoy the moment (watching tennis matches on TV with her spouse or working on a *New York Times* crossword puzzle), knowing she was living on borrowed time, medically speaking. I was privileged to visit with her right until the end of her life.

After Toni's death, I had the honor of offering her husband bereavement care for several months through the hospice bereavement group I was leading. His first wife had died many years before, so his presence in the group was beneficial and healing on several levels: his current loss; the earlier loss of his first wife whose death, he realized, he had not adequately grieved; and his process of "reinventing" his life without Toni. In addition, he was an important and valuable member of the group because he was willing to share his feelings about his loss and his wisdom and strategies for coping with grief and readjusting to life without his spouse. Thanks to his generosity of spirit, he became a resource for others in the group who were able to benefit from his experience. Had I adhered to the oppressive rules of managed health care, therefore, many people would have been the poorer: Toni, who I would have had to abandon; her husband and the bereavement group, who would have lost the opportunity to benefit from one another's healing presence; and the hospice team, including me, who would not have learned from Toni all the wisdom that we did in fact learn.

I began this chapter, as I do my work, with the premise that pastoral care, and in particular hospice pastoral care, is not only deeply spiritual and holy but also inextricably linked to justice and compassion. As caregivers, therefore, we have a sacred responsibility to do everything in our power to help our patients and their families free themselves from whatever has burdened them during the dance of life so that they can experience the dance of death as truly liberating. To this end, I can think of no better or wiser advice for those who wish to engage in "pastoral care as if oppression matters" than to remember, always, the words of Micah 6:8-9: "What does the LORD require of you but to do justice and love mercy and walk humbly with your God."

TWENTY-TWO

Making (Ritual) Sense of Our Own Lives

Elaine J. Ramshaw

Laura, a white female college student, was at a communion service in the college chapel. Members of the congregation in this place knelt to receive communion, and the usual practice was to receive the host on one's tongue. However, Laura, who was in spiritual direction, was trying to come to a new, more positive evaluation of her own neediness. Her director was encouraging her to think that God welcomed her need; that it was good for her to ask for what she needed. So she held up her hands to reach for the bread, actively asking for it by her gesture. The white male presider, who had definite ideas about such things, shoved the host into her mouth.

What was he thinking? Astoundingly, he was trying to enact the grace of Christ as clearly as possible. He believed that the only way we could know the unmerited grace of God was to be purely passive in receiving the signs of God's love, and that to him meant opening your mouth but not stretching out your hands.

Of course, there were many other factors at work here, besides his belief about the "right" way to receive communion. There was his deep cluelessness, his inability to imagine what his action would feel like to Laura. There were societal, church, and university structures that gave him power over Laura, power he was privileged to remain largely unconscious of in the liturgical setting. He was a tenured professor; she was a student. The college's denomination did not ordain women, so the liturgy was led by a phalanx of vested (white) men. The God-language was entirely male. The chapel architecture as a whole, along with the practice of kneeling at the communion rail, placed the leaders (and the Christ-image) above and at a distance from the layfolk. These and other factors contributed to the presider's power to treat Laura this way, to his ability to fool himself into believing he was acting in her best interest, and to her limited options for resistance.

As disturbing as this encounter was for Laura, it could have been much worse. What if she had been a survivor of childhood sexual abuse? Then what would this mildly violent and physically intrusive action have meant to her? The profound disrespect of the presider's action would likely have been amplified by the history of much worse intrusive violence she had suffered. What if she had been African American? Then his action would have ramified into the history of whites' bodily and spiritual abuse of people of color. Though his treatment of her would not have been a response to her color, for her his action would have borne echoes of the countless acts of physical dishonor or violence, which are an essential part of systemic racism.

If we want our religious ritual lives to bear the liberative power of our faith stories, and not to collude in oppression, we need to look at many dimensions of the ritual experience. We need to do far more than vet the ritual language for inclusivity—note that words played no role in the ritual abuse Laura experienced. What are the sources of oppression in our religious ritual, and how might each of those sources be addressed and challenged in our ritual practice? Let's begin here with that question. Then I will move on to some constructive proposals for how to empower everyone to "speak" ritually out of the truth of their own lives.

Sources of Injustice in Religious Ritual: You'll Find It in the Bible

First of all, there is injustice in our religious ritual that goes right back to our founding stories, texts, and communal patterns. The patriarchy and androcentrism of the societies in which the biblical material developed is one clear example. Power adheres to maleness; men take center stage, and women's stories are marginalized. In the Bible, no divine promise is ever fulfilled by the birth of a girl.[1] God, who is not just "a god" or "our national god" or "top god of the pantheon" but the ground of being, the source and sustainer of the entire universe, is nonetheless spoken of as "he." Jewish and Christian ritual carry on this heritage of patriarchy, in the gender imbalance in the stories we tell, in the male God-language, in the historic practice of giving ritual authority in the worshiping community to men. The task of challenging this heritage of patriarchy and androcentrism has been a central mission of Jewish and Christian feminism.

If we want our religious ritual to be as fully liberative for girls and women as for boys and men, we need to do feminist biblical interpretation, feminist recovery of women's stories, and feminist critique of androcentric language. Some of this has been happening on a denominational level and within the ecumenical liturgical movement, and our official ritual books, hymnody, ecumenical lectionary, and the gender composition of church leadership all show results of this. All this has a direct effect on the extent to which our ritual can provide liberative pastoral care for girls and women.

There are other forms of oppression besides patriarchy that can find support in the texts and stories and practices at the core of our religious traditions. The purity codes stigmatize people with disabilities or deformities. The ancient Near Eastern negativity about homosexuality shows up in those codes and elsewhere. The household codes in the New Testament seem to put the divine imprimatur on Roman kinship structure and its hierarchy, including slavery. Some of these forms of oppression show up in our present-day ritual practice more than others, but all of them need the corrective of a constant process of critique analogous to the feminist critique.

Faithful Christian and Jewish feminists generally hold that the tradition itself, including the Bible, bears the grounds for critique as well as the means of oppression. The Bible intentionally reinforces and unconsciously reflects societal power assumptions; it also critiques and challenges societal power assumptions. Kings are divinely anointed; but God didn't want kings in the first place. A great man leads the Hebrew people out of slavery in Egypt; but Exodus begins with the stories of the four women and one girl who preserve that man's life. The Israelites are more important to God than other peoples; but the book of Jonah is a joke on ethnocentrism. Having bad things happen to you is a sign of God's disfavor; but in Job God disavows that conventional theodicy. Women should keep silent in church; but baptism trumps gender disparity. One of the most life-giving things about the Bible is precisely its internal critique, the way it holds contrasting voices in tension.

This means that we shouldn't consider the critique of oppressive aspects of the tradition as a move from a messed-up past to a cleaned-up future. Rather, we understand ourselves to be continuing the internal critique that has always been contained within the canon (though not always recognized in our history!). We can't make oppression-free ritual, not this side of the eschaton. But we can practice ritual that constantly questions the oppressive elements it can't help but carry. When we plan ritual for people with particular needs, for instance, we ask if those people are being ritually defined out of power. Why do we bless the sick person and not ask the sick person to bless us? Does the children's sermon use the children to entertain the adults? Does Youth Sunday empower the young people, or confine their leadership to one day a year? Should we really be trying to integrate people who are cognitively disabled into our worship—or should we be trying to integrate ourselves into their worship?

Sources of Injustice in Religious Ritual: Malformed Theology

Some oppressive elements in our ritual practice derive not from our founding stories, texts, and practices but from theology gone wrong. In Western Christian history, some of the theological drift from the sources was directly linked to Christianity's becoming the state church, first of the Roman Empire and later of nation-states. Entanglement with the powers that be kept the church from speaking the social critiques found in the prophets, the Gospels, and early church practice.

One theological casualty of establishment was a vital, corporate/cosmic eschatology. The key petition in Jesus' prayer, "Your kingdom come," asks God to change the world utterly, so that the divine will might be done on earth as in heaven. Many Christians have been taught to pray "Your will be done" rather as a divine certification of whatever happens to me today. The New Testament expectation of God's future was pushed off entirely into a separate, heavenly realm, to be reached after death.[2] The second coming came to be thought of as the death of this world, not its resurrection.

Without a vital, corporate eschatology, people who are suffering are likely to be advised to accept their suffering as God's will, and to look to the next world for salvation. There is still some of this sort of theology in church rituals of care—and still way too little of the radical societal critique of corporate eschatology.

What difference would it make for ritual pastoral care if we really prayed in the Lord's Prayer for God to come and change the world? Suppose people were experiencing a corporate crisis or loss—the local factory being moved overseas, or a natural disaster poorly handled by the government, or the revelation of sexual abuse by a trusted pastor, or an episode of mass violence.

A ritual life shaped by a vital, corporate eschatology would give people who are suffering three things. It would provide ways to pray (starting with the Lord's Prayer itself!) that would recognize how far the systems of this world are from the will of God, and ask God to change them. People would not be limited to praying for comfort for the afflicted and for the ability to forgive individual wrongdoers. Second, a corporate eschatology would through symbolic language put the victims' crisis in touch with the groaning of the world for redemption. Third, it would give them grounds for hope, even for hopeful ritual and social action. In the words of the executed activist, playwright, and poet Ken Saro-Wiwa of Nigeria: "Dance, my people, dance away sorrow; dance, dance, for we have seen tomorrow!"[3] When we have been to the mountaintop and seen the promised land, we can take action out of hope, even when we cannot be sure whether we ourselves will get there in this life. When Christian ritual grounds us in God's future, it empowers us to live in the present with hope and to live and work toward that future.

A vital, corporate eschatology would also improve the ritual pastoral care we could provide for individuals who are suffering a more personal crisis. When an individual is sick, for example, the question always arises of how and even whether to pray for physical healing. Should we pray for physical healing only if it seems possible to the medical establishment? Should we always hedge a prayer for healing with the phrase, "if it be your will"? What if we pray for healing and it doesn't happen? All these questions are profoundly transformed if we pray for and with a sick person in the context of a vital, cosmic eschatology. The specific healing we request is one small but irreducibly important piece of the healing of the universe, which we know to be the will of God. If it happens according to our prayers, it will be an Easter experience: like Jesus' resurrection, it will be a preview of the cosmic healing to come, a bit of God's future coming to be ahead of time. If physical healing does not occur, we will pray in the knowledge that we live with Easter hope in a Good Friday world, an unhealed world, which groans with us for God's future.

Another huge area in which dominant-culture Western Christian theology went in an unfortunate direction was the definition of the human problem. While many theologians had sophisticated understandings of "sin" that included corporate, social evil and individuals' unconscious predilections along with individual wrongdoing, the common understanding of sin came to be individual wrongdoing (or wrong thinking), which engenders individual guilt. This understanding also was the most prevalent in the dominant-culture church ritual practice.[4] Again, one of the influences on this development may have been the identification of the church with the powers that be: if the problem is always one of individual guilt, no boats need be rocked.

The narrowness of this definition has all sorts of negative ramifications for pastoral care. Social sin is not recognized, so it can't be named or challenged. Whatever form of inchoate badness I feel gets interpreted as that personal sin which rightly brings guilt. My feelings of badness may have more to do with shame, or captivity to addiction, or what Koreans call han—the mixture of shame and helpless rage experienced by the oppressed (Park 1993). But popular Christian theology, and especially dominant-culture Christian ritual practice, will try to force that "badness" into the category of personal sin, which we know how to deal with.[6] In the process, systemic evil gets a free pass and the victim too often gets blamed.

In the process of writing this essay, I asked a churchgoing gay male friend for his thoughts on ritual, pastoral care, and oppression. We eventually talked about the need for occasional rituals that speak to the passages and relationships unique to gays and lesbians; but the first thing he named as oppressive was the focus on personal guilt. The problem is that you are bad, sinful, guilty. The problem is that there is something deeply wrong with you. He loves his (Canadian Anglican) parish, but he finds it difficult to go there even during Lent.

We need to look to a variety of sources to develop a more adequate theological and ritual naming of the human problem. The biblical writings comprise many understandings of the human problem, from the prophets' naming of social sin to the psalmist's recognition of the suffering of the innocent. Luke may focus in on the forgiveness of sins, but in Mark, Jesus' ministry speaks just as strongly to the problem of social shame, as Jesus breaks purity boundaries to touch the unclean and to party with those with the social status of "sinners."[7] There are also broader definitions of the human problem, as I've indicated, in the writings of Western theologians, while Eastern Orthodox theologians thought of the human problem not just as sin/guilt, but as mortality. We need to pay attention to Christians of cultures very different from our own, where the "sin/guilt" paradigm has not been established. If their culture is more a "shame-oriented" than a "guilt-oriented" culture, what resources have they found in the tradition or developed for themselves that image grace as a response to shame? If their culture has a more corporate understanding of responsibility than ours, how does that manifest itself in their ritual practice? Also within Christianity in the United States, there are ethnic and denominational groups whose ritual practice addresses the communal dimension of both sin and healing from sin. In some African American Pentecostal churches, for instance, when an individual's sin becomes known, another person may become spirit-possessed in order to cleanse the community.

Finally, we can look at rituals Christians have recently developed to address aspects of the human problem other than personal sin and guilt. The Good Friday Walks for Justice, an adaptation of the Stations of the Cross, where people walk through the city and stop at sites that are associated with systemic injustice, are one way to ritually name and address social sin (Ruether 1985). In *Women-Church*, Rosemary Radford Ruether advocates having a rite of repentance for the sins of the church (ibid., 117–18, 241–51). While I don't think the one she proposes is very broadly usable, her discussion of this need made me think of the times recently that a Roman Catholic bishop has made public apology on behalf of the church for the harm done by priestly sexual abuse. I wonder whether there might be ways, in public or private ritual, for a person who has been harmed in or by the church to receive a ritual apology from a clergyperson not implicated in that harm, who would be speaking on behalf of the church. This could be a healing ritual encounter for some people.[10] Another set of rituals to consider would be those developed by and for survivors of sexual abuse or violence. Some of these rituals include a symbolic cleansing (perhaps with echoes of baptism) to address the feelings not of personal guilt but of shame and defilement (ibid., 151–53).[11]

Among recent developments in the ritual life of the church is the revival of the biblical practice of individual and corporate lament. For centuries, Western Christian liturgical practice included praying the "lament psalms," but they were interpreted christologically, which often meant that since only Jesus was truly innocent in his suffering, only Jesus had the grounds on which to lament. The loss of lament as a faithful way of praying protest was tied up with the limited and limiting definition of the human problem as personal sinfulness. Happily, Christians in other parts of the world or in nondominant cultural settings sometimes learned lament from the Bible, and were able to name to God evils other than their own sin. I remember an occasion at Trinity Seminary in Columbus, Ohio, after the November 1980 bombing of the printing press of the Evangelical Lutheran Ovambo-Kavango Church in Namibia. During the prayers when people were invited to speak their petitions, a Namibian student spoke a strong lament: "How could you let this happen, O God? We have been faithful!"[12] This was not a way that the North American Lutherans in the room had learned to pray!

Since at least the 1980s, voices in the ecumenical liturgical movement have been advocating a recovery of lament.[13] This is connected with a recovery of a cosmic eschatology—that we are not living in a God's-will world, but in a not-yet world. It is also connected with a recognition of systemic evil, and an awareness of the need to pray honestly out of the experience of victimhood, suffering, and unreason. Getting free of bad theology and (re-)finding ways to pray the whole of our human experience go hand in hand. In recent decades, a number of people have written about how to help suffering people and survivors pray their laments (see Anderson 2005; Billman and Migliore 1999; Fraser

2005; Henderson 1994; Tanner 2001; Silva 2001). This literature provides one clear example of how Christian ritual might more faithfully hold the experience of the oppressed.

Sources of Injustice in Religious Ritual: Society beyond the Church

Some forms of oppression that surface in our religious practice derive not from the sources of the tradition or from theology but from the influence of oppressive systems and prejudices at large in our societies. The racial separation of Christian worshiping communities in segregated America is one example. The ableism we practice through our imagery, our unstated criteria for worship participation, and our architectural inaccessibility comes more from societal assumptions than from theological tenets. Age discrimination would be the clearest example of a form of oppression that cannot be legitimated from Scripture or tradition. When the elderly are marginalized in the worship life of a community, when they are seen only as ritual recipients and never as leaders or planners or caregivers, it is a fairly recent societal prejudice at work. In all such cases, the greatest danger is that we will not be aware of the injustice we do at all, because we, and everyone around us, take these attitudes for granted. The power of these prejudices means that, along with the hard, ongoing work of critical biblical interpretation and theology, we need to be critical anthropologists toward our own culture.

The best safeguard against these and all forms of oppressive treatment in our religious ritual is the empowerment of the oppressed to define and determine their own ritual action. When Laura had the host shoved into her mouth, there were two main problems at work: the presider's inadequate sacramental theology and interpersonal skills, and his power over Laura in the ritual setting. If society and church had not given him so much power over her in that setting, it would not have been possible for him to treat her so badly without even recognizing his own violence. One of the most positive developments in modern Western culture has been the coming together of persons with a common experience of need or oppression to name their own reality and to speak out to the rest of society about the conditions of their lives. Much of the most effective, newly developed rituals for pastoral care have been developed by people coming together to share and name their own experience. For instance, rites to mourn after a miscarriage were identified as a need by grieving parents themselves; only later did hospitals and, finally, the church develop institutional ritual responses. In the rest of this essay,

I will turn to the question of how we can move toward giving power to the "least of these" to ritually name their own reality before God.

Barriers to Ritual Empowerment: Clericalism, Individualism, and Consumerism

One of the main goals of the ecumenical liturgical movement from its beginnings was to have the liturgy recognized as the work of the people (one way to define the word *leiturgia*), not a clerical performance put on for a lay audience. Clericalism has deep roots, though, both in historical church practice and in human nature, and it is hard to get beyond it. Laypeople cede their own ritual responsibility to the clergy, and clergypeople may unconsciously need to hang on to control. It's a problem in our communal worship, and it's even more of a problem in "occasional services," the rituals designed for situations of pastoral care, for times of transition or crisis. The weekly worship service can become more communally owned to the extent that the community learns how to do it over time. Rituals of pastoral care are more likely to be unfamiliar to the layfolk involved—the persons in crisis or transition themselves. In denominations with liturgical books, the book with the Sunday liturgy is usually familiar to the laypeople, while the occasional services book is owned, controlled, and brought into the situation by the pastor. This makes it even more of a challenge to give agency within pastoral care rituals to the entire worshiping community (whether that's just one pastor and one sick individual, or several leaders and a large gathering at a wedding or funeral).

In U.S. culture particularly, the challenge of empowering the community is complicated by our individualism. Many factors make it difficult for us to make and sustain organic community in the United States, and where there is no organic community, there is only an audience. Individualism also gives many Americans an antiritual bias, a negative reaction to the idea of ritual that goes back at least to the turn of the twentieth century. We may still want rituals at certain significant times (such as after public tragedies), but we resist the call to become ritual makers because we are suspicious of ritual in general, seeing it as a threat to our values of spontaneity, genuineness, individuality, and freedom.

Perhaps the most pervasive and insidious threat to ritual empowerment in our culture is consumerism. This is not just a matter of spending money; it is a question of our very identity as consumers. In our economy, we exist to consume, even more than to work. (We work in order to have the wherewithal to consume.) We do not make art, or music, or clothing; we consume it. We don't play instruments ourselves; we buy perfect recordings of music produced by professionals. Think what this means, say, for the celebration of weddings. We don't make the gown or the suits, the festal food or the music at the reception, the decorations or the invitations. We pay professionals to provide those things (the average wedding in the United States now costs two thirds of the average American annual salary!). Too often the music at the reception is not music that people of all ages can dance to (if they all even understand themselves as capable of dancing), so that the only festive action left to many attendees is literal consumption: eating and drinking. One of the reasons why alcohol becomes so important in our partying is that for many of us, it is the only festal activity left, the only thing that makes us feel like we're having fun.

Consumerism deprives us of a repertoire of creative activity for rituals, and it also makes us turn to professionals to provide things for us, including rituals. This is the new clericalism. If I need something religious, I'll turn to a religious professional and expect her or him to provide it. It should be easily accessible, it should be of high quality, and I should be able to tell quickly whether or not it suits my needs. If it doesn't, I'll shop elsewhere. All of these attitudes and expectations militate against my feeling my way into a commonly created ritual life.

Ritual Empowerment When People Have a Ritual Repertoire

Let me begin with two stories of house blessings.

In a Roman Catholic, Yup'ik village in Alaska, Bruce Morrill, a priest who has spent enough time there to be integrated into the community when he visits, was asked by a couple he knew to do a house blessing. All five of their children had moved out to big cities, and the parents were legitimately worried about their welfare—and grieving the loss of their daily presence. Bruce listened to their stories and concerns for some time, and understood that their request for a house blessing was based on their concern for the integrity and well-being of their entire family. He took note of the symbols the couple had set out on a table to use for the ritual: a photo of the entire family, a much-read (dog-eared, Post-It-noted) family Bible, and a certain candle. The couple had ready the tundra grass that the Yup'ik use for incense (like other Native Americans' smudging). As they walked around the house for the ritual, the woman carried it, smoking in a small dish, as she walked ahead of Bruce, who sprinkled holy water around. The adjacent Sunday's Gospel was read: Mary of Bethany anointed Jesus' feet, and

Bruce used that to talk about Christ's presence in the family's life. He chose to read Psalm 84, and when the psalmist spoke of yearning for the dwelling place of God, the woman of the couple groaned with her own yearning. He left plenty of room for intercessory prayer. In the couple's storytelling, they had conveyed the sense that since his mother and her father had died, things kept going wrong. Knowing how vivid the spirits of the ancestors are in traditional Yup'ik culture, Bruce prayed with the couple for their ancestors, especially the two that had recently died.[15]

Ivis LaRiviere-Mestre, a Lutheran pastor serving a Latino/Mestizo community in an American city, has done much work to develop rituals of pastoral care for her community's needs. To address the needs of children who had expressed a fear of going to bed at night due to an incident of violence in their home or neighborhood, she developed a rite of "Angelical Blessings." She would meet with the family ahead of time to go over the ritual and make adjustments, to invite children into leadership roles, and to ask them to have the child's baptismal candle and a comforting bedtime object or song available. On the day of the ritual, she began by drawing with the children so they could express their fears. After a prayer requesting angelic protection (drawing on Latino popular piety), a comforting Bible story was read by one of the children. Then the whole family was invited to breathe in the Spirit and "puff away" the monsters, which they did all around the children's rooms, and baptismal water was splashed around. Finally, in view of the importance of a parental blessing in many Latino communities, the parents were given oil to anoint their children's foreheads, and the ritual ended with their anointing of their children.[16]

Both Ivis LaRiviere-Mestre and Bruce Morrill did exemplary pastoral ritual care in these respective house blessings. Working with people who were culturally and personally at risk, they showed great respect for culture and person alike. They listened well before they made their ritual choices and shared ritual leadership with the family. Ivis even knew how to give the children a say, getting them to "speak" their fears by drawing. The two pastors each used the symbols that the family provided, integrating those into the ritual action. They didn't come in and "do" a preset ritual; they cocreated a ritual with the family. They validated the family's or the child's experience by addressing their fears in meaningful, symbolic ways. Both rituals made use of elements of the family's cultural symbolic heritage (the tundra grass, the ancestors; the angels, the parental blessing) in concert with the common symbols of the Christian tradition. The pastors "midwifed" a ritual experience that made a place for the family's needs and fears and brought a sense of renewed wholeness and confidence.

The ritual pastoral care of these two pastors is a fine model for pastors everywhere. Some of their approach—the listening, the involvement of the others in planning and doing, the use of the family's own symbols—could be used in almost any cultural setting.

There is one way, though, in which these two examples are not at all representative of what many American pastors would face in their ministry with families. In both cases, the family had a vital repertoire of cultural/religious ritual symbols at hand. The pastor had to be sensitive to that cultural world of meaning in order to incorporate pieces of it into the ritual; but at least there was a cultural world of meaning to be sensitive to. Many dominant-culture Americans have lost most of the ethnic religious traditions that once shaped everyday life. Pluralism, the mixing up of ethnicity in families, the lack of valuing of the past, the individualist resistance to ritual expectations, the way we experience time, and many other factors have led to this loss. Dominant-culture Americans have little repertoire of ritual activity because they consume art and music rather than making it; and they have little repertoire of ritual activity because they have not carried on the folk traditions of their ancestors.

Ritual Empowerment for People without a Ritual Repertoire

How do we empower people to name their own reality before God when they don't have much of a ritual repertoire, and aren't positively aware of the repertoire they do have? I will suggest here five things we can do in our religious communities to lay the groundwork for pastoral ritual care that empowers the care-receiver.

1. In our weekly worship, we can repeatedly include certain elements that are particularly well suited for use in times of crisis or celebration outside the community setting. In Christian Sunday worship, we could sing hymns or Taizé chants that would be appropriate to sing at times of transition, loss, or celebration (or at least learn tunes to which other texts are set that would be appropriate at such times). We could (several times a year) pray the sort of litanies—short lines followed by a repeated simple response—that work well as a way to pray at a deathbed or while waiting anxiously at a time of crisis. We could incorporate simple symbolic actions, such as touching the

water in the font and bringing it to your forehead (sometimes it works best to teach such actions first to the children).

2. We can make ritual agency one of the goals of all of the committee meetings and small group meetings and Sunday/Saturday school classes in the life of the community (though I wouldn't name it that way—people won't feel a need to be "ritual anythings"!). We can start by going around the circle and having everyone say a short prayer (inviting petition or thanksgiving or lament). Then we can ask people to bring some sort of physical symbol as a sign of their hope or worry, or to make a symbol by drawing a picture or by shaping some modeling substance (colored beeswax feels good). We can draw them into music making by getting them to sing or chant unaccompanied. If they get used to doing such things in a small-group setting, they'll be much more likely to be able to do them at home or in the hospital.

3. When, as denominations or congregations, we offer resources to people for home ritual, they should not be only in the form of books or booklets with set rituals. We should offer make-your-own-ritual resources: recipes with lots of options of things to do and say and invitations to fill in the blanks with your own personal or familial symbols, vignettes of different ways various people have adapted the recipe in different settings, physical symbols to use (a family blessing cup, a baptismal candle, a make-it-yourself Advent wreath). Generally speaking, home-based ritual is considered women's work in our gendered world; design-your-own-ritual computer software might help get men involved in planning. We can offer mini-workshops on making bedtime safe, or on celebrating the holidays after a death in the family, or on how to handle the transitions when a dual-custody child is transferred from one parent to another.

4. We have much to learn from those family therapists who help families create rituals for transitions, losses, or other special needs.[17] We should pay attention to the sorts of transitions and crises for which they find ritual to be helpful: old losses that were not able to be mourned at the time; a family that can't launch a young adult child; a child's night fears after her parents' divorce. We can learn from the therapists how they introduce the idea of ritual making to the family. They can give us a sense of a kind of common human ritual repertoire that seems meaningful to most people, for instance, how

destroying a symbol of something can help us recognize and accept the reality of an ending. Most of all, they can teach us how to elicit from people their own symbols and meaningful actions, and how to integrate those into the ritual. Family therapists who use ritual are probably the best guides for this kind of ritual facilitation. Other teachers, though, might include the "death midwives" who help mourners design and carry out home funerals,[18] authors of books on creating family traditions,[19] and even some of the more sensible New Age-style ritual mavens.[20]

5. Instructed by such ritual facilitators, we can train clergy and other religious leaders to be ritual midwives rather than ritual masters. As in the field of congregational studies we teach seminarians to listen to the congregation's story before leading, and as in pastoral care we teach caregivers to listen first, last, and in between, so in worship classes we can teach them to listen, to draw out from people their own symbols, to see how they structure their time, to pick up on the culture-specific symbolic language, and to use all that in cocreating with them rituals that make sense out of their own lives. The surest route to greater justice in the church's ritual life is to empower every last person to speak the truth of her or his life to God.

APPENDIX

<h1 style="text-align:center">Some Definitions</h1>

For the purposes of establishing some common terminology throughout this book, the following definitions are operative. Pastors should note that not all persons in any given congregation are necessarily from the United States. While racial and ethnic oppression exists worldwide, the impact it has on persons living in a specific context varies. For instance, racism as it is experienced in the United States is a result of a particular set of historical circumstances that may be similar, but not identical, to the oppression experienced by others elsewhere. Moreover, people of color who come to the United States from other countries will face racism in this context even if they are members of "the majority" in their home countries. These definitions have been adapted and expanded from two sources: The National Dialogues on Anti-Racism: Expanded Version (New York: Episcopal Church Center, 1999), 17–20; also, Valerie Batts, "Modern Racism: New Melody for the Same Old Tunes," Episcopal Divinity School Occasional Papers (1968), 6–12.

African American or Black (not of Hispanic origin)—Persons who are of African descent or who have African ancestry. Though the terms are used interchangeably, some prefer reference to geographic origins rather than skin color.

American Indian/Alaskan Native—Persons who have descended from or who have ancestral connections to any of the original (indigenous) peoples of North America. In some contexts, the term Native American is preferred.

Anglo or Anglo-American—Pertains to English-rooted culture in the United States. Refers to a language group. Because of the fundamental nature of the English language within American culture, this term is often used to signify the mainstream or dominant culture.

Asian American/Pacific Islanders—Persons who have origins in the people of the Far East, Southern Asia, or the Pacific Islands.

Bigotry—An intensive and negative form of prejudice usually marked by fear, intolerance, hatred, or suspicion.

Cross-cultural—Refers to the interaction, communication, or connection between people from two or more different cultures.

Culture—The body of learned beliefs, traditions, behavior patterns, communication styles, concepts, values, institutions, and standards that are commonly shared among members of a particular group, and that are socially transmitted to individuals and to which individuals are expected to conform. Persons belong to a variety of cultural groups simultaneously, for example, racial cultures, ethnic cultures, religious cultures, regional cultures, and so forth.

Cultural Identity—The part of each of us that relates to the cultural groups to which we belong, also referred to as social location. Each person, in fact, encompasses multiples identities in that they relate to a variety of cultural groups, including race, ethnicity, gender, nationality, sexual identity, and so forth.

Diversity—Differences among people or peoples reflected in a variety of cultural forms, included but not limited to race, ethnicity, gender, age, religion, class, and so forth. Technically, to state that a group or a congregation is "diverse" does not assume that there are relationships between people across differences.

Dominant Culture—That which is considered mainstream American culture, a term used synonymously with white culture; the historic and institutionally recognized set of cultural patterns.

Ethnic or Ethnicity—Refers to a people who share a group identity because of common racial, national, tribal, religious, linguistic, or cultural characteristics.

European American—Persons who are of European descent or have their origins in the peoples of Europe.

Genocide—The destruction of, or conspiracy to destroy, a group because of their cultural, racial, ethnic, national, or religious identity.

Hispanic American or Latino/Latina—Persons of Spanish-speaking cultures of origin such as Mexican, Puerto-Rican, Dominican, Central or South American. Latino/Latinas or Hispanic Americans are from a variety of racial groups. The terms Hispanic or Latino are sometimes used interchangeably; often people from particular countries or locales will favor one of the terms over the other.

Internalized Oppression—The response of a marginalized individual or group that reinforces the oppressor's view of that individual or group. For instance, a person of color cannot technically be a racist, yet people of color are challenged by internalized racism, or the racist view of their identity. Similarly, women struggle with internalized sexism, or a patriarchal view of their identity.

Multicultural—A term describing the coexistence of a variety of distinct cultures within a given group of people. Technically, the term multiculturalism alone does not assume that a group or a congregation is antiracist, or has worked to correct the power imbalance between whites and people of color in a given context.

Oppression—The use of power by one group against another.

People of Color—A collective term, including African Americans, Asian Americans, American Indians, and Hispanic Americans. Although commonly used, the term *minorities* is a misnomer; persons within these groups are the numerical majority in the world and in parts of the United States. Although this term continues to be a source of debate, it is preferable to "nonwhite," which only describes what other racial groups are not.

Pluralism—A state where members of diverse groups maintain autonomous participation in both a common society and separate cultural groups.

Prejudice—A prejudgment that is directed against others before one has all the facts. Prejudice can be positive or negative.

Race—A social (rather than biological) construction based on differences in skin color and facial features imposed by Europeans in North America in order to justify colonization.

Racism—The systematic oppression of one race over another. In the United States, racism operates on personal, interpersonal, institutional, and cultural levels, and as a system differentiates between whites and people of color. Because the social systems and institutions within the United States are controlled by white people, they have the social power to make and enforce decisions, and have greater access to resources. Racist attitudes and behaviors can be intentional or unintentional.

Power—The capacity to have control, authority, or influence over others. In the context of cultural competence and white racism awareness, social power refers to the capacity of the dominant (white) culture to have control, authority, and influence over people of color. Social power plus prejudice equals oppression.

Prejudice—A preconceived judgment or opinion that is directed against all members of a group with insufficient grounds.

Stereotype—An oversimplified and usually inaccurate belief about a group that is projected upon all members of that group.

White—A political (rather than cultural) construct used to describe the racial identity of European Americans. It was first used in seventeenth-century Virginia by upper-class persons (the numerical minority), in an effort to have lower-class "whites" identify with themselves, rather than with blacks or indigenous persons. Previously, legal documents referred to "ethnic" identities such as English, German, Dutch, African, and so forth.

CONTRIBUTORS

Editors

Sheryl A. Kujawa-Holbrook is the Academic Dean and the Suzanne Radley Hiatt Professor of Feminist Pastoral Theology and Church History at the Episcopal Divinity School. She is the author of numerous books and articles, including *Seeing God in Each Other; A House of Prayer for all Peoples: Congregations Building Multiracial Community;* and *Deeper Joy: Lay Women and Vocation in the Episcopal Church.* An Episcopal priest, she served as the chair of the Anti-Racism Committee of the Executive Council of the Episcopal Church for seven years. She lives with her husband and their daughter in Cambridge, Massachusetts, and Tucson, Arizona.

Karen B. Montagno is Dean of Students and Community Life at Episcopal Divinity School in Cambridge, Massachusetts. She is a faculty member in pastoral theology, and teaches courses in pastoral care, antioppression, vocational discernment, and blacks and the Episcopal Church. Her publications include artwork on spirituality, worship, and women in the Bible. She has written curriculum for the Episcopal Curriculum for Youth and articles and meditations on spirituality and everyday life. An Episcopal priest, she lives in Cambridge, Massachusetts, with her family.

Authors

William Blaine-Wallace has spent over thirteen years as a counselor to dying and bereaved persons and was executive director of the health-care organization that opened the nation's first acute inpatient center for persons with HIV/AIDS. He consults with private and public agencies that make policies for the care of the terminally ill. He currently serves as the multifaith chaplain at Bates College.

Webb Brown is a chaplain with the VNA Care Network Hospice. She has spent over fifteen years with hospice, offering pastoral care, counseling, and bereavement follow-up to terminally ill patients and their families in Cambridge and Needham, Massachusetts, and surrounding areas. Committed to both the spiritual and justice dimensions of hospice ministry, she serves also as an advocate for those who are terminally ill.

Donald M. Chinula is the chair of the department of religion and philosophy at Stillman College, and has degrees in law and theology from the University of Minnesota Law School, Columbia University School of Law, the Interdenominational Theological Center, and the School of Theology at Claremont. He is author of *Building King's Beloved Community: Foundations for Pastoral Care and Counseling with the Oppressed*.

Howard Cohen is a graduate of the Reconstructionist Rabbinical College, and is currently on the faculty of the American Hebrew Academy, the first and only pluralistic Jewish boarding school. His rabbinic career includes twelve years as a congregational rabbi in rural Vermont, and before that, he served for five years as a prison chaplain in a maximum-security facility.

Miguel A. De La Torre is associate professor for social ethics and director of the Peace and Justice Institute at Iliff School of Theology in Denver. A scholar-activist and an ordained Southern Baptist minister, he is author of over a dozen books, including the award-winning *Reading the Bible from the Margins*; *Santería: The Beliefs and Rituals of a Growing Religion in America*; and *Doing Christian Ethics from the Margins*.

Cheryl Giles is the Francis Greenwood Peabody Professor of the Practice in Pastoral Care and Counseling at Harvard Divinity School. She is a licensed clinical psychologist specializing in teaching and providing culturally competent clinical care to underserved populations. Giles has extensive experience in the treatment of children, adolescents, and families with significant mental illness, high-risk behaviors, and traumatic stress disorder.

Brita L. Gill-Austern is Austin Philip Giles Professor of Psychology and Pastoral Theology at Andover Newton Theological School, where she also serves as director of the program and Summer Institute in Faith, Health and Spirituality. She is coeditor of *Feminist-Womanist Pastoral Theology* and author of articles on health and spirituality, the psychology of women, pastoral theology, and pastoral care and the role of congregations in healing.

Ahmed Nezar M. Kobeisy is currently the Imam and Director of the Islamic Center of Capital District in Schenectady, New York. He is the Muslim chaplain at Syracuse University, and a faculty member at Le Moyne College, State University of New York at Oswego (SUNY), and at Hartford Seminary. He is the author of *Counseling American Muslims: Understanding the Faith and Helping the People.*

Eric H. F. Law is an internationally known consultant, teacher, and trainer in building inclusive community. An Episcopal priest, his numerous books include *The Wolf Shall Dwell With the Lamb*; *The Bush Was Blazing but Not Consumed*; *Sacred Acts, Holy Change*; *The Word at the Crossings*; *Inclusion*; and most recently, *Finding Intimacy in a World of Fear.*

Kenneth Leech founded Centrepoint, one of the main agencies for young homeless people in the United Kingdom. He serves as Honorary Research Fellow in Social and Pastoral Theology in the University of Manchester, and as adjunct lecturer at the Nazarene Theological College, Manchester. He is the author of *Through Our Long Exile: Contextual Theology and the Urban Experience*; *Soul Friend*; *Spirituality and Pastoral Care.*

Christopher Medeiros is the director of admissions, recruitment, and financial aid at Episcopal Divinity School, where as adjunct faculty he teaches classes around queer issues. He holds a Master of Divinity degree from EDS and a Master of Arts in Counseling Psychology from Lesley University. Chris was director of the Stepping Stone Day Treatment clinic in Boston where he led spirituality groups with chronically mentally ill adults.

Sara Gibb Millspaugh is a Unitarian Universalist minister currently serving as adult programs director for the Unitarian Universalist Association of Congregations. A graduate of Harvard Divinity School, her background includes work on the *Our Whole Lives* sexuality education program for faith communities and pastoral care with people living with HIV/AIDS. She lives in Orange County, California, with her husband.

Mikel Ryuho Monnett is a member of the Zen Peacemaker Order and the Karma Kagyu lineage of Tibetan Buddhism. An ardent advocate of Buddhist chaplaincy, he is a member of the Buddhist Chaplains Network of the ACPE and currently serves as the Heart Services Anchor Chaplain at Barnes-Jewish Hospital at Washington University Medical Center in St. Louis, Missouri.

Greer Anne Wenh-In Ng is associate professor emerita of Christian Education at Emmanuel College, Victoria University, in the University of Toronto, and faculty coordinator of its Centre for Asian Theology. An ordained minister of the United Church of Canada, she is editor of *Our Roots, Our Lives: Glimpses of Faith and Life from Black and Asian Canadian Women* and *That All May Be One: A Resource for Educating Toward Racial Justice*.

Altagracia Perez is rector of Holy Faith Episcopal Church in Inglewood, California, and has been actively involved in the fight against HIV/AIDS since 1985, especially among youth and Latinas. She served as writer and consultant for the educational resource *Episcopal Guide to TAPS: Teens for AIDS Prevention*, and was a member of President Clinton's Advisory Council on HIV/AIDS, serving as cochair of the Racial and Ethnic Minorities Subcommittee.

Janet L. Ramsey is associate professor of Congregational Care Leadership at Luther Seminary in St. Paul. A former parish pastor and nursing home chaplain, she is on the staff of the Center for Aging, Religion and Spirituality in St. Paul. She is first author of the book *Spiritual Resiliency in Older Women: Models of Strength for Challenges through the Life Span*.

Elaine Ramshaw is a spiritual director and parish pastoral care coordinator, and teaches online courses for seminaries scattered across the country. She taught pastoral care full-time for sixteen years (at Methodist, Lutheran, and Episcopal seminaries) until the sugar maples called her home to New England in 2001. She is the author of *Ritual and Pastoral Care* and *The Godparent Book*.

Carolyn R. Thompson serves on the Disabilities Ministries and the Wider Church Ministries Boards of the United Church of Christ (UCC), and on the Reference Committee for the Ecumenical Disability Advocates Network (EDAN) of the World Council of Churches. A person with a lifelong disability, she works for the Commission for Persons with Disabilities in Cambridge, Massachusetts.

Marsha I. Wiggins is Professor of Counseling Psychology and Counselor Education at the University of Colorado at Denver and Health Sciences Center. An ordained United Methodist minister, her research and writing focus is on multicultural counseling and the integration of spirituality and counseling. She is the author of *Integrating Religion and Spirituality into Counseling: A Comprehensive Approach*.

Carmen Braun Williams is assistant vice president for diversity at the University of Colorado. She also is associate professor in counseling psychology at the University of Colorado at Denver and Health Sciences Center, former associate dean of the UCDHSC School of Education, and a licensed clinical psychologist. Her research area is racial and cultural factors in psychotherapy and higher education.

Joel Glenn Wixson is currently assistant professor in the Graduate School of Arts and Sciences in the division of Counseling and Psychology of Lesley University. He is a licensed clinical psychologist and a licensed alcohol and drug counselor. He has worked in the field of human services for over fifteen years, primarily with people who are homeless and are struggling with mental illness and addiction.

NOTES

1: Midwives and Holy Subversives

1. These colleagues, my community voices of wisdom (including myself), are: The Rev. Karen B. Montagno, Dean of Students and Community Life, Episcopal Divinity School, Cambridge, Mass.; The Rev. Dr. Alan Robinson, rector, St. James Episcopal Church, Baltimore, Md.; The Rev. Brian Jemmott, rector, Episcopal Church of the Holy Cross, Decatur, Ga.; The Rev. Shariya Molegoda, interim priest, St. James Episcopal Church, Cambridge, Mass.; The Rev. Belva Brown Jordan, associate dean for admission and student services, Phillips Theological Seminary, Tulsa, Ok.; The Rev. Lynn Washington, director of Peter and Paul Development Center, Richmond, Va.; The Honorable Byron Rushing, Massachusetts House of Representatives, 9th Suffolk District; The Rev. Nelson Foxx, rector, St. Bartholomew's Episcopal Church, Cambridge, Mass.; Marie-Therese "Tess" Browne, SCN, Quincy, Mass.; The Rev. Canon Edward W. Rodman, Professor of Pastoral Theology and Urban Ministry Carpenter Visiting Professor of Racism Studies and Social Change, Episcopal Divinity School, Cambridge, Mass.; Henry A. Lewis III, correctional facility education instructor, Suffolk County House of Corrections at South Bay; Dorothy E. Dottin, church activist, mentor, former president of the Union of Black Episcopalians, Massachusetts Chapter.

2: Love and Power

1. Statistics from Teaching Tolerance, a project of the Southern Poverty Law Center, "Ten Ways to Fight Hate," http://www.tolerance.org/10_ways/index.html; and U.S.

Census Bureau, "Population Profile of the United States: 2000," http://www.census.gov/prod/cen2000/index.html, (both accessed December 5, 2008).

2. "Race as a Target Variable," VISIONS, Inc., Roxbury, Massachusetts, n.d.

3. These criteria have been adapted and expanded from *The National Dialogues on Anti-Racism: Extended Version* (New York: The Episcopal Church Center, 1999), 127 & appendix.

3: Engaging Diversity and Difference

1. This chapter is based in part on the Schmiechen Lecture I gave at Eden Theological Seminary on October 10, 2005, entitled "Fostering Healing Connections that Build Communities without Borders."

2. This quote is attributed to a radio interview with poet Carl Sandburg (National Public Radio, n.d.).

3. This section on the work of Miroslav Volf draws upon an article entitled "Practices of Exclusion Fuel the Global AIDS Crisis: The Fire that Keeps Burning," *The Journal of Pastoral Theology* 17, no. 1 (Spring 2007): 36–53.

4. In the United States in 1976, the top 1 percent owned 22 percent of the wealth, the bottom 99 percent earned 78 percent. Twenty-five years later, in 2001, the top 1 percent increased their earnings by 16 percent for a total of 38 percent of the wealth, while the bottom 99 percent decreased their resources by 16 to 62 percent (see Collins and Yeskel 2005, 54).

5. Robert Bellah et al. (1985) described lifestyle enclaves as places where people are characterized by some shared feature of private life: "Members of a lifestyle enclave express their identity through shared patterns, appearance, consumption, and leisure activities, which often serve to differentiate them sharply from those with other lifestyles. They are not interdependent" (335). These are places where people gather in "a narcissism of similarity."

6. John De Graaf et al. tell us that Americans have reached a new milestone in that the United States now has more cars (204 million) than registered drivers (2005, 33).

4: Pastoral Care from the Latina/o Margins

1. All scriptural quotes in this chapter are my own translation from the original Hebrew or Greek.

2. It is important to note that other minority groups also participate in a time of testimonies during their worship service. Even some European American churches, as in

the case of Pentecostal congregations and charismatic Roman Catholic liturgies, have a similar testimony period as part of their worship.

6: North American Asian Communities

1. This is Clinebell's statement. The six aspects from Clebsch and Jackie are "Enlivening one's mind; Revitalizing one's body; Renewing and enriching one's intimate relationships; Deepening one's relationship with nature and the biosphere; Growth in relationship to the significant institutions in one's life; and Deepening and vitalizing one's relationship with God." Quoted in Clinebell 1984, 31.

2. Stephen Pattison cites in particular the example of a chaplain in a poorly run psychiatric hospital who ignores the low standard of care and indeed abuse suffered by patients as he goes about his pastoral care ministry with individual patients. For an argument to hold both aspects in tension, see Leas and Kittlaus 1981.

3. The Chinese Immigration Act of 1923 was not repealed till 1947. In Canada, there was the additional discrimination of imposing a "head tax" on Chinese applicants only, beginning with $50 in 1885 and ending with $500 in 1923—a sum that in those days would have purchased two modest houses. For more detailed historical accounts of these "first wave" Far East Asian immigrants, see Takaki 1989; Fong 1992; S. Kim 1996.

4. A survey of 1,216 (presumably non-Asian) adults by the Committee of 100 at the time of the 2000 U.S. census found that fully 25 percent would disapprove of a family member marrying a Chinese person, and 17 percent would be upset if a substantial number of Asian Americans moved into their neighborhood (Sue and Sue 2003, 329).

5. For an in-depth study of recent development of what Russell Jeung calls "Asian American panethnicity," with concrete cases for both evangelical and mainline denominations, see Jeung 2005.

6. Such support has been established by most major American Protestant denominations either as Asiamerican Ministry (Episcopal Church, United Methodist Church, etc.) or as part of multicultural or intercultural ministry (Evangelical Lutheran Church of America), and ecumenically in joint efforts such as PAACCE (Pacific Asian American Canadian Christian Education Ministries).

7. For "a continuum for churches" on becoming antiracist institutions, see the chart developed by Ronice Branding, Baily Jackson, Rita Hardiman, and Andrea Ayvazian reproduced in *Making Waves: an ecumenical feminist journal* [of the Women's Interchurch Council of Canada], 4/2 (Summer 2004), 48.

8. Internalized racism is discussed in "Raising Awareness for Aboriginals and People of Colour" in G. Ng 2004b, 48–52.

9. For an exposition of a continuum of high and low context cultures as applied to North American society, see Herberg 1993, 29–68.

10. This is how Young Lee Hertig names her bilingual (English and Korean) study of contemporary Korean immigrant life; see Lee Hertig 2001.

11. Of Chinese, Korean, and Japanese ancestry, these five authors are Jeannette Yep, Peter Cha, Susan Cho Van Riesen, Greg Jao, and Paul Tokunaga. See their experiences in Yep et al. 1998).

12. For a historical account and some contemporary Asian North American manifestations of these values, see G. Ng 1997b.

13. Hope S. Antone gives a succinct exposition of this theological quagmire based on a public lecture given by Rita Nakashima Brock in Hong Kong in October, 2003, in Antone 2003. Brock's thesis may be followed in Brock and Parker 2003.

14. The irony of such exclusion stares one in the face when one recalls that it was a female Chinese Anglican, Florence Tim Oi Lee, who was the first woman in the worldwide Anglican communion to be ordained priest, under wartime conditions by the bishop of Hong Kong in 1943. For a contemporary discussion by a group of Asian young adults, see Toyama and Gee 2006.

15. Asian feminist theologian Kwok Pui-lan's pioneering work in applying a postcolonial lens to "majority" feminist biblical interpretation can be found in Kwok 2005, esp. 77–99.

16. My attempt at inviting bilingual Asian pastors and theologians in North American to begin addressing this null curriculum is found in G. Ng 1997a, 21–36.

17. A short, basic introduction can be found in G. Ng 2004a. An edited volume that deals in particular with biblical interpretation for Asians is Liew 2002.

18. R. S. Sugirtharajah provides a list of goals for postcolonial biblical interpretation, among which this is one, in Sugirtharajah 2001, 99.

19. An exposition of the power flower as a social analysis tool may be found in Arnold et al. 1991. An adaptation of the tool for antiracism work is found in "A Tool for Everyone: Revelations from the Power Flower," in G. Ng 2004b: 53–55.

20. Basing their formulations on earlier models developed by R. T. Carter and J. E. Helms, Derald Wing Sue and David Sue have come up with a five-stage process for whites that mirrors their racial-cultural development model for minorities. This process begins with an initial conformity status (to white superiority and privilege as norm), moves to a status of dissonance (caused by contradictions arising from personal experience such as parental response to interracial dating), passes through a status of dissonance and immersion (beginning to question and challenge one's own racism, possibly overidentifying with racial-cultural minorities) and of introspection (accepting responsibility and honestly confronting one's biases and white privilege), ultimately arriving at an integration status (achieving release from racist memories and deciding to

change oneself and other whites) that results in conscious commitment to action that aims at eradicating systemic racism in institutions and in social policies (Sue and Sue 2003b, 235–64; implications for clinical practice are found on 263–64).

21. The model from monocultural to multicultural may be found in D. W. Sue 2006, 236, and Sue and Sue 2003a, 447–50. The continuum from exclusive to inclusive for churches is taken from a chart developed by Ronice Branding, Baily Jackson, Rita Decision, and Andrea Ayvazian of Mediation Service and is reproduced under the title "A Continuum for Churches: Becoming an Anti-Racist Institution," in *Making Waves* 4, no. 2 (Summer 2004): 48. Such building of cross-racial alliances can take many forms, and can be practiced both within one's own denomination and ecumenically. The former would include the Episcopal Church's "Seeing the Face of God in Each Other" antiracism thrust, or The United Church of Canada's antiracism policy, "That We May Be One," adopted in 2000. In Canada, the Canadian Ecumenical Anti-Racism Network (CEARN, since 2002) has produced and promoted a packet of educational, immersion, and action resources for a Racial Justice Week around March 21 in 2006. For Asian North Americans, observing Asian Heritage Month in May, as well as the International Day to Eliminate Racial Discrimination on March 21, can signal their church's acknowledgement of racial injustice suffered and bring them hope. In the same way, the observance of International Women's Day on March 8 can acknowledge a willingness on their church's part to recognize women's histories and contributions.

7: Pastoral Care from a Jewish Perspective

1. Translations of biblical passages that are not my translations are from *Etz Hayim: Torah Commentary* (New York: The Jewish Publication Society, 2001).

2. *Kol Hanishamah Daily Prayerbook* (New York: Reconstructionist Press, 1994).

3. *Halacha* (*halachic*): Rules and teachings pertaining to everyday activities observed by pious Jews. The degree of force these rules have over one's life is determined either by personal choice or movement affiliation. Within Halachic Judaism there is a whole category of special laws pertaining to marital relations referred to as "family purity laws." For more information contact a rabbinic authority.

8: Pastoral Care for Muslims

1. It is for this very reason that some colleagues and I have launched a publication, *The Journal of Muslim Mental Health* (published by Taylor and Francis) in collaboration with the Department of Global Health at New York University. In this journal, we have a

section called "Faith Based Practice" to discuss issues related to chaplaincy, pastoral care, counseling, and therapy among other professions and practices as they relate to Muslims.

2. Although the study was made on Muslims in counseling, pastoral counseling should not be any different except in the stronger link to religion and spirituality.

3. Many thanks and gratitude go to Dr. Hani Midani for his assistance on medical issues. Religious rulings on issues related to medical rules in specific conditions and on end of life care are based on the resolutions of Muslim World League Fiqh Council (Council of Jurisprudence).

9: A Buddhist Approach to Pastoral Care

1. The disciplines are Right Understanding, Right Resolve, Right Speech, Right Acts, Right Livelihood, Right Effort, Right Mindfulness, and Right Concentration. For anyone desiring to learn more about the basic tenets of Buddhism, I heartily recommend Walpola 1959 as a terrific introductory text for those who have no previous knowledge of Buddhism.

2. For a first-person account of the development of the School for Social Service in Vietnam, please read Kong 1993.

3. Anyone wishing to learn more about Engaged Buddhism as a movement and in its practical applications should read Kotler 1996.

4. The development of the Peacemaker Community (now Peacemaker Circle International), is detailed in Glassman 1998.

5. A fascinating account of how this process can ruin the lives of medical professionals is detailed in Shapiro 2004.

11: Never at Ease: Black, Gay, and Christian

1. Interview with Thomas G. Burke, December 28, 2004, from "The Soldier's Heart," *Frontline*, Public Broadcasting System, http://www.pbs.org/wgbh/pages/frontline/shows/heart/interviews (accessed October 30, 2008).

2. Ibid.

3. Ibid.

12: Addiction, Power, and Powerlessness

1. Unless I am quoting persons, I will use quotation marks to connote ideas satiated in AA traditions. In this instance, for example, I am using quotes to underscore the idea that constructing problems with substances as a disease is one possible way to think about these problems. It is also the way AA traditionally constructs these problems.

2. By sociopolitical power, I am referring to that form of power that prioritizes some forms and styles of living over others, and functions to marginalize alternate ways of being.

3. The notion of "identification" is a complex one, and I use the term here to connote the idea that an insider and an outsider would not be thought to share experiences from the same perspective.

4. I will not attempt to represent an entire list of symptoms said to be associated with the disease of alcoholism; however, I will mention a few. Symptoms typically associated with the disease of alcoholism are minimizing, blaming, rationalizing, and having difficulty with change. The complexity of the relationship between the Steps and the construction of the disease cannot be overstated. The idea of denial is mentioned nowhere in the Steps, yet it figures prominently in the process of treatment said to be based on the Steps. Symptoms said to result from the disease of alcoholism are mentioned, for the most part, in the "Big Book" (as *Alcoholics Anonymous*, the Program's basic sourcebook, is popularly called), where the Steps are also found (AA 1976).

5. This account represents an amalgam of people's lives with whom I have been privileged to engage.

6. A related topic that I will not cover here is the issue of disclosure. Currently, in the field of substance abuse treatment there is much discussion about the utility of disclosing one's personal history of problems with substances. There are, in fact, many treatment facilities where disclosing one's relationship to substances is strongly discouraged. This discussion will not address this additional issue.

7. For a further discussion of modernism, see Freedman and Combs 1996.

8. For a more complete description of the positioning of rich descriptions in opposition to naturalistic assumptions, see White and Epston 1994.

9. This letter is an example of letter writing informed by narrative practice. This tradition of letter writing is more fully described elsewhere (see Epston and White 1990).

10. In many locations in the United States meetings are available up to three times every day. You may contact AA Central Services for specific times and meeting locations.

13: A Liturgical Approach to Pastoral Care

1. For the full translation with commentary on the Nican Mopohua, which tells the story of the Guadalupe event in verse, see Elizondo 1997, 1–22.

2. For a full description of the *Community Bible Study* process see Law 1993, 121–29. I have also developed a half-hour process that I use in most gatherings. You can download it from the Web site of the Kaleidoscope Institute for Competent Leadership in a Diverse Changing World: http://www.ladiocese.org/ki (accessed October 31, 2008), in which suggested discussion questions for each Sunday's Gospel are updated every month.

3. For a description and theological understanding of why the Mutual Invitation process is essential for empowerment see Law 1993, 79–88.

15: Pastoral Care with Persons Living with HIV/AIDS

1. There are a great number of places where basic HIV/AIDS information can be found. Among them are Web sites such as http://hivinsite.ucsf.edu (accessed November 3, 2008), at the University of California, San Francisco, geared toward specific populations with resources appropriate for each.

2. Costs of treatment vary and there is some financial help through government programs supported. See "Ryan White Care Act," http://www.hab.hrsa.gov (accessed November 3, 2008).

3. At the beginning of public awareness of HIV in 1985 I was working in a parish-based leadership program for young women. As part of their training I led a workshop on HIV/AIDS thinking that it would be new information for them. I was surprised to find out that they already knew people who were infected and that one had an uncle who had died of AIDS. They believed the method of infection was injection drug use (IDU) since the people they knew were addicted to injection drugs. This population was infected from the beginning of the epidemic but did not receive media attention until later in the epidemic.

4. See "The Leadership Campaign on AIDS" (TLCA), U.S. National Institutes of Health, http://gateway.nlm.nih.gov/MeetingAbstracts/ma?f=102252578.html (accessed December 10, 2008).

5. See http://www.aids.org and the CDC Web site, http://www.cdc.gov/hiv (both accessed November 3, 2008).

6. See the Florida Department of Health Web site, http://www.doh.state.fl.us (accessed November 3, 2008).

7. For the history of the Gay Men's Health Crisis, see http://www.gmhc.org, accessed November 3, 2008.

8. For research on AIDS/HIV and gender issues, see http://www.who.int/en/, the Web site of the World Health Organization (accessed November 8, 2008).

9. See http://www.unaids.org (accessed November 8, 2008).

10. See http://www.cdc.gov/hiv/ (accessed November 8, 2008).

11. "Mental Health: Culture, Race, Ethnicity," Supplement to Mental Health: A Report of the Surgeon General, U.S. Department of Health and Human Services, 2001, http://mentalhealth.samhsa.gov/cre/default.asp (accessed November 3, 2008).

12. Ibid.

13. "The Tuskegee Study of Untreated Syphilis in the Negro Male," 1932–1972, U.S. Public Health Service.

14. For background on sterilization issues, see "Sterilization Abuse: A Task for the Women's Movement," The Chicago Committee to End Sterilization Abuse (CESA), January 1977, at http://www.cwluherstory.org/CWLUArchive/cesa.html (accessed December 10, 2008).

15. See http://www.aidsinfo.nih.gov, "Health Topics," under "Specific Populations" (accessed December 10, 2008).

16. For statistics on young gay men and AIDS/HIV, see http://www.avert.org/statindx.htm (accessed November 3, 2008).

17. Ibid.

18. For information on CDC faith-based initiatives, see http://www.cdc.gov/omhd/Partnerships/resourcesFai.htm (accessed December 10, 2008).

19. See http://www.pocaan.org (accessed November 3, 2008).

20. "Healing Begins Here: A Pastor's Guidebook for HIV/AIDS Ministry Through the Church," 2004, available for download through http://www.arkofrefuge.org/guidebook.html (accessed November 3, 2008).

21. Denominational Web sites carry a wide variety of resources for AIDS/HIV ministries; for example, see *Youth Ministry in the Age of AIDS*, available through the National Episcopal AIDS Coalition, http://www.neac.org/articles/000427.html (accessed December 10, 2008).

16: Ableism

1. Justice-For-All e-mail posting, Feb. 13, 2007: Information Bulletin #197, available at http://www.jfanow.org/jfanow/index.php?mode=A&id=3105;&sort=D (accessed November 4, 2008).

2. For information on prisoners with mental illness in New York prisons, see Sarah Kershaw, "New Rules in NY for Confining People with Mental Illness," New York Times, in Justice-For-All email posting, April 26, 2007, http://www.jfanow.org/jfanow/index.php?mode=A&id=3238;&sort=D (accessed November 4, 2008).

17: Pastoral Care with Transgender People

1. Student homily, National Coming Out Day worship service, Harvard Divinity School, Cambridge, Mass., October 13, 2000.

2. Barb Greve, personal interview, October 18, 2000.

3. Ibid.

4. http://www.uua.org/obgltc (accessed November 5, 2008).

18: Senior Adults and a New Story for Pastoral Care

1. I include older adults on class panels, videos, interviews, and on-site classes.

2. Humor, when it is not at the expense of someone or some group, is, of course, a great coping device at any age.

3. One of the most effective ways to accomplish this, while expanding student's crosscultural imagination, is to read classical literature, such as Shakespeare's *King Lear*, Paula Gunn-Allen's *Spider Woman's Granddaughters*, and Maya Angelou's "Our Grandmothers" in *I Shall Not be Moved*. See further, Burton 1991.

4. I did not, of course, encourage Heidi to act on these desires (with a new man) any more than I would with a young person.

5. This diversity also makes it very challenging to conduct research (especially quantitative research) and to create deep theory in gerontology. It also points to the importance of being careful when interpreting results if pluralism has not been taken into account.

6. Often older persons are themselves quite ageist, since they have lived for many years in an ageist culture and internalized these attitudes. For a thorough overview of ageism, see Nelson 2002.

7. I also write as a Lutheran pastor, counselor, and teacher of the church, and as a sixty-one-year-old mother and grandmother who grew up in an ageist, Western culture.

8. Consedine et al. 2004. These researchers found that older European Americans spoke of "adapting" whereas older African Americans were more likely to talk about

"surviving." They also found African Americans to be, overall, more resilient in the face of aging-related physical losses.

9. This occurs very early, beginning shortly after age three. See further, Montepare and Xebrowitz 2002.

10. In this article, I use the word *vocation* to mean "the call to be a child of God." In the Lutheran tradition, this word comes from the German word *Beruf*, which includes but is not limited to one's occupation. See further, Wingren 1957.

11. Academic findings about psychological factors, too, would seem to dispute the language of oppression. For example, most qualitative research studies conclude that life satisfaction does not decline with age. See further, Larson 1978.

12. See further, Gist and Hetzel 2004.

13. For example, in Minnesota during fall 2005, increases in fuel prices meant that demands on the food bank were sharply increased during the cold winter months of 2006. (I discovered this while volunteering at a food bank in St. Paul.)

14. *Federal Interagency Forum on Aging-Related Statistics*, "Older Americans 2004: Key Indicators of Well-Being," http://agingstats.gov/Agingstatsdotnet/Main_Site/Data/2004_Documents/entire_report.pdf (accessed November 5, 2008).

15. Harold Bloom, Shakespeare's *King Lear* (New York: Riverhead, 2005), 44.

16. Shakespeare, *King Lear*, act 2, scene 4. These are typically the persons who have difficulty asking for help when they need it, thus adding to difficulties for their family caregivers.

17. The Fifth Commandment is, of course, the only one that includes a promise along with the command, thus demonstrating its high importance: "Honor your father and your mother, that your days may be long in the land the LORD your God is giving to you" (Exod. 20:12).

18. Hans Küng commented recently that "Globalization of the economy, technology and communication has to be accompanied by the globalization of ethics" (*Santa Clara Magazine*, Summer 2005).

19. Moving five years ago to the Twin Cities in Minnesota from a small city in the South, I was struck by the more advanced educational background of many older members of my new congregation and by the more challenging educational materials that this diversity required.

20. We are typically motivated to see our own group more positively than others, but this is more difficult for a lower-status group, such as older adults. See further, Kite and Wagner 2002.

21. Depression is actually found at lower rates in older adults than in the general population. For an example of basic and accessible information about depression in older adults, see http://www.healthyplace.com/Communities/Depression/elderly.asp (accessed November 5, 2008).

22. Volf believes that embrace, not inclusion (which ignores differences), is the best term for our goal of being together in Christian love. See further, Volf 1996.

23. Kegan has described this transformation as that which "entails a reconstruction of basic forms of the distribution of energy or information or production"; see Debold 2006.

24. These include Anna, who speaks out against ethnic discrimination in her little town in Northern Germany; Alex, whose religiously mixed marriage has taught him the dangers of denominational prejudice; and Rebecca, who now is confined to a chair but whose life is busy with a prayer ministry. See further, Ramsey and Blieszner 1999 and forthcoming.

25. As of the 2000 census, thirty-five million Americans were over sixty-five. See further, Gist and Hetzel 2004.

26. Research has repeatedly confirmed the importance of religious faith for this age group. See, for example, Idler and Kasl 1997.

27. This is by no means an inclusive list. Please see further, Kimble et al. 1995 and 2003. Both volumes have excellent materials on pastoral care and aging. Also, many denominations now have their own Web sites for aging ministries, such as http://archive.elca.org/evangelizingchurch/congregations/senioradultministry.html (accessed November 5, 2008).

28. Including meeting times; too often congregations hold meetings at night, when elderly people can't drive.

29. Reverse ageism assumes that older people all know how to pray. Researchers have demonstrated that this is not the case. See further, Eisenhandler 2003.

30. In narrative therapy, we often speak of "externalizing the problem." See further, White and Epston 1990.

31. The work of Rabbi Dayle A. Friedman is particularly helpful here. See further, D. A. Friedman 2003.

32. For example, in one Lutheran congregation in St. Paul, older members were among those most supportive to the pastor when she introduced the possibility of becoming a Reconciling in Christ congregation (openly welcome to gay, lesbian, bisexual, and transgendered persons).

21: Loss, Death, and Dying: A Hospice Perspective

1. For some years, the stages of grief identified by Elizabeth Kübler-Ross in the context of people who had been diagnosed with a terminal disease were transferred to the grief experienced by people who had lost loved ones. Recent work by grief and loss counselors, such as William Worden and Jin Doka, offer another paradigm for the grief

that accompanies loss. Instead of naming them "stages," which can make us feel like puppets being manipulated by a power beyond ourselves, Worden and Doka talk about the "tasks" of grief, which are intertwined and follow no particular linear order.

22: Making (Ritual) Sense of Our Own Lives

1. In Christian tradition, the tropes of a sacred birth narrative get applied to a girl only in the apocryphal material about the birth of Mary, Jesus' mother. Not that I think the mythos surrounding the Virgin Mary was an unmixed gift to womankind!

2. I do not think there is any incompatibility between a corporate/cosmic eschatology and a belief in a future for the individual after death; Paul had both. The problem in my view came not with views of heaven so much as with the lack of expectation that God would change this world.

3. Quoted in the song "Sarowiwa" by Terry Leonino and Greg Artzner (on the CD "Guide My Feet" by Kim & Reggie Harris and Magpie, Appleseed Records, 1999).

4. There were rituals of corporate repentance, triggered by natural disasters or outbreaks of the plague, but I wouldn't see the deuteronomistic theodicy behind these rituals (something bad has happened; it must be punishment for our sin) as a liberative resource.

6. Robert Albers' pastoral theological book, *Shame* (Albers 1995), begins with the story of Jan, who seeks a word of forgiveness from her pastor, but for whom the rite of confession and absolution is a pastoral failure. The pastor expects and intends that the clear word of grace will free her, but after the absolution Jan feels worse than ever, not believing that she deserves to be forgiven. This is one clear example of how the overly narrow understanding of the human problem that dominates much of Western Christian practice can lead to placing an extra burden on people who already feel bad about themselves.

7. When we hear that Jesus associated with "sinners," we understand that word within our cultural framework, and think that they were persons who had done bad things or lived immorally. However, in Jesus' day, "sinner" was a word applied to classes of people who did not live a properly observant way of life from the point of view of religious authorities.

10. I have sometimes fantasized that this ritual role, that of apologizing on the behalf of the church to its victims, would be made part of the job description for all bishops and judicatory leaders.

11. See also the "Service of Cleansing" in M. W. Zimmerman 1995, 62–72. From p. 71: "By water and the Spirit, may you be cleansed from the power of the abuse that was done to you. May your soul be refreshed, your spirit uplifted and your vision cleared to see the pureness of your own heart."

12. For more such African Lutheran lament, see Kameeta 1986.

13. See, for example, Lathrop 1984; and Sparkes and Rutherford 1986. Westermann 1974 helped bring this to the fore.

15. Bruce Morrill, personal communication, April 5, 2007.

16. Ivis LaRiviere-Mestre, "God's Language of Hope: Children's Rituals as a Pastoral Care Tool," paper for my class "Ritual Care in Times of Transition or Crisis," Lutheran Theological Seminary at Philadelphia, spring 2006.

17. The classic books here are: Imber-Black et al. 1988; Imber-Black and Roberts 1992; Imber-Black 1991; and van der Hart, 1988).

18. See the Web site http://www.finalpassages.org for information on the approach pioneered by Jerrigrace Lyons (accessed November 7, 2008).

19. Of the many such books, I particularly like Cox 2003.

20. I learned things from the ritual vignettes in Biziou 1999 and from J. T. Johnson 2001.

BIBLIOGRAPHY

Adams, Maurianne, Warren J. Blumenfeld, Rosie Casteñeda, Heather W. Hackman, Madeline L. Peters, Ximena Zúñiga, eds. 2000. *Readings for Diversity and Social Justice: An Anthology on Racism, Antisemitism, Sexism, Heterosexism, Ableism, and Classism.* New York: Routledge.

Ahmed, G. M. 1991. "Muslim Organizations in the United States." In Haddad 1991, 11–24.

Albers, Robert. 1995. *Shame: A Faith Perspective.* New York: Haworth.

Alcoholics Anonymous. 1976. *Alcoholics Anonymous.* New York: Alcoholics Anonymous World Service.

Al Faruqi, I. 1984. *Islam.* Brentwood, Md.: International Graphics.

Al-Krenawi, Alean, and John R. Graham, eds. 2003. *Multicultural Social Work in Canada: Working With Diverse Ethno-racial Communities.* Toronto: Oxford University Press.

All Consuming Passion: Waking Up from the American Dream. 1998. Pamphlet. Seattle: New Road Map Foundation and Northwest Environmental Watch.

Altareb, Belkeis Y. 1996. "Islamic Spirituality in America: A Middle Path to Unity." *Counseling & Values* 41, no. 1 (October): 29–38.

Andersen, Tom, M.D. 2002. *A Collaboration, what some call psychotherapy; bonds filled of expressions, and expressions filled of meaning.* Unpublished manuscript.

Anderson, Herbert. 2005. "Violent Death, Public Tragedy, and Rituals of Lament." In Dirk Lange and Dwight Vogel, eds., *Ordo: Bath, Word, Prayer, Table,* 188–200. Akron, Ohio: OSL Publications.

Angelou, Maya. 1975. *Oh Pray My Wings Are Gonna Fit Me Well.* New York: Random House.

Antone, Hope S. 2003. "Making Sense of Christ's Atonement," *In God's Image* 22, no. 4 (December): 35–38.

Arnold, Rick, Bev Burke, Carl James, D'Arcy Martin, and Barb Thomas. 1991. *Educating for a Change*. Toronto: Doris Marshall Institute of Education and Action and Between the Lines Press.

Asad, Talad. "Anthropological Conceptions of Religion: Reflections on Geertz." *Man: The Journal of the Royal Anthropological Institute* 83 (1983): 237–59.

Augsburger, David W. 1986. *Pastoral Counseling Across Cultures*. Philadelphia: Westminster.

Bagby, Ihsan, ed. 1994. *Muslim Resource Guide*. Fountain Valley, Calif.: Islamic Resource Institute.

Baker-Fletcher, Karen. 1993. "Tar-Baby and Womanist Theology." *Theology Today* 50:29–38.

Baltes, Margaret. 1996. *The Many Faces of Dependency in Old Age*. New York: Cambridge University Press.

Baltes, Paul, and Margaret Baltes. 1990. "Psychological Perspectives on Successful Aging: The Model of Selective Optimization with Compensation." In Paul B. Baltes and Margaret M. Baltes, eds., *Successful Aging: Perspectives from the Behavioral Sciences*, 1–34. New York: Cambridge University Press.

Bateson, Mary Catherine. 2001. *Composing A Life*. New York: Grove Press.

Batts, Valerie A. "Modern Racism: New Melody For the Same Old Tunes." 1998. EDS Occasional Papers, no. 2. Cambridge: Episcopal Divinity School.

———, and Jocelyn Landrum-Brown. 2003. "VISIONS, Inc: Assumptions and Definitions." Arlington, Va.: Visions, Inc.

Beck, Martha. 1999. *Expecting Adam: A True Story of Birth, Rebirth, and Everyday Magic*. New York: Crown.

Bellah, Robert N., Richard Madsen, William M. Sullivan, and Ann Swidler. 1985. *Habits of the Heart: Individualism and Commitment in American Life*. Berkeley: University of California Press.

Bernstein, Nina. 2001. "Waiting to Sleep: For Family in Shelter System, Living From Bench to Bench." *The New York Times*. March 25.

Billman, Kathleen D. 1996. "Pastoral Care as an Art of Community." In *The Arts of Ministry: Feminist-Womanist Approaches*, ed. Christie Cozad Neuger, 10–38. Louisville: Westminister John Knox.

———, and Daniel Migliore. 1999. *Rachel's Cry: Prayer of Lament and Rebirth of Hope*. Cleveland: United Church Press.

Bishop, Anne. 2005. *Beyond Token Change: Breaking the Cycle of Oppression in Institutions*. Halifax, Nova Scotia: Fernwood.

————. 2002. *Becoming an Ally: Breaking the Cycle of Oppression in People.* 2nd ed. Halifax, Nova Scotia: Fernwood.

Biziou, Barbara. 1999. *The Joys of Everyday Ritual: Spiritual Recipes to Celebrate Milestones, Ease Transitions, and Make Every Day Sacred.* New York: Saint Martin's Griffin.

Black, Kathy. 1996. *A Healing Homiletic: Preaching and Disability.* Nashville: Abingdon.

Blount, Brian K., and Gary W. Charles. 2002. *Preaching Mark in Two Voices.* Louisville: Westminster John Knox.

Bohjalian, Chris. 1998. *Midwives.* New York: Random House.

Bons-Storm, Riet. 1996. "Pastoral Care." In *Dictionary of Feminist Theologies*, ed. Letty M. Russell and J. Shannon Clarkson, 202. Louisville: Westminster John Knox.

Botcharova, Olga. 2001. "Implementation of Track Two Diplomacy." In Raymond G. Helmick, S.J., and Rodney L. Petersen, eds., *Forgiveness and Reconciliation: Religion, Public Policy and Conflict Transformation*, 279–304. Radnor, Pa.: Templeton Foundation.

Boyd-Franklin, Nancy. 1989. *Black Families in Therapy: A Multisystems Approach.* New York: Guilford.

Brandon, David. 1991. *Zen in the Art of Helping.* London: Routledge.

Brock, Rita Nakashima, and Rebecca Ann Parker. 2003. *Proverbs of Ashes: Violence, Suffering, and the Search for What Saves Us.* Boston: Beacon.

————, Jung Ha Kim, Kwok Pui-lan, and Seung Ai Yang, eds. 2007. *Off the Menu: Asian and Asian North American Women's Theology and Religion.* Louisville: Westminster John Knox.

Brown, Sally A., and Patrick D. Miller, eds. 2005. *Lament: Reclaiming Practices in Pulpit, Pew, and Public Square.* Louisville: Westminster John Knox.

Brueggemann, Walter. 2001. *The Prophetic Imagination.* 2nd ed. Minneapolis: Fortress Press.

————. 2006. *The Word That Redescribes the World.* Minneapolis: Fortress Press.

Burton, Linda. 1991. "Creating Culturally Relevant Ways of Thinking about Diversity and Aging," *Generations* 15:67–72.

Butler, Robert N. 1969. "Age-ism: Another Form of Bigotry." *Gerontologist* 9, no. 3:243–46.

Cannon, Katie Geneva. 1988. *Black Womanist Ethics.* Atlanta: Scholar's.

Carter, Richard B., and Amelia El-Hindi. n.d. *Understanding the Issues Faced by Islamic Families: A Study to Inform School Counselors and Teachers.* Mini-grant Proposal, Texas Tech University, College of Education.

Carter, Robert T. 1998. *The Influence of Race and Racial Identity in Psychotherapy: Toward a Racially Inclusive Model.* New York: John Wiley.

CELAM. 1968. *La iglesia en la Actual transformacion de America Latina a la luz del concilio, II Conclusiones.* 3rd ed. Bogata: Secretariado general del CELAM.

Charlton, James I. 1998. *Nothing About Us Without Us: Disability Oppression and Empowerment.* Berkeley: University of California Press.

Chinula, Donald M. 1997. *Building King's Beloved Community: Foundations for Pastoral Care and Counseling with the Oppressed.* Cleveland: United Church Press.

Clancy, John. 1961. "Procrastination: A Defense Against Sobriety." *Quarterly Journal of Studies on Alcohol* 22:269–76.

Clebsch, William A., and Charles R. Jaekle. 1964. *Pastoral Care in Historical Perspective.* Englewood, N.J.: Prentice-Hall.

Clinebell, Howard. 1984. *Basic Types of Pastoral Care and Counseling: Resources for the Ministry of Healing and Growth.* Rev. and enl. ed. Nashville: Abingdon.

Collins, Chuck, and Felice Yeskel. 2005. *Economic Apartheid in America: A Primer on Economic Inequality and Insecurity.* Rev. and updated ed. New York: New Press.

Collins, Patricia Hill. 2000. *Black Feminist Thought: Knowledge, Consciousness, and the Politics of Empowerment.* 2nd ed. New York: Routledge.

Combahee River Collective [CRC]. 1983. "A Black Feminist Statement." In Cherrie Moraga and Gloria Anzaldua, eds., *This Bridge Called My Back: Writings by Radical Women of Color,* 210–18. London: Persephone Press.

Comstock, Gary David. 2001. *Whosoever Church: Welcoming Lesbians and Gay Men into African-American Congregations.* Louisville: Westminister John Knox.

Conde-Frazier, Elizabeth. 1997. "Hispanic Protestant Spirituality." In José David Rodríguez and Loida I. Martell-Otero, eds., *Teología en Conjunto: A Collaborative Hispanic Protestant Theology,* 125–45. Louisville: Westminster John Knox.

Consedine, Nathan S., Carol Magai, and Francine Conway. 2004. "Predicting Ethnic Variation in Adaptation to Later Life: Styles of Socioemotional Functioning and Constrained Heterotopy." *Journal of Cross-Cultural Gerontology* 19:97–131.

Constantine, Madonna G. 2002. "The Intersection of Race, Ethnicity, Gender, and Social Class in Counseling: Examining Selves in Cultural Contexts." *Journal of Multicultural Counseling and Development* 30:210–15.

———, and Derald Wing Sue., eds. 2005. *Strategies for Building Multicultural Competence in Mental Health and Educational Settings.* Hoboken: Wiley.

Couture, Pamela D., and Rodney J. Hunter, eds. 1995. *Pastoral Care and Social Conflict: Essays in Honor of Charles V. Gerkin.* Nashville: Abingdon.

Cox, Meg. 2003. *The Book of New Family Traditions: How to Create Great Rituals for Holidays and Everydays.* Philadelphia: Running Press.

Crawford, A. Elaine. 2004. "Womanist Christology and the Wesleyan Tradition." *Black Theology: An International Journal* 2:213–20.

Croteau, James M., Donna M. Talbot, Teresa S. Lance, and Nancy J. Evans. 2002. "A Qualitative Study of the Interplay between Privilege and Oppression." *Journal of Multicultural Counseling and Development* 30:239–58.

Daloz, Laurent A. Parks, Cheryl A. Keen, James P. Keen, and Sharon Daloz Parks. 1997. *Common Fire: Leading Lives of Commitment in a Complex Age.* Boston: Beacon.

Davie, Ann Rose, and Ginny Thornburgh. 1992. *That All May Worship: An Interfaith Welcome to People with Disabilities.* Washington, D.C.: National Organization on Disability.

Davis, Richard H. 1984. "TV's Boycott of Old Age: Advertisers are Most Interested in the 18 to 55 Audience." *Aging* 346 (August–September):12–17.

Debold, Elizabeth. 2006. "Epistemology, Fourth Order Consciousness, and the Subject-Object Relationship .or . . . How the Self Evolves." In *What Is Enlightenment: Refining Spirituality for an Evolving World* 34, http://www.wie.org/j22/kegan.asp (accessed November 5, 2008).

De Graaf, John, David Wann, Thomas H. Naylor, and Vicki Robin. 2005. *Affluenza: The All-Consuming Epidemic.* San Francisco: Berrett-Koehler.

De La Torre, Miguel A. 2003. *Reading the Bible from the Margins.* Maryknoll, N.Y.: Orbis.

——————, and Edwin Aponte. 2001. *Introducing Latino/a Theologies.* Maryknoll, N.Y.: Orbis.

Denny, Frederick M. 1995. *Islam.* San Francisco: HarperSanFrancisco.

DiCicco, Lena, Hilma Unterberger, and John E. Mack. 1978. "Confronting Denial: An Alcoholism Intervention Strategy." *Psychiatric Annals* 8:596–606.

Diller, Jerry V. 2004. *Cultural Diversity: A Primer for the Human Services.* Belmont, Calif.: Wadsworth.

Dimensions of Faith and Congregational Ministries with Persons with Developmental Disabilities and Their Families. 2000. A Bibliography and Address Listing of Resources for Clergy, Laypersons, Families and Service Providers. Piscataway, N.J.: Building Community Supports Project.

Doka, Kenneth J. 1966. *Living With Grief: After Sudden Loss Suicide, Homicide, Accident, Heart Attack, Stroke.* Washington, D.C.: Hospice Foundation of America.

Douglas, Kelly Brown. 1999. *Sexuality and the Black Church: A Womanist Perspective.* Maryknoll, N.Y.: Orbis.

Dozier, Verna. 2006. "My Father had a Searching Mind." In Cynthia L. Shattuck and Fredrica Harris Thompsett, eds., *Confronted By God: The Essential Verna Dozier,* 13–36. New York: Seabury.

Dube, Musa W. 1998. "Go Therefore and Make Disciples of All Nations (Matthew 28:19A): A Postcolonial Perspective on Biblical Criticism and Pedagogy." In Fernando

F. Segovia and Mary Ann Tolbert, eds., *Teaching the Bible: The Discourses and Politics of Biblical Pedagogy*, 224–46. Maryknoll, N.Y.: Orbis.

———. 2000. *Postcolonial Feminist Interpretation of the Bible*. St. Louis: Chalice.

———. 2002. "Reading for Decolonization (John 4:1-42)." In Musa W. Dube and Jeffrey L. Staley, eds., *John and Postcolonialism: Travel, Space and Power*, 51–75. Sheffield: Sheffield Academic Press; New York: Continuum.

Du Bois, W. E. B. 2005 (1903). *The Souls of Black Folk*. New York: Pocket.

Eade, John, and Christopher Mele, eds. 2002. *Understanding the City: Contemporary and Future Perspectives*. Malden, Mass.: Blackwell.

Ebaugh, Helen Rose, and Janet Saltzam Chafetz, eds. 2000. *Religion and the New Immigrants: Continuities and Adaptations in Immigrant Congregations*. Walnut Creek, Calif.: AltaMira.

Ecumenical Disability Advocates Network, Justice, Peace and Creation Team (drafters). 2003. *A Church of All and For All: An Interim (Theological) Statement*. Document #PLEN 1.1. Geneva, Switzerland: Central Committee of the World Council of Churches.

Eglit, Howard. 2005. "Elders on Trial: Age and Ageism in the American Legal System." *Florida Bar Journal* 79:52.

Eiesland, Nancy. 1994. *The Disabled God: Toward a Liberatory Theology of Disability*. Nashville: Abingdon.

Eisenhandler, Susan A. 2003. *Keeping the Faith in Late Life*. New York: Springer.

Elias, Marilyn. 2006. "USA's Muslims Under a Cloud." *USA Today*, August 10.

Elizondo, Virgil. 1997. *Guadalupe, Mother of the New Creation*. Maryknoll, N.Y.: Orbis.

Epston, David, and Michael White. 1990. *Narrative Means to Therapeutic Ends*. New York: Norton.

Esposito, J. 1995. "Islam: An Overview." In Esposito, J., chief ed., *The Oxford Encyclopedia of the Modern Islamic World* 2:243–54. New York: Oxford University Press.

Everly, George S., Jr. 2000. "Pastoral Crisis Intervention: Toward a Definition." *Journal of Emergency Mental Health* 2, no. 2:69–71J.

Farah, Caesar E. 1994. *Islam*. 5th ed. Hauppauge, N.Y.: Barron's.

Feinberg, Leslie. 1998. *Trans Liberation: Beyond Pink or Blue*. Boston: Beacon Press.

Fong, Rowena. 1992. "A History of Asian Americans." In Furuto et al. 1992, 23-49.

Frame, Marsha W., and Carmen Braun Williams. 1996. "Counseling African Americans: Integrating Spirituality in Therapy." *Counseling and Values* 41:16–28.

———, ———, and Evelyn L. Green. 1999. "Balm in Gilead: Spiritual Dimensions in Counseling African American Women." *Journal of Multicultural Counseling and Development* 27:182–92.

Fraser, Lyn. 2005. *Prayers from the Darkness: The Difficult Psalms*. New York: Church Publishing.

Freedman, Jill, and Gene Combs. 1996. *Narrative Therapy: The Social Construction of Preferred Realities.* New York: Norton.

Friedman, Rabbi Dayle A. 2003. "An Anchor amidst Anomie: Ritual and Aging." In Kimble et al. 2003, 134–44.

Friedman, Edwin H. 1985. *Generation to Generation.* New York: Guilford Press.

Furuto, Sharlene Maeda, Renuka Biswas, Douglas Chung, Kenji Murase, and Fariyal Ross-Sheriff, eds. 1992. *Social Work Practice with Asian Americans.* Newbury Park, Calif.: Sage.

Gans, Herbert. 1995. *The War Against the Poor.* New York: Basic Books.

Ghayur, M. Arif. 1981. *Muslims in the United States: Settlers and Visitors.* Fort Worth: Texas Christian University Press.

Giddings, Paula. 1994. *Where and When I Enter: The Impact of Black Women on Race and Sex in America.* New York: William Morrow.

Gist, Yvonne J., and Lisa I. Hetzel. 2004. "We the People: Aging in the United States," *Census 2000 Special Report,* CENSR-19. Washington, D.C.: U.S. Census Bureau, U.S. Department of Commerce. http://www.census.gov/prod/2004pubs/censr-19. pdf (accessed November 6, 2008).

Glassman, Bernie. 1998. *Bearing Witness.* New York: Bell Tower.

Glenn Wixson, Joel. 2000. "Letters in the Street: A Narrative Based Outreach Approach." *Gecko* 2:50–58.

Goizueta, Roberto S. 1995. *Caminemos con Jesús: Toward a Hispanic/Latino Theology of Accompaniment.* Maryknoll, N.Y.: Orbis.

Gold, Steve. 2002. "Beyond Pity and Paternalism." *The Other Side* (September-October): 19.

Golub, Sarit A., Allan Filipowicz, and Ellen J. Langer. 2002. "Acting Your Age." In Nelson 2002, 277–94.

Gomes, Peter J. 1996. *The Good Book: Reading the Bible with Mind and Heart.* New York: Avon.

González, Justo L. 1999. *For the Healing of the Nations: A Book of Revelation in an Age of Cultural Conflict.* Maryknoll, N.Y.: Orbis.

Graham, Elaine L. 1996. *Transforming Practice: Pastoral Theology in an Age of Uncertainty.* London and New York: Mowbray.

Graham, Larry Kent. 1992. *Care of Persons, Care of Worlds.* Nashville: Abingdon.

———. 1997. *Discovering Images of God.* Louisville: Westminster John Knox.

Grandin, Temple. 2006 (1996). *Thinking In Pictures: And Other Reports from My Life.* Exp. ed. New York: Vintage.

Greene, Beverly. 1994. "African American Women." In Lillian Comas-Diaz and B. Greene, eds., *Women of Color: Integrating Ethnic and Gender Identities in Psychotherapy,* 10–29. New York: Guilford.

Greve, Barb, ed. 2003. *Crossing Paths: Where Religion and Transgender Meet.* Boston: Unitarian Universalist Association Office of Bisexual, Gay, Lesbian, and Transgender Concerns. http://www.uua.org/documents/obgltc/crossingpaths.pdf (accessed November 5, 2008).

————, and Keith Kron. 2000. *Transgender 102.* Boston: Unitarian Universalist Association.

Gross, Sally. 2000. "Intersexuality and Scripture." October 23. http://www.freeessays.cc/db/39/pnl53.shtml (accessed November 5, 2008).

Grossman, David. "The Power of 'We're Sorry.'" *The Los Angeles Times,* February 8, 2005.

Haddad, Yvonne Yazbeck, ed. 1991. *The Muslims of America.* New York: Oxford University Press.

————, and Adair T. Lummis. 1987. *Islamic Values in the United States: A Comparative Study.* New York: Oxford University Press.

Hall, Douglas John. 1996. *Confessing the Faith: Christian Theology in a North American Context.* Minneapolis: Fortress Press.

Harley, Debra A., Kristine Jolivette, Katherine McCormick, and Karen Tice. 2002. "Race, Class, and Gender: A Constellation of *Positionalities* with Implications for Counseling." *Journal of Multicultural Counseling and Development* 30:216–23.

Harris, E. Lynn. 2003. *What Becomes of the Brokenhearted.* New York: Doubleday.

Hayhurst, Christine. 2002. "Focal Point." *Engineering Management* (August/September).

Heidegger, Martin. 2008 (1962). *Being and Time.* New York: Harper.

Helms, Janet E. 1990. "Generalizing Racial Identity Interaction Theory to Groups." In J. Helms, ed., *Black and White Racial Identity: Theory, Research, and Practice,* 187–204. New York: Greenwood.

Henderson, J. Frank. 1994. *Liturgies of Lament.* Chicago: Liturgy Training Publications.

Henry, Frances, Carol Tator, Winston Mattis, and Tim Rees. 1998. *The Colour of Democracy: Racism in Canadian Society.* 2nd ed. Toronto: Nelson/Thomson.

Herberg, Dorothy Chave. 1993. *Frameworks for Cultural and Racial Diversity: Teaching and Learning for Practitioners.* Toronto: Canadian Scholars Press.

Hobgood, Mary Elizabeth. 2000. *Dismantling Privilege: An Ethics of Accountability.* Cleveland: United Church Press.

Hockenberry, John. 1995. *Moving Violations: War Zones, Wheelchairs, and Declarations of Independence.* New York: Hyperion.

hooks, bell. 1995. *Killing Rage: Ending Racism.* New York: Henry Holt.

————. 2000. *Where We Stand: Class Matters.* New York: Routledge.

Hoover, Theressa. 1979. "Black Women in the Churches: Triple Jeopardy." In James Cone and Gayraud Wilmore, eds., *Black Theology: A Documentary History,* 1:380–81. Maryknoll, N.Y.: Orbis.

Hopkins, Dwight N. 1993. *Shoes That Fit Our Feet: Sources for a Constructive Black Theology.* Maryknoll, N.Y.: Orbis.

———. 2005. "A Black Theology of Liberation." *Black Theology: An International Journal* 3:1–31.

Hoshmand, Lisa Tsoi. 2001. "Psychotherapy as an Instrument of Culture." In Brent D. Slife, Richard N. Williams, and Sally H. Barlow, eds., *Critical Issues in Psychotherapy,* 99–113. London: Sage.

Howell-Baker, Maxine E. 2005. "Towards a Womanist Pneumatological Pedagogy: An Investigation into the Development and Implementation of a Theological Pedagogy by and for the Marginalized." *Black Theology: An International Journal* 3, no. 1:32–54.

Idler, E. L., and S. V. Kasl. 1997. "Religion Among Disabled and Nondisabled Persons I: Cross-sectional Patterns in Health Practices, Social Activities, and Well-being." *Journal of Gerontology* 52: S291–93.

Imber-Black, Evan. 1991. "Rituals and the Healing Process." In Froma Walsh and Monica McGoldrick, eds., *Living Beyond Loss: Death in the Family,* 340–57. New York: Norton.

———, and Janine Roberts. 1992. *Rituals for Our Times: Celebrating, Healing, and Changing Our Lives and Our Relationships.* New York: HarperCollins.

———, ———, and Richard Whiting, eds. 1988. *Rituals in Families and Family Therapy.* New York: Norton.

Iwamura, Jane Naomi, and Paul Spickard, eds. 2003. *Revealing the Sacred in Asian and Pacific America.* New York: Routledge.

Jencks, Christopher. 1994. "The Crack Epidemic." Chapter 4 in *The Homeless,* 41–48. Cambridge: Harvard University Press.

Jeung, Russell. 2005. *Faithful Generations: Race and New Asian American Churches.* New Brunswick, N.J.: Rutgers University Press.

Johnson, Allan G. 1997. *Privilege, Power, and Difference.* New York: McGraw-Hill.

Johnson, Harriet McBride. 2006. *Too Late to Die Young: Nearly True Tales from a Life.* New York: PicadorUSA.

Johnson, Julie Tallard. 2001. *The Thundering Years: Rituals and Sacred Wisdom for Teens.* Rochester, Vt.: Bindu Books.

Jordan, Janice M. 1991. "Counseling African American Women: 'Sister-friends'." In Lee and Richardson 1991, 51–63.

———. 1997. "Counseling African American Women from a Cultural Sensitivity Perspective." In Courtland C. Lee, ed., *Multicultural Issues in Counseling: New Approaches to Diversity,* 2nd ed., 109–21. Alexandria, Va.: American Counseling Association.

Kameeta, Zephania. 1986. *Why, O Lord? Psalms and Sermons from Namibia.* Philadelphia: Fortress Press.

Kasser, Tim, and Richard M. Ryan. 1996. "A Dark Side of the American Dream: Correlates of Financial Success as a Central Life Aspiration." *Journal of Personality and Social Psychology* 65:410–22.

Kawuki Mukasa, Isaac. 2005. *Belonging: Constructing A Canadian Theology of Inclusion.* Toronto: Kamu Kamu Press.

Kegan, Robert. 1998. *In Over Our Heads: The Mental Demands of Modern Life.* Cambridge, Mass.: Harvard University Press.

Kendall, Frances E. 2006. *Understanding White Privilege: Creating Pathways to Authentic Relationships across Race.* New York, London: Routledge.

Kickman, Martha W. 1998. *Healing after Loss: Daily Meditations for Working Through Grief.* New York: Avon.

Kiefer, Heather Mason. 1994. "Gays in the Military: Public Says Go Ahead and Tell." Gallup Poll, December 21, 2004. http://www.gallup.com/poll/14419/Gays-Military-Public-Says-Ahead-Tell.aspx (accessed October 30, 2008).

Kim, Ai Ra. 1996. *Women Struggling for a New Life: The Role of Religion in the Cultural Passage from Korea to America.* Albany: State University of New York Press.

Kim, Grace Ji-Sun. 2002. *The Grace of Sophia: A Korean North American Women's Christology.* Cleveland: Pilgrim.

Kim, Jung Ha. 1997. *Bridge-Makers and Cross-Bearers: Korean American Women and the Church.* Atlanta: Scholars.

———. 2006. "What's with the Ghosts? Portrayals of Spirituality in Asian American Literature." *Spiritus* 6, no. 2 (Fall): 241–48.

Kim, Stephen S. 1996. "Seeking Home in North America: Colonialism in Asia, Confrontation in North America." In D. Ng 1996a, 1–24.

Kimble, Melvin A. 2003. "Final Time: Coming to the End." In Kimble et al. 2003, 449–60.

———, Susan H. McFadden, James W. Ellor, and James J. Seeber, eds. 1995, 2003. *Aging, Spirituality, and Religion: A Handbook, Volumes 1 and 2.* Minneapolis: Fortress Press.

King, Martin Luther, Jr. 1967. "Where Do We Go from Here?" Address to the Southern Christian Leadership Conference, August 16, 1967. In Washington 1991, 245–52.

Kingsley, Jason, and Mitchell Levitz. 1994. *Count Us In: Growing Up with Down Syndrome.* San Diego: Harcourt Brace.

Kite, Mary E., and Lisa Smith Wagner. 2002. "Attitudes toward Older Adults." In Nelson 2002, 129–62.

Kleinman, Arthur, Leon Eisenberg, and Byron Good. 1978. "Culture, Illness, and Care." *Annals of Internal Medicine* 88: 251–58.

Kobeisy, Ahmed. 2004a. *Counseling American Muslims: Understanding the Faith and Helping the People.* Westport, Ct.: Praeger.

———. 2004b. "Shame in the Context of Illness: An Islamic Perspective." Spirituality, Religion, Wisdom and the Care of the Patient. *The Yale Journal of Humanities in Medicine.*

Kong, Sister Chan. 1993. *Learning True Love.* Berkeley: Parallax.

Kornfield, Margaret. 1998. *Cultivating Wholeness: A Guide to Care and Counseling in Faith Communities.* New York: Continuum.

Kotler, Arnold, ed. 1996. *Engaged Buddhist Reader.* Berkeley: Parallax.

Kozol, Jonathan. 1991. *Savage Inequalities.* New York: HarperCollins.

Kübler-Ross, Elisabeth. 1969. *On Death and Dying: What the Dying Have to Teach Doctors, Nurses, Clergy, and Their Own Families.* New York: Macmillan.

Kujawa, Sheryl A. 1995. *Resource Book for Ministries with Youth and Young Adults in the Episcopal Church.* New York: Episcopal Church Center.

Kwok, Pui-Lan. 2001. "Feminist Theology at the Dawn of the Millennium: Remembering the Past, Dreaming the Future." *Feminist Theology: The Journal of Britain & Ireland School of Feminist Theology* 27:6–21.

———. 2005. *Postcolonial Imagination and Feminist Theology.* Louisville: Westminster John Knox.

Lai, Alan. 2003. "Dragon Talk: Providing Pastoral Care for Chinese Immigrants." *Journal of Pastoral Care and Counseling* 57, no. 1 (Spring): 46–52.

Lane, Belden. 1998. *The Solace of Fierce Landscapes: Exploring Desert and Mountain Spirituality.* New York: Oxford University Press.

Larson, Reed. 1978. "Thirty Years of Research on the Subjective Well-Being of Older Americans." *Journal of Gerontology* 33:109–25.

Lartey, Emmanuel Y. 2003. *In Living Color: An Intercultural Approach to Pastoral Care and Counseling.* 2nd ed. London & New York: Jessica Kingsley.

Lathrop, Gordon. 1984. "A Rebirth of Images: On the Use of the Bible in Liturgy." *Worship* 58:291–304.

Law, Eric H. F. 1993. *The Wolf Shall Dwell with the Lamb.* St. Louis: Chalice.

Leas, Speed, and Paul Kittlaus. 1981. *The Pastoral Counselor in Social Action.* Philadelphia: Fortress Press.

Lebacqz, Karen, and Joseph D. Driskill. 2000. *Ethics and Spiritual Care: A Guide for Pastors, Chaplains, and Spiritual Directors.* Nashville: Abingdon.

Lee, Courtland C., and Bernard L. Richardson, eds. 1991. *Multicultural Issues in Counseling: New Approaches to Diversity.* Alexandria, Va.: American Counseling Association.

Lee, Jung Young. 1995. *Marginality: The Key to Multicultural Theology.* Minneapolis: Fortress Press.

Lee Hertig, Young. 2001. *Cultural Tug of War: The Korean Immigrant Family and Church in Transition.* Nashville: Abingdon.

Lee, Sang Hyun, and John V. Moore, eds. 1993. *Korean American Ministry: A Resource Book.* Expanded English ed. Louisville: General Assembly Council, Presbyterian Church (U.S.A.).

Leech, Kenneth. 1993. *Race, Class and Homelessness in Britain and the USA.* London: Catholic Housing Aid Society.

Legge, Marilyn J. 1992. *The Grace of Difference: A Canadian Feminist Theological Ethic.* Atlanta: Scholars.

Lévinas, Emmanuel. 1999. *Alterity and Transcendence.* New York: Columbia University Press.

Lewis, Marjorie. 2004. "Diaspora Dialogue: Womanist Theology in Engagement with Aspects of the Black British and Jamaican Experience." *Black Theology: An International Journal* 2:85–109.

Liew, Tat-siong Benny, ed. 2002. *The Bible in Asian America. Semeia* 90–01. Atlanta: Society of Biblical Literature.

Linton, Simi. 2005. *My Body Politic: A Memoir.* Ann Arbor: University of Michigan Press.

Lipsky, Suzanne. 1991. "Internalized Oppression." In Gerald L. Mallon, ed., *Resisting Racism: An Action Guide,* 94–99. San Francisco: National Association of Black and White Men Together.

Logan, Pat. 2002. *The Joy of the Journey.* London: UNLEASH.

Longmore, Paul K. 2003. *Why I Burned My Book and Other Essays on Disability.* Philadelphia: Temple University Press.

Lopes, Tina, and Barb Thomas. 2006. *Dancing on Live Embers: Challenging Racism in Organizations.* Toronto: Between the Lines.

Lowe, Lisa. 2003. "Heterogenity, Hybridity, Multiplicity: Marking Asian-American Difference." In Jane Evans Braziel and Anita Mannur, eds., *Theorizing Diaspora,* 132–55. Malden, Mass.: Blackwell.

MacIntyre, Alasdair. 1981. *After Virtue.* Notre Dame, Ind.: University of Notre Dame Press.

Maddox, George. 1991. "Aging with a Difference." *Generations* 15:7–11.

Marquand, Robert, and Lamis Andoni. 1996. "Muslims in America: Finding Their Place." *The Christian Science Monitor,* January 22, 9–10.

Matsuoka, Fumitaka. 1998. *The Color of Faith: Building Community in a Multiracial Society.* Cleveland: United Church Press.

———, and Eleazar S. Fernandez, eds. 2003. *Realizing the America of Our Hearts: Theological Voices of Asian Americans.* St. Louis: Chalice.

Mays, Vickie M. 1985. "Black Women and Stress: Utilization of Self-Help Groups for Stress Reduction." *Women in Therapy* 4, no. 4:67–79.

Mazrui, Ali Al'Amin. 1991. "Multiculturalism and Comparative Holocaust: Educational and Moral Implications." Annex to the Report of the New York Social Studies Review and Development Committee.

Mbiti, John S. 1990. *African Religions and Philosophy.* 2nd ed. Portsmouth, N.H.: Heinemann.

McFague, Sallie. 1993. *The Body of God: An Ecological Theology.* Minneapolis: Fortress Press.

McGoldrick, Monica. 1995. *You Can Go Home Again: Reconnecting with Your Family.* New York: Norton.

McIntosh, Peggy. 1990/1998. "White Privilege: Unpacking the Invisible Knapsack." *Independent School.* Winter 1990. 31–36. Also in Monica McGoldrick, ed., *Re-Visioning Family Therapy: Race, Culture, and Gender in Clinical Practice,* 145–52. New York: Guilford.

Mele, Christopher R. 2000. *Selling the Lower East Side: Culture, Real Estate, and Resistance in New York City.* Minneapolis: University of Minnesota Press.

Melton, J. Gordon. 1993. *The Encyclopedia of American Religions.* 4th ed. Detroit: Gale Research.

Metz, Johann Baptist. 1980. *Faith in History and Society: Toward a Practical Fundamental Theology.* New York: Seabury.

Meyers, Bryant L. 1999. *Walking with the Poor: Principles and Practices of Transformational Development.* Maryknoll, N.Y.: Orbis.

Miles, Margaret R. 1990. *Practicing Christianity: Critical Perspectives for an Embodied Spirituality.* New York: Crossroad.

————. 1999. *"Religion and the Common Good."* Baccalaureate address, Stanford University, June 12. Stanford Online Report, June 16, 1999. http://news-service. stanford.edu/news/1999/june16/baccspeech-616.html, accessed December 8, 2008.

Mitchell, Ella P., and Henry H. Mitchell. 1989. "Black Spirituality: The Values in That Ol' Time Religion." *Journal of the Interdenominational Theological Center* 17, nos. 1/2: 98–109.

Molsberry, Robert F. 2004. *Blindsided by Grace: Entering the World of Disability.* Minneapolis: Augsburg.

Monk, Gerald, John Winslade, Kathie Crocket, and David Epston. 1997. *Narrative Therapy in Practice: The Archaeology of Hope.* San Francisco: Jossey-Bass.

Montepare, Joann M., and Leslie A. Xebrowitz. 2002. "A Social-Developmental View of Ageism." In Nelson 2002, 77–125.

Moore, R. C., and T. C. Murphy. 1961. "Denial of Alcoholism as an Obstacle to Recovery." *Quarterly Journal of Studies on Alcohol* 22:597–609.

Moradi, Bonnie, and Linda Mezydlo Subich. 2003. "A Concomitant Examination of the

Relations of Perceived Racist and Sexist Events to Psychological Distress for African American Women." *The Counseling Psychologist* 31:451–69.

Morrissey, Paul F. 1995. *Let Someone Hold You: The Journey of a Hospice Priest.* New York: Crossroad.

Muwakkil, Salim. 2006. "Black Men: The Crisis Continues." *In These Times* 30, no. 5, April 27. http://www.inthesetimes.com/article/2621/black_men_the_crisis_continues/ (accessed October 28, 2008).

Nelson, Todd D., ed. 2002. *Ageism: Stereotyping and Prejudice against Older Persons.* Cambridge, Mass.: Bradford.

Nerney, Catherine, and Hal Taussig. 2002. *Re-Imagining Life Together in America.* Chicago: Sheed & Ward.

Ng, David, ed. 1996a. *People on the Way: Asian North Americans Discovering Christ, Culture, and Community.* Valley Forge: Judson.

———. 1996b. "Varieties of Congregations for Varieties of People." In D. Ng 1996b, 281–300.

Ng, Greer Anne Wenh-In. 1989. "The Dragon and the Lamb: Chinese Festivals in the Life of Chinese Canadian/American Christians." *Religious Education* 84, no. 3 (Summer): 368–83.

———, ed. 1995. *Generations Trying to Live Together, with study guide.* Toronto: Division of Mission in Canada, The United Church of Canada.

———. 1996a. "Asian North American Relationships with other Minority Cultures." In D. Ng 1996a, 228–37.

———. 1996b. "Asian Socio-Cultural Values: Oppressive and Liberating Aspects from a Woman's Perspective." In D. Ng 1996a, 63–103.

———. 1996c. "One Faith, One Baptism—One Liturgy? Worship in a Multicultural, Multifaith Context." *Reformed Liturgy and Music* 30, no. 3:28–31.

———. 1996d. "The Asian North American Community at Worship: Issues of Indigenization and Contextualization." In D. Ng 1996a, 147–74.

———. 1996e. "Toward Wholesome Nurture: Challenges in the Religious Education of Asian North American Female Christians." *Religious Education* 91, no. 2 (Spring): 238–54.

———. 1997a. "Inclusive Language in Asian North American Churches: Non-issue or Null Curriculum?" *Journal of Asian and Asian American Theology* 2, no. 1 (Summer): 21–36.

———. 1997b. "Pacific-Asian North American Religious Education." In *Multicultural Religious Education*, ed. Barbara Wilkerson, 190–234. Birmingham: Religious Education Press.

———. 1998. "Toward Gender Justice: Challenges in Human Living from a Confucian-Christian Perspective." *Cheng Feng: A Journal of Chinese Religion and Culture* 41, nos.

3-4 (September-December): 345–61.

———. 2002. "Leadership in East Asian Women in Asia and the Diaspora." *In God's Image* 21, no. 1 (March): 34–37.

———, ed. 2003. *Our Roots, Our Lives: Glimpses of Faith and Life from Black and Asian Canadian Women*. Toronto: United Church Publishing House.

———. 2004a. "Reading with New Eyes: Feminist Postcolonial Perspective for Anti-Racism Work." *Making Waves* 4, no. 2 (Summer): 25–27.

———, ed. 2004b. *That All May Be One: A Resource for Educating toward Racial Justice*. Toronto: United Church of Canada, 2004.

———. 2004c. "Beyond Bible Stories: The Role of Culture-Specific Myths/Stories in the Identity Formation of Nondominant Immigrant Children." *Religious Education* 99, no. 2 (Spring): 125–36.

———. 2006. "The Place of Asian Resources in Festivals and Liturgies in Christian Churches." *Spiritus* 6, no. 2 (Fall): 249–54.

———. 2007. "Salmon and Carp, Bannock and Rice: Solidarity between Asian Canadian Women and Aboriginal Women." In Brock et al. 2007, 197–216.

Olsen, Sharon L., ed. 2000. *Your Gift: An Educational, Spiritual, and Personal Resource for Hospice Volunteers*. Traverse City, Mich.: Seasons Press.

Pak, Su Yon, Unzu Lee, Jung Ha Kim, and Myung Ji Cho. 2005. *Singing the Lord's Song in a New Land: Korean American Practices of Faith*. Louisville: Westminster John Knox.

Palmer, Parker J. 2005. *The Politics of the Brokenhearted: On Holding the Tensions of Democracy*. Kalamazoo, Mich.: The Fetzer Institute.

Paris, Peter J. 1995. *The Spirituality of African Peoples: The Search for Common Moral Discourse*. Minneapolis: Fortress Press.

Park, Andrew Sung. 1993. *The Wounded Heart of God: The Asian Concept of Han and the Christian Doctrine of Sin*. Nashville: Abingdon.

———. 2001. "The Bible and Han." In Park and Nelson 2001b, 45–60.

———. 2003. "A Theology of Tao (Way): Han, Sin and Evil." In *Realizing the America of Our Hearts: Theological Voices of Asian Americans*, ed. Fumitaka Matsuoka and Eleazar S. Fernandez, 41–54. St. Louis: Chalice.

———, and Susan L. Nelson. 2001a. "Introduction." In Park and Nelson 2001b, 1–23.

———, and ———, eds.. 2001b. *The Other Side of Sin: Woundedness from the Perspective of the Sinned Against*. Albany: State University of New York Press.

Parlagreco, Joseph, dir. 2005. *Call Me Malcolm*. Video. New York: Filmworks; and Cleveland: United Church of Christ. http://www.callmemalcolm.com (accessed November 5, 2008).

Pattison, Stephen. 1988. "Politics and Pastoral Care." In Stephen Pattison, *A Critique of Pastoral Care*, 82–105. London: SCM.

Patton, John. 2005. *Pastoral Care in Context*. Louisville: Westminster John Knox.

Paz, Octavio. 1985. *The Labyrinth of Solitude*. New York: Grove/Atlantic.

Phan, Peter C., and Jung Young Lee, eds. 1999. *Journeys at the Margin: Toward an Autobiographical Theology in American-Asian Perspective*. Collegeville, Minn.: Liturgical.

Pharr, Suzanne. 2000. "Reflections on Liberation." In Adams et al., eds., *Readings for Diversity and Social Justice*, 450–56.

Pinderhughes, Elaine. 1990. *Understanding Race, Ethnicity and Power: The Key to Efficacy in Clinical Practice*. New York: Free Press.

Pinn, Anthony B., and Dwight N. Hopkins, eds. 2004. *Loving the Body: Black Religious Studies and The Erotic*. New York: Palgrave Macmillan.

Quarles, Benjamin. 1964. *The Negro in the Making of America*. New York: Macmillan.

Ramsey, Janet L. 2006. "Holy Friendship: Reimaging Ministry with Homebound Older Adults." *Word and World* 26, no. 3:259–68.

———, and Rosemary Blieszner. 1999. *Spiritual Resiliency in Older Women: Models of Strength for Challenges through the Life Span*. Thousand Oaks, Calif.: Sage.

———, and ———. *Aging and Spiritual Resiliency: Everyday Stories, Remarkable Strength*. Forthcoming.

Ramsey, Nancy J., ed. 2004. *Pastoral Care and Counseling: Redefining the Paradigms*. Nashville: Abingdon.

Rando, Theresa A. 1988. *How to Go on Living When Someone You Know Dies*. Lexington, Mass.: Lexington Books.

Rashid, Abdul. 1985. *The Changing Profile of Canadian Families with Low Incomes, 1970–1985*. Ottawa: Ministry of Supply and Services, Canada.

Rashid, Hakim Muhammed. 1990. *In Search of the Path: Socialization, Education and the African Muslim*. Capitol Heights, Md.: Imania Publications.

Recionos, Harold J. 1992. *Jesus Weeps: Global Encounters on Our Doorstep*. Nashville: Abingdon.

Remen, Rachel Naomi, M.D. 2000. *My Grandfather's Blessings*. New York: Riverhead.

Rich, Adrienne. 1979 (1971). "When We Dead Awaken: Writing as Re-Vision." In *On Lies, Secrets, and Silence: Selected Prose 1966–1978*, 33–50. New York: Norton.

Richardson, Bernard L. 1991. "Utilizing the Resources of the African American Church: Strategies for Counseling Professionals." In Lee and Richardson 1991, 65–75.

Ruether, Rosemary Radford. 1985. *Women-Church*. New York: Harper & Row.

Sachedina, A. 1997. "What Is Islam?" *The World & I* 12, no. 9: 45–49. Washington, D.C.: The Washington Times.

Sachs, Jeffrey D. 2005. *The End of Poverty: Economic Possibilities for Our Time*. New York: Penguin.

Said, Edward. 1981. *Covering Islam*. New York: Pantheon.

Sassen, Saskia. 1991. *The Global City: New York, London, Tokyo*. Princeton: Princeton University Press.

Savin-Williams, Ritch C. 2005. *The New Gay Teenager*. Cambridge: Harvard University Press.

Schreiter, Robert J., C.P.P.S. 1998. *The Ministry of Reconciliation: Spirituality and Strategies*. New York: Orbis.

Schüssler Fiorenza, Elisabeth. 1983. *In Memory of Her: A Feminist Theological Reconstruction of Christian Origins*. New York: Crossroad.

Servicemembers Legal Defense Network [SLDN]. 2004. "Conduct Unbecoming: The Tenth Annual Report on "Don't Ask, Don't Tell, Don't Pursue, Don't Harass." http://dont.stanford.edu/commentary/sldn.10.pdf (accessed October 30, 2008).

Shapiro, Dan. 2004. *Delivering Doctor Amelia: The Story of a Gifted Young Obstetrician's Error and the Psychologist Who Helped Her*. New York: Vintage.

Shapiro, Joseph. 1993. *No Pity: People with Disabilities Forging a New Civil Rights Movement*. New York: Times Books.

Shilts, Randy. 1987. *And the Band Played On: Politics, People, and the AIDS Epidemic*. New York: St. Martin's.

Silva, Larry. 2001. "The Cursing Psalms as a Source of Blessing." In Stephen Breck Reid, ed., *Psalms and Practice: Worship, Virtue, Authority*, 220–30. Collegeville, Minn.: Liturgical.

Smith, Bill. 1993. "Locating My Theology in Sacred Places." In David Batstone, ed., *New Visions for the Americas: Religious Engagement and Social Transformation*, 159–71. Minneapolis: Fortress Press.

Sobrino, Jon. 1994. *The Principle of Mercy: Taking the Crucified People from the Cross*. Maryknoll, N.Y.: Orbis.

Soelle, Dorothee. 1975. *Suffering*. Trans. Everett R. Kalin. Philadelphia: Fortress Press.

———, and Sarah Katherine Pinnock. 2003. *The Theology of Dorothee Soelle*. New York: Trinity Press International.

Sparkes, Robert, and Richard Rutherford. 1986. "The Order of Christian Funerals: A Study in Bereavement and Lament." *Worship* 60:499–510.

Stone, Carol L. 1991. "Estimate of Muslims Living in America." In Haddad 1991, 25–36.

Stringfellow, William. 1973. *An Ethic for Christians and Other Aliens in a Strange Land*. Waco: Word.

Sue, Derald Wing. 2003. "What Must People of Color Do to Overcome Racism? A Personal Message to My Brothers and Sisters of Color." In Derald Wing Sue, *Overcoming Our Racism: The Journey to Liberation*, 254–76. San Francisco: Jossey-Bass.

———. 2004. "Crossing the Barriers of Internalized Racism and Cross-Racial Hostility." In G. Ng 2004b, 49–50.

———. 2006. *Multicultural Social Work Practice*. Hoboken: Wiley.

———, Patricia Arredondo, and Roderick J. McDavis. 1992. "Multicultural Counseling Competencies and Standards: A Call to the Profession." *Journal of Counseling and Development* 70 (March/April): 477–86.

———, and David Sue. 2003a. *Counseling the Culturally Diverse: Theory and Practice*. 4th ed. New York: John Wiley.

———. 2003b. "White Racial Identity Development: Therapeutic Implications." In Sue and Sue 2003a, 235–64.

Sugirtharajah, R. S. 2001. *Postcolonial Criticism and Biblical Interpretation*. New York: Oxford University Press.

———. 2003. *Postcolonial Reconfigurations: An Alternative Way of Reading the Bible and Doing Theology*. London: SCM; St. Louis: Chalice, 2003.

———, ed. 1998. *The Postcolonial Bible*. Sheffield: Sheffield Academic Press.

Sundberg, Norman D., and David Sue. 1989. "Research and Related Research Hypotheses about Effectiveness in Intercultural Counseling." In Paul B. Pedersen, Juris G. Draguns, Walter J. Lonner, and Joseph E. Trimble, eds., *Counseling Across Cultures*, 335–70. Honolulu: University of Hawaii Press.

Sung-Kim, Young I. 1992. "Battered Korean Women in Urban United States." In Furuto et al. 1992, 213–26.

Swedish, Margaret, and Marie Dennis. 2004. *Like Grains of Wheat: A Spirituality of Solidarity*. Maryknoll, N.Y.: Orbis.

Takaki, Ronald. 1989. *Strangers from a Distant Shore: A History of Asian Americans*. New York: Penguin.

Tanner, Beth LaNeel. 2001. "How Long, O Lord! Will Your People Suffer in Silence Forever?" In Stephen Breck Reid, ed., *Psalms and Practice*, 143–52. Collegeville, Minn.: Liturgical.

Taylor, Carrie. 2000. "The Divine Edge: Living with Manic Depression." *Theology Today* 57, no. 2:211–16.

Thomas, David A., and Robin J. Ely. 1996. "Making Difference Matter: A New Paradigm for Managing Diversity." *Harvard Business Review* 74:79–90.

Thompson, Neil. 1993, 1997. *Anti-Discriminatory Practice*. London: MacMillan.

Thornton, Sharon. 2002. *Broken Yet Beloved: A Pastoral Theology of the Cross*. St. Louis: Chalice.

Thurman, Howard. 1981. *Jesus and the Disinherited*. Richmond, Ind.: Friends United Press.

Tigert, Leanne McCall, and Maren C. Tirabassi, eds. 2004. *Transgendering Faith: Identity, Sexuality, and Spirituality*. Cleveland: Pilgrim.

Toyama, Nikki A., and Tracey Gee, eds. 2006. *More Than Serving Tea: Asian American*

Women on Expectations, Relationships, Leadership and Faith. Downers Grove, Ill.: InterVarsity.

Turner, Clevonne W. 1997. "Clinical Applications of the Stone Center Theoretical Approach to Minority Women." In Judith V. Jordan, ed., *Women's Growth in Diversity: More Writings from the Stone Center,* 74–90. New York: Guilford.

Tutu, Desmond. 1999. *No Future Without Forgiveness.* New York: Random House.

Ty, Eleanor, and Donald C. Goellnicht, eds. 2004. *Asian North American Identities.* Bloomington: Indiana University Press.

United Church of Canada. 2000. *Justice and Reconciliation: The Legacy of Indian Residential Schools and the Journey toward Reconciliation.* Toronto: The United Church of Canada.

VandeCreek, Larry and Arthur Lucas, eds. 2001. *The Discipline for Pastoral Care Giving: Foundations for Outcome Oriented Chaplaincy.* New York: Haworth.

van der Hart, Omno, ed. 1988. *Coping with Loss: The Therapeutic Use of Leave-Taking Rituals.* New York: Irvington.

Volf, Miroslav. 1996. *Exclusion and Embrace: A Theological Exploration of Identity, Otherness and Reconciliation.* Nashville: Abingdon.

Walker, Alice. 1979. "One Child of One's Own: A Meaningful Digression Within the Work(s)." *Ms* 8 (August): 47–50, 72–75.

———. 1987. *In Search of Our Mother's Gardens.* London: The Women's Press.

Walpola, Rahula. 1959. *What the Buddha Taught.* New York: Grove.

Warner, R. Stephen, and Judith G. Wittner, eds. 1998. *Gatherings in Diaspora: Religious Communities and the New Immigration.* Philadelphia: Temple University Press.

Washington, James M., ed. 1991. *A Testament of Hope: The Essential Writings and Speeches of Martin Luther King, Jr.* New York: HarperCollins.

Wassermann, J. A. 2002. "Leaving." *Phi Delta Kappan* (June), 83.

Watkins, Carroll A. 1999. *Survival and Liberation: Pastoral Theology in African American Context.* St. Louis: Chalice.

Waugh, Earle H., Sharon McIrvin Abu-Laban, and Regula Burckhardt Qureshi, eds. 1991. *Muslim Families in North America.* Ontario: University of Alberta.

Waun, Maurine C. 1999. *More than Welcome: Learning to Embrace Gay, Lesbian, Bisexual, and Transgendered Persons in the Church.* St. Louis: Chalice.

Way, Peggy. 2005. *Created by God: Pastoral Care for All God's People.* St. Louis: Chalice.

Weaver, Matt. 2003. "Rough Justice." *The Guardian,* 27 August.

Webb-Mitchell, Brett. 1994. *Unexpected Guests at the Banquet: Welcoming People with Disability into the Church.* New York: Crossroad.

Wegela, Karen Kissel. 1996. *How to Be a Help Instead of a Nuisance.* Boston: Shambhala.

Welch, Sharon D. 2000. *A Feminist Ethic of Risk.* 2nd ed. Minneapolis: Fortress Press.

Westermann, Claus. 1974. "The Role of Lament in the Theology of the Old Testament." Trans. Richard N. Soulen. *Interpretation* 28, no. 1 (January): 20–38.

White, Michael. 1999. "Reflecting Team as Definitional Ceremony." *Gecko* 2:55–82.

———. 2000. *Reflections On Narrative Practice: Essays and Interviews.* South Adelaide: Dulwich Centre Publications.

———, and David Epston. 1990. *Narrative Means to Therapeutic Ends.* New York: Norton.

———, and ———. 1994. *Experience, Contradiction, Narrative and Imagination: Selected Papers of Michael White and David Epston, 1989–1991.* South Adelaide: Dulwich Centre Publications.

White Paper. 2003. *Winning Back Our Communities.* London: Her Majesty's Stationery Office.

Williams, Carmen Braun, and Marsha Wiggins Frame. 1998. "Race, Gender and Spirituality: Key Themes in Therapy with Black Clients." *Awareness* 25, no. 1:11–15.

———, and ———. 1999. "Constructing New Realities: Integrating Spiritual and Cultural Traditions in Therapy with African American Women." *Pastoral Psychology* 47:303–14.

———, and ———. 2001. "Womanist Interventions: Working with African American Women in Couples and Families." In Richard E. Watts, ed., *Techniques in Marriage and Family Counseling* 2:39–44. Alexandria, Va.: American Counseling Association.

———, and ———, and Evelyn Green. 1999. "Counseling Groups for African American Women: A Focus on Spirituality." *Journal for Specialists in Group Work* 24:274–87.

Williams, Delores S. 1993. *Sisters in the Wilderness: The Challenge of Womanist God-Talk.* Maryknoll, N.Y.: Orbis.

Williams, Terry Tempest. 1991. *Refuge: An Unnatural History of Family and Place.* New York: Vintage.

Wilson, Henry S., Takatsoo Mofokeng, Judo Poerwowidagdo, Robert A. Evans, and Alice Frazer Evans. 1996. *Pastoral Theology from a Global Perspective: A Case Method Approach.* Maryknoll, N.Y.: Orbis.

Wimberly, Edward P. 1997. *Recalling Our Own Stories: Spiritual Renewal for Religious Caregivers.* San Francisco: Jossey-Bass.

———. 2000. *Relational Refugees: Alienation in African American Churches and Communities.* Nashville: Abingdon.

Wingren, Gustaf. 1957. *Luther on Vocation.* Philadelphia: Muhlenberg.

Wink, Walter. 1992. *Engaging the Powers: Discernment and Resistance in a World of Domination.* Minneapolis: Fortress Press.

Winslade, John, and Lorraine Smith. 1997. "Countering Alcoholic Narratives." In Monk et al. 1997.

Wittgenstein, Ludwig. 1953. *Philosophical Investigations.* Oxford, UK: Blackwell.

Worden, J. William. 2002. *Grief Counseling and Grief Therapy: A Handbook for Practitioners.* New York: Springer.

Wormser, Richard. 1994. *American Islam: Growing Up Muslim in America.* New York: Walker.

Ye-Myint, Carolyn. 1992. *Who's Hiding.* London: No Fixed Abode.

Yep, Jeannette, Peter Cha, Susan Cho Van Riesen, Greg Jao, and Paul Tokunaga. 1998. *Following Jesus Without Dishonoring Your Parents.* Downers Grove, Ill.: InterVarsity.

Yoo, David K., ed. 1999. *New Spiritual Homes: Religion and Asian Americans.* Honolulu: University of Hawai'i Press.

Yoong, K. K., and T. Heymann. 2005. "Colonoscopy in the Very Old: Why Bother?" *Postgraduate Medical Journal* 81: 2357–365.

Young, Iris Marion. 1990. *Justice and the Politics of Difference.* Princeton: Princeton University Press.

———. 2000. "Five Faces of Oppression." In Adams et al. 2000, 35–49.

Young-Eisendrath, Polly. 1997. *The Resilient Spirit: Transforming Suffering into Insight and Renewal.* Reading, Mass., Perseus.

Zhou, Min, Carl L. Bankston III, and Rebecca Y. Kim. 2002. "Rebuilding Spiritual Lives in the New Land: Religious Practices Among Southeast Asian Refugees in the United States." In Pyong Gap Min and Jung Ha Kim, eds., *Religions in Asian America: Building Faith Communities*, 37–70. Walnut Creek, Calif.: Altamira.

Zimmerman, Jeffrey L., and Victoria C. Dickerson. 1996. *If Problems Talked: Narrative Therapy in Action.* New York: Guilford.

Zimmerman, Mari West. 1995. *Take and Make Holy: Honoring the Sacred in the Healing Journey of Abuse Survivors.* Chicago: Liturgy Training Publications.

INDEX